The governance of the
Single European Market

MANCHESTER
UNIVERSITY PRESS

European Policy Research Unit Series

Series Editors: *Simon Bulmer* and *Mick Moran*

The European Policy Research Unit Series aims to provide advanced textbooks and thematic studies of key public policy issues in Europe. They concentrate, in particular, on comparing patterns of national policy content, but pay due attention to the Europeran Union dimension. The thematic studies are guided by the character of the policy issue under examination.

   The European Policy Research Unit (EPRU) was set up in 1989 within the University of Manchester's Department of Government to promote research on European politics and public policy. The Series is part of EPRU's effort to facilitate intellectual exchange and substantive debate on the key policy issues confronting the European states and the European Union.

Titles in the series also include

The politics of health in Europe   Richard Freeman

Mass media and media policy in Western Europe   Peter Humphreys

The regions and the new Europe   ed. Martin Rhodes

The European Union and member states   ed. Dietrich Rometsch and Wolfgang Wessels

Political economy of financial integration in Europe   Jonathan Story and Ingo Walter

The governance of the Single European Market

Kenneth A. Armstrong and Simon J. Bulmer

Manchester University Press

Manchester and New York

Distributed exclusively in the USA by St. Martin's Press

Published by Manchester University Press
Oxford Road, Manchester M13 9NR, UK
and Room 400, 175 Fifth Avenue, New York, NY 10010, USA

Distributed exclusively in the USA by
St. Martin's Press, Inc., 175 Fifth Avenue, New York,
NY 10010, USA

Distributed exclusively in Canada by
UBC Press, University of British Columbia, 6344 Memorial Road,
Vancouver, BC, Canada V6T 1Z2

British Library Cataloguing-in-Publication Data
A catalogue record for this book is available from the British Library

Library of Congress Cataloging-in-Publication Data
Armstrong, Kenneth A.
    The governance of the Single European Market / Kenneth A. Armstrong and
Simon J. Bulmer.
        p.   cm. – (European policy research unit series)
    "Distributed exclusively in the USA by St. Martin's Press and in Canada by UBC
Press."
    IBSN 0–7190–4456–1 (cloth). – ISBN 0–7190–4457–X (pbk.)
    1. European Union countries–Economic policy.   2. Europe–Economic integration.
I. Bulmer, Simon.   II. Title.   III. Series.
HC240,A834   1998
337.1'42–dc21   97–20798

ISBN   0 7190 4456–1 *hardback*
        0 7190 4457–X *paperback*

First published 1998

01 00 99 98   10 9 8 7 6 5 4 3 2 1

Typeset in 10/12pt Sabon
by Graphicraft Typesetters Ltd., Hong Kong
Printed in Great Britain
by Biddles Ltd, Guildford and King's Lynn

Quite early in life, events taught me that human nature is weak and unpredictable without rules and institutions.

Jean Monnet (1978: 37)

Contents

Abbreviations

ACE	Association des Compagnies Aériennes de la Communauté Européene
ACP	African, Caribbean and Pacific
AEA	Association of European Airlines
AECMA	Association Européene des Constructeurs de Matériel Aérospatial
AIE	International Association of Electrical Contractors
ANEC	European Association for the Co-ordination of Consumer Representation in Standardisation
APEC	Asia–Pacific Economic Cooperation
ASB	Associated Standardisation Body
BEUC	Bureau Européen des Unions des Consommateurs
BKartA	Federal Cartel Office (Germany)
BTS	Technical Standards Board
CAA	Civil Aviation Authority
CAP	Common Agricultural Policy
CBI	Confederation of British Industry
CEC	European Commission
CEECs	central and eastern European countries
CEN	Comité Européen de Normalisation
CENELEC	Comité Européen de Normalisation Électrotechnique
CFI	Court of First Instance (of the European Communities)
CFSP	Common Foreign and Security Policy
COFACE	Confederation of Family Organisations in the EC
COMPAS report	Competition in Air Services report
COREPER	Committee of Permanent Representatives
CREW	Centre for Research on European Women
DG	Directorate General
DIN	Deutsches Institut für Normung
EAP	Environmental Action Programme

EC	European Community/ies (including references to articles of the European Community treaty)
ECAC	European Civil Aviation Conference
EC-CCC	Consumer Consultative Council of the EC
ECISS	European Committee on Iron and Steel Standardisation
ECJ	European Court of Justice
ECMA	European Computer Manufacturers' Association
EcoFin	Council of Economics and Finance Ministers
Ecosoc	Economic and Social Committee
ECSC	European Coal and Steel Community
ECTEL	European Telecommunications and Professional Electronics Industry
EEA	European Economic Area
EEB	European Environmental Bureau
EEC	European Economic Community (including references to treaty articles)
EFTA	European Free Trade Association
EMS	European Monetary System
EMU	Economic and Monetary Union
ENOW	European Network of Women
EOC	Equal Opportunities Commission (UK)
EOTC	European Organization for Testing and Certification
EP	European Parliament
EPRU	European Policy Research Unit (University of Manchester)
ERA	European Regional Airlines Association
ERRA	European Recovery and Recycling Association
ESF	European Social Fund
ESPRIT	European Strategic Programme for Research and Development in Information Technology
ESRC	Economic and Social Research Council
ETSI	European Telecommunications Standards Institute
ETUC	European Trade Union Confederation
EU	European Union
Euratom	European Atomic Energy Community
EUROCOOP	European Community of Consumers Cooperatives
EUROPACABLE	European Confederation of Associations of Manufacturers of Insulated Wires and Cables
EUROPEN	European Organisation for Packaging and the Environment
EWL	European Women's Lobby
EWOS	European Workshop for Open Systems
FATUREC	Federation of Air Transport Users' Representatives in the EC

FEAD	Fédération Européene des Activités des Déchets
GATT	General Agreement on Tariffs and Trade
IATA	International Air Transport Association
ICAO	International Civil Aviation Organisation
IEO	International Electrotechnical Organization
IGC	inter-governmental conference
IOCU	International Organisation of Consumers' Unions
IR	international relations (theory)
ISO	International Standardisation Organisation
IT	information technology
JHA	Justice and Home Affairs
M&A	merger and acquisition
MCR	Merger Control Regulation
MEP	Member of the European Parliament
MMC	Monopolies and Mergers Commission (UK)
MTF	Merger Task Force
NAFTA	North American Free Trade Agreement
OECD	Organisation for Economic Cooperation and Development
OFT	Office of Fair Trading (UK)
OIML	International Organisation of Legal Metrology
ONP	Open Network Provision
PASP	Protocol and Agreement on Social Policy
PIC	prior informed consent
prEN	draft European standard
PSO	public-service obligation
QMV	qualified majority voting
R&D	research and development
SAP	Social Action Programme
SEA	Single European Act
SECO	Secrétariat Européen de Coordination pour la Normalisation
SEM	Single European Market
SLIM	Simpler Legislation for the Internal Market
TC	Technical Committee
TEDs	Tenders Electronic Daily
TEU	(Maastricht) Treaty on European Union
UK	United Kingdom
UNEP	United Nations Environmental Protectional
UNICE	Union of Industries of the European Community
UNIPEDE	International Union of Producers and Distributors of Electrical Energy
USA/US	United States of America/United States
WTO	World Trade Organisation

Acknowledgements

This book is the product of a research project on 'rule-making in the Single European Market (SEM)', itself part of a wider project, on regulatory institutions and practices in the SEM, conducted in the European Policy Research Unit (EPRU) of Manchester University's Department of Government. The research was funded by the Economic and Social Research Council (ESRC), within its single market initiative, under award number L113251014. We are pleased to acknowledge the ESRC's generous support.

The research was initiated during the period 1992–93. From March 1992 to August 1993 Kenneth Armstrong worked as research officer within EPRU. For his part, Simon Bulmer was relieved of teaching duties during the academic year 1992–93. During 1992–93 we undertook several research visits to Brussels to conduct interviews and gain access to additional documentary material. In the subsequent period attention has focused upon writing up the research, reflecting upon the implications of the data for our analysis, and upon the way the single market 'agenda' has evolved in the aftermath of its notional completion on 31 December 1992. Some follow-up research has also been undertaken in the run-up to submission of the manuscript.

We would like to thank all those officials of the European/national institutions and interest groups who gave up their time to speak to us. We would also like to thank some 'facilitators' who opened up additional avenues of research or data collection in Brussels, including Richard Corbett, David Earnshaw, Francis Jacobs, David Spence and Michael Wood.

Within the research we developed a division of labour in terms of both the analytical and empirical components. Kenneth Armstrong worked particularly on the analysis of the regulatory issues, discussed in Chapters 10/11, as well as on the case studies relating to public procurement, the harmonisation of technical regulations and standards and the regulation of shipments of waste. Simon Bulmer concentrated on the new institutionalist analysis, outlined in Chapters 2/3, and on the other three case studies (merger control, air transport and the Maternity Directive). However, as a collaborative project between a lawyer and a political scientist, there have been many cross-disciplinary exchanges across this division of labour.

We have had the opportunity on a number of occasions to discuss the research findings with others working in the broad area. We would, therefore, like to thank those who helped us refine our ideas in the EPRU research seminar, at the comparative competition policy institutions conference in Exeter, the European Community Studies Association conference in Washington (1993), the University of Keele, Manchester Metropolitan University, the end-of-project workshop at Manchester University, the Conference of Europeanists in Chicago, the University of Tübingen, the Max-Planck-Institut für Gesellschaftsforschung in Cologne, the Law and Society conference in Phoenix, the ESRC single market COST A4 conference in Exeter, and seminars at the Centre d'Etudes et de Recherches Internationales (Paris), the University of Hull and the Université Libre de Bruxelles. We are grateful for the financial support offered by various sources to enable these discussions of our work. Discussion of various aspects of the single market with other researchers in the ESRC single market initiative, co-ordinated at the time by David Mayes, also animated our research.

We have benefited from many discussions on new institutionalism and its (by some contested) value to the study of the European Union (EU) with individual fellow-researchers both within our university departments and beyond. We would particularly mention Martin Burch, Jeff Collin, Charlie Dannreuther, Peter Hall, Peter Katzenstein, Andrew Moravcsik, Paul Pierson, Mark Pollack, Dietrich Rometsch, Vivien Schmidt, Jo Shaw, Marina Strezhneva, Dan Wincott, Joseph Weiler, Wolfgang Wessels and Ekaterini Yiantsios. In addition, Laura Cram, Hussein Kassim, Anna Murphy, Jacqueline Nonon, John Peterson, Joanne Scott, Colin Scott, Julia Sohrab and Handley Stevens commented on drafts of individual chapters. We are also very grateful to Michael Moran for reading the manuscript and for his encouragement of the research.

Simon Bulmer would like additionally to thank David M. Farrell and Peter Humphreys for taking responsibility for teaching duties on European integration during his absence on research leave. Kenneth Armstrong would like also to acknowledge the British Academy for additional support through a personal research grant (APN4635) and the Faculty of Law, University College Dublin for accommodation during a sabbatical in 1996. The manuscript was completed while Armstrong was employed at Keele University. Thanks and best wishes go to his former colleagues.

Despite the many acknowledgements we take full responsibility for what follows.

Finally, we are grateful to, successively, Richard Purslow and Nicola Viinikka, for their support at Manchester University Press.

Kenneth A. Armstrong and Simon J. Bulmer
Keele and Manchester

Introduction

In 1985, at the Milan meeting of the European Council, the Member States of the European Community (EC) agreed to the programme presented by the Commission for the completion of the internal market.[1] For much of the rest of the decade this objective was a major matter of concern for economists, political scientists and legal analysts of European integration, not to mention practitioners in these three domains. Moreover, the scope of the project ensured that many analysts whose work had previously been confined to individual Member States thenceforth had to take full account of the impact of European integration upon their interests. Similarly, economic actors in several Member States – for instance, in France and the United Kingdom (UK) – were subjected to awareness-raising campaigns on the new challenges and opportunities afforded by the internal market. Thus, the internal market lay at the heart of new interest in European integration.

Over a decade later, what has become of the Single European Market (SEM)? In terms of its place in public perceptions of European integration, it has subsided from view. Even before the end-1992 deadline for completion of the SEM had passed, the subject had been replaced by the protracted national debates about the Maastricht Treaty on European Union (TEU) and its ratification. There then followed concern with the enlargement of the European Union (EU) to include applicants from the European Free Trade Association (EFTA). More recently, two parallel concerns have developed in respect of European integration. The approach of the 1998 decision on proceeding to the third stage of monetary union has dominated the economic agenda. At the same time, the debate associated with the 1996/97 inter-governmental conference (IGC) on further constitutional reform of the EU has occupied centre-stage in the political debate.

In the light of the way in which the focus of attention has shifted away from the SEM it is pertinent to ask what its significance was. Was it all froth but no substance?

The significance of the SEM

The creation of the SEM was a major development in the history of European integration. The motives behind the project were various but common to all of them was a wish to give the (then) EC a new relevance to meeting the economic challenges of the era. A minimalist interpretation of the SEM is that it was a programme of legislation developed with a view to achieving one of the original goals of the 1957 Treaty of Rome: the creation of a common market. A maximalist interpretation, however, is that the programme provided a platform for a major revival of European integration itself. It triggered policy activism in a range of policy areas beyond the SEM itself. It also contributed in no small measure to the 1995 enlargement of the EU, as other European states felt it in their interest to be full participants in the integration project. Over the longer term the SEM programme raised important questions about the legitimacy of the integration process. These questions came to the fore in the early 1990s when public opinion and political forces in several Member States began to question whether European integration was a juggernaut out of control. The SEM programme thus has an absolute centrality to the recent development of integration in Europe.

As the breadth of these issues displays, the SEM project cannot simply be regarded as a self-contained, time-limited episode that was brought to an end at midnight on 31 December 1992, the target-date for agreement on the legislation. To begin with, the whole issue of putting the SEM into operation had barely begun. Moreover, the ramifications of the SEM upon economic and political actors would take time to become clear, so that much of the jockeying for power and control in the new market-place will take years to play out. Above all, the SEM could not be seen as an hermetically-sealed entity; it was in substantial part a response to global economic developments and the internal market would have to continue to respond to new international challenges.

But the SEM project has a much wider empirical significance. In terms of policy dynamics it was accompanied by such flanking policy measures as increased regulation of working conditions as well as increased transfer payments, via the structural funds, to the industrially weaker Member States. It provided the initial impetus towards monetary union before that momentum was further increased in the aftermath of German unification in 1990. There was a further indirect link between the SEM and some of the policy initiatives contained in the TEU, signed in 1992 and brought into effect from November 1993, for instance the attempt to increase the scope for social regulation.

Alongside these policy linkages, the SEM was closely linked institutionally with the first round of comprehensive institutional reform, embodied in the Single European Act (SEA). In formal terms the institutional changes of the SEA provided improvements to the EC's machinery of government so as to achieve more efficient decision-making. The impact of the SEA upon the policy-making environment was, in fact, pervasive. The Commission saw new opportunities to exploit the renewed momentum of integration with a view to further deepening integration. The European Parliament (EP) and its Members sought to deploy the new powers granted in the SEA. More widely, the policy-making 'community' – defined in the broadest sense – became more heavily populated. The SEM's impact upon new areas of economic activity triggered the formation of new interest groups, the development of new lobbying strategies. Existing groups had to reconsider their strategies. Within the Council of Ministers the new rules providing for qualified majority voting (QMV) resulted in changes to the tactical considerations of national governments. The transfer from the Council to external agencies of one important area of regulation – that concerning technical standards – represented a further shift in the character of governance. Whether governmental or non-governmental; whether national, sub-national or supranational: economic and political actors were obliged to rethink their relationship with, and role in, the EC.

Alongside the changes in the policy-making arena, there were important implications for, and developments in, legal integration. The law of the single market had developed significantly in the period prior to the adoption of the SEM programme (Green, Hartley and Usher 1991). Indeed, some of the key principles of European law had been defined in cases relating to single market issues. With the political emphasis upon the goal of a single market, an increased burden was placed upon the legal system of the EC. The Court of First Instance of the European Communities (CFI) was provided for in the SEA as one response to the increased pressure. It did not come into being until 1989 but already new challenges were posed for the European Court of Justice (ECJ) concerning the interpretation of the Treaty of Rome and its provisions for market integration. Key rulings in the ECJ's jurisprudence fed into the the legislative policy process, thereby reinforcing the interaction of the judicial and legislative processes: an often underexplored area of integration. It goes without saying, then, that practising lawyers were not to be left on the sidelines by the emerging single market. Further downstream in the policy process, the whole issue of the transposition of EC legislation into national law, and the further stage of ensuring compliance, were brought into focus.

If the implications for the EC as a system of governance were great, they were for the Member States as well. Important areas of economic and social regulation at the national level were either lost to the supranational level or had to be shared. National rules were increasingly subject to scrutiny, in national and Community courts, for compatibility with EC law. Policy areas from waste disposal to regulating air transport became Europeanised. Many interest groups had to liberate themselves from a predominantly national mode of operating and become accustomed to multiple tiers of lobbying. It was no longer just in a federal state such as Germany that the phenomenon of multi-level governance was the order of the day. This trend was especially pronounced in respect of sub-national government's response to the increased size of European structural funds (Marks, Hooghe and Blank 1996). However, there was also a sense in which European regions had to become more competitive with each other in pursuit of inward investment within the SEM (Rhodes 1995).

Beyond the EC/EU the SEM has had a wider impact. The creation of the European Economic Area (EEA) to allow European states not wishing to join the EC itself to participate in the SEM project was one step. However, the EEA's significance was subsequently reduced when Austria, Finland and Sweden chose to become full members of the EU. The impact of the SEM to the east has been assured by the EU's pre-accession strategy for the central and eastern European states. That strategy entails an alignment on the part of those states with the rules of the SEM.

Beyond Europe, the SEM programme initially occasioned concerns in the USA about the possible development of a 'fortress Europe', which would place traders from the outside at a disadvantage. However, the SEM occasioned other responses. For instance, it was one factor which led to other economic regions developing their own forms of market integration: for example, the North American Free Trade Agreement (NAFTA) and Asia-Pacific Economic Cooperation (APEC). This economic regionalism in turn provided a backdrop for trade negotiations in the Uruguay Round, in which the tensions between regional and multilateral rules of trade came to the fore (Woolcock 1994; Woolcock and Hodges 1996). The SEM was closely linked with these wider developments.

Whether on a European, national or international scale, the significance of the SEM was striking. Conceived as a project for transforming the European economy, the SEM was at the heart of a dynamic period during which the political and legal contexts of economic governance were also transformed. It is the political and legal contexts which form the central focus of this study.

The research agenda

For the analyst of European integration – whether lawyer, political scientist or economist – the SEM programme is arguably *more* relevant at present than in 1985. The 'hype' of the SEM, as symbolised by the UK Department of Trade and Industry's 'power breakfasts' on the SEM, has been forgotten. Now, the extent to which this single market has been achieved can be examined in a more detached manner. Research data are increasingly available. Paradoxically, in the academic community examination of these data has not kept pace, since the analysis of European integration has again displayed its event-driven character. Many analysts are concerned with more 'current' policy issues. What are the analysts' tasks in reviewing the achievements of the SEM?

For economists, they entail assessing the economic effects of the legislation agreed as well as measuring the broader economic impact alongside those projections made in the Cecchini report (summarised in Cecchini, Catinat and Jacquemin 1988). For political scientists, they involve examination of the political struggles that accompanied the formulation of the measures associated with the SEM and of the resultant policy. Moreover, what has been the impact of these developments for economic governance in the EU? For lawyers, it entails particularly the examination of the legal form taken by the SEM but also the issues of the implementation and enforcement of single market rules.

An important definitional problem needs to be resolved at the outset of our study: what do we mean by the SEM? Do we take it to be simply the White Paper on the internal market? In fact, the internal market programme was part of a wider endeavour. Less clearly defined, and therefore sometimes politically contested, this wider endeavour incorporated two extra components. The first was made up of flanking policies which were part of the linked bargain struck at Milan but only finding written expression in the 1986 SEA. The second consisted of various policy measures conceived as part of creating a functioning internal market but which did not happen to be in the White Paper. It is this wider endeavour which interests us in this study, and which we refer to as the SEM. We recognise that there are some difficulties in defining what aspects of integration may be considered part of the SEM and what lies outside.

How have we addressed these issues? First, we need to explain why this study is not just concerned with the internal market White Paper. Important as it was, the White Paper was never going to provide a comprehensive regulatory framework. It needed to connect up with competition legislation and was bound to have broader repercussions, such as on the environment. To take the White Paper as sufficient to create a single market would have been to adopt an arbitrarily bounded understanding of market integration. Equally, one could take such an inclusive understanding of the SEM, and go so far as to include monetary union. Ours is an intermediate position: we have taken the scope of the SEM to encompass the integration of economic markets, and the associated regulatory arrangements. Our overview chapters as well as the choice of case studies (see Chapter 3) reflect this understanding. So much for the terrain of study, what of our research objectives?

In this study of the governance of the SEM we have five aims.

The first of these is to give an impression of the reality of the SEM. The study is not, in consequence, concerned with measuring the economic impact of the SEM but, rather, with what has happened so far in terms

of the construction of the necessary regulatory arrangements. We look at
the formulation of single market policy. We look at the inputs made by
political actors. And we look at the character of the resultant EC policy.
Moreover, we do this by taking both an overview of the single market
programme and by undertaking in-depth analysis of a selection of some of
the necessary steps taken as part of completing the SEM. As already noted,
our case studies are not confined to the almost 300 items of legislation
contained in the Commission White Paper.

The second objective is to disaggregate the SEM. Usually presented as an
integrated programme – particularly when equated with the White Paper
– the single market project did indeed entail interconnections between
individual measures. Some of these interconnections will be seen in subsequent chapters. However, in terms of how policy was made and put into
practice, there was a significant degree of diversity. Thus, some parts of the
programme required QMV in the Council of Ministers; others did not.
Some parts of the programme were subject to the more extensive legislative consultation of the EP, the 'cooperation procedure'; others were not.
Some parts of the programme have vested regulatory authority in the
supranational institutions themselves; others rely on national authorities to
enact and implement legislation; still others, notably on technical standards, pushed the burden of responsibility into supervised self-regulation.

This taste of the diversity within the SEM programme is not an end in
itself. Rather, it is designed to indicate that the politics of constructing the
single market did not follow a single path. Thus, there cannot be a fixation
with one set of political tactics for those participating in the policy process:
not, at least, if regular success is to be achieved in negotiating SEM legislation. Thus, to use a soccer analogy, the 'Route One' approach of long
balls delivered to a burly centre forward may quickly prove to be coun-
terproductive in a league in which other teams have realised the need to
adopt more sophisticated tactics: tactics which may have to vary from one
game to another in the light of the opportunities they may offer.

Or to put the diversity into the terms of a wider debate about the governance of the EU, the differentiation between the measures entailed in
creating and running a single market offers considerable illustration of the
EU's complex decisional processes: a complexity which is an important
facet of the EU's lack of transparency.

This leads on to a third and important objective of the study, namely the
wish to make some kind of contribution to the analysis of European
integration. The SEM and the linked SEA represented only one staging-
post on the long and winding road of integration. Thus, there are difficulties in abstracting from this set of decisions in order to test hypotheses
about the integration process as a whole.[2] As a result, we do not have
ambitious goals in respect of testing or exploring integration theories.
Instead, our attention is focused on the analysis of governance in the EC/
EU, and specifically as illustrated by the SEM.

Creating the SEM was a 'meso-level' phenomenon. Thus, the SEM should be seen as having an intermediate scope between the broad macro-framework of integration and cooperation across many policy areas of the EU, on the one hand, and the micro level of individual items of legislation, on the other. The SEM and the SEA represented an important step in the integration process but our interest is not with developing 'grand theory' based on this experience but with the more limited aspect of how they transformed the governance of the EC/EU. How did the SEM and SEA affect the character of governance in the EC/EU? How did they affect the governance capacity of the EC/EU?

The general approach adopted in the study is to examine the governance of the SEM by drawing upon the analytical tools of law and political science. The broad context for drawing upon these literatures is the fact that European integration has now produced a system of government with state-like features. The puzzle is: with what kind of state can the EU be compared? To be sure, it is not with the traditional notion of the West-phalian state where a monopoly is held over the legitimate use of force, for the EU remains distant from meeting that requirement (see Caporaso 1996). Perhaps the EU is a kind of post-modern state or what Ruggie terms a 'multiperspectival polity', characterised by the unbundling of the traditional state patterns of territoriality (Ruggie 1993a: 172).

Our contention is that as supranational governance has become increasingly complex, so the traditional international relations frameworks have become less able to encapsulate the nuances and differentiation of EU governance.[3] Approaches such as neo-functionalism and inter-governmentalism offer single narratives of the integration process but fail to encapsulate the complex dynamics and interplay of forces which characterise governance in the EU (Armstrong forthcoming). In attempting to bring some analytical order to an untidy situation, we eschew the endeavour to develop fully-blown grand theory. Quite simply, existing grand theories do not seem to us to be capable of explaining the dynamics of the SEM. Instead, we advance an institutionalist approach. This methodology seeks to assign explanatory power to the role of institutions in shaping the pattern of integration.

The approach which we adopt draws on the work of the 'new institutionalist' political scientists in the USA. As utilised here, this approach is based on the simple presumption that, in the process of formulating EC/EU rules and policy, institutional arrangements matter. Further elaboration of this perspective can be deferred to Chapter 2. But we should point out here that we take institutions to have a wider meaning than the 'formal institutions of government'. They are taken, instead, to include treaty provision, procedural codes, the norms, values and identities embedded in the institutions, deriving from landmark judgments of the ECJ, so-called 'soft law', bureaucratic culture and so on. Our argument is to reject a pure choice-based view of politics that sees policy outcomes as the rational product of competing interests. Rather, it sees institutions as occupying an intermediating position: shaping the ways interests are articulated; occasionally shaping the interests themselves; but invariably affecting the policy in some way.[4]

The connection with legal aspects conveniently leads us to a fourth objective of the study. Many past studies of the dynamics of European integration have failed to take due account of the interaction of law and politics. This book is the product of cooperation between a legal scholar (Armstrong) and a political scientist (Bulmer). Not surprisingly, therefore, it aims to rectify this kind of failing. The jurisprudence of the ECJ has contributed much to the process of integration, and this situation is no less applicable to the specific context of the SEM. We shall ensure that the legal dimension is given full account but will aim to do this in an manner which is accessible to those who do not possess, or wish to possess, an encyclopedic knowledge of the case law of the ECJ. New institutionalism, we believe, is an appropriate vehicle for bringing together both disciplines to study European integration.

The single market is an economic policy area shaped by politics and law. So, can the interaction of these three disciplines be brought together within the institutionalist context identified earlier? We believe so, and this leads to the fifth objective of the study. The single market was essentially a programme for regulatory reconstruction within the EC/EU. Thus rule-making, regulatory institutions and regulatory practices assume a centrality in the analysis that follows.

The '1992' programme did not amount to the launching of a new policy area, for the creation of a common market was originally set down in the 1957 Treaty of Rome. Rather, it was the development of a new phase in the attempt to achieve that goal. It was a new phase in regulatory development. This interpretation coincides with one well-established meaning of the term 'regulation', namely the activity of system-steering. The fact is that, by the mid-1980s, the institutional structures and administrative mechanisms of the Community had failed to deliver the common market provided for in the 1957 Rome Treaty. Hence the SEM White Paper reformulated the objectives and gave the all-important deadline which served as a motivating target date for policy-makers and economic actors (businesses, trade unions, etc.). The SEA was complementary in that it reformed the institutional and procedural route to achieving the common market and gave a wider purpose to the SEM goal, as well as providing necessary side-payments to Member States and other sectors of society that felt threatened by market liberalisation. In this sense, the SEM programme represented regulation as system-steering.

The SEM programme was launched at a time when a different notion of regulation had assumed prominence. This notion was the idea of the deregulation of economic markets that had assumed prominence in the 1980s. The move towards this 'de-regulation' was motivated by the wish to liberalise market access and to increase competition. It was not a phenomenon shared with equal vigour throughout the Community; its main ideological proponent was the British government of Margaret Thatcher. Pressure for this de-regulation, however, did not just come from a few Member States within the EC, but was given assistance by the effects of 'contagion'. The de-regulation policies of the Reagan administrations (in the case of air transport, of the Carter administration) had affected the international and European trading environment. So, too, had the communications revolution, which had begun to undermine existing regulatory arrangements.

Thus the SEM programme must be seen in terms of regulatory reform in a second meaning, namely an economics-derived one of regulating market access and competitive behaviour. Member States held, and continue to hold, different views along this particular 'scale' of regulation. Similarly, it is beginning to become clear that the impact of the SEM upon individual Member States has differed according to the extent to which the market-orientated thrust of the SEM has been congruent with prevailing national patterns of state–market relations (on France, see Schmidt 1996).

The third widely accepted definition of regulation concerns the specifics of rule-making. It is in this connection that the interface of law and politics is at its clearest. How are rules set? How are regulatory practices effected? These debates may often appear to be very technical but, cumulatively, they form the pieces of the jigsaw of regulatory reconstruction. Moreover, these technical debates are quite closely related to the economic debates about regulatory change. One of the principal ways in which economic governance develops is through the control over property rights exercised by 'the state'. As will be seen in this study, the SEM programme has gone hand-in-hand with a widening of the scope, and a tightening of the application, of supranational competition rules. These rules and their detailed application are now having an increasing albeit subtle impact upon economic governance in Europe. This aspect of regulation is a recurrent theme in our study.

A fourth component, related to the three outlined above, concerns the level at which economic activity is regulated. Is regulation undertaken at the sub-national, national or supranational level? This dimension of regulation includes the three discussed already. It helps explain how the SEM programme could at one and the same time be seen as both *de*-regulation (under our second, economic understanding) and *re*-regulation in the sense of powers being transferred to a strengthening, supranational level of control. Thus, the SEM programme was about liberalising markets through removing obstacles to the exercise of the four freedoms (the free movement of goods, persons, capital and of services). However, it was not about creating a neo-liberal 'paradise', since the supranational level has become more important in the role of shaping markets, for example through deciding on issues of property rights.

As part of our fifth objective we argue that, by locating the single market into a debate about regulation, we can contribute to some of the work that is beginning to appear on the EU as a 'regulatory state' (see, for instance, Majone 1996). This conception emphasises that the Community has a rather limited set of policy instruments. The absence of large-scale financial resources strongly influences the methods it can employ in achieving its goals. Similarly, the absence of supranational field agencies in the Member States means that national authorities are responsible for putting into practice the majority of EC legislation. Finally, the regulatory character of the EC pillar generally and of the SEM in particular, has arguably come about because policy developed in this way less easily identifies the winners and losers than revenue-raising and spending programmes (Peters 1992: 77).

This regulatory context ties in with the institutionalist approach which we will employ in the study. This is so because it is precisely the institutional form which integration has taken – in terms of formal organisation, policy responsibilities and so on – that has led to the EC being perceived as a regulatory state. Furthermore, the substance of rules, regulatory reconstruction, and the removal of organisational barriers to market access: all these dimensions of regulation can be seen in institutional terms.

Finally, what is this book *not* about?

It is not centrally about implementation and enforcement of the single market rules, although we do deal with the strategies which have emerged to make the SEM's operation more effective. These are key issues, since the member governments could place obstacles in the way of completion of the internal market by dilatoriness or deliberate obstructionism in enacting national legislation. Moreover, the simple enactment of legislation is insufficient. Implementation also necessitates enforcement of the legislation and a change in behaviour of economic and political actors. Compliance with the single market legislation is crucial to its success.

Having stressed the importance of compliance, why is it not a central interest here? The answer to this question is twofold. First, the empirical component of the research project was already extensive, with the examination of six discrete case studies. In addition, the timing of our research was such that some of our cases studies had not been put fully into operation. In air transport liberalisation, for example, full liberalisation occurred only in April 1997. Add some derogations negotiated for certain Member States and it soon becomes clear that we can only address the issue of compliance in a more general manner.

And the book is not about the economics of the single market. That is clearly an exercise best undertaken by specialist economists. However, an awareness of the type of the institutional parameters posed by the rules of the single market, we believe, is important to such economic studies. Creating the single market has not been an exercise in creating a laboratory for neo-classical economics. It has been politicised, with individual Member States, interest groups and individual companies seeking power and control. Moreover, the EU's competition policy rules, with their impact on property rights, also serve as factors affecting the patterns of economic governance. The creation of the SEM and the widening of application of European competition rules have gone some distance towards the creation of a set of framework rules for the supranational governance of the European economy, towards a European economic constitution. Thus, our neglect of the economics of the single market does not mean that our study does not address matters of concern to economists.

Structure

How is the book organised?
In Chapter 1 we offer a review of the origins of the SEM programme and its interaction with broader developments in the integration process during the mid-1980s. We also offer a brief review of existing interpretations of the SEM as a way of setting the scene for the introduction of our own approach. The latter task is undertaken in Chapter 2, where we set out our historical institutionalist framework and indicate what it has to offer in the understanding of EU governance. Chapter 3 represents a dissection of EU governance, at systemic and sub-systemic levels, and is designed to give an institutional context for the case studies which follow. Chapters 4–9 comprise our six case studies of the SEM: merger control, public procurement in the utilities sector, the removal of technical barriers to trade, air transport liberalisation, transfrontier shipments of waste, and the protection of pregnant women at the workplace. Chapter 10 reverts to a wider focus, namely on the broad theme of governance and regulation in the SEM, an issue of continuing importance, and distinguishes again between the narrower White Paper programme and our broader understanding of the SEM. Chapter 11 takes a wider focus still by assessing the SEM in its current context. The Maastricht Treaty and its implementation, the 1996/97 IGC, projected eastern enlargement, new norms of subsidiarity and administrative simplification: these developments mean that the SEM is still evolving in important ways. It is evolving as the systemic political and institutional context of the EU as a whole evolves. In our concluding chapter we summarise the development of the SEM, as the most significant development in integration to date, and take stock of the contribution offered by historical institutionalism.

Notes

1 Throughout this study, which straddles the date when the European Union (EU) was created (1 November 1993), we use the term European Community

(EC) to refer to the situation prior to that date, and subsequently to the EC 'pillar' of the EU as well as to EC law. The term European Union or EU is employed under all other circumstances in the period from November 1993. The putting into effect of the Treaty on European Union (TEU) brought with it a further complicating factor concerning treaty terminology. The 1957 treaty founding the European Economic Community (EEC) was re-named the European Community (EC) Treaty, and some articles were re-numbered. References to the EEC Treaty and EC Treaty thus relate to the situation prior to November 1993 and the situation thereafter respectively.

2   Helen Wallace (1996a) sees the SEM/SEA episode – termed by her as the 'cooption method' – as having been supplanted by a more diffuse approach to integration in the post-Maastricht period. Taking this to be so, a wider theoretical endeavour would need to look at post-Maastricht data, which are data not addressed in this study.

3   This is not to deny other insights into the phenomenon of integration offered by international relations (IR) theory. See Carlsnaes and Smith (1994) for an attempt to use IR theory to grasp developments in the EU. Significantly, none of the chapters really analyses governance issues. However, Michael Smith's contribution (Smith 1994) recognises the problems the EU poses for IR theory in that 'the state' – traditionally at the core of IR debates – is not so clear to identify in a multi-tiered EU. See Hix (1994) and Hurrell and Menon (1996) for conflicting views on the utility of IR theory in the context of the EU. For a good overall survey, see Risse-Kappen (1996).

4   For a general contrast between choice-based and new institutionalist analysis, see March and Olsen (1996).

1

The single market in context

Introduction

How do we best contextualise and analyse the single market objective? In this chapter we undertake this task in four sections. In the first we look at the contours and origins of the political bargain. Hence we focus on the emergence of the agreement on the White Paper, *Completing the Internal Market*, at the Milan European Council in June 1985 (CEC 1985a). But we also examine the background to the SEA, for the latter was clearly linked to the former.

The second section of the chapter briefly sets out the contents of the SEM/SEA bargain. This material is reasonably well known but is needed for the sake of comprehensiveness of our study. In section three we review some of the existing literature analysing the origins of the SEM and SEA. The purpose of this critique is to try to identify some of the strengths and weaknesses of existing accounts. In particular, the goal is to set out certain analytical considerations of our own – undertaken in section four – upon which we shall build an alternative focus and analytical approach in Chapter 2.

Origins of the single market

Before looking at the the origins of the SEM we need to give consideration to what exactly we mean by the 'single market' itself. It is potentially misleading to look at the single market in a narrow, legalistic manner. The White Paper bundled together a set of proposed measures which would undoubtedly lay the foundations of a single market. However, it would be wholly incorrect to presume that the passage of these measures alone would suffice to create a single market. More important still are two important linkages with the SEA.

The first linkage was that the SEM and the SEA formed part of the same political bargain. To be sure, the SEA was not agreed at the 1985 Milan summit and only came into effect from July 1987. However, the process leading to treaty revision was initiated at that summit, for the Dooge Report on institutional reform was tabled at the European Council meeting alongside the White Paper. Moreover, in terms of the bargaining dynamics at the Milan European Council meeting, the constitutional reform process was able to satisfy those Member States who wanted institutional reform and/or linkages with other policy developments (environment, economic and social cohesion and so on) *as a complement to, or even in preference to*, the market liberalisation of the White Paper.

This linkage, it should be pointed out, came about in part by accident. There was no grand plan to assemble this package; rather, the component parts happened to be 'on the negotiating table' in Milan. If it had not been for the decision of the Italian presidency at the meeting to force through the convening of an IGC (in which the SEA was negotiated) through a majority vote, the course of history might have been quite different. Who knows whether the SEM legislation could have been agreed without the shift to increased provision for QMV in the Council later embodied in the SEA?[1]

Secondly, one of the central goals of the SEA was specifically to facilitate the attainment of the SEM by reforming the decision-making process. Thus, in a study of the governance of the SEM, it is impossible to ignore such institutional reforms and the wider package deal embracing both the SEA and the SEM.

So, bearing in mind this wider nature of the package deal, what were its origins?

Several different accounts exist of the origins of the SEM and SEA (Cameron 1992; Corbett 1987; Garrett and Weingast 1993; Kirchner 1992: Ch. 3; Moravcsik 1991; Sandholtz and Zysman 1989).[2] Why add another account to an already comprehensive literature? Our defence is based on two arguments.

Our first contention is intrinsic to our research task. A book on the governance of the single market would be incomplete without explaining how the initiative came about and what the various motivations were. Thus, a comprehensive account of the SEM must include its origins. However, the origins are an insufficient basis for analysis of the SEM. The SEM was not a moment in the history of integration but is a continuing development.

Hence our second contention is that we believe we can offer a more encompassing perspective than some of the earlier accounts: one of the benefits of hindsight, of course! Moreover, we seek to provide a new focus in our analysis of the emergence of the package deal, and 'profile' this against some of the explanations that have been offered hitherto. The new focus, which emphasises the role of institutions, ideas and norms in the formulation and operationalisation of the package, will be developed as an analytical framework in Chapter 2 and then utilised in the individual case studies.

The EC before the SEM/SEA package

The roots of the package lie in two related contexts: those of the systemic evolution of integration as a whole; and those of the sub-systemic context of market integration in particular.

The process of integration lacked dynamism in the 1970s, as a result of the assault upon the supranational institutions launched by President de Gaulle during the 1960s, in his efforts to restore pride in the French nation state (see H. Wallace 1996a: 45–7). The ensuing 'dark ages' period was characterised by only limited progress in the deepening of European integration: notably, the creation of an own resources budget (1970); the introduction of foreign policy cooperation in 1970; the introduction in 1979 of the European Monetary System (EMS); and the first direct elections to the European Parliament, also in 1979.[3] As Keohane and Hoffmann put it, however, such developments were overshadowed 'by the Community's ineffectual response to the 1973 oil crisis, decisionmaking gridlock in the Council, and fears of Eurosclerosis' (1991: 8). Other cautious integrative advances were recorded in the development of EC policy on environmental, social, regional and technology matters, which – like the EMS – had little if any clear rooting in the existing treaties. In consequence, decisionmaking was hampered procedurally by the need to make creative use of Article 235 (EEC). This article – the EC's 'flexible friend' – enabled the Community to do things which were not otherwise specified in the treaty. But Article 235, like Article 100 on the approximation of laws relating to the common market, entailed unanimous voting in the Council and placed the Commission in a relatively weak role in the policy process.

Apart from the inauguration of direct elections, there were no major initiatives for institutional reform in the 1970s. The European Council had been established in 1974 and, from its first meeting in March 1975 in Dublin Castle, had presided over reports on possible institutional changes, for example, the 1976 Tindemans Report; the 1979 report by the Committee of the Three Wise Men (respectively *Bulletin of the EC* Supplement 1/76; *Bulletin of the EC* 11/79: 25–8). However, these developments largely represented tinkering around the edges, for there was an unwillingness to discuss basic objectives in integration for fear that this would open up unmanageable divisions between the national governments. And at this stage the European Council had no formal constitutional status, for it was not embodied in the treaties.

It is worth adding some brief comments on the European Council. Its establishment in 1974 created an institutional arrangement which evolved into the arena for 'defining the guidelines of integration' (Bulmer and Wessels 1987: 85–90).[4] If it did not distinguish itself in the execution of this function in its first decade of operations, it *did* stake its claim to play this role in the future (Bulmer 1996). As we shall explain below, the European Council played a crucial role in constructing, and delegating the construction of, the SEM/SEA package. This role was developed further in subsequent integrative developments during the late-1980s, in the further round of reforms embodied in the TEU, and continued in preparing and supervising the work of the 1996/97 IGC on further treaty revisions.

The early 1980s scarcely gave much indication that the 1970s approach of 'muddling through' would give way to a qualitative change in the character of integration later in the decade. The protracted dispute between Britain and her fellow Member States over contributions to the EC budget created an air of crisis. And the most integrated EC policy area – the Common Agricultural Policy (CAP) – was associated with an inefficient use of resources due to surplus production.

Market integration had also become bogged down. The customs union had been established in 1968, with the removal of tariffs and quotas on intra-EC trade and the creation of the Common External Tariff. Beyond that, however, progress was quite modest on the many other steps needed to create a common market along the lines provided for in the founding EEC Treaty. For instance, attempts to harmonise product standards were limited because behind apparently technical discussions could lie major entrenched national interests. These interests were of crucial importance when legislation was discussed. The requirement to achieve unanimity in the Council of Ministers meant that many Commission proposals were blocked and often eventually shelved. Overall, measuring Community decisions and their domestic implementation against treaty prescriptions, Pelkmans and Robson concluded in 1987 that, 'the *acquis Communautaire* with respect to market integration falls far short of Treaty obligations' (1987: 182).

At the same time, as technology advanced, each new set of legal requirements and/or technical standards associated with new products tended to be agreed at the national level, reflecting the interests of the national industry(ies) concerned. In some instances, particularly in high tehnology, national standards not only reflected the preferences of a national industry but entailed significant financial investment by the government concerned. Thus, far from making progress towards the creation of a common market, in line with treaty goals, fragmentation was becoming more pronounced.

Frontier controls, discrepancies in fiscal arrangements and a range of other 'technical barriers' added to the shortcomings in meeting the aspirations of the EEC Treaty. Other deficiencies included the persistence of capital controls, differences in the regulation of corporate governance, obstacles to labour mobility and the lack of measures to open up a European market in service provision, In sum, a customs union had been created but a common market had not. Arguably, the only institution which was apparently advancing market integration was the European Court through its accumulated jurisprudence (see, for instance, Green, *et al.* 1991). This situation reflects the way in which it is important to bear in mind both the 'political-decisional' dynamics of integration but also the 'judicial-normative' ones associated with the ECJ (see Weiler 1982).

The roots of economic and political reform

Despite an inauspicious start to the 1980s for the EC, it is to that period which we must look in order to trace the path to the SEM/SEA package deal. As early as the June 1981 meeting of the European Council in Luxembourg, the government heads expressed concern that the intentional or unintentional erection of trade barriers, along with excessive state subsidies, was undermining the internal market. In consequence, the European Council agreed that concerted efforts should be undertaken to develop a free internal market for goods and services (*Bulletin of the EC* 6/1981). This was, then, the placing of a first 'marker' on the lengthy route to the June 1985 commitment to this goal. Many a statement made in the conclusions to European Council meetings has later disappeared without trace, for that body's record on overseeing the implementation of its goals has been weak (Bulmer and Wessels 1987: 99–100). However, statements were made repeatedly in the conclusions of summit meetings. An examination of the conclusions shows that such statements were made on the occasion of nine out of thirteen European Council meetings between June 1981 and June 1985.[5]

One concrete effect of these statements came with the convening in November 1982 of a special session of the Council of Economics and Finance Ministers (EcoFin) devoted to the internal market. This led on to a second development, namely the creation in January 1983 of a specific Council of Internal Market Ministers (Cockfield 1994: 22).

In one sense, there was nothing surprising about the statements made by the European Council on the internal market objective. After all, the Member States had all signed up to the EC treaties, so completing the internal market was not a new commitment in the general form set out in European Council conclusions. On the other hand, these were the same governments which were obstructing the individual items of legislation proposed by the Commission for its attainment! Further, the election of President Mitterrand and a socialist government in 1981 did not suggest a French endorsement for such measures of market liberalisation. Their priority was rather the reverse: a programme of nationalisation of large private-sector enterprises.

Repeated rehearsal of policy commitments can lead to the embedding of ideas in institutions; to the creation of new norms and values. To us, this appears to be a feature that has been overlooked in analysis of the SEM programme hitherto. Cameron, to be sure, refers to several of the occasions when the European Council encouraged further reports to be drawn up by the Commission on the subject (1992: 32–5). He also refers to the government heads' encouragement (at Copenhagen, December 1982) to the Council of Internal Market Ministers, followed – at the Stuttgart summit meeting in June 1983 – by an expression of dissatisfaction at their progress (Cameron 1992: 35). And he gives particular attention to the roles of the institutions in developing a momentum towards the SEM goal.

The market liberalisation ideas pertaining to the SEM programme were on the European Council's agenda, therefore, but they were not yet prior-itised. The explanation for this was to be found in the government heads' preoccupations with crisis-management. The makings of a solution to the British budgetary problem, carrying out policy and institutional reform, clearing the way for Iberian enlargement and advancing other issues such as the internal market, were some time in coming. The Stuttgart European Council may be seen as the forerunner to eventual agreement, for the Solemn Declaration on European Union addressed reform issues, whereas the 'Stuttgart Declaration' set out some possible solutions to the proble-matic policy issues. In his account of the development of the SEM, Lord Cockfield, one of the central actors in the episode, asserts that: 'If any spe-cific event can be described as "relaunching the European Community" it was undoubtedly the Solemn Declaration' (Cockfield 1994: 23).[6]

It was not until the June 1984 Fontainebleau meeting of the European Council, however, that the path was cleared for a reform agenda, with resolution of the British budgetary issue and other matters. The internal market was again stated as a goal in the summit's conclusions. Moreover, the Commission was invited to prepare a report on progress in drawing up internal market proposals for the following year and to indicate certain priority areas (*Bulletin of EC* 6/1984: 8–9). Securing a parallel process with the request for a report on the internal market, the European Council set up a committee of personal delegates of the heads of state or govern-ment to examine institutional reform (on which, see Keatinge and Murphy 1987). As Moravcsik puts it, 'Fontainebleau became the moment when momentum toward a package deal containing internal market liberaliza-tion and decision-making reform became unmistakeable' (1991: 57). Thus it was that two reports were tabled for the Milan European Council, thereby providing a potential – and then actual – linkage between the SEM and SEA in a package deal.

The picture as presented thus far has emphasised the role of the Euro-pean Council. Two points need to be made at this point. First, whilst the national governments were the key players in the European Council, their positions were shaped by domestic circumstances deriving from national political debates, ideas and lobbying. National governments may have had some autonomy in advancing their wishes in the European Council but they had to be in touch with their respective domestic contexts. Secondly, we do not see the European Council in crude principal–agent terms. In other words, the European Council's resolutions were not the mere prod-uct of the rational working-through of national governments' policies. In fact, the European Council provided an institutional opportunity for the

European Commission to make an input into shaping the guidelines of integration. The skill of President Jacques Delors in exploiting his role in the European Council to advance the goals of the Commission was a striking feature of this era. The opportunity was the product of the institutional configuration of the European Council, and something which intergovernmentalist accounts underplay. These two points have important implications. They mean that the European Council was at the pinnacle of a multi-level policy-making apparatus. Moreover, they indicate that the European Council was not a mere neutral arena within which political goals were reconciled. Rather, the European Council's profile had an impact on who could participate in shaping goals and on the outcomes themselves.

In one respect we do find a marked distinction between the dynamics behind the SEM and those behind the SEA. In the former case, the advocacy of completion of the internal market was undertaken by certain governments but also by a set of transnational interests with close links to the European Commission. In the case of the SEA, however, the interested parties primarily consisted of the national governments and the supranational institutions (the EP and the Commission).

The emergence of a coalition of elites supporting completion of the internal market has been well charted by Sandholtz and Zysman (1989) and by Cowles (1995). The background to this coalition was the increased perception by leading European industrialists of a serious technological lag behind Japanese counterparts in a structurally changed international economy (Sandholtz and Zysman 1989: 103–6). An elite coalition came together initially in the area of information technology (IT). A motivating factor was the ever-increasing cost of corporate research and development (R&D) in a fragmented market, where no single company could draw the economic benefits from a large domestic market as a consequence of its product innovation: something that placed European IT companies at a disadvantage compared to their Japanese and American competitors. The coalition brought together twelve major electronics companies from the EC in collaboration with European Commissioner Viscount Davignon, who held responsibility for the research and technology portfolio. The European Strategic Programme for Research and Development in Information Technology (ESPRIT), which was agreed in 1982, was one specific outcome (Sandholtz 1992). Cross-national R&D collaboration was supported as a way of overcoming market fragmentation.

The parallel to this development in respect of the internal market was the lobbying undertaken by the European Round Table of Industrialists (Cowles 1995). It brought together industrialists from the largest European companies and campaigned for completion of the internal market. In this respect it proved rather more effective than the established representative group for business in the EC, the Union of Industries of the European Community (UNICE). The Round Table's goals were more strategically focused because it was less involved in seeking to influence the minutiae of EC legislation. Hence it proved to be a valuable ally of the Commission in advancing the White Paper.

For its part, the Commission was able to capitalise on a number of developments which suggested that the internal market programme could offer a useful core to its work. It was not just the support of the Round Table, for that would not have been sufficient for success. It included the all-important positions of key national governments (see below). However, there were also the lessons which it was able to draw from the jurisprudence of the ECJ on internal market matters, notably the *Dassonville* and *Cassis de Dijon* cases, which indirectly provided a potential new route map to the goal of a common market. The route comprised mutual recognition of products rather than the much more centralised approach attempted hitherto. That approach had necessitated the agreement of legislation on free movement in the Council of Ministers. However, the need to take decisions by unanimous vote had been a major factor in the lack of progress on the necessary legislation. The *Cassis* case made clear that only under certain circumstances could national legislation hinder trade and that such hindrances would be deemed 'suspect' until approved in the courts (Armstrong 1995). The way was cleared for a much lighter-touch regulatory approach to the single market.

The implications of the 1979 *Cassis* judgment had been clear to the Commission for some time. Indeed, it stimulated the development of many internal market proposals during the Thorn Commission (1981–84). Apart from the support offered by the so-called Kangaroo Group of Members of the European Parliament (MEPs), established in 1981, there was little resonance beyond DG III (then industrial affairs and internal market) of the Commission. Nevertheless, it was the work conducted during this period which greatly contributed to the White Paper (see Cameron 1992: 52).

The crucial factor for the Commission was the appointment of the new team of commissioners to take office with Jacques Delors at the start of 1985. Delors sought a programme with which to make an impact, particularly since the budgetary stalemate of the EC had been removed by agreement at the June 1984 Fontainebleau summit. Delors' preferences were for strengthening monetary integration. However, Lord Cockfield quickly appreciated the opportunity available to construct an internal market programme, drawing upon the measures which had been developed under his predecessor Karl-Heinz Narjes, as the centre-point of the new Commission's work programme (see Cockfield 1994).

It was still necessary for much work to be done by the Commission to build up a kind of 'advocacy coalition' supporting the programme.[7] Crucial to this was the ability of Delors to deploy his political skills within the European Council. Although this institution is usually regarded as the quintessentially inter-governmental institution of the EC, in reality it also offers a potentially important channel through which a Commission president can secure a direct line to the European leadership: something which was not provided for in the founding treaties. As Ludlow puts it, 'Far from being a threat to the Commission or its President in their efforts to provide the Community with leadership, the European Council is an indispensable aid' (Ludlow 1991: 113). Thus, in the post-Fontainebleau period Delors was able to utilise the Commission's access to the government heads to respond to their earlier hand-wringing statements about the poor performance in progress towards an internal market. Cockfield refers to Delors' work as 'inducing' the government heads to support the completion of the internal market (1994: 43).

The Commission's role and its support from transnational actors would have been of much less importance were it not for endorsement of the single market objective by certain national governments (as well as the endorsements given earlier by the European Council as a whole). The principal supporters were the UK government of Mrs Thatcher, the Dutch government of Mr Lubbers and Chancellor Kohl's coalition in Germany. These and other governments had come into office in the period from 1979, and displayed greater ideological-political preference for a neo-liberal political agenda (Cameron 1992: 56–9). The UK government had already embarked on a domestic programme of economic de-regulation and privatisation, so support for the SEM objective was consistent in terms of economic ideas. Indeed, at the Fontainebleau European Council meeting it presented a paper on the development of European integration, in which liberalisation of the internal market was a key component (HM Government 1984). Moreover, the strong domestic financial-services sector in the City of London, itself undergoing liberalisation in the 'big bang' of the mid-1980s, was advocating the liberalisation of the service sectors in the EC so as to open up markets hitherto closed to its products. The Federal Republic of Germany, traditionally the protagonist of (conditional) economic liberalism, was also ready to embrace the objective.

The vital additional member of the coalition was the French government. As has been well charted, its policy reversal in March 1983, when it abandoned 'Keynesianism in one country' in favour of joint European action, led on to growing support for internal market liberalisation. This support was somewhat fragile but was facilitated by the EC's actions in developing research and technology policy, a policy area which bore some resemblance to the French domestic policy of picking 'industrial champions'. Research and technology policy was one of the policy areas placed on a more secure constitutional footing in the SEA.

We have outlined the mainsprings of the SEM programme. However, we need to be aware of the wider context, including the negotiation of the SEA. First, this context was inextricably linked with putting the SEM into practice, for the SEA made important procedural changes to the decisional capacity of the Council of Ministers. Thus, if mutual recognition and the White Paper changed the route map towards a single market, the SEA helped clear up some of the 'gearbox problems' of the decision-making process so that progress could be facilitated. Secondly, the SEA came to form part of 'the new European bargain'. Thus, economic and social cohesion, technology policy, environmental policy as well as increases in the power of the EP and other institutional reforms were bound up with the SEM goal.

The SEM/SEA package deal

Outlining the contents of the package deal is essentially a descriptive exercise. However, it is an important exercise for three reasons.

First, since we have argued that the SEM cannot be seen as being confined to the White Paper on the internal market, and has to be interpreted more widely, the setting out of the wider contours of the package is important for understanding the policy dynamics in the case studies which follow. The overall package reflected an aggregation of Member States' interests, but refracted through the EC's institutional structure, and embodied in a delicate consensus reached in 1985/86. How far could this consensus be maintained when it came to the agreement on the measures needed to achieve the SEM goal over the subsequent years? How far would linkages with other aspects of the SEA come into play in the negotiations?

A second issue concerns reviewing the analyses which have been made hitherto of the package deal (undertaken in the next section). How far do they present a balanced view of the package? Do these analyses in fact encompass the breadth of the SEM/SEA package deal?

Thirdly, the SEM/SEA package brought about a major transformation in the governance of the EC. It represented a step-change in the EC's institutional capacity. This step-change was not confined to the SEM but was part of a wider pattern. Thus, in order to encapsulate the transformation of governance, we need to be familiar with the wider picture of constitutional and institutional change.

The White Paper and the internal market

A central part of the SEM/SEA agreement derived from the programme to complete the internal market by the end of 1992 was enshrined in two ways. First of all, it was set down in the conclusions of the June 1985 Milan meeting of the European Council, which endorsed the Commission's White Paper as a programme for achieving the goal. However, this agreement did not have an authoritative, constitutional quality. Hence, when it came to the negotiation of the SEA, treaty modifications were needed to take account of the way in which the internal market goal amended the pre-existing commitments to a common market. Hence the goal was a product of the Milan European Council but was given greater force in the SEA. This dual provenance was a key reason why the SEM and the SEA could not be separated in political terms.

The White Paper set forward a strategy for completing the internal market that was driven by an attack on barriers and obstacles. In consequence, it did not follow the division of labour within the Treaty of Rome of separating out the so-called four freedoms (of goods, services, labour and capital). Rather, it used the attack on frontiers and barriers as a specific strategy. Cockfield justifies this approach in the following terms:

> If the Community was to become a United Europe ... the frontiers and the controls associated with them would have to go. It is useless simplifying the controls and leaving the frontiers in place. As long as the frontiers are there they will attract controls: each control will be the excuse for some other control. (Cockfield 1994: 41)

This approach had the secondary advantage that it did not discriminate between the four freedoms. Hence it did not present the opportunity for the Member States to continue, for instance, to neglect the creation of a completed internal market in services: an area where progress had been negligible in the past.

The White Paper itself was structured around the different types of barriers: physical, technical and fiscal. In all, it comprised some 300 legislative proposals but was later reduced to 282.

Physical barriers related to the largely administrative controls conducted at frontier posts. Such controls included varying national customs documentation (subsequently standardised in the Single Administrative Document in 1988); formalities relating to taxation documentation; controls over the movement of EC/EU citizens; and a range of veterinary and phyto-sanitary controls over such matters as animal diseases and pesticide residues. Technical barriers referred to the many divergent national requirements affecting the cross-frontier sale of goods or services. Some of these barriers took on a legal form, that is they originated in national legislation. Others arose from national industry standards, set in many cases by agencies with independence from the national governments. The common effect of these technical barriers, whatever their character, was to fragment the EC market. In other words, goods which could be sold in one Member State could not be sold in another, thus disrupting the possibilities for deriving the maximum benefit from economies-of-scale production. These technical barriers were pervasive with major economic costs (see Cecchini *et al.* 1988).

The third category – fiscal barriers – related to the impact of divergent excise duties and indirect taxation regimes upon cross-border trade in the EC, as well as certain aspects of corporate taxation which affected trans-frontier activities.

These three categories are well known from the literature on the internal market. As noted above, this categorisation was in part the product of Cockfield's attempt to tackle the balkanised character of the European market in a manner which was neutral in respect of the four freedoms and of individual economic sectors. Viewed from a somewhat different perspective, however, the internal market entailed a focus on a set of specific areas. These included:

- opening up public procurement to ensure that the purchasing activities of public-sector bodies would be open to similar cross-border competition comparable to the private sector;
- extension of cross-border competition to the service sectors, including transport and financial services;
- adopting a new approach to the legal requirements associated with product safety and the norms associated with technical standards; and
- progress on the mutual recognition of professional qualifications as a means of promoting intra-EC labour mobility.

Not much of this detail was carried forward into the internal-market-related amendments contained in the SEA. Essentially these comprised the insertion into the EEC Treaty of the goal of completing the internal market and a range of more procedural adjustments to provide for a move to QMV in the Council of Ministers on specific aspects of the White Paper (on the latter, see below).[8] One point worth emphasising here is that the date for completing the internal market – 31 December 1992 – was weakened somewhat by a declaration attached to the SEA, stating that the deadline did not have automatic legal effect. The governments of France, Greece and Ireland were reported to have opposed the automatic legal effect (Corbett 1987: 245). Despite the declaration, it was to have little significant impact on the preparations by economic actors (see also Snyder 1993: 21).

Institutional change
The principal areas of institutional change all affected the policy process in connection with the internal market legislative programme. These were the changes relating to:

- the voting arrangements in the Council of Ministers;
- the role of the EP in policy-making; and
- the Commission's powers.

In addition to these three areas of change, there were two more minor developments. One was the formalisation for the first time of the regular summit meetings – the European Council – in the SEA. The other was provision (included at the request of the ECJ) for the creation of a Court of First Instance to alleviate some of the burden on the ECJ. This step would have an indirect effect on the internal market programme in the sense that relief of the ECJ itself could enable that court to concentrate on the key cases – many related to the internal market – arising from litigation in the national courts and referred to the ECJ under Article 177.

The working practices of the Council of Ministers had long been regarded as the root of much of the EC's so-called Eurosclerosis. The political need to reach a consensus amongst all the governments on all legislation – regardless of whether or not the treaty provided for decisions by QMV – had been the legacy of the empty-chair crisis and its *dénouement* in the 1966 Luxembourg Compromise (Teasdale 1993). Thus, 'before 1986 majority votes in the Council rarely reached double figures in a full year' (Allen 1992: 42). In order, therefore, to improve the Council's decisional efficiency and, in consequence, that of the EC as a whole, member governments had to undertake reforms. During the 1985 IGC negotiations the governments were also mindful of the Iberian enlargement taking effect at the start of 1986 and the accompanying possibility of increased decisional gridlock in a Community with twelve sets of national vested interests.

The SEA introduced QMV in two distinct ways. First, it revised the existing EEC Treaty by changing the voting arrangements specified in several policy areas:

- the alteration or suspension of the common customs tariff (Article 28, EC);
- mutual recognition of qualifications amongst the self-employed (Article 57(2), EC, further revised by the TEU);
- liberalisation of capital movements (Article 70, EC);
- liberalisation of the service sector for nationals of third countries (Article 59, EC); and
- the regulation of air and maritime transport (Article 84, EC).

Secondly, the SEA introduced some changes in competences, and at the same time provided for the use of QMV in these areas. Of central importance to the internal market programme was the introduction both of the new Article 100a, which was the central means of obtaining the broad objective of completing the internal market, as set out in Article 8a (after the TEU, Article 7a), and of QMV as the means of decision-making. Relating to the approximation of legislation in Member States with a view to creating the internal market, Article 100a with QMV offered a more rapid legislative route than the existing Article 100, which necessitated unanimous voting in the Council and had been one of the root causes for poor progress. It must be mentioned, however, that fiscal measures, the free movement of persons and the rights and interests of employed persons were specifically excluded from QMV at the behest of several national governments under Article 100a(2) (for details, see Corbett 1987: 245). Moreover, Article 100a(4) permitted national derogations provided these were not employed in a manner that would be discriminatory. Elsewhere in the SEA, QMV was introduced into what might be termed second-order legislation relating to environmental policy and research and technological development.[9] QMV was also extended to legislation on the working environment (Article 118a, EC).

The overall purpose of these moves to QMV was to facilitate progress on the internal market and on the other policy areas. Bearing in mind this book's concern with a wider notion of the SEM rather than just with the contents of the White Paper, it must be noted that the SEA did not introduce constitutional change relevant to some important adjacent areas, such as competition policy.[10] Nevertheless, the increased potential use of QMV had a wide dynamic effect on the EC's legislative output.

The EP's powers were extended principally through two measures. First, a new cooperation procedure was introduced. This procedure was to apply, *inter alia*, to the approximation of internal market legislation under Article 100a, as well as to legislation on the working environment (Article 118a). The cooperation procedure involved adherence to a specific time-table for the legislative process, thus reinforcing the efforts to accelerate internal market law-making. The procedure enabled the EP to be involved in two readings of affected legislation. We will not outline the operation of this procedure here – see Chapter 3 – but the EP derived political resources enabling it to become involved in trilateral horse-trading (chiefly with the Council but with the Commission as a kind of mediator). Further increases in EP power came through articles requiring parliamentary assent on enlargement of the EC and on international agreements.[11]

The changes to the Commission's powers were less striking in the SEA. First of all, in those policy areas that were formally added to Community competence, such as environmental and technology policy, the Commission was given clearer standing to initiate the policy process than had existed beforehand.

Secondly, the Commission was given extended powers to manage and implement policy under Article 145. This development gave birth to the phenomenon of 'comitology'. Essentially, unless the Council reserved powers to itself, the Commission was responsible for policy management using one of three different types of committee. Each type of committee comprises a different balance of power between the Commission itself and national governments. A 1987 Council decision established the arrangements for comitology but the EP was unhappy at the limited scope afforded for parliamentary supervision (Jacobs, Corbett and Shackleton 1992: 230–5). The EP sought to challenge the procedures in the decision by way of an annulment action before the ECJ, though the action was declared inadmissible on procedural grounds.[12] Comitology has proved to be an area of ongoing inter-institutional conflict.

And thirdly, the Commission's mediatory powers were increased because of new responsibilities in seeking compromises between the EP and the Council where disagreements over legislation arose in the operation of the new cooperation procedure.

Overall, the purpose of the institutional reforms was to increase the decisional capacity of the EC in the light of the internal market programme and the new treaty powers conferred in other policy areas. Linked to the institutional reforms were a series of substantive changes to specific policy goals, to which we now turn our attention.

Social policy
The SEA contained two developments in the area of social policy. One was the attempt to develop employer–employee 'social dialogue' (Article 118b). The second change, in Article 118a, was designed to provide a floor level of standards in the working environment, largely on health and safety matters; individual Member States would be able to set higher national standards. The thinking behind this treaty change was to seek to prevent increased competition within the internal market giving rise to declining standards in the working environment. As will be seen (Chapter 9), this new treaty provision was utilised in an expansive manner by the Commission with a view to breaking the long-standing blockage of EC social legislation. The situation was further complicated by subsequent developments in the TEU, which provided a different legislative route to social legislation – albeit without British participation – by means of the Protocol and Agreement on Social Policy.

Environmental policy
The SEA's provisions on environmental policy built on the considerable amount of legislative activity which the EC had undertaken in the period since the early 1970s. Three Environmental Action Programmes (EAPs) had already been agreed before the EC gained explicit powers to legislate in the policy area! Articles 130r–t, which were subsequently revised in the TEU, set out the objectives of environmental legislation and the details of the policy. A potential conflict existed between the treaty's environmental provisions and those relating to the internal market. Not only could some issues of environmental regulation be considered as falling under Article 130s but they could also be considered as a matter of approximation of national legislation designed to provide a 'level playing field' in the internal market, and thus covered by Article 100a (see Chapter 8 below; also see Jacobs *et al.* 1992: 188). The fact that the two articles had different policy-making procedures led to a number of disagreements on the legal base of Commission proposals (see Chapter 8).

Research and technology policy
Here, as with environmental policy, the SEA served to codify an area of activity which was well established, albeit using Article 235. Already prior to signature of the SEA one EC Framework Programme had been agreed and put into effect. As with environmental policy, the SEA set out policy

objectives, policy modalities and the policy-making process. Collective action in this policy area was seen as a necessary complement to the internal market programme itself. Thus, the fragmentation of the internal market was not just a matter of eliminating the barriers outlined earlier but of going further upstream in the production process to encourage collective collaboration before new technologies assumed readiness for the market. Such collaborative research, it was hoped, would avoid some of the duplication of effort between companies in different Member States that, in turn, limited the scope for economic returns later in the production process.

Economic and social cohesion

Economic and social cohesion arose in discussions at the IGC because of the concern that peripheral economic regions would be especially exposed to new competitive threats in a completed internal market. The wish to include new treaty provisions was actively supported by Greece, France, Ireland and the Commission itself (Corbett 1987: 248). Article 130a contains a general commitment to the EC's pursuit of actions strengthening economic and social cohesion. In fact, there was no elaboration in the new section of the treaty to explain what social cohesion really meant. Instead, the specific details of the subsequent articles really reinforced the role of the structural funds as instruments of economic re-distribution.

It is important to note that some Member States saw the treaty's cohesion commitments as intrinsic to the new economic bargain of the SEM/ SEA. It is only an overly formalistic reading of events in the mid-1980s which detaches cohesion from the internal market programme. Even in the internal Commission politics leading up to the launch of the White Paper clear links were drawn with the need to promote economic convergence. Lord Cockfield, while denying formal 'linkage', puts it thus:

> The agreement I made with my colleagues [i.e. Commissioners] from the South was that in return for their support for my Internal Market Programme, I would support them in their demands that the Structural Funds be doubled. (Cockfield 1994: 45)

Those politicians and analysts who ignored the connection between the two policy areas, and saw the internal market as an entirely free-standing issue, risked a major misjudgment of the character of the new 'bargain' struck in the mid-1980s. Indeed, with Spain and Portugal acceding to the EC in the month before the SEA was signed, the political momentum on cohesion was further strengthened.

Monetary capacity

The final area of substantive change in the EEC Treaty concerned its so-called monetary capacity. In one sense this amendment to the treaty had little impact; it simply recognised the existence of the EMS, which had developed outside the formal treaty framework in the period since 1979.

However, it was clear that the Commission and some member govern-ments wished to go further. Indeed, the SEA's preamble included EMU as an objective of the EC. The policy connection with economic and mon-etary integration was, at this stage, embryonic. It was not until the June 1988 Hanover European Council meeting that the EMU objective was firmly placed on to the EC's policy agenda as an issue linked to completion of the internal market. The momentum of EMU was accelerated from 1990 as it became associated with the wish to deepen integration in the context of German unification.

European Political Cooperation

One last policy area strengthened by the SEA was European Political Cooperation (EPC), albeit in a separate, inter-governmental part (or title) of the SEA. The treaty changes on EPC naturally enough reflected the interests of certain Member States within the broad package deal of the SEM/SEA (for details, see Allen 1992: 47–50). However, the connection between EPC and the internal market thereafter was negligible, so we can leave this aspect of the SEA aside.

Summary

Overall, the SEM/SEA package deal covered a broad range of policy and institutional issues. It was not a free-standing neo-liberal economic agenda but contained several countervailing steps. The strengthening of research and technology policy could be seen as enhancing the status of a policy area with a more mercantilist character. The cohesion issue strengthened notions of economic re-distribution. And there were also limited hints at the need to have more socially solidaristic flanking measures for the internal market, even if they were initially confined to regulation of the working environment. What was common to the package as a whole was the enhancement of both the EC's governance competence and capacity by increasing the efficiency of the decision-making machinery. The focus on governance capacity of the EC will be central to the main body of this study. Thus, we shall examine how the SEM/SEA package affected policy- and decision-making in specific areas. Our focus, therefore, will be upon the policy dynamics and the issues of governance: a somewhat different research agenda from existing analysis, which we now review. Finally, we would underline the fact that we see the SEM – as we use the term – as going beyond the White Paper and encompassing a broader notion of market integration.

Analytical perspectivies on the SEM/SEA

What are the key analytical approaches which have been used hitherto with a view to explaining the dynamics of the SEM and the SEA? Of course, some accounts have concentrated in presenting a full account of events and of their significance, most notably in a succinct article by Jacques Pelkmans (1994) and in a more studied chapter by Helen Wallace and Alasdair Young (1996). Attempts to provide more theoretically-driven accounts of the SEM have had rather more mixed results. In many respects the mixed results are reflective of the shortcomings of integration theory more generally.

Institutional inter-governmentalism

Andrew Moravcsik's work has been particularly influential in the analytical debate on integration within recent political science (Moravcsik 1991). After a brief discussion of 'supranational institutionalism', an approach which approximates the assumptions of neo-functionalism, Moravcsik sets out his own favoured interpretation: inter-governmental institutionalism. This approach he sees as based upon three key characteristics: inter-governmentalism (the important role of the leading Member States in EC bargaining); lowest-common-denominator bargaining; and the protection of national sovereignty (Moravcsik 1991: 46–8). He then applies this approach to the empirical evidence and finds that it has more explanatory power than the alternative of supranational institutionalism. It is worth pointing out that Moravcsik's 1991 article does not have much methodological specification of the domestic dimension of the shaping of the SEM/SEA package. However, in a subsequent article (Moravcsik 1993), he then develops his framework to incorporate that dimension. Now termed 'liberal intergovernmentalism', his approach uses liberal theory to explain how national preferences are formed within Member States, while retaining an inter-governmentalist perspective on upper-tier bargaining.[13]

First of all, we share Moravcsik's understanding of the *scope* of the agreement itself, namely a balanced one perceiving the SEM and the SEA as part of a package deal. But what of the analysis and interpretation? Clearly, a view of European integration which places the nation states at the centre of evolution has to correspond to reality, at least where major constitutional reforms are concerned, for the unanimous agreement of national governments is required. However, several questions may be posed beyond agreement upon this point:

- Does Moravcsik's analysis underestimate important aspects of supranational institutional input?
- What exactly is the contribution of the 'institutionalism' in his framework of intergovernmental institutionalism?
- Does he overrationalise a much more haphazard process?
- Does his approach only have validity for the grand political bargains of European integration but then display weaknesses in explaining the more routine phases of policy-making and implementation?

• Is it valid to examine the phenomenon of integration with reference only to the episodic grand bargains?

Clearly, these questions suggest critical answers, so what are they?

First, we would argue that Moravcsik does indeed underestimate important aspects of supranational institutional input. His view that the EP played a limited role in negotiations is not disputed fundamentally. The EP's contribution was twofold. On the SEM the Kangaroo Group gave the oxygen of publicity – at least within EC circles – to the desirability of breaking down (or leaping over) national frontiers. Similarly, the EP's work under Spinelli, culminating in the 1984 Draft Treaty Establishing the European Union, gave some momentum to constitutional reform but played only a background role in the negotiation of the SEA. The EP's cotribution was in the background, shaping the agenda to a limited extent.

Moravcsik devotes rather more attention to the Commission but is ultimately unpersuaded of its critical importance (Moravcsik 1991: 65–7). Thus, Lord Cockfield's White Paper is seen as simply being a response to an invitation from the European Council. Even allowing for Cockfield perhaps seeking to aggrandise his role, Moravcsik's account does not correspond to that offered by the former commissioner, who saw the incoming Commission as identifying the internal market as the basis upon which to advance economic integration towards some of the EC's original goals (Cockfield 1994). Further, and as already indicated, the European Council had been issuing statements on the internal market since 1981; the mere commissioning of a report does not of itself justify an explanation of the SEM/SEA which gives all the credit to government heads. Several reports have been requested by the European Council, particularly in its early years, that were actually designed to fudge an issue and *remove* it from the agenda. The Tindemans Report and the Report of the Three Wise Men are two that come to mind (Bulmer and Wessels 1987). So it seems questionable to use such evidence to dismiss the Commission's role in the shaping of the SEM. The Commission is reduced, in Moravcsik's account, to a virtual puppet-on-a-string pulled by the national governments.

We need to bear in mind some alternative possibilities too. What would have happened if the Commission had failed to put forward an acceptable White Paper? Would the European Council have knocked it into shape over their short two-day meeting in order to ensure that the Commission's shortcomings did not disrupt their combined national preferences? Such an explanation seems highly unlikely. In our view the Commission was astute in putting forward a programme which largely eschewed direct clashes with Member States over national sovereignty. And where Member States did feel some unease over challenges to national sovereignty, such as the UK government did on indirect tax harmonisation, they reserved the matter for unanimous voting during the subsequent negotiations leading to the SEA.

We also need to consider the *anti-monde* of life without the European Council. The Council of Internal Market Ministers had already been criticised as early as 1983 for its lack of response to the government heads' encouragement. And the governments had already had since 1958 to construct the common market! One of the key problems for the Commission had been that it was very difficult for it to launch major policy initiatives within the EC institutional structure. The reaction to Hallstein's proposals in 1965 – namely the 'empty-chair' crisis – had weakened precisely the Commission's ability to launch major initiatives. The European Council offered a new route for the Commission to do so, and the Commission under Delors learned how to make the most of this possibility. Moravcsik neglects the contribution of the European Council, as an institution offering its own opportunity structures, to securing the package, including offering the Commission a voice in the critical negotiations. We argue that that institutional context matters.

Arguably an even greater omission in Moravcsik's account is the role of the ECJ. Despite his recognition (1991: 43) that the European Court is one of the potential sources of EC reform, there is only one other reference to it in the article. On a general level the ECJ's establishment of the principles of supremacy and direct effect of EC law (see Weiler 1991 and below) could ensure that the whole SEM initiative would have a qualitatively different, direct impact at the national level, and thus be distinct from other international legal arrangements. Furthermore, in the specific context of the internal market, it was precisely the jurisprudence of the Court, and in particular its *Cassis de Dijon* ruling, which paved the way for a new regulatory strategy for completing the SEM. And this was of critical importance in two specific senses.

One was its introduction of mutual recognition as a means towards achieving a more complete SEM. Mutual recognition is a much more sovereignty-friendly approach than the prior expectation that a single market could only be achieved by legislative harmonisation: the much-disliked legislation on 'Euro-beer', 'Euro-sausages' and so on that offended national tastes and traditions. In the single market domain more than any other, the interpretations of the ECJ have played a significant role in shaping policy. Its judgments were an integral part of a multi-faceted pattern of developments that led up to the SEM programme.

The other, indirect contribution of the ECJ was precisely that its jurisprudence did not go unnoticed in the Commission. That institution recognised the new possibilities which had been opened up towards achieving the original goals of the EEC Treaty. The Commission's response would appear to be a suitable case for empirical testing of the literature of 'policy learning': the capacity of government or institutions to learn from its own (or others') experiences (Rose 1993; Sabatier 1988). Although that task is not attempted here, the fact remains that it was during the Thorn presidency that the Commission Directorate General responsible for the internal market began work on various proposals following the new approach. And thus it was that Cockfield's White Paper – despite its somewhat arbitrary contents – could be assembled quickly and provide an acceptable strategy for the European Council.

It is our contention, therefore, that Moravcsik underestimates the role of the supranational institutions. What, then, of the contribution of 'institutionalism' to Moravcsik's account?

Here we can be briefer. Empirically, inter-governmental *institutionalism* comprises three core features: inter-governmentalism, lowest-common-denominator bargaining and protection of sovereignty (Moravcsik 1991: 47–8). However, the latter two features were already well established in the literature on inter-governmentalism (see, for instance, Webb 1983). *Plus ça change?* Theoretically, Moravcsik links his approach to Keohane's 'modified structural realist' view of international relations. That may account for the wish to use a different title from mere inter-governmentalism. However, the approach appears to offer no analytical insights into the contribution of the institutions and their configuration to explaining the SEA outcome. In this respect, Moravcsik does not give attention to the burgeoning literature in comparative politics (and in economic analysis) that sees institutional configurations as playing an important role in shaping policy-makers' preferences, policy itself or, indeed, economic behaviour.[14] We shall return to this 'new institutionalist' literature in Chapter 2.

A third observation about Moravcsik's interpretation is the obverse of this point. If institutions are deemed to have no impact upon the shaping of the SEA, then there is a strong assumption that the agreement was a rational outcome of negotiations. But this view encounters one of the problems of rational actor analysis, namely that a disorderly process of negotiations looks overly tidy when viewed with the benefit of hindsight. We have already pointed out that the Italian presidency's unprecedented use of a procedural vote to call the IGC leading to the SEA was not predestined. In other words, the IGC was convened almost as much as a result of accident than of strategy. Moreover, as Garrett and Weingast have argued, ideas and institutions provide important information in constructing the shared belief systems necessary to a such a major step as the SEM/SEA (Garrett and Weingast 1993). Although Moravcsik does not totally neglect the role of ideas and institutions, they are not employed in an analytical sense to explain how it was that the SEM/SEA came to be agreed at that particular juncture. We would argue, therefore, that there is a danger in Moravcsik's analysis that it overly rationalises the negotiation process through a reductionist emphasis on the role of national governments.

What is the validity of inter-governmental institutionalism more widely?[15] Can it be applied to the more routine phases of EC/EU policy-making or is it at its most valuable in respect of the grand bargains? Certainly, the greater attention given by Moravcsik to the domestic level in his 'liberal intergovernmentalism' (1993) helped increase the viability of Moravcsik's explanation of the integration process, for the role of interest groups at domestic and supranational levels is much greater than presented in his account of the SEA. We have already argued that Moravcsik's account underemphasises the contributions of the supranational institutions. However, on more routine policy the supranational institutions have much greater autonomy to influence the policy agenda and content. This finding will be illustrated in our case studies.

It is the three core elements of inter-governmental institutionalism which present the problems when the focus of attention shifts from the 'grand bargains' like the SEM/SEA and the TEU to more routine policy-making. In this routine policy-making the Commission is much more clearly empowered as the initiator of policy; decision-making in the Council may be by QMV; the EP enjoys greater power; transnational interest groups, corporate actors and sub-national government are much more organised. These circumstances run against the principal assumptions of inter-governmental institutionalism. Thus, we take the view that both inter-governmental institutionalism and liberal inter-governmentalism are best suited to explaining the major political bargains of the EC/EU. Our view is echoed by Peterson (1995), who sees Moravcsik's analysis as best suited to 'history-making' decisions in European integration.[16] At the level of routine policy-making, assumptions about the retention of sovereignty and about lowest-common-denominator solutions intuitively appear questionable. Indeed, decisional complexity may render the premises of inter-governmentalism untenable in many policy areas. We shall address some of these points in the specific context of our case studies.

It would be unjustified to criticise Moravcsik for not giving attention to the question of the implementation of the SEM/SEA. His concentration is on the constitutive politics of the SEA and not on the politics of putting it into practice. However, it is dangerous to only consider the role of domestic politics in the shaping of national preferences which in turn shape the package deal reached through inter-state bargaining. Intrinsic to the constitutive politics phase is ratification of the bargain. The Danish and Irish referenda and the parliamentary ratification procedures did not in fact obstruct the SEM/SEA but the problems experienced with the Maastricht Treaty indicate that this dimension is neglected by both analysts and national governments at their peril. To put it another way, it would be faulty policy analysis to examine how a specific area of EC policy is made and then neglect how it is put into practice. Should constitutive politics be exempt from this concern?

In summary, institutional inter-governmentalism may offer a valuable and parsimonious account of European integration. But it is a single narrative; it relies on a somewhat selective reading of events; and it is best attuned to the grand bargains rather than to developments in between.

Transnational relations: 'recasting the European bargain'

An earlier account of the origins of the single market was offered by Sandholtz and Zysman (1989). Their interpretation emphasises two key components, namely the role of elite bargains and of Commission entrepreneurship (1989: 96–7). Their arguments bear some resemblence to Moravcsik's 'supranational institutionalism' but, in reality, are an account based on the perspectives of transnational relations theory. Hence Sandholtz and Zysman's account essentially revolves around the changes in the international economy, with particular reference to technological change, and how these then led to changes in the thinking of transnational European business elites and in the Commission.[17] Clearly, it would be quite wrong to discount these developments, which serve as a useful corrective for the state-centred interpretation offered by Moravcsik. Nevertheless, Sandholtz and Zysman's interpretation of how the elite bargains and the Commission's entrepreneurship translated into the SEM/SEA is underspecified.

Three specific observations may be made about their argument. First, what is the role of national politics in the forming of the SEM? A domestic politics explanation is rejected *a priori* as inadequate (Sandholtz and Zysman 1989: 100) but the role of the Member States and domestic politics in shaping the bargain is simply not spelled out. It is one thing to reject an explanation resting solely on Member State politics but it is unconvincing not to integrate them into an explanation.

Secondly, for an article presenting Commission entrepreneurship as a motor behind the SEM, it is strange indeed that there is no detail on how this entrepreneurship affected the ultimate 'bargain'. How was the White Paper drawn up? How did it come to be accepted by the European Council? These central aspects of Commission entrepreneurship are not even considered. Instead, there is empirical detail concerning analogous developments in telematics. Yet the circumstances are quite different. Creation of a common market was part of the original treaty objectives; research and technology policy was not. Thus, the jurisprudence of the ECJ in the *Cassis* case was one factor opening up scope for the Commission to employ its entrepreneurship. But *that* crucial aspect of Commission entrepreneurship is also neglected! In short, the telematics case has some interesting parallels in abstract terms but was not subject to the same policy dynamics, for technology policy was new and scarcely subject to the jurisprudence of the ECJ. Or, to put it another way, the SEM was not new, it was merely a re-formulation of existing treaty goals. In that respect it had much to do with 'policy learning': learning from the failures of the old approach, from the lessons of the *Cassis* judgment.

A third problem arises from the interesting argument that the '1992 movement' can be analysed as a hierarchy of bargains. As Sandholtz and Zysman argue, the fundamental bargains are embodied in the SEA and the White Paper. However, the SEA is not given any sustained analysis as part of their study of 'recasting the European bargain'. It was this omission which enabled Moravcsik (1991) to respond with his inter-governmental institutionalist explanation, which we have already examined.

In short, Sandholtz and Zysman's piece is the proverbial curate's egg. It puts forward two important hypotheses for explaining the SEM/SEA – elite bargains and Commission entrepreneurship – but then fails to explore all the appropriate empirical material to support them. Instead, there is some interesing material on parallel developments in technology policy but these, ultimately, are somewhat spurious. Additionally, there is the important pointer to the importance of transnational business elites: something which has been taken up further in the work of Maria Green Cowles (Cowles 1995).

Ideas, interests and institutions

Garrett and Weingast (1993) offer a rather different kind of explanation for the EC's success in agreeing to the SEM programme. It rests upon the assumption that, 'ideas, social norms, institutions, and shared expectations may influence both the way actors choose to cooperate and the stability of these arrangements over time' (176). Institutions are seen as playing an important role in providing information and in helping to construct a shared belief system. Proceeding from these assumptions, and with supportive prisoner's dilemma explanations, Garrett and Weingast come on to a specific application to the SEM. Rejecting overly rationalised explanations, they see the *Cassis* decision as providing an essential focal point in ideas (i.e. mutual recognition) that was critical in explaining how the Member States were able to agree on the SEM. In particular, the role of the European legal system and of the ECJ as guarantors of the SEM is regarded as explaining why Member States were prepared to place their trust in the functioning of the system.

Garrett and Weingast's emphasis on the importance of ideas and institutions brings into focus an important additional facet of the SEM. However, two particular points of criticism may be directed at their study. The first is that the focus of their analysis is essentially upon the SEM. They argue that the role of the legal dimension was important for ensuring that certain key Member States felt their interests would be guaranteed in the courts. However, this explanation is partial. Other Member States signed up to the SEM/SEA for other benefits: because of a broad commitment to deeper integration; because of anticipated side-payments embedded in the idea of cohesion; because of an anticipated strengthening of Europe's technology policy; and so on. Thus, by concentrating on the SEM, they arguably give only a partial explanation of actors' motivations. For some Member States it was the encompassing nature of the SEM/SEA bargain rather than the ECJ that explained their commitment to the programme of action.

A second observation is that the faith in the European legal structure is perhaps a little overdone. On the one hand, one gains the impression that much of the litigation within the EC pillar of the EU is to stop Member States cheating. In reality the vast majority involves private economic actors. Moreover, many of the proceedings initiated under Articles 169 and 170 (EC) concerning the treaty compatibility of Member States' actions do not in fact reach the ECJ but are resolved politically between the Commission and the member government concerned (see Snyder 1993). On the other hand, in the minority of cases where court proceedings do concern whether a state is 'cheating', a non-compliant Member State is aware that such proceedings can be protracted. Hence, several years may have elapsed by the time the cheating is eventually unmasked. Moreover, one might question whether Garrett and Weingast take due account of the different legal procedures in the Member States, so that the route to seeking redress – e.g. whether damages are payable – differs considerably from one state to another.[18] Hence the idea that the ECJ and EC law serve as guarantors for inter-state trust in the SEM is perhaps viewed too uncritically.

Thus, whilst we will argue that the role of institutions and ideas is important, we have some reservations about the match between the analysis of Garrett and Weingast and empirical reality.

Incomplete narratives: the neo-functionalist and neo-realist accounts
In a different type of account David Cameron (1992) aims to examine what insights into the origins of the SEM initiative can be offered by two theories: neo-functionalism and neo-realism. Empirically, this account presents a very balanced view of the dynamics of reform, although the focus on the SEM to the exclusion of the SEA is somewhat artificial for the reasons outlined earlier in this chapter. Nevertheless, Cameron includes the all-important inter-state bargaining; the role of the ECJ; the role of the European Council; the evidence concerning Commission entrepreneurship (including some which was omitted by Sandholtz and Zysman); and he acknowledges the role of transnational interests, although noting that their influence is a source of disagreement amongst analysts.

Ultimately, Cameron concludes, quite briefly, that both approaches offer valuable insights and that the situation was more complex than either neo-functionalist or neo-realist interpretations can accommodate (Cameron 1992: 64–5). He has much to say empirically about the policy-making institutions but makes no analytical suggestions in that direction. In short, it is a balanced empirical account but its contribution to the theoretical debate is principally to reveal the shortcomings of any single account using one or other of the dominant paradigms.

There are of course other accounts of the dynamics of the SEM/SEA which we are unable to consider here. However, in our view the accounts examined are either influential or representative of the existing theoretical approaches (or both). A striking omission is the use of an analytical approach sensitive to comparative social science. Such an approach, we believe, can offer valuable insights. First of all, it may help overcome the lack of dialogue between scholars of political science and of the law. Secondly, it may contribute to the growing literature on 'comparative politics' approaches to understanding the EU (see Hix 1994). What are the key considerations that such an approach should have?

Analytical lessons: towards a new method?

In our review of existing analyses a number of critical observations were made which can serve as guidelines for an alternative perspective.

- The analytical approach not only must be able to include – and preferably explain! – the major constitutive decisions of European integration but must also be capable of application to the more routine decision-making: the 'bread and butter' of the EU's work. Qualitatively the former decisions are important because constitutive decisions may create step-changes in governance capacity. However, routine decision-making is quantitatively more important for that is where changes in governance capacity become apparent. If no impact were felt upon routine decision-making, the constitutive political decisions would have been to no avail.

- Analysis must be confined not only to policy-making but must also be capable of application to the putting of policy goals into practice. Analysts of the key constitutive decisions have tended to neglect this aspect: something which was shown to be methodologically problematic by the problems associated with ratification of the TEU. This consideration might be held to demonstrate how research on European integration is often largely event-driven. However, in public policy and legal analysis there are well-established literatures on this dimension. The fundamental problem may in fact lie elsewhere, namely in epistemology. EU analysts' predominant reliance upon international relations theory, which is based, literally, on a whole world of experience, is likely to downplay the implementation of agreements precisely because the EU is _sui generis_ in this respect. However, it is only _sui generis_ if compared with other international organisations; comparison with federal and confederal political systems is arguably more valuable. Hence a reliance on the methods of comparative social science can help overcome these deficiencies.

- Analysis must be able to strike a balance between the political, economic and legal dimensions of integration. Too often the three areas are seen as independent of each other, as discrete. However, it is clear that perceived changes in the international economy acted as impulses for reviving the EC. The enhancement of the latter's governance capacity was designed to manage new international economic developments.

But the legal dimension is also critical and will be strongly underlined in our study. Too many scholars of economics and political science have neglected the legal dimension of integration (see Armstrong forthcoming; Weiler 1982; 1991). Political scientists in particular saw the 1960s as the epoch of stagnation in the integration process. Period. In reality, this was precisely the era when the key advances in legal integration took place. Without such advances it would not have been possible to rely on the ECJ and EC law to make a major contribution to the realisation of the SEM project. Moreover, as we will demonstrate in our case studies, the interaction between ECJ jurisprudence and the policy process is quite close. Within the EC pillar of the EU the law is central to the normative component of integration: it is often the 'currency' in which the policy debate has to be conducted. It is perhaps the most important EC/EU-specific normative 'social structure' with which policy actors must engage.

- A further consideration relates to the historical dimension of the policy process. It would be quite false to assume that the SEM programme started in 1985. In reality, the White Paper was simply a new means to an end stated in the 1957 Treaty of Rome, and only modified slightly in the SEA. Not only was the White Paper heavily influenced by the experience of trying to create a common market but so were many of the individual items of legislation. We need, therefore, to have an analytical method which is sensitive to history. In this way we can build into analysis of the policy process the interaction with earlier jurisprudence of the ECJ. Approaches which focus on the highly visible politics of treaty revision tend to freeze change at one time-point when, in reality, developments in ECJ jurisprudence may be creating more subtle, evolutionary change in governance regimes. Thus, the SEM/SEA may have brought about a kind of 'punctuated equilibrium' (Krasner 1984), that is a discontinuity, in the governance capacity of the EC. They did not, however, create a complete rupture with the past.
- In examining the governance of the EC/EU our approach gives considerable attention to institutional structure. One disadvantage of grand theories, such as neo-realism or neo-functionalism, is that they inevitably have some *a priori* assumptions about the institutional profile of the EU. Such assumptions can be unhelpful, for we risk ending up with conclusions that different theories – with quite different assumptions – can explain different policy case studies. If the theories are fundamentally incompatible with each other, however, this pick-and-mix approach has serious limitations in promoting a coherent intellectual understanding of the governance of the EU. Hence, we must adopt an approach which does not prescribe particular institutional forms. Instead, it may be more appropriate to ascribe the different patterns of power in different EU policy areas to different institutional attributes. And these

attributes will also differ between constitutive decisions on the overall development of integration, with the European Council normally the key body involved, and the more regulative, day-to-day decisions, where the Council, Commission, the ECJ and the EP are the principal institutions involved.

- The institutional structure, we argue, plays a major role in shaping the strategies of political forces. Interest groups and politicians adapt their strategies to the locus of political power. Hence we can provide a focus on the institutional structure of the EC/EU without de-politicising a fundamentally political process. This is *not* an approach which brings institutions in but then downplays political forces. It seeks to achieve an analytical balance between agency and structure: something which has not been achieved in the predominant paradigms (see Armstrong forthcoming).
- Finally, although they are still young, the institutions of the EU are not free of values. Embedded within them are values and norms which evolve gradually over time through learning-by-doing. Institutional norms can have a significant impact on how functions allocated to the EU are in fact operationalised. But these norms and values may also be subject to stronger, political change. That was the effect of the SEM/SEA package in increasing the presence of neo-liberal values in the work of the EC. Institutional change is unlikely to take place without changes in ideas and values. This relationship must also be taken into account in any study of governance, whether of the EU or of a nation state. We cannot talk of an EU political culture as yet. That is some way off. However, that does not mean that ideas, norms and values have no explanatory value in analysing the governance of the EU.

To conclude, we have set out a number of considerations which lead us to believe that a comparative social science method may offer valuable insights into the governance of the SEM. After all, most of these considerations would apply to the analysis of policy developments in the national context. More specifically, we will deploy some of the insights offered by the method of new institutionalism. Our attention now turns to outlining that approach.

Notes

1 The relationship between the provision for, and the use of, QMV will be discussed further in Chapter 3.
2 We confine discussion largely to English-language studies, although there is, of course, a rich literature in French and German on the subject.
3 In addition to these developments, there were abortive ones, notably the first attempt at Economic and Monetary Union (EMU). In respect of widening the EC, the first enlargement (1973) brought in Denmark, Ireland and the UK.

4 Only with the SEA did the meetings of the European Council formally become recognised. However, the formalist argument that it was not, therefore, an institution is unhelpful due to the achievements made during its first, informal decade, notably the creation of the EMS.

5 In fact, this can be regarded as nine occasions out of eleven European Council meetings, for at the December 1983 meeting in Athens, and at the March 1984 meeting in Brussels, no conclusions could be issued due to the disagreement concerning British budgetary payments. This logjam was cleared eventually at Fontainebleau in June 1984.

6 Cockfield's view finds specific support in the opening of the preamble to the SEA, which states:

> MOVED by the will to continue the work undertaken on the basis of the Treaties establishing the European Communities and to transform relations as a whole among their States into a European Union, in accordance with the Solemn Declaration of Stuttgart of 19 June 1983 . . .

Many commentators in the UK were quick to dismiss the Solemn Declaration as of little value. However, such an approach is to fall precisely into the trap of not recognising that even 'mere' declarations can reflect a shift in the norms and values embedded in the European institutions. Of course, UK observers (and ministers) might then compound the problem by arguing that treaty preambles are mere 'Eurobabble'. But, as Church and Phinnemore point out, 'many continental jurists accept them as meaningful commitments' (1994: 51). Thus, the relationship between ideas, norms and rhetoric, on the one hand, and institutions, on the other, is perceived rather differently between the UK and continental Member States.

7 On advocacy coalitions generally, see Sabatier (1988).

8 These changes were incorporated into Articles 7a, 7b, 7c, 28, 57(2), 59, 70(1), 84, 99, 100a and 100b of what is now – following consolidation of changes brought about by the TEU – the *EC* Treaty. For full details of the changes brought about by the SEA, and then by the TEU, to the original *EEC* Treaty, see Church and Phinnemore (1994: 516–27).

9 In environmental policy the Council would decide unanimously on what areas could subsequently be determined by QMV. In technology policy the multi-annual framework programmes would be decided unanimously, whilst the individual component programmes would be subject to QMV.

10 The eventual creation of the CFI, in 1989, did lead to changes in the judicial process, however.

11 Under Articles 237 and 238 (EEC). Article 237 has now become Article O of the TEU; Article 238, EC is the product of further amendment by the TEU.

12 It is to be noted that the procedural impediments to annulment actions by the EP have now been removed.

13 The empirical material used to support liberal inter-governmentalism is rather more diffuse than in the earlier article; the SEM/SEA are not the primary focus.

14 On this point, see also the comments of Leon Lindberg on Moravcsik's liberal inter-governmentalism article (Lindberg 1994).

15 Full judgment on this point must await publication of Moravcsik's forthcoming study, 'The Choice for Europe'.

16 We do not share Peterson's view that new institutionalism cannot be used to analyse history-making decisions (see Peterson 1995: 84). All levels of decision-making require an institutional framework – formal or informal – therefore new institutionalist analysis should simply be adjusted to take account of the different scope of the decisions concerned.

17 The emphasis by Sandholtz and Zysman upon changes in the international economy indicates that they cannot be seen as orthodox neo-functionalists. Neo-functionalism perceived the dynamics of integration to be endogenous.

18 This situation thus questions the assertion by Garrett and Weingast that 'the [EC legal] system works because the courts and the member states share a common framework about how the "internal market" should be applied in specific cases' (Garrett and Weingast 1993: 202).

2

Analysing the governance of the single market

Introduction

The purpose of this chapter is to set out the framework, or analytical method, which we will employ in this study of the governance of the single market. Although our analytical focus is institutional in character, it is part of a broader view of the political process of collective problem-solving: hence our use of the term 'governance'.[1]

In the first part of the chapter we consider how far the institutional structure of the EU may be viewed in a manner analogous to nation states, including federally organised states. There are, of course, many potential traps in undertaking such a comparison, for the EU does not have all the prerequisites of statehood, including the all-important reservoir of popular legitimacy. We also need not to have in mind too fixed a notion of 'the state' in the EU context, for it is multi-levelled, fluid and complex (Smith 1994). Nevertheless, as a system of governance the EU is assuming some limited maturity, albeit rather fragile in character.

The second part of the chapter underlines our focus upon the institutional characteristics of the EU. It reviews the literature on institutions and governance that has emerged in comparative politics over the last two decades. We concentrate on that branch of the literature which is categorised as 'new institutionalism'. In reality, it has developed a number of sub-branches, and we review these as part of the task of outlining the method which we will follow in the study. In short, we believe that this method, drawn from comparative politics and comparative social science, is sensitive to many of the considerations outlined at the end of the previous chapter.

One of the key characteristics of the 'new institutionalism', as we shall see, has been that it has been applied most typically to explain why policy does *not* change; why policy decisions often represent a sub-optimal response to given circumstances; and why the 'baggage of history' creates a kind of path-dependency or 'lock-in' in the policy process (see also Pierson

1996). How, then, can we integrate such an approach into an explanation of the circumstances surrounding the SEM/SEA bargain, for the latter represented a step-change in the character of European integration? How can we incorporate the role of institutions and the state in an account of the significant reconstruction, first, of state–economy relations and, second, of the national–supranational balance of power in Europe that the SEM/SEA programme represented? The answer is that institutionalist analysis must be incorporated into a model of change. This approach does not imply that we throw the proverbial baby out with the bath-water and neglect interests. Rather, we must take into account the role of institutions as 'shapers' of interests and ideas.

The governance of the EU in comparative context

The emergence of the EU as a developed system of supranational governance has been one of the striking developments in post-war European politics. Analyses of this development from a structuralist vantage point have been few and far between.

Alan Milward (1992) has utilised historical source material to explain how the first transfers of policy responsibility came about. One of his central theses is that the integration process was a way of rescuing the nation state. Thus, the attempted resolution of awkward domestic political problems, such as agricultural protection, has entailed Europeanisation. In Milward's view, the resultant reconstruction of state authority reinforced the power of the nation state. Milward's analysis is insightful and convincing.

However, Milward's analysis is not beyond critique. There is quite heavy reliance on national and supranational archives which may have a bias in favour of accounts of national governments' actions, neglecting the domestic economic and social forces prompting such action. Moreover, Milward's analysis tells us very little about whether the European integration process, empowered by the nation states, subsequently *remained* subservient to their interests. Unintended consequences abound in practical politics: could it be that the supranational tier of government assumes its own dynamics and begins to pursue self-serving goals? Milward confines his empirical analysis to the rationale behind transfers of national power to an upper, supranational tier. But what happens to the powers which have been transferred to the upper tier?

That task was not part of Milward's research agenda but it leaves the same gap in our understanding of supranational governance that arises from Moravcsik's analyses of the SEM/SEA and the Maastricht Treaty. In other words, nation states or national governments may demonstrably have had control over what powers were transferred to the upper tier at the stage of constitutive politics. But have they retained control over the powers thus transferred when it comes to the day-to-day utilisation of those powers? Readers of Milward (1992) and of Milward, Lynch, Romero, Ranieri and Sørensen (1993) will find very little about the legal dimension of European integration. Yet the law is central to the notions of statehood and sovereignty: key themes in those studies.

Constructing a new European state?

If one wanted to put an opposing argument, namely that the supranational tier of governance has developed its own autonomy, it would presumably run along the following lines. The national governments did indeed resort to supranational solutions to awkward domestic political issues. However, the result of such transfers of power was to build a new European state. Milward would presumably not dissent from Stephen Skowronek's view that, '[S]hort of revolutionary change, state building is most basically an exercise in reconstructing an already established organization of state power' (1982: ix). Skowronek continues, 'Success hinges on recasting official power relationships within governmental institutions and on altering ongoing relations between state and society.'

The subject of Skowronek's research, however, was the expansion of the national administrative capacities of the *United States* in the period 1877–1920, a development which he considers to be, 'a rather remarkable achievement in political reform claiming a special place in the comparative study of state development' (Skowronek 1982: viii). We leave aside for the time being the contentious issue of regarding the EU as a state, for there are some interesting parallels between the dynamics of state reconstruction in America and Europe. Clearly, the stimuli for such reconstruction will differ between the two cases, since European developments have taken place in a different geographical context and in a different age. Moreover, the European nation states have heterogeneous traditions and these differ qualitatively from the experiences of the states of the Union. However, despite these distinctions between the two cases, comparisons remain.

A first possible comparison relates to the abstract pattern of state reconstruction. Skowronek puts things in the following terms:

> State building is prompted by environmental changes, but it remains at all times a political contingency, a historical-structural question. Whether a given state changes or fails to change, the form and timing of the change, and the governing potential in the change – all of these turn on a struggle for political power and institutional position, *a struggle defined and mediated by the organization of the preestablished state.* (Skowronek 1982: 285, our italics)

This view is one which we believe applies to the evolution of European integration.

In specific terms, we can see changes in the international economic environment and in the Member States as generating pressures for the creation, *inter alia*, of an internal market. Moreover, the reconstruction of the EC through the SEM (and SEA) was defined and mediated by the pre-established 'state'. Where we would depart from the approach of Milward and Moravcsik on the reinforcement of the nation states through integration is by pointing out that 'the pre-established state' comprised not merely the nation states but also the EC's *acquis communautaire*, i.e. the accumulation of supranational legal and political integration, and supranational institution-building. Thus, in concrete terms the SEM was built upon the Treaty of Rome's founding commitment to a common market;[2] the White Paper's strategy for completing the internal market was in part a product of the jurisprudence of the ECJ; and the institutions and procedures of the EC – including the Commission and particularly the European Council – left their imprint on the new structure of the 'European state'. Hence, if additional (supranational) layers of authority have been 'fused' onto the nation state, as Wolfgang Wessels (1992; 1997) has asserted, then we need to incorporate the dynamics of *all* these layers into an analysis of the dynamics of state-building. The 'European state' no longer consists of single-tiered nation states: the supranational layer may also provide dynamics for change. Similarly, sub-national layers of authority may provide such dynamics, as the German *Länder* did in pressing for the creation of the Committee of the Regions and other changes in the TEU (see Jeffery 1994; Marks, Nielsen, Ray and Salk 1996).

A second comparison lies in the terrain of state reconstruction. Skowronek's study of the US experience concentrates upon three areas: the re-organisation of business regulation; the development of the army; and the reconstitution of civil administration. Certainly, the first of these is analogous to the re-building of state power in Europe concerning the single market. That is the essence of a view of the SEM programme as an exercise in regulatory reconstruction: the move from a situation where nation states retained control in shaping state–market relations to one where the EU has assumed a more prominent, and in some cases a pre-dominant, role. Thus, the fragmentation of the European 'common market' was a spur to regulatory reform. The creation of a new set of rules, via the SEM, was an explicit attempt to create a new supranational regulatory framework. The parallels are not exact along all dimensions, but the entrenched patterns of nineteenth-century US business regulation, with control lodged in the individual states, proved unable to contend with the emergence of a national railroad system: one of the stimuli for national-level business regulation (Skowronek 1982). In both cases, therefore, reconstruction arose from the inability of the existing state authorities to regulate cross-frontier problems.[3]

A third comparison lies in the role of the courts in the reconstruction of state power. Most strikingly, it is constitutional courts which inevitably play a role in policing the boundaries of regulatory authority. However, their importance is wider than that. Skowronek terms the early American state 'a state of courts and parties' (1982: 24). State lawyers exerted an invisible influence and formed an important reservoir of political values. Skowronek argues that the 'transformation in the intellectual constitution of the American state may be traced through an examination of its most important intellectual resource – the lawyers' (Skowronek 1982: 12).

In the development of American economic governance, the courts played a particularly major role. In their analysis Lindberg and Campbell put it thus:

> For much of American history, the courts were the only state institution that could stand outside of political party domination and claim to perform an integrative statelike function. Courts determined the meaning and effect of laws passed by the legislature, shaped the boundaries of intergovernmental relations, invoked the state's prerogatives over the economy, and became the chief source of economic surveillance. The courts became the American surrogate for the administrative apparatus familiar in European states. (Lindberg and Campbell 1991: 357)

Their study pays particular attention to the way in which the law–economics interface in respect of property rights shaped patterns of economic behaviour (Lindberg and Campbell 1991).

Once again, it is possible to identify parallels between American experience and that in Europe but we cannot take these too far. The European Courts have not played as large a role as in the USA in the reconstruction of state power and in the transformation of economic governance. Nevertheless, they have played an often underestimated role. Joseph Weiler (1982), for instance, has pointed out that when political scientists were at their most pessimistic concerning the process of integration, namely at the time of the 1965 'empty-chair' crisis and in its immediate aftermath,

> from the legal point of view, Europe . . . made its greatest integrationalist steps forward which not only gave 'supranationalism' a new reinforced meaning (which even the framers of the Treaties could not have envisaged), but which also led the Community . . . to a structure akin to a federal constitution. (40–1)

Weiler was referring, of course, to the major principles established in judgments of the ECJ (also see Weiler 1991). The ECJ was establishing its own constitutional theory and practice, while superficially deriving its legitimacy from its function of adjudicating on what the founding fathers intended when drafting the founding treaties. The ECJ established through various landmark decisions important legal norms and principles which have had a profound impact on the subsequent evolution of European integration.[4] Weiler is far from being alone among legal scholars in seeing the ECJ as facilitating a kind of constitutionalisation of the Treaty of Rome (see Stein 1981; see also Weiler, 1997).

Legal scholars are divided on the way in which the ECJ (including its judges, Advocates General and support staff) has used discretionary

action. Have its judgments been 'legalist' interpretations of EC law? Or
has a more activist interpretation of the law been made, with the result
that supranational competences have been strengthened? Burley and Mattli
(1993), Garrett (1995), Mattli and Slaughter (1995), Weiler (1994) and
Wincott (1995) are amongst those who offer varying interpretations of the
ECJ's role.

Finally, noting Lindberg and Campbell's perception of the American
courts as a surrogate for the administrative apparatus characteristic of
European states, we should note that such an apparatus is also absent
at the supranational level (Lindberg and Campbell 1991: 357–8). The EU
institutions are very modestly staffed – despite the frequent jibes about
'Brussels bureaucracy' – and are reliant on national and sub-national administrative agencies for putting policies into practice. Moreover, EC law is
highly dependent upon its administration in the national court structures,
utilising organisational linkages such as the Article 177 preliminary reference procedure. With the ECJ at the apex of this court structure, at least
where EC legal issues are concerned, it is not too fanciful to regard legal
integration as playing a key role in shaping the governance of the EU and
in state reconstruction.

A fourth parallel exists in the resultant structures of state authority in
the EU. Although criticism became more pronounced during ratification of
the TEU than of the SEA, a highly complex system of government has been
emerging. Characterised by a multitude of different policy-making procedures, supranational governance has lacked transparency and popular legitimacy. However, a lack of transparency is not exclusively an EU problem.
Skowronek, indeed, refers to 'modern institutional politics in America [as]
a politics distinguished by incoherence and fragmentation in governmental
operations and by the absence of clear lines of authoritative control' (1982:
viii). One comparison may be attributed to the accountability problems associated with 'the regulatory state', an EU characteristic accelerated by the
SEM's development (see Caporaso 1996: 39–44).

The EU is certainly *not* a state of parties, to recall the other component
in Skowronek's characterisation of the early American state. A supranational
party system is far from reaching maturity, and that is a contributory
factor to the EU's weak popular legitimacy. These deficiencies are particularly critical because of the weakness, indeed absence, of a European identity. If the EU has some of the trappings of a state, it certainly does not
correspond to any popular perception of it as such, nor does it have broad
political engagement in its policy processes (Featherstone 1994).

The weakness of popular orientation to European integration presents
clear difficulties for comparison with the US experience. However, those
wishing to put the best possible 'gloss' on the EU might wish to look at
another literature on political development. The crisis-sequence school
is exemplified by the work of Tilly (1975), who identified a pattern in

continental European state formation whereby state activities developed ahead of a popular, democratic groundswell of support for the process. Is the development of the EU also following this pattern?

It is not our purpose to pursue the theme of supranational state-building further. Rather, we have been concerned to make several points, which we now summarise.

- First, it is easy in a study of a specific policy area such as the SEM to lose sight of the wider political canvas on which events are taking place.[5] Hence the need to recall that European integration is a process of state development. Transfers of power to a supranational level are invariably a product of national (or sub-national) agencies being unable to achieve desired goals. This view is one we share with commentators such as Milward (1992), Moravcsik (1991) or Wessels (1992). And the SEM/ SEA must be seen as a key phase in European state reconstruction.
- Secondly, our comparisons with the US experience are designed to show that the dynamics of European state development are not wholly *sui generis*. Making allowances for the different geographical and temporal contexts, there are parallels between American and European developments. Whether European developments will lead to the construction of a new supranational state in Europe remains to be seen. We make no presumptions on this point. But we *do* believe that the supranational level of government has some kind of institutional autonomy: that it is not merely an instrument of the nation states; and that the *acquis communautaire* has a strong normative component. Might not those analysts who interpret the integration process through a methodology based on interviewing in the Member States, on national archives and on the rationale behind transfers upwards of national authority, predispose themselves to a nation-state-centred view of the EU?
- Thirdly, state reconstruction is the product of multiple dynamics, at least when undertaken in peacetime conditions. Underlying causes are normally economic, technological or societal in character. However, reconstruction is dependent on these causes assuming political salience. Of central importance, *institutions matter*.
- Fourthly, there is our caveat. States are usually associated with an emergent political identity. Levels of citizens' attachment and identification with the EU remain much weaker than with the national and regional levels, so that there is no clear parallel in this respect (see Reif 1993).
- Finally, we need to make some comments about our usage of the term 'the state'. The EU has state-like qualities. It has an array of legislative competences, set down in the treaties, and has come to act in core 'state activities', such as on citizenship, foreign and security policy and policing. Caporaso examines the circumstances from a different

perspective and comes to the view that the EU is best regarded as 'an international state' (1996: 33). Nevertheless, the issue of the EU's statehood is one which could easily become a distraction from our core interests in the governance of the SEM. We do not wish to be ensnared in semantics about statehood nor in polemics about an emergent European 'super-state'. Moreover, we recognise that there are different forms of the state; for instance, Westphalian, regulatory and post-modern variants (Caporaso 1996). As James Caporaso notes, all three are able to illustrate particular facets of the EU's character. Our general view, therefore, is to interpret the SEM/SEA initiative as an exercise in reconstructing state authority.

It is against this backdrop of changing state power that we examine the specific theme of the governance of the SEM. How best, then, to analyse this more detailed subject-matter? Does the governance of the SEM have core attributes?[6] Or do these vary according to the specific legislation or policy issue? Which institutions hold power: the national governments (in the Council), the Commission, the ECJ or the EP? What is the role and influence of political forces in single market policy-making? Where do ideas fit into the policy process? These are the central issues of this study and, to analyse them, we need a method of investigation. This method is outlined in the next section.

Institutional analysis and the governance of the single market

The EU is located, in analytical terms, at the intersection of the sub-disciplines of international relations and comparative politics. International-relations-based analyses have predominated in the study of European integration hitherto, just as they have in the specific context of the SEM/SEA (see Chapter 1). But what of comparative politics and comparative social science? Can these literatures offer insights into the substance of integration?

The approach which we utilise in this study, namely new institutionalism, stems from comparative politics and social science. It is a middle-range theoretical approach. Unlike neo-functionalist and neo-realist (or inter-governmentalist) theories this institutionalist focus does not entail a teleology of integration. Rather, new institutionalism offers a more modest starting-point: a methodology for research. This methodology generates research questions and orientations rather than mapping out a 'scientific' model of integration. The core assumption of this approach is that *institutions matter*.

This assumption, it should be noted, is shared with the 'institutionalists' in international relations theory. Particularly linked to the analysis of international regimes, this view of international relations argues that institutions represent 'persistent and connected sets of rules (formal and informal) that prescribe behavioral roles, constrain states, and shape expectations' (Keohane 1989: 3). Although we only utilise international relations literature intermittently in this study, we do emphasise the existence of this intellectual link. By adopting a comparative approach we do not wish to contribute to the balkanisation of social science, for we believe that, in the past, the analysis of European integration has suffered from such fragmentation. The *sui generis* assumptions of some political integration theory and the lack of interdisciplinary dialogue have risked confining European integration to an intellectual 'ghetto' within the social sciences.

New institutionalism

New institutionalism is one of the principal methodological approaches to have emerged in the recent comparative social science literature. There are different variants of new institutionalism, so it should be regarded as something of an umbrella term. The most obvious question is: what is 'new' about the approach? Two aspects are particularly distinctive to new institutionalism.[7]

One is a wider interpretation of what constitutes institutions. Thus, there is a shift away from formal constitutional-legal approaches to government, with their tendency to be configurative. It is possible to take into account some of the less formalised arenas of politics. A new institutionalist concern, therefore, encompasses these broader aspects of governance: a wider remit than the formal institutions of state or government. In including the less formal arenas of politics new institutionalism can be sensitive to the valuable findings of the 'policy community' and 'policy network' literature that has exposed the interconnectedness between formal state organisations and communities and networks of actors with an expertise and interest in a given policy area (see Peterson 1995).

A second distinction is a concern with the 'beliefs, paradigms, codes, cultures and knowledge' embedded within the institutions (March and Olsen 1989: 26). This concern with institutional values is important, for the machinery of government is steeped in norms and codes of conduct and it is difficult to isolate formal institutional rules from the normative context. Of course, nobody would read the EU treaties and expect to gain an accurate impression of the operation of the institutions: witness the divergence of the practice of decision-making in the Council from treaty rules following the Luxembourg Compromise. To be sure, we did not need the invention of new institutionalism to provide that insight. On the other hand, it helps organise analysis of the evolution of ideas within institutions; of differing institutional cultures embedded within different parts of, say, the European Commission; of the change in institutional values brought about by the commitment to complete the SEM by the end of 1992 (which, it will be recalled, had no automatic legal effect); and similar normative changes.

New institutionalism places the analytical focus on the polity. We can understand politics as comprising three separate components: politics, polity and policy. The presumption is that the polity structures the inputs of social, economic and political forces and has a consequential impact on the policy outcome.[8]

POLITICAL FORCES → POLITICAL STRUCTURES → POLICY

In such an approach institutions play a key role. What do we consider to be 'institutions' for the purposes of this study? They are taken as meaning formal institutions; informal institutions and conventions; the norms and symbols embedded in them; and policy instruments and procedures. This definition helps us to incorporate the traditional constitutional-legal notions of governance. But it also enables us to bring in the culture of political institutions; the informal decisional arenas – the 'smoke-filled rooms' of politics; the accumulation of jurisprudence and the development of legal norms as factors contributing to institutional norms; and finally, it allows us to incorporate the role of 'soft law' and political declarations as further influences upon policy outcomes.

An additional issue upon which we must comment is that of institutional autonomy: of how much autonomy institutions possess in the political process. Most analysts see institutions as playing a mediating role. That is why the simple model of politics outlined above sees political (and socio-economic) forces as the starting point of governance. We certainly are not proposing that institutions provide the fundamental dynamics of politics. However, we do not see institutions as neutral arenas within which political forces are played out. First, institutions structure the access of political forces to the political process, creating a kind of bias. Thus institutional rules, norms, resources or symbols shape actors' behaviour. Secondly, institutions can themselves develop endogenous institutional impetuses for policy change that exceed the role of mere institutional mediation. This second aspect enables us to take into account the active contributions of the ECJ to the governance of the EU or of the Commission as an agenda-setter (see, respectively, Weiler 1991 and Peters 1994).

Historical institutionalism   Following these general remarks on new institutionalism, we now adopt a specific variant from within this literature, and examine the kinds of issues which it can help analyse. The approach adopted is historical institutionalism, which has a particularly encompassing interpretation of the role of institutions, as will be seen below. The particular distinction made here is with so-called rational choice institutionalism, which takes into account institutions and their rules but only in so far as they modify an essentially rational choice model of politics (see

Thelen and Steinmo 1992: 7–10).[9] That essentially rationalist approach may be described as being at the 'thin' end of institutionalism. By contrast our historical institutionalism is at a 'thicker' end of institutional analysis by virtue of including the normative and cultural dimensions which go beyond rationalist calculations. We argue that historical institutionalism can highlight some important analytical issues in the governance of the SEM. Of course, new institutionalism is not without its critics (see, for instance, Cammack 1989). None the less, it is our contention that the analysis of governance in the context of the EU remains underdeveloped (but see the survey in H. Wallace 1996b), and that historical institutionalism has something to offer.

In order to show the potential insights of historical institutionalism, we identify four particular dimensions of EU governance which it can help 'capture': systemic change, governance structures, policy evolution, and the role of values and norms.

Historical institutionalism and systemic change An important research terrain of new and historical institutionalism has been concerned with the state's role in macro-social change. Reacting to the society-centred, behavioralist analysis of the 1950s and 1960s, some political scientists moved, in the 1980s, to 'bring the state back in' as the focus of analytical attention (see Evans *et al.* 1985). These analysts were particularly concerned with the evolution of political systems, and with the question of the degree of state autonomy in such developments.

The European integration literature has concentrated in particular on the issue of macro-level change: on the patterns of overall development. However, the attention paid to the role of the supranational institutions or to the embryonic European 'state' has been skewed by the two predominant narratives. Neo-functionalism tended to underplay the reconstruction of state capabilities in the integration process. One of the first studies in this vein to attribute importance to systemic transformation and the institutional capacity of the EC institutions was Lindberg and Scheingold's *Europe's Would-Be Polity* (Lindberg and Scheingold 1970: especially Ch. 4). In general, however, neo-functionalists saw a reconstruction of state capabilities as the outcome of what they were examining rather than as an explanatory focus of the integration process.

A concern with the state is much more at the heart of realist or neo-realist interpretations of the integration process (see, for example, Hoffmann 1966; 1982). In such analyses, however, it is the resilience of the *nation states* that is the focus of attention. In other words, European integration is seen as a dependent variable of state development at the *national* level. In terms of comparative politics this kind of interpretation is unusual since the phenomenon being explained (supranational integration) is on a different level from that of the analysis (the nation state). Nevertheless, this approach has enjoyed something of a resurgence in the last decade, notably through the historical research of Alan Milward (1992) and Andrew Moravcsik (1991; 1993; 1994). Their work, with its emphasis upon the 'rescue' and 'strengthening' of the nation state respectively, argues a particular line about where state power lies.

What does historical institutionalism have to offer in this context of systemic transformation? Essentially it places the focus upon those formal and informal institutions where systemic change is negotiated. Moreover, it presupposes no particular teleology of development. Hence, whilst the research agenda may be compatible with those of Milward and Moravcsik, the prescriptions of historical institutionalism are not concentrated on whether nation states are the winners or losers of the process but more neutrally on the way in which the negotiating fora shape the outcome of negotiations in a process of state reconstruction (see Bulmer 1996). The process of state reconstruction is a multi-level phenomenon. Hence there is not a zero-sum game between nation states and the EC/EU. Indeed, the process of integration involves a reconstruction of state responsibilities and activities at multiple levels, as officials and politicians from British local government or the German *Länder* will attest.

In the context of systemic change a historical institutionalist perspective comes closest to the work of analysts who examine the reconstruction of state authority over time. The work of Wolfgang Wessels, with its strong rooting in continental European writing on the state, displays consistency with historical institutionalism. The connection is formed by the emphasis which Wessels places on how the EU is the product of the 'logic' of the European state system, with supranational solutions being sought for the problems of managing welfare states in an increasingly interdependent Europe (Wessels 1992; 1997). Although his work uses the terminology of 'fusion', which implies a convergence of state power on one level, he does take into account multiple levels of governance. Marks, Hooghe and Blank (1996) advocate a multi-level governance explanation of integration, and this too displays strong consistency with a historical institutionalist approach, for they not only look at the inter-governmental institutions but also examine the role of supranational and sub-national institutions and actors. Paul Pierson (1996) explicitly employs historical institutionalism to explain characteristics of the integration process. He offers a corrective to inter-governmental analysis and does so by explaining the importance of evolutionary change at the systemic level.

The principal value of historical institutionalism in respect of systemic change is twofold. It can explain, through institutionalist lenses and without a teleology of integration, the involvement of key actors in the transfers of competence at particular junctures of the integration process. That is how we sought to re-interpret the SEM/SEA package in Chapter 1. It can also explain systemic change between those crucial episodes of integration, such as the SEM/SEA, the TEU and so on, for much systemic change is evolutionary in character and judicial-normative in form, and consequently omitted from the research focus of those who only examine history-making decisions (Dehousse and Weiler 1990; Pierson 1996; Weiler 1982).

Historical institutionalism and governance structures   Historical institutionalism is not only an analytical approach which is helpful to examining systemic change, it can also assist analysis of sub-systemic governance. In this case the emphasis is upon how different institutional *configurations* – between political systems or between policy sub-systems – can impact upon governance capacity.[10] In the context of the governance of the SEM, two particular research issues are highlighted in this way.

The first is in the governance capability of the EC/EU. Weaver and Rockman (1993a: 5–7) have identified various ways of measuring governance capability, and how the structural properties of the decision-making system may affect that capability. The SEM/SEA package deal was a specific attempt to increase the EC's governance capability, both generally and with a view to ensuring the necessary legislation for the SEM programme. It is important, therefore, that we review performance in achieving that goal. Did the SEM/SEA package enhance the governance capability of the EC; and how? Thus, an institutionalist agenda is concerned with the impact of the polity upon putting the SEM into operation.

The second research issue is one which is well established in the literature on policy-making in the EC, namely the variable performance of the EC/EU in executing its various policies (Wallace and Wallace 1996; Wallace, Wallace and Webb 1983). The interest in differing sectoral policy dynamics is thus well developed but the particular contribution of historical institutionalism is to attribute varying policy outcomes to the different institutional arrangements. In order to highlight the different character of these arrangements, we term them 'governance regimes'. Each of our policy case studies – Chapters 4–9 – is associated with a governance regime.

Historical institutionalism and policy evolution   Historical institutionalism emphasises the cumulative nature of policy-making, a feature explored by Pierson (1996). Thus, initial policy choices may restrict subsequent evolution so that a kind of path-dependency influences a change of course in policy. The result may be a policy which outlives its usefulness, or which does not correspond to the requirements of a new era. Nevertheless, it may have its own internal 'logic'. The CAP may be seen in these terms. With an emphasis upon institutions, an interpretation of the CAP's character would be that those engaged in agricultural policy-making were able to isolate themselves from broader issues of public policy – including the financial aspects – and thus exploit supranational policy-making to enhance their own power resources. Only with the 1988 reform package were agriculture ministers, and the farm lobby influencing them, formally required to reconcile their policy decisions with those of EC budget ministers. According to such analysis, the result, both before 1988 and since, has been a sub-optimal CAP which none the less corresponds to the internal logic of the prevailing governance regime (see also Rieger 1996).

Although historical institutionalism is not confined to policy analysis, that is the context to which we apply it in what follows, namely in the six case-study chapters. Historical institutionalism offers a number of valuable insights into the dynamics of the policy process.

First, it helps us to organise an exercise in process-tracing in the case studies. Much policy-making is iterative and incremental. Thus, most of the legislation associated with the White Paper and with many of the flanking measures did not simply emerge in the mid-1980s. Rather, new strategies were adopted to achieve goals already set out in the Treaty of Rome. And a new 'bargain' gave renewed political impetus. Thus, whilst historical institutionalism often reveals path-dependency and policy solutions outliving their usefulness, there is the more positive possibility that lessons may be drawn from past experience, resulting in new strategies being put forward. This situation combined with the enhanced governance capability to create the new policy dynamics of the SEM. New strategies were attached to achieve existing goals.[11] Thus, the rationality of policy changes is a bounded rationality based on the endogenous construction of experience: 'learning by doing'. Accordingly, we place emphasis in our case studies on the 'construction' of the particular policy issue, for this is influential in determining the 'logic' of the issue to be addressed.

At the policy level, we are able to encapsulate this iterative process by examining the development of the corresponding 'governance regime'.[12] From the modest beginnings of the first Commission initiative in a policy area, itself preceded by a phase of agenda-setting, interest groups establish their claims to consultation.[13] National governments and civil servants are engaged in many meetings before the first piece of legislation is agreed. Gradually a governance regime is established. Then comes the learning process of how implementation by the national authorities corresponds to intentions. Further, ECJ jurisprudence develops legal norms. New legislation may be proposed, reflecting pressure from affected interests and incorporating the benefits of institutional learning. And so policy evolves in a manner which is structured by the institutional capacity of the EU generally and of the specific governance regime as well.

In this way a historical institutionalist perspective rejects the idea that European integration is just about the SEA and the Maastricht Treaty. Those negotiations represent the tip of an iceberg; we need to look at the nine-tenths of the iceberg which are below the waterline. Moreover, a historical institutionalist perspective focuses on the evolution of policy. It rejects the notion that politics can be separated from public administration, for the putting of policy into practice is an essential part of the whole: the experience of administration may start a new cycle of policy development.

Secondly, historical institutionalism helps forge a link between jurisprudence of the European Court and the legislative process. Unlike some areas of EU activity, notably the second (Common Foreign and Security Policy) and third (Justice and Home Affairs) pillars established under the TEU, the first (EC) pillar is regulated by EC law. In consequence, disputes between private parties, or disputes involving the supranational institutions or the member governments can lead to the establishment of important policy principles. Since the Commission's role is to act as conscience of 'Europe', it follows that its staff closely monitor the work of the European Courts (the ECJ and the CFI). Indeed, they may have intervened in litigation brought before the Court and thus be well placed to draw lessons from consequent jurisprudence. Historical institutionalism offers a framework for understanding the judicial and legislative processes as complementary to one another. This situation is illustrated by the Commission seizing upon mutual recognition as a regulatory strategy for market integration in the wake of the *Cassis de Dijon* judgment.

A third contribution of historical institutionalism is through illustrating the ways in which institutions structure the policy process. Here we expand on the point made earlier on new institutionalism generally: that institutions are not mere neutral arenas.

In their analysis of the governance of the American economy, Lindberg and Campbell alert us to three ways in which the institutional structure shapes the policy process (Lindberg and Campbell 1991: 357–61).[14] The first means of influence derives from the fact that the supranational institutions do not provide equal access for influencing the policy process. Thus the strong position of the Council of Ministers privileges national governments and their civil servants in the policy process, although increased power-sharing with the EP and varying rules on voting in the Council qualify this statement. Another instance of bias deriving from the institutional structure can be shown by another reference to the CAP. The weakness of consumer responsibilities within the Commission and, for that matter, in national governments, has been another factor explaining why broad public interests, as well as those of taxpayers, have scarcely been heard in the CAP governance regime.

A second means of institutional influence derives from the fact that the supranational institutions are not mere arbitrators but are key *players* in their own right. The Commission is an obvious example, for it is charged with finding supranational solutions to policy problems. As the initiator of policy, it has useful cards to play in setting the policy agenda (Peters 1994). So, too, do other institutions: the European Council, as was seen in the last chapter, but also the presidency of the Council of Ministers (see below).

A third means of institutional influence derives from the fact that 'the state' has its own distinctive configuration which predisposes it to certain types of activity. Within the EC pillar that distinctive configuration is its regulatory character. Hence the whole character of the White Paper was to legislate or regulate within the context of a small EC budget. Regulatory costs are borne by the Member States and the regulated. They are hardly borne by the supranational institutions at all, since implementation is left overwhelmingly to national arrangements, apart from in competition policy. As Peters (1992) puts it:

> Regulatory policy may ... minimize (although not eliminate) national, re-
> gional, and even class conflicts over Community policy. The choice [of policy
> instrument] also enhances the relative powers of the Commission and the
> bureaucracy. (93)

The configuration of the EU institutions and the rather untypical set of policy instruments available predispose the EU to certain types of policy action but limit the scope for others, especially involving large financial transfers. This situation provides a specific illustration of Schattschneider's general observation that organisation is the mobilisation of bias (Schatt-schneider 1960: 71).

The three ways in which institutions influence the policy process – as identified by Lindberg and Campbell (1991) – represent elements of institutional autonomy within the EU. They comprise the third and final contribution of historical institutionalism to the analysis of policy evolution.

Historical institutionalism and the norms of governance   A major intellectual input into new institutionalism derives from the work of James March and Johan Olsen (March and Olsen 1984; 1989). Their work has rather different origins from that described thus far, for its roots are in organisation and decision theory. For example, they criticise rational choice assumptions that political and administrative action is the product of calculated self-interest. In short, their criticism is of the utilitarianism implicit in much of the existing literature rooted in neo-classical economics. March and Olsen, like other analysts considered here, place emphasis upon institutions. Their view of institutional analysis is perhaps best encapsulated thus:

> political actors are driven by institutional duties and roles as well as, or
> instead of, by calculated self-interest; politics is organized around *the con-*
> *struction and interpretation of meaning* as well as, or instead of, the making
> of choices; routines, rules, and forms evolve through history-dependent pro-
> cesses that do not reliably and quickly reach unique equilibria; the institutions

of politics are not simple echoes of social forces; and the polity is something different from, or more than, an arena for competition among rival interests. (March and Olsen 1989: 159, our italics)

We find several new institutionalist preoccupations in this passage. However, what is particularly distinctive to their work is the importance of norms, values and routines embedded within institutions; and what they term a 'logic of appropriateness' that shapes individuals' actions within institutions (March and Olsen 1989: 160–2). What, then, can historical institutionalism offer by highlighting the normative dimension of EU governance?

Three contributions are particularly worthy of note. The first is to go beyond the idea of the institutional structure of the EC/EU being important and to look at the internal organisational features of individual institutions. This 'micro-institutional' (or *organisational*) analysis allows us to focus on the routines, norms and symbols within individual institutions. Thus, the internal processes of decision-making in the European Commission, the committee structure of the EP, comitology and a range of other specific organisational features may help explain policy outcomes. These features, or what Burch and Holliday have termed the 'disposition of an institution', also privilege certain policy actors over others because they define a pattern or distribution of power potential (Burch and Holliday 1995). In one sense this is simply giving a micro-level focus to institutionalism. However, the addition of March and Olsen's second contribution – the role of norms and values – goes beyond mere structure to include such aspects as administrative culture.

March and Olsen highlight the norms and values held within organisations. Cultural explanations of the politics of the EU are problematic because we cannot identify a European culture.[15] However, within individual institutions norms and values accumulate and create a kind of institutional culture. These institutional norms, codes of conduct and values provide some kind of stability to a potentially fluid political system. We can identify systemic norms associated with the EU, for example efforts by all institutions to respect the subsidiarity principle. Equally, norms and values may be attached to individual institutions. For example, they explain the informal voting practices in the Council of Ministers whereby attempts are made to reach a consensus and not overrule 'significant minorities', even where QMV is specified in the treaty rules. Taking another example, the Commission has a pro-integration mission which is partly inculcated by its rules and partly by its institutional culture. Lord Cockfield, responsible in the first Delors Commission for the SEM programme, adopted such a missionary approach that he was deemed by the Thatcher government to have 'gone native'. He adopted the institutional role and culture of the Commission to such an extent that he was not re-nominated for a further term. It is by linking together the micro-institutional and normative dimensions of March and Olsen's work that one can also analyse the different values held in different parts of the same institution (see Bulmer 1993: 363–4).

Thus, to take an illustration relating to air transport, we find that state aids in this sector of economic activity are handled by Directorate General (DG) VII (transport policy). This situation is quite different from what applies to state aids in general, for they are dealt with by DG IV (competition policy). This division of responsibility means that airlines seeking approval of state aids are dealing with a DG and a set of officials whose task is to oversee a functioning transport infrastructure. Their institutional remit is thus different from that of DG IV, whose concern is with competition rules. DG VII has traditionally been seen as more industry-friendly and more likely to be sympathetic on state aids than DG IV. The precise significance of state aid decisions in air transport policy will be discussed in Chapter 7. Suffice it to note here that the organisational role – the organisational logic and administrative culture – of DG VII staff may affect the character of their decisions. Organisational roles are reinforced by the different norms and values embedded in the DGs. Organisational roles, norms and values affect the access points open to lobbyists and other political forces.

A third normative issue which historical institutionalism can highlight extends March and Olsen's work into the domain of ideas, an area which has been examined by Jachtenfuchs (1995). Particular institutional configurations can facilitate the spread of policy ideas if they possess suitable resources.[16] One pertinent example of that was the decision taken in early 1986 by internal market commissioner, Lord Cockfield, to ask Paolo Cecchini, a former Deputy Director General of DG III, to undertake a report on the benefits of creating the SEM (Cockfield 1994: 90). Cecchini's findings, *The European Challenge 1992. The Benefits of a Single Market* (Cecchini *et al.* 1988), succeeded in constructing positive values around the SEM programme at a very crucial stage in the White Paper's operationalisation. Not only did this report have a wide impact on economic actors but it proved to be a major factor in giving purpose to DG III itself. Together with the White Paper and other studies on 'the costs of non-Europe', it became a crucial factor shaping the administrative culture of DG III.

Historical institutionalism – a summary   There is an analytical core which runs through the four dimensions of EU governance discussed above. Centrally, the analysis is institution- or state-centred rather than being actor-centred and behavioural in character. For March and Olsen a more organisational focus is adopted, with the endogenous organisational features structuring politics (1984; 1989). Further, informal and formal institutions are seen as structuring actors' political behaviour. Another recurrent

Box 2.1: Historical institutionalist insights into the SEM/SEA package

---

- How the SEM/SEA package came to be agreed (systemic change)
- How changes to the EC's institutional structure contributed to the realisation of the SEM (governance structures)
- How institutional structures shape the governance of individual policy areas and issues into governance regimes (governance structures)
- How EC/EU policy is shaped over time as the product of both rule-making and judicial methods of regulation (policy evolution)
- How the institutional structure of the EU is not purely and simply a neutral arena but structures the policy process (policy evolution)
- How organisational disposition as well as institutional norms, values and ideas shape policy outcomes (normative dimension)

---

feature is a historical focus; past choices restrict subsequent policy action. Finally, the values and norms embedded within institutions are ascribed explanatory value. *Emphatically, none of this means that our empirical concern is just with institutions.*

Historical institutionalism is not applied in this study as some kind of grand theory but, rather, as a theory of the middle range. That is not a deficiency in the context of European integration and specifically of the governance of the SEM. Attempts at grand theory within European integration have been shown to be highly problematic (Caporaso and Keeler 1995). Moreover, the EU is not yet a state with a stable institutional system, so the development of a convincing grand-theoretical explanation of its governance seems to be highly unlikely. Nevertheless, historical institutionalism offers a method for deriving analytical insights. And this method allows us to focus on different aspects of the SEM/SEA, summarised in Box 2.1. We pick up these various insights in different parts of the book. Above all, historical institutionalism offers a method which helps bring together the high-profile politics of the SEA and the TEU, on the one hand, and the day-to-day policy-making and policy-administration of the EC pillar, on the other.

Finally, how does historical institutionalism help pull together the 'social science' of the governance of the EC/EU? At the cost of parsimony, it emphasises the multi-levelled and multi-faceted nature of governance. In referring to the reconstruction of state authority, and by dropping the teleological presumptions that the trend is for that authority to flow in one direction (or not to flow at all), we necessarily are describing a phenomenon of *multi-level governance*. Our perception of the governance of the EU is broadly consistent with that of Marks, Hooghe and Blank (1996), although we take a different route to reach our conclusions.

The importance of seeing the governance of the EU as multi-level governance is important for the social sciences. By contrast with the narratives of integration offered by neo-functionalism and neo-realism, multi-level governance facilitates a discourse with those social scientists whose primary focus is the national political arena into which the supranational level has intruded. This multi-levelled character of governance is also important for linking up the political science and legal analysis of the EU. The matrix of relationships between national courts, national legislatures, supranational courts and supranational legislatures can also be examined. And these relationships are central to 'bringing the legal dimension in'. Thus, just as we can consider the issue of the autonomy of the EU's political institutions, so we can examine the way in which the institutionalisation of legal norms has created some autonomy for the EC legal system. The interaction of the legal and political systems is facilitated in a way that is not possible with the predominant approaches (see the review in Armstrong forthcoming).

Conclusion

In this chapter we have undertaken two tasks. First, we have sought to present the integration process as an exercise in the reconstruction of state power. We have suggested that it can be helpful and illuminating to look comparatively at other experiences.

Secondly, we have reviewed the new institutionalist literature. The insights which it offers will be examined in different parts of the remainder of the book. It should be clear that we consider that historical institutionalism helps address some of the concerns outlined at the end of Chapter 1. Thus, an institutional focus enables us to link up the constitutive decisions of integration with the daily routine of putting a programme such as the SEM into operation. We do not need to resort to different research methodologies for different scales of analysis (as advocated by Peterson 1995: 84).[17] Further, we have suggested that historical institutionalism can link up the politics of the process with both the important public-administration dimension of policy as well as with the judicial process. Historical institutionalism does not present some grand theory of integration; it makes no predictions of the path ahead. Rather, it remains neutral on this point and offers instead a middle-range analytical view.

There are two links with the empirical material contained in this study. First, we have made explicit the institutionalist approach which underlined our (more embracing and comprehensive) account of the origins of the SEM programme, outlined in Chapter 1. We will return to this concern with the SEM as state reconstruction in Chapter 12. Secondly, in the six case studies which are examined below, we look at the dynamics of policy change in the particular area of policy. We ascribe explanatory importance to the EC/EU institutional structure. But we do not ignore the role of socio-economic interests, of technological development, of extra-EC developments and so. Before we apply the analytical approach set out in this chapter, however, we offer a brief overview of the institutional structure of the EC/EU.

Notes

1 For further discussion of the suitability of the term 'governance' for analysis of the SEM, see Chapter 10.

2 However, Pescatore, a former judge of the ECJ, went so far as to see the SEA as potentially *threatening* the existing EEC objective of a common market and the work of the ECJ in helping to make that a reality (Pescatore 1987). For him the common market was achievable within the existing treaty structure.

3 A major distinction between European and US experience lies in the role of external actors. The reconstruction of state authority associated with the SEM/SEA was prompted in part by the concerns about European competitiveness in a global economy. These exogenous environmental factors were not applicable to the business regulation considered by Skowronek, because American economic development was not located in an environment of global interdependence. We are grateful to Mark Pollack for making us sensitive to this distinction.

4 Two key case were: *NV Algemene Transport en Expeditie Onderneming Van Gend en Loos* v. *Nederlandse Administratie der Belastingen*, Case 26/62, which established the doctrine of direct effect; and *Costa* v. *Ente Nazionale per l'Energia Elettrica*, Case 6/64, which established the doctrine of the supremacy and autonomy of EC law over national law. The doctrine of direct effect was elaborated in subsequent cases.

5 It is one of the striking features of the British political debate about the EU's development that Euro-sceptics are well aware of this wider constitutional aspect even if the discourse is somewhat hysterical.

6 A wider issue, of course, is whether the governance of the EU as a whole has core attributes (see Chapters 3 and 10 on this). See also Bulmer (1993) for a new institutionalist analysis.

7 On new institutionalism in general see the surveys by Hall and Taylor (1996); Lowndes (1996); and March and Olsen (1996). For applications of new institutionalism to different aspects of European integration, see Armstrong (1995; forthcoming); Armstrong and Bulmer (1996); Bulmer (1993; 1994; 1996); Kerremans (1996); Pierson (1996); Wincott, (1995).

8 This view corresponds to German institutional theory: see Göhler 1987: 15–47. For a more elaborate development of this chain in connection with the issue of governance capabilities, see Weaver and Rockman 1993a: 7–11.

9 This distinction between rational choice institutionalism and a 'thicker' variant which sees institutions embedded in norms, values and even identity is also present in the international relations literature. The former approach is illustrated by Keohane (1989); the latter, for example, by Ruggie (1993b) or Young (1989).

10 For an application of this approach, comparing the American political system with others, see Weaver and Rockman (1993b). One well-known study of EC decision-making which, by virtue of its comparative dimension, could be seen as structural institutionalism is that by Scharpf (1988).

11 The situation was not quite as straightforward as suggested here, since the notion of an 'internal market' was not identical to that of a 'common market'. In truth, there were elements of all of the explanations for change put forward by Thelen and Steinmo (1992: 16–18).

12 See also Campbell and Lindberg (1991). Their analysis of the governance of the US economy has contributed to our thinking here.

13 This illustration is just that: it does not claim to incorporate all the possible variations in the development of governance regimes.

14 We substitute the term 'institutional structure' for what, in an American context, they term 'the state'.

15 Different national cultures do meet in the Council of Ministers, of course. See Shackleton (1991) for an application of cultural analysis to the EU.

16 For an illustration of this in British economic policy – namely the shift from Keynesianism to monetarism – see Hall (1992). Also see Finnemore (1993) for discussion of how international organisations may 'teach norms' to states.

17 Peterson suggests the use of macro-theories such as inter-governmentalism to explain the 'history-making' decisions like the SEM/SEA; new institutionalism for systemic decisions; and policy network analysis for meso-level decisions. Whilst new institutionalism and policy network analysis display some methodological compatibility – see Lowndes (1996) – these two approaches have a fundamentally different methodological perspective from inter-governmentalism.

3

Policy-making, the legal system and the single market

Introduction

Understanding the governance of the single market requires two things. First, it necessitates a dissection of the systemic characteristics of the EU that can be connected up to the dynamics of the policy issues of the SEM. Secondly, we need to insert the roles of institutions, policy actors as well as the policy 'toolkit' into this survey.

We divide what follows into three parts. In the first part we identify different scales of the policy arena: from the systemic properties of the EU as a whole to the more specific properties of a particular policy issue. Our argument is that the latter must be located in the context of the former. Thus, when changes occur at the systemic level, so there are bound to be ramifications for individual policy issues. Cumulatively, changes at the policy level can influence the systemic governance. In the second part of the chapter we give an overview of the institutions and other policy actors engaged in SEM policy-making, placing particular emphasis on the period between the SEA and the TEU, since this is the period in which the principal events in our case histories are played out. In a final part of the chapter we introduce the case studies.

Policy scale: of systemic and sub-systemic properties

All political systems have overarching characteristics. This point is well established in comparative political science (see, for instance, Katzenstein 1978). However, this emphasis upon national characteristics or national 'policy styles' (Richardson 1982) led to an adverse reaction on the part of some analysts. The idea that there were 'strong' states and 'weak' states was resisted by these critics. Examination of different policy cases revealed examples which did not fit with the supposed national profile. This kind of approach was one source of a burgeoning literature on policy networks and communities (Atkinson and Coleman 1989; Freeman 1985; Wilks and

Wright 1987; Wright 1988). This literature was a new 'take' on Lowi's argument that policy shapes politics: that the character of politics is shaped by the policy concerned (Lowi 1964).

This debate about the scale of analysis confronts us again in any survey of the policy framework of the EC/EU. Is there an EU policy style: a predominant character to the policy process? Alternatively, are there multiple political and legal sub-systems, each the product of a specific set of policy dynamics? As is so often the case, reality is less clear-cut. There are indeed systemic properties of the EU; but there are also policy-specific properties. The trick is to find a balance reflecting the different scales of analysis. An institutional perspective can assist here, since some institutions, procedures, norms and values are system-wide, whilst others are more specific to a particular policy sector.

Systemic properties
The systemic properties of the EC/EU are those which cross policy sectors.[1] They are set down to some extent in the EU treaties but also derive from accumulated norms and practices. They evolve over time, being modified most dramatically by constitutive changes such as the SEA and the TEU. However, constitutive change is not just a matter of 'history-making' political bargains. It can come about without something as formal as an IGC, as was demonstrated when the 1966 Luxembourg Compromise brought about a change to EC decision-making practice, bringing in the so-called veto culture that obstructed agreement in the Council of Ministers and caused such stagnation in the integration process. Having no constitutional-legal status, the Luxembourg Compromise became a new systemic norm of EC policy-making. Constitutive change can also come about as a result of developments in the legal domain. ECJ jurisprudence has been responsible for fundamental, systemic changes in the character of integration through some of its landmark decisions. What, then, may we regard as the key systemic features of the EC/EU?

- *The EU is a multi-level system of governance: a confederation located between inter-state and intrastate patterns of rule* (see Forsyth 1981). Admittedly there is not a tidy fit with a confederal pattern of governance. The doctrine of direct effect in EC law, with its conferring of rights on individuals and not just on states, is a federal principle. However, the EU does not possess statehood, so it lacks a necessary qualification for being truly federal. Nor is there a clear catalogue of competences – national and supranational – occasionally advanced in German reform proposals for the EU; such a catalogue would give the EU a more federal component.[2] Equally, and setting aside activities in the Common Foreign and Security Policy (CFSP) and Justice and Home Affairs (JHA) domains, the EU is not just another international organisation. We reject the notion that its actions are simply exercising power delegated, and controlled, by the member governments. In particular, the legal component of the EC pillar is particularly distinctive. The best judgment which can be reached, therefore, is that we are dealing with a multi-level system of governance which best approximates to a confederation.

- *The systemic properties of the EU are particularly subject to evolution over time.* This feature is the product of the EU's fragile legitimacy. In consequence, the EU-as-confederation is much more subject to change over time in its character than, by comparison, most federal states (Belgium excluded!). It might be argued that this fragility merely confirms that supranational integration is the delegated authority of the Member States. That inter-governmentalist position is not ours, for we see the EC/EU as being more than the sum of governments' wishes. However, we recognise that the purposes of integration can be adjusted. Indeed, in the case of the SEM, the original purpose of the Treaty of Rome, namely the creation of a common market, was virtually reinvented with the SEM programme. Reflecting the patterns of evolution in the character of supranational governance, Helen Wallace has identified four phases: the Monnet method of partnership; the Gaullist method of negotiation; the cooption method of the SEA; and the competing policy methods of the post-Maastricht era (for details, see Wallace 1996a). In addition to the phases which she identifies, we believe it important to bear in mind that the character of supranational governance has also been affected by the path-breaking decisions of the ECJ.

- *The systemic properties of the EU at any one time are the balance between the conflicting dynamics of 'cooperative confederalism' and the territorial principle.* What is meant here by cooperative confederalism is a tendency on the part of the Member States to seek supranational policy solutions to problems which are less efficiently resolved at the national level.[3] It is precisely this creeping confederalisation, based on efficiency grounds, which lay behind the impulses to completing the SEM. As in any multi-level polity, however, there is a tension between finding efficient policy solutions and meeting the demands of democratic governance. This situation is no less apparent in the EU. And democratic governance continues to remain firmly rooted in territorial politics of the Member States (see Sbragia 1993). The European identity is weakly developed. Moreover, the democratic legitimacy of the EU's non-territorial political institutions (the Commission and the EP) is problematic. Thus, the systemic institutional properties of the EU at any one time reflect the balance between conflicting social, economic and political forces. The concern with subsidiarity in the negotiations leading up to the Maastricht Treaty and thereafter reflects the latest phase in balancing out these dynamics. That concern was present as much in the British government's criticisms of 'Brussels centralism' as in the concerns on the part of German *Länder* about the erosion of their powers.

- *A core of constitutionalism lies at the heart of the EC pillar of the EU.* In addition to the institutional ground-rules set out in the treaties, the jurisprudence of the ECJ has contributed extensively to a constitution- alisation of the EC pillar. Examples of the relevant judgments would be the landmark decisions on direct applicability, direct effect, the suprem- acy of EC law and on proportionality (see Weiler 1991). A further example would be the establishment of individual entitlement to dam- ages where EC obligations are not properly implemented, as set down in the *Francovich* ruling and fleshed out in the *Factortame* and *Brasserie du Pêcheur* decisions. Cases such as these have shaped the constitutional- legal order of the EC pillar beyond what the founding treaties provided for. The cases are as much part of its systemic properties as the found- ing treaties, the reforms introduced by the SEA and the TEU, and those under discussion in the 1996/97 IGC. This constitutionalism has served as a kind of 'hard core' to supranational governance.[4]

- *The prevailing pattern of EU governance is the product not only of formal rules but also of informal procedures and 'rules of the game'.* The impact of treaty revisions on the EU is well known. The informal procedural politics of the EU are less well systematised. The search for consent and solidarity in the Council even where QMV is provided for; the projection of national interests in European 'clothing'; the predom- inant respect on the part of national governments for rulings of the European Courts; and legal norms such as proportionality: these are all part of the workings of governance in the EU. They make up a kind of sociological dimension to the institutions (Jachtenfuchs 1995). Beha- viour within this informal system is overwhelmingly 'rule-governed': this is necessitated by the need to build trust in a multinational polity. We argue that rules (e.g. as set out in inter-institutional agreements) and norms in the system serve the function identified for them by Kratochwil, namely as 'guidance devices which are designed to simplify choices and impart "rationality" to situations by delineating the factors that a decision-maker has to take into account' (Kratochwil 1989: 10).

- *The EU's small administrative apparatus places a large burden on national administrative resources in both the policy-making and policy- implementation stages.* The European Commission is a small agency for the running of EC-pillar policy for a population of some 370 mil- lion inhabitants. It relies on national executives to assist its work. It requires advisory input from national civil servants in the policy- formulation stage. It requires the administrative cooperation of national civil servants in the various types of committees falling under the heading of 'comitology' (see below). And it is reliant on national and sub-national executives for the implementation of EC law. Despite the conflicting dynamics outlined earlier, the EU can only work effectively if all tiers of government are cooperating to achieve the same policy goals.

- *Governance in the EU is executive-dominated.* The multi-level form of governance taken on by the EU – termed *Politikverflechtung* (interlocking politics) by German scholars – privileges the executive branch of government. This is because the making, administration and implementation of EU policy entails the existence of a large number of two-tiered or multi-level inter-governmental committees.[5] Making these multi-level committees democratically accountable is very difficult, since parliaments are elected at one level only and can only call to account the executive at 'their' level. The EP's difficulties in calling the Council of Ministers to account is indicative of the problem, for it has very limited sanctions in this respect.[6] Equally, few national parliaments have generated especially effective ways of calling ministers to account over their actions in the Council; the Danish parliament's European Affairs Committee being a possible exception (see Norton 1996).

- *The policy instruments of the EU are very restricted owing to its limited budgetary resources.* The EU has strikingly modest budgetary resources: in 1996 they amounted to 1.2 per cent of EU GDP. Deficit spending is not permitted. In consequence, there are major constraints upon the nature of activity which the EU can support. Spending programmes are frequently merely supportive of national or sub-national programmes, such as with the structural funds, or of private sector spending in the case of research and technology funds. There is no scope (or competence) for one of the functions of public budgets, namely macroeconomic stabilisation. For another function – that of re-distribution – the sums available are very limited.[7]

- *The predominant form of policy in the EC pillar is regulatory.* This state of affairs has been well charted by Majone.[8] Regulatory policy requires little by way of a central budget, for the direct costs of such a policy are largely administrative. In addition, the EU has never engaged in the ownership of industry or of other economic activities, unlike other levels of European government. The resultant regulatory form of policy fits well with the budgetary circumstances outlined above. As Majone notes:

> the real costs of most regulatory programmes are borne directly by the firms and the individuals who have to comply with them. Compared with these costs, the resources needed to produce the regulations are trivial.
> (Majone 1991: 96)

Moreover, a regulatory type of policy is less controversial for a fragile polity such as the EU. As Guy Peters puts it,

regulative instruments tend to mask the effects of policies and make winners and losers less visible than expenditure programs do. Regulatory
policy may thus minimize (although not eliminate) national, regional and
even class conflicts over Community policy. (1992: 93)

This regulatory form of policy is particularly prominent in the EC
pillar of the EU, and is absolutely the character of policy exhibited by
the single market (but see also Chapter 10).

- *The predominant pattern of rule in the EC pillar is legal in character.*
Owing to the problems of legitimacy associated with the EU, regulation
by law serves as a kind of substitute for some of the less formal trust
which might be built into a more developed polity. In British politics,
for example, there had been a long tradition of tackling particular
policy issues, such as the rules on takeovers, through informal means:
through self-regulation rather than statutory regulation. This situation,
it is worth noting, prevailed in a state with a long tradition of evolutionary development and which lacks a codified constitution. For a
young, multinational polity like the EU there is insufficient trust to use
more voluntary approaches to regulation except under specific circumstances. The principal exception relates to the regulation of technical
standards; the old approach of regulation by law proved to be so slow-
moving and ineffective that it had to be modified in favour of a mix of
legislation on minimum safety requirements, accompanied by standards-
setting by private agencies. Coincidentally this exception to the rule
forms one of the case studies (see Chapter 6). A related point is that
the ECJ has come to be seen as a source of legal legitimacy for EC pillar
activity, making up for deficiencies in political legitimation.

- *The EU's policy-making machinery is particularly fragmented.* This feature was heightened by the three-pillar character of the EU, as embodied
in the Maastricht Treaty. However, this feature is also well established
within the EC pillar, which is our concern here. If one were to adopt
Lowi's perspective on public policy, this fragmentation would be attributed to the character of the policy/ies in the EC pillar. Thus, regulatory politics (in the USA) was identified by him as being disaggregated,
decentralised, interest-orientated and localised (Lowi 1972): characteristics also pertinent to EC-pillar governance. Our own approach is to
attribute the fragmentation to the institutional make-up of the EU.
Thus, fragmentation is brought about by a range of factors of which
the following are especially significant:

  - the closely defined competences in the European Commission and
the relatively weak horizontal coordination in that institution;
  - the organisation of the EP, i.e. in its committee structure, follows
a pattern which largely mirrors the Commission's organisation;

- the creation of specialised advisory and management committees on legislation with issue-specific responsibilities;
- the weak coordination of the work done in the different 'technical' Councils of the EU;
- the different sets of policy-making rules (affecting voting in the Council or the extent of the EP's involvement);
- the different patterns of institutional interaction derived from the legal bases for action; and
- the range of conventions and norms associated with each policy-specific admixture of these differentiated ingredients.

These factors explain why we argue that the fragmentation of the policy process can clearly be attributed to institutional features of the EC.

Sub-systemic properties
We have outlined some of the systemic characteristics of EU governance in the previous section and concluded by considering the fragmentation of governance. This characteristic is particularly important for our case studies, for we argue that the EU is characterised by a plethora of policy- or issue-specific *governance regimes.*[9]

Just as an institutionalist perspective can assist us at the systemic level, so it can do so at the sub-systemic level. March and Olsen recognised this in arguing that:

> Many of the rules within political institutions are essentially devices for partitioning politics into relatively independent domains ... By suppressing links across partitions, the division of labour creates significant barriers between domains of legitimate action – areas of local rationality ... and responsibility. (1989: 26)

This is recognition that policy sub-systems can be focused on from an institutionalist perspective. But what do we mean by governance regimes in the EU context?

- *Governance regimes define the 'rules of the game' for individual policy issues.* They reflect Krasner's well-known definition of international regimes:

> Regimes can be defined as sets of implicit or explicit principles, norms, rules, and decision-making procedures around which actors' expectations converge in a given area of international relations. (1983: 2)

The reference to 'governance' reflects our concern not only with the formal aspects of the EU but with its less formal parts too. The EU represents a classic case of governance without a formal government (see Chapter 10).

- *Governance regimes each reflect one admixture of rules, procedures and norms embedded within the systemic context.* Procedurally, each governance regime comprises the prevailing admixture of institutions, rules and norms together with the relevant policy 'players': socio-economic actors, national civil servants and ministers, Commission officials, MEPs and so on. The prevailing admixture varies over time: system-wide reforms may have repercussions on the governance regime, such as through the EP being granted rights to participate in legislation by co-decision; an overarching norm such as subsidiarity may have to be given serious consideration; or court rulings may clarify relevant legal bases and policy procedures. Important tasks in examining any governance regime include identifying the boundaries of the governance regime, its characteristics and the participants.
- *Policy-makers follow the rules prevailing in 'their' governance regime.* We regard policy-making participants as orientating themselves to the specific regime characteristics in developing their own policy strategies. This may occur both strategically and tactically. This situation applies to interest groups, MEPs, the Commission and national governments alike. The characteristics of the governance regime are thus an important factor. They may influence calculations on the choice of appropriate forum for agenda-setting. Equally, they may influence a government's negotiating tactics and strategy in the Council of Ministers and its preparatory committees.
- *Governance regimes each reflect a particular policy inheritance.* Policy development is iterative and incremental. At some point a policy 'comes onto the agenda' perhaps in the form of discussions leading to a political declaration. Repeated declarations may be made, having the form of 'soft law' (Wellens and Borchardt 1980). After the passage of time, and if there is sufficient momentum for more formal measures, a number of possibilities may provide the basis for such action. Legislation might be proposed on the basis of Article 235, EC, i.e. on grounds that action is needed as part of creating a common market; and/or the explicit granting of competence to the EU through a reform package might take place. An alternative scenario is that ECJ jurisprudence might declare that the treaties already provide the basis on which to act. Momentum develops in the policy area; the amount of legislation increases; new focuses might develop, thereby creating sub-groups of activity. Actors who had to compromise on their objectives in the first round of legislation will re-enter the fray in the second round. Moreover, the growth of Court jurisprudence contributes to the substance of policy and at this level an evolution of legal norms can be identified (see Armstrong 1995; also Chapter 6). This legal dimension interacts with the policy process. Past policy decisions influence subsequent legislation. This cumulative development, drawing upon political and legal processes as

well as formal and informal integration, characterises the substance of a governance regime. But this development remains situated in the wider, systemic context outlined earlier in the chapter.

- *Policy implementation is an important part of a governance regime.* Improving the implementation of legislation may well be part of the lesson-drawing of incremental policy-making. In any case, it is essential for the success of policy that there are arrangements or incentives present to ensure that the substantive component is put into practice. Unlike other international organisations the EU – and specifically its EC pillar – is comparatively well developed in its compliance mechanisms, with established routes for seeking redress. Nevertheless, the transposition of EC law into national law remains far from perfect and there are divergent patterns between the Member States. Ensuring that EC law is adhered to is more difficult still. The Commission lacks the resources to supervise compliance systematically. Member governments may have a vested interest not to do so, since they may be the subjects of the law concerned. Finally, redress in the courts by private parties, whose vigilance may serve as another support for compliance, may be expensive. Moreover, the opportunities and rewards for action through the courts vary according to the national systems of civil and criminal justice concerned. The 'mature' governance regime takes the procedural and substantive issues of compliance into account but these aspects may be neglected at first.

Institutions, policy actors and the toolkit of governance: an overview[10]

We have outlined some of the principles of governance in the EU, and especially its EC pillar. What of the roles of the individual institutions and other policy actors?

The European Commission
The Commission has the potential to play a major role in EC-pillar activities. It has important power resources but these are dependent on the general normative context of integration, i.e. the upswings and downswings in integrative momentum. Also important is the role of personalities, for it is important to underline that the Commission is not just a bureaucracy consisting of Directorates General but has a political leadership, namely the individual Commissioners, and collectively the College of Commissioners. Individual Commissioners are able to use their *cabinets* as part of an apparatus for pursuing policy ideas and for trying to complement work undertaken in the regular administrative structure. During the period under study here Jacques Delors was President of the Commission. He played a key role, exploiting the full potential of the presidency with the assistance of his *cabinet* (Ludlow 1991; Ross 1995). He played an

important part in inserting his ideas into discussions of the European Council. He also sought to energise the workings of the Commission in a number of key policy areas which he gave priority to himself. This work, reinforcing the specific efforts of Internal Market Commissioner Lord Cockfield and his *cabinet*, headed by Adrian Fortescue, was important in dynamising the work of the 'services' of the Commission: the relevant Directorates General.

The European Commission is regarded as having six roles: initiating policy, mediating between Member States, administering policy, representing the EU to third parties, acting as guardian of the treaties, and playing the role of supranational conscience. These roles, each of which has a grounding in the treaties, are of varying importance. Moreover, all of these Commission roles are shared with other institutions, whether formally or informally.

In the EC pillar it is the Commission which initiates formal legislative proposals. However, its proposals are often in response to invitations made by the governments in either the European Council or the Council of Ministers. The White Paper on the single market was a Commission initiative but in part responding to governments' promptings in the European Council. Due to its slender resources the Commission is dependent on outside advice, whether it be in the form of abstract ideas, technical expertise or more naked lobbying from pressure groups. This dependency makes it exposed to the risks of 'agency capture' by producer groups, especially where countervailing interests are weak and where a policy is isolated from wider examination, as was illustrated by the CAP. A factor sometimes neglected is that the EP may exert an influence at the formative stage when the Commission is drafting legislation (see Earnshaw and Judge 1997).

The mediation function in the policy process entails the Commission having to compromise between what it originally proposed and what it can feasibly secure in the Council, also taking into account the EP's views during the legislative phase. This function of mediation – especially between Member States – is shared with the Council presidency, which has its own resources in this respect. Where it administers policy, the Commission is still reliant on outside expertise from national civil servants. This reliance is expressed in the phenomenon of comitology, which was given more attention following the SEA. On the one hand, the Member States wanted the Commission to be able to take speedy administrative decisions, such as in competition policy. On the other, they wanted to retain control over the form of the decisions taken. Comitology is the umbrella term for the various committees which bring the Commission and national civil servants together. Different types of committee exist, each reflecting a different balance of power between the Commission and national officials.[11] The EP generally favours a more supranational form of committee because it has better opportunities to intervene, and because it can much better call the

Commission to account. There are power struggles surrounding comitology and the work of the individual committees. The latter aspect comes into play once legislation has been agreed, so does not receive systematic attention in our case studies (but see Chapter 11).

The Commission's role of acting as guardian of the treaties is important to the functioning of the SEM but this means of ensuring compliance can only be limited, given the Commission's slender personnel resources. The member governments and private parties also have to be relied on to ensure that the treaties are adhered to (see below). Although generally important, the Commission's role in external relations is less relevant to a study of the *internal* market. However, there are important issues relating to the compatibility of SEM rules with those of the World Trade Organisation (WTO), and it is here that the Commission's external negotiating role comes into play. The extent of the Commission's authority to negotiate on these matters has been contested.

The Commission's last role, that of acting as the conscience of the EC/EU, is worthy of more attention. Essentially, we are dealing with a normative context for the Commission: its 'mission' is to find supranational solutions to policy problems. However, if that serves as the general normative context for the Commission, its internal fragmentation means that individual Directorates General have their own norms. Officials working on the internal market (in DG III until January 1993 and thence in DG XV) were preoccupied with breaking down the barriers to the four freedoms of goods, labour, capital and services. Their objectives had a neo-liberal tinge. However, they had to work in conjunction with other DGs. The 'mission' of DG XI (Environment) was much more concerned with ensuring good environmental practice. The removal of frontier controls, as part of the internal market logic, opened up the possibility for trafficking in environmentally hazardous material. This situation brought the two sets of values into conflict and complaints from DG XI at the failure to assess the environmental consequences of the SEM (see Chapter 8). This situation of conflicting norms of individual DGs arose in several of our case studies. Thus, the Commission may generally favour supranational solutions: but different DGs may be normatively predisposed to different forms of solution. Amongst the other DGs relevant to SEM matters are DG IV (Competition Policy); DG V (Industrial Relations and Social Affairs, including health and safety and equal opportunities); DG VII (Transport); DG X (Audiovisual Sector and Information); DG XIII (Telecommunications and Information Technology); DG XXI (Customs Rules and Fiscal Matters); and DG XXIII (Small and Medium-sized Enterprises).

The European Council

The European Council is the institution which is most able to provide a political lead in changing the systemic character of the EC/EU (see Bulmer and Wessels 1987; Werts 1992). Thus, its major importance to this study is in terms of its exhortations on completing the internal market, followed by the agreement on the Commission's White Paper and supervision of the negotiations leading to the SEA (see Chapter 1). These two developments brought about important institutional and normative changes to European integration. However, the European Council had no direct involvement in the routine policy-making on the SEM: that was left to the Council of Ministers. Later on during the creation of the SEM, the Social Charter, the Maastricht Treaty and negotiations on subsidiarity had an impact on the systemic framework, with implications for internal market legislation. The European Council's two main functional contributions to the SEM were as a *demandeur* of progress on the internal market, and as the principal source of systemic change of EC/EU governance.

The Council of Ministers[12]

The Council is centrally concerned with the substance of policy-making. It is therefore the forum in which much of the politics of our case studies is played out. However, 'the Council' is an umbrella term covering separate bodies. The Council meets in some twenty formations, and our case studies were not confined to the Council of Internal Market Ministers. Beneath the Council of Ministers in the hierarchy is the Committee of Permanent Representatives (COREPER) and a multitude of working groups (which should not be confused with those discussed earlier as part of comitology).[13]

The Council is a two-faced institution: it seeks collective solutions but it is made up of Member States with vested national interests. For Hayes-Renshaw and Wallace it is multi-faceted: it is both executive and legislature, European and national, multi-issue and sectoral, and a forum for both negotiation and decision (1996: 4–8). The new momentum in integration in the mid-1980s and the reforms of the SEA brought about changes to the functioning of the Council that are relevant to the SEM. A number of policy areas became subject to QMV, and this figure was further increased with the Maastricht Treaty. In addition, changes to the Rules of Procedure in 1987 facilitated the calling of majority votes by the presidency. The veto culture of the period since the 1965 empty-chair crisis was left behind and national governments could no longer rely on a policy of blocking decisions (Marks, Hooghe and Blank 1996: 362–3). That did not mean that QMV was widely practised either. Rather, individual governments became much more conscious of the need to form majority or blocking alliances; either way unilateral policy positions became less prominent. The importance of QMV was to reduce the incentives for unilateral blocking tactics. It was not about individual ministers sitting in the Council making rationalist calculations, such as with the Shapley-Shubik power index, to determine their coalition and voting behaviour in the Council.[14]

Apart from facilitating decision-making, the new rule-derived practices in the Council accelerated decisional speed. The momentum towards completing the SEM 'lubricated' decision-making by facilitating package deals (Engel and Borrmann 1991: 242). In fact, Engel and Borrmann show that the SEM and SEA had the effect of galvanising decisional speed not only in the Council, where legislation subject to the cooperation procedure was to adhere to a specific timetable, but in the EP and during the initial stages of policy development within the Commission (see also Sloot and Verschuren 1990).

The Council presidency also has significance in respect of decision-making. It can play a facilitatory role in securing agreement. When the internal market programme was at its height, presidencies became keen to achieve good 'scores' in securing agreement on White Paper measures. Individual states might swallow hard and withdraw objections to a particular proposal if they, as president, could claim the prize of agreement (see the French government's behaviour in respect of merger control, Chapter 4). Sequences of presidencies can also be significant. Thus, the successive Dutch and UK presidencies in 1986 gave the opportunity for two neo-liberal governments to push for neo-liberal solutions to airline regulation (Stevens 1997; see also Chapter 7).

Overall, the Council retains a central role in the policy process. However, the period following the 1985 internal market commitment and the SEA saw important changes in its dynamics. It departed from a purely inter-governmental mode of operation due to changes in procedural rules, practices and norms. This change was complemented by more intensive inter-institutional bargaining brought about by the cooperation procedure.

The European Parliament

The EP has tended to be regarded as the weakest of the main policy-making institutions. Its legislative powers tended to be particularly weak: until the SEA it only needed to be 'consulted', and its only sanction – arising from the 1980 *Isoglucose* ruling – was that its opinion had to be issued before the Council could decide on legislation, so in extreme circumstances it could use delaying tactics (see Jacobs, Corbett and Shackleton 1992: 180–2). With the SEA the introduction of the cooperation procedure brought the EP into the legislative process in a significant way.[15] Two readings were needed for legislation affected by the procedure. The co-operation procedure applied initially to ten articles of the Treaty of Rome, including internal market legislation and some social policy matters: about one-third of the legislation considered by the EP (see Jacobs *et al.* 1992: 185; also Earnshaw and Judge 1997). Under the original consultation procedure, the EP gives an opinion on legislation proposed by the Commission but has no real influence over the Council. Thus, its opinions under the consultation procedure are much less significant than under the cooperation procedure where the Council is required to give due consideration to proposed amendments.

The cooperation procedure requires the EP to act much more in a law-making mode. At the end of the first round of consultation the Council agrees on a 'common position'. This position is then sent back to the EP which has a three- or four-month period to decide on its further action. It may do one of the following:

- reject the common position, but this action may be overruled by a unanimous vote of the Council;
- propose new or reinstate earlier amendments, which are referred to the Council for its final decision; or
- accept the common position.

In each case there are specific voting rules for both the EP and the Council. The Council remains the final decision-maker but its autonomy is restricted significantly by the need to engage in an inter-institutional dialogue with the EP, and with the Commission acting as mediator. A further consequence of the cooperation procedure has been much better inter-institutional information on why a particular position had been adopted.

The different parliamentary procedures give different levels of opportunity for the EP to influence legislation. In consequence, MEPs prefer the Commission to use legal bases which provide the most generous opportunities where there is any discretion over the matter.[16]

Under the Maastricht Treaty the policy areas subject to the cooperation procedure were re-assigned, with some new areas coming in, and some being transferred out to the newly established co-decision procedure (see Jacob *et al.* 1992 for details). This new procedure added a further stage to proceedings by permitting the EP to reject legslation under specified conditions, albeit with referral to conciliation. These developments under the TEU do not bear upon the specific legislation discussed in the case studies, since the TEU was not then in effect.

The EP's scope to bring issues into wider debate had been difficult historically because of its relatively weak profile. That did not prevent it from seeking to shape the policy agenda even before its powers were extended in the SEA. This situation is clear in two cases: air transport and women's rights. In the former case the British MEP Lord Bethell sought through the EP to draw attention to the anti-competitive behaviour of the European airline industry well before the issue really gained momentum. The case of women's rights is somewhat different. As Chapter 9 indicates, the existence of an EP committee with this portfolio – a departure from the regular 'Commission-shadowing' structure of its committees – played an important part in developing policy momentum. When legislation on the Maternity Directive was introduced on the legal base of health and safety, the EP was able to exploit the prevailing cooperation procedure in order to engage in inter-institutional bargaining.

There is of course much more that could be written about the EP's procedures and powers, including its supervisory and budgetary ones. There is also the relationship of the EP with the democratic deficit in the EU. Our concern here is somewhat narrower, so we must set that issue aside. Suffice it to indicate that MEPs are concerned not only with influencing policy substance but also with ensuring that the EP's influence is as strong as possible in inter-institutional relations.

The Court of Justice and the Court of First Instance

The ECJ, unlike the other institutions discussed thus far, is not overtly concerned with policy-making. The ECJ's concerns are with interpretations of EC law and ensuring that it is obeyed. However, these functions are important to any policy cycle, the SEM included. The ECJ is currently comprised of fifteen judges and assisted by nine Advocates General, all of these being assisted by personal *cabinets* of lawyers. Cases are heard either before the 'Full Court' (eleven or thirteen judges) or in Chambers (three or five judges).[17] The collegiate nature of the Court is evidenced by the secrecy of its deliberations and the production of a single judgment without dissenting opinions. Where there are disagreements between the judges, a vote will be taken and the majority view will prevail. The existence of dissent is not published. The veil of secrecy is increased by the sometimes brief nature of the Court's judgments. Even though the ECJ's judgments are preceded by an opinion of the Advocate General acting in the case, this does not bind the Court. Thus, there is further opaqueness in those (relatively rare) cases when the Court and the Advocate General reach different conclusions, especially if the Advocate General gives a lengthy reasoned opinion and the Court gives a rather cursory judgment. Another variant of this ambiguity arises where they reach the same conclusion but through different legal reasoning.

The SEA expanded the Court structure by providing for the creation of the CFI. Created in 1989, the CFI currently comprises fifteen judges (but no Advocates General). A growing body of cases has been transferred to the CFI. The scope of the CFI's jurisdiction is, however, limited. Originally, the CFI only possessed jurisdiction in staff cases and competition cases brought by non-privileged applicants (i.e. applicants other than Community institutions or Member States). Its jurisdiction has been expanded to include all direct actions brought by non-privileged applicants (see Bellamy 1997; Brown and Kennedy 1994: 74–6; Weatherill and Beaumont 1995: 187–90). Accordingly, there is now a jurisdictional division between direct actions brought by the institutions and the Member States, which are heard before the ECJ, and direct actions brought by individuals and companies, which are heard before the CFI (though with a right of appeal

to the ECJ).[18] What this means in practice is that some SEM-related litigation is heard by the CFI. To give a specific illustration, if British Airways
complains about state aids to Air France its case will go before the CFI.
If the British government complains, however, its case will go to the ECJ.

The establishment of the CFI can be seen as one step in the process of
reform to the 'judicial architecture' of the Community.[19] The need for reform
arises from a variety of related pressures: the sheer number of cases now
coming before the Court has placed enormous strains on the Court's resources and on litigants' patience; the persistence of cases ranging from the
very specific to those where constitutional jurisprudence is at issue; and the
fact that the enlargement of the EC/EU brings with it an increased caseload.

The creation of the CFI has only provided a limited solution to these
reform presures. In the specific context of the SEM it has to be noted that
justice postponed may well be justice denied. Given that the SEM programme vests new EC-law rights in individuals, the long delays experienced
with the Article 177 preliminary ruling procedure may serve to undermine
the legal framework of the SEM. In short, the reform to the *legislative*
institutions of the EC brought about by the SEA could be undermined by
failure to reform the *judicial* institutions.[20] Both the ECJ and the CFI made
submissions to the 1996/97 IGC concerning the future judicial architecture.

The exact way in which cases reach the Courts varies according to the
form of action taken. However, we can distinguish between direct and
indirect actions as set out in Box 3.1. We cannot go into the full details

Box 3.1: Types of actions before the Community Courts

Direct actions

Article 169: actions brought by the Commission against a Member
              State;

Article 170: actions brought by a Member State against a Member
              State;

Article 171: actions declaring a failure to comply with a previous
              judgment of the ECJ (with the possibility of the impo-
              sition of a fine);

Article 173: actions seeking judicial review of the legality of acts by
              institutions;

Article 175: actions declaring a failure to act on the part of a
              Community institution;

Article 215: actions regarding the non-contractual liability of the
              Community.

Indirect actions

Article 177: references from national courts for a preliminary ruling.

of these procedures here. However, it might be worth illustrating how the procedures that are most typically used in conjunction with the single market work.

It is Article 169 which gives the Commission the power to, for instance, bring actions alleging a failure to transpose or otherwise implement legislation, including legislation on the SEM. Only a small percentage of infringement proceedings instituted by the Commission actually reaches the Court (Snyder 1993). Instead, bargained solutions tend to be reached between the Commission and the Member State. In the context of the SEM, the Commission has held so-called 'package meetings' with Member States at which complaints and alleged infringements are discussed. This has given rise to an increase in the number of infringement actions which have been terminated prior to the case coming before the ECJ (CEC 1996a). The Commission has also placed increased emphasis on proper transposition and enforcement of SEM legislation, and the number of infringements detected by the Commission has increased (CEC 1996a). There is a tendency to think of Article 169 as *the* mechanism for forcing Member States to abide by their obligations. Yet, this is to ignore the vast numbers of infringements which are alleged before *national* courts and which are brought before the ECJ using the Article 177 preliminary ruling procedure. While there is a clear advantage for a disgruntled company to make a complaint to the Commission rather than seeking to litigate directly in the national courts – Article 169 actions use up the Commission's rather than the company's resources – the trade-off is a loss of control over the legal action, and an inability to obtain legal remedies (e.g. damages) other than a declaration of the infringement. Thus, in important SEM areas such as the free movement of goods and services, it is actions brought directly in national courts, and where necessary referred to the ECJ under Article 177, that are of extreme importance.[21] One other procedure particularly relevant to our study is Article 173, which is used to establish the legality of acts of the EC institutions. This procedure has been used in a number cases relevant to our study, for example to clarify the legal base for legislation. Because the legal base determines the procedures of policy-making, it can be seen that rulings on Article 173 cases can have important consequences for the making of policy. Finally, under Article 228, EC the ECJ may be asked for an Opinion regarding the compatibility with the Treaty of draft international agreements.

The Courts and the judicial process are important factors in the shaping of the substantive and procedural policy rules of a governance regime. Neglect of their importance gives only a partial view of policy dynamics on the SEM.

Other institutions
Other institutions have limited importance for a study of the SEM. The Economic and Social Committee (Ecosoc) was consulted on much of the

SEM legislation. The impact of its work on the resultant legislation is very difficult to gauge. It was certainly another forum within which the substance of policy was discussed but it was overshadowed by the increased legislative importance of the EP. Other institutions, such as the Court of Auditors, have little direct relevance to our concerns. The Committee of the Regions, created following the TEU's ratification in 1993, largely falls outside our time-frame. In any case, its activities are geared towards spatial policies, such as the structural funds.

Interests and interest groups

Although we have concentrated on institutions thus far, we are in no sense interested in them to the exclusion of all else. However, we are arguing that interests and interest groups are rule-followers. This argument is a variant of Mazey and Richardson's invocation of the rule that lobbyists 'shoot where the ducks are' (Mazey and Richardson 1993). In other words, socio-economic interests – whether individual companies, interest groups or whatever their form of organisation – turn their attention to those points in the policy process, formal and informal, where their influence counts most.

The SEM and the SEA, as major reforms to the institutional rules and to prevailing norms, consequently had a significant impact on such activity. Two broad consequences can be identified. First, the transfer of new competences and the enlivenment of existing areas of competence led to a shift in their orientation towards the EC level of governance. Well over 500 European-level groups existed at the start of the 1990s: a doubling since the 1970s, according to Mazey and Richardson (Mazey and Richardson 1993, p. 37). Further associated phenomena of this period of integration were the growth of consultancy companies undertaking quasi-lobbying activity and the growth of large individual companies represented in Brussels. It was not only the growth of supranational legislation that was responsible but also a recognition that the provision for QMV meant that the national lobbying route, i.e. of targeting the appropriate national government, might not be a successful strategy for influencing legislation. Secondly, there has been some re-balancing in the targets of lobbying amongst the supranational institutions, with increased attention being directed to the EP due to its increased legislative powers. An increase in the Brussels-based interest groups and a change in their tactics represent the key developments. And whilst producer groups remain the best resourced of the groups, we also find other promotional groups being created, such as the European Women's Lobby (EWL) (see Chapter 9).

Political parties

Transnational political parties played rather less of a role in connection with our case studies. Truly transnational parties – i.e. party alliances operating *outside* the EP – had little importance in connection with the decisions on the SEM and SEA. Their importance increased in the period from 1990 through their holding caucus meetings prior to sessions of the European Council (see Hix 1995). Party groups inside the EP, by contrast, came to play a more important role at this time. This was for the simple reason that the increased legislative role of the EP placed a greater premium on turnout levels in the EP and upon the securing of majorities for amendments and other actions in plenary votes. In some economic and social policy issues a left-right spectrum can be identified across the parliamentary parties. However, territorial-national politics continue to play a part within the EP.

The policy-making toolkit

It is worth making some observations about the policy-making toolkit available in the context of the EC pillar. We can identify the following means by which governance is conducted, and it will be noted that they are both informal and formal, and in the latter category legislative and judicial.

- *Treaties* provide the legal competence to act and can be interpreted by the ECJ. The treaties also set out the rights and duties for states, EU institutions and private actors.
- *EC legislative acts* comprise the secondary legislation adopted by the EC institutions. The principal forms of this legislation are well known to students of integration: Regulations and Directives (see, for instance, Nugent 1994: 210–13). The decision to employ a Regulation rather than a Directive, or vice versa, may be related to the mode of governance prevailing in the particular policy situation. Thus in competition policy the preferred policy instrument is the Regulation. This reflects a range of factors: the fact that the principles of the policy are set down in the EEC Treaty, so only their implementation is required; the fact that the Commission's competence is strong in this policy area; the need to have uniform application of the law; the fact that the law is addressed to private economic actors rather than to the Member States; and so on. Directives, by contrast, introduce some limited discretion as to how the EC's wishes are administered and operationalised in Member States. Thus the choice between using a Directive or a Regulation is likely to be closely linked to the prevailing form of governance for the particular subject-matter. Directives have to be transposed into national law, thus providing a strong link between the national and supranational legal systems. Since much of the legislation associated with the White Paper on the internal market was in the form of Directives, the Commission took a strong interest in checking transposition rates. A final form of EC legislative act is the Decision. Typically, this

is the way in which the EC institutions – principally the Commission – implement their own legislation. To take the competition policy area once again, it is by means of legally binding Decisions that the Commission may find companies guilty of transgressions of competition law and, where appropriate, impose a fine on them. Generally, Decisions are employed by the Commission where it enjoys a regulatory role, i.e. where it has some discretionary power of its own.

- *Jurisprudence* of the ECJ is important in establishing and clarifying legal principles – as part of the constitutionalism identified above. It is also important for clarifying more policy-specific points of law: what the treaty intended, whether an institution has acted within its powers, whether a Member State is in breach of its obligations, or something similar. Sometimes such judgments have a broader rhetoricised effect beyond their immediate legal circumstances. Examples of this might be the *Cassis de Dijon* or *Dassonville* cases. In narrow terms these simply resolved specific legal disputes. However, their impact was not confined to the specifics of the two cases. Rather they established principles which the ECJ was able routinely to use in its development of its internal market jurisprudence. Further, the Commission was able to appeal to the *Cassis* principle of mutual recognition in seeking agreement on its new approach to the removal of technical barriers to trade (see Chapter 6). Similarly, in the case of merger control the *Philip Morris* judgment made a specific ruling on a case affecting an agreement between enterprises in the tobacco industry. However, in effect it also gave the Commission regulatory powers (see Chapter 4).

- *Soft law* represents a grey area between legislative acts and non-binding political declarations (see Wellens and Borchardt 1980). In simple terms it relates to rules of conduct that are not legally enforceable but none the less have a legal scope in that they guide the conduct of the institutions, the Member States, individuals and undertakings (Wellens and Borchardt 1980: 285). Examples of soft law include Commission practice notes and memoranda, declarations attached to the treaties, and statements recorded in the minutes of the Council of Ministers but not normally published. Although they have the status of soft law, they can nevertheless make an important contribution to the operation of policy (see Chapter 4 for examples in merger control; see also Bulmer 1993: 368).

- *Political agreements* are included by Wellens and Borchardt (1980) in their exploration of 'soft law'. We see them as worthy of mention in their own right, and identify two categories. First, broad constitutive agreements, such as the 1983 Solemn Declaration on European Union, can have a normative impact across the integration process. However, the impact of these efforts at non-treaty reform may be difficult to measure. We might include in this category the 1992 Edinburgh European Council declaration on subsidiarity, again political in nature and trans-sectoral in impact on the form of policy action. As a result of the latter, the supranational institutions were required to think about whether policy can better be carried out at EU level, regardless of the policy area. Of procedural significance are inter-institutional agreements or other agreements on the rules of the game, such as the Ioannina Declaration on interpreting QMV after the 1995 enlargement (Hayes-Renshaw and Wallace 1996: 55–6, 313). Secondly, there are also narrower, policy-specific political agreements. Typically, these might be policy declarations, recommendations or opinions. They have no legal status. For many years these were the form which policy action took in some aspects of equal opportunities. But it would be mistaken to dismiss them as having no relevance simply because they had no legal status. As soon as new opportunities arise, for example a new legal base, the substance of the declarations might become a legislative proposal (see Chapter 9 for examples).

Policy-making in practice

We have given an overview of governance in the context of the single market. Necessarily, this has been a somewhat static and synoptic view. In the case studies a more dynamic picture can be presented: the way in which national governments lined up in the Council of Ministers, the role of interest groups, inter-institutional politics, the role of ideas, and similar issues. What then are the case studies and how were they selected?

Six case studies of the single market

First of all, how did we select the case studies? As outlined in our Introduction, we have understood the SEM as the integration of economic markets rather than in terms of the somewhat arbitrary contents of the White Paper. This document, whilst of key importance to understanding the dynamics of the wider SEM, was narrower in its purview. Market integration clearly entails the breaking down of national barriers: the focus of the White Paper. Accordingly, two of our case studies focus on such policy issues that were prominent in that document: public procurement and the free movement of goods. However, market integration is not just a matter of such horizontal issues but also has a sectoral dimension. In order to capture this, a further case study is concerned with air transport liberalisation. The liberalisation of this sector was mentioned in the White Paper but in limited terms. In the event it took on greater significance. It is also emblematic of other sectoral programmes of market integration that are still evolving: in telecommunications and electricity for example. This sectoral dimension is now seen as a key part of the SEM.

Market integration needs a regulatory framework to govern corporate behaviour. That function is normally provided through competition rules. The EC already possessed strong competition policy powers when the White Paper was launched. However, in one area a coherent set of rules was absent, namely in respect of mergers and acquisitions. The White Paper was scarcely concerned with competition rules but they form an integral part of the regulatory arrangements for market integration. Accordingly, we examine the emergence of the EC's rules for merger control: rules which were needed to regulate the industrial restructuring which the White Paper aimed to induce.

We have argued that the SEM was closely bound up with the SEA. The latter included a number of treaty reforms which were specifically designed to regulate possible consequences of the internal market programme. Prominent amongst these were the strengthening of treaty provision, and thereby EC competence, in the area of health and safety and of environmental policy. Both these areas may be seen as classic areas of social regulation: seeking to limit the consequences of market integration for the worker, consumer or citizen. Accordingly, our two final case studies concern such issues: respectively the provision of health and safety rules concerning pregnant workers, and transfrontier shipments of waste.

It can be seen, then, that our understanding of the SEM is wider than the White Paper. We have explained the analytical basis for our scope in terms of regulating market integration. Empirically, it is worth noting that the Commission came to understand the SEM in these wider terms over the ensuing decade (see the Conclusion). By way of introduction we briefly set out the issues at stake in the six case studies which follow.

Chapter 4 examines the regulation of mergers and acquisitions in the single market. To reinforce the point that we are not concerned with the single market simply in terms of the White Paper, we commence with a case study which was not part of that programme. The chapter traces the search for a regulatory instrument from the first efforts in the early 1970s through to agreement on the Merger Control Regulation (MCR) in 1989. We examine how the MCR has worked in practice and review the subsequent efforts to strengthen the legislation.

Chapter 5 is concerned with public procurement, specifically in the utilities sectors (water, energy, transport and telecommunications). Regarded in the pre-SEM era as the 'excluded sectors', this position became untenable under the new conditions. It could scarcely be justified that government purchasing in these sectors could be excluded from the new impulses towards a more competitive market that the governments were advancing in the private sector. We also examine how this legislation – which *was* provided for in the White Paper – interacted with a number of other single market issues, such as sectoral liberalisation in telecommunications and the regulation of technical standards.

Chapter 6 is concerned precisely with the issue of technical regulations and standards. We review the evolution in the Community's policy from its traditional approach of legislative harmonisation to the new approach brought in with the SEM. This evolution was at the heart of facilitating a single market with a much lighter legislative load, and with emphasis being placed on the transfer of much standards-setting work to outside agencies. The chapter reflects a core issue of the White Paper. The interaction of standards with other issues is also examined.

Chapter 7 deals with air transport liberalisation. Mentioned in a limited way in the White Paper, the sector nevertheless became infused with the objective of creating a single aviation market. The chapter charts how this new momentum was achieved, culminating in the creation of a fully liberalised system from 1 April 1997. We examine how the attention has shifted from the three liberalisation packages of the 1980s and early 1990s to a new focus on state subsidies and access to airport infrastructure. Although many of the dynamics of this case study are airline-specific, it is illustrative of the liberalisation of sectors which traditionally were regarded as sectors excluded from liberalisation.

Chapter 8 addresses shipments of waste. Not included in the White Paper, it gradually became clear that the removal of trade barriers could permit unmonitored, cross-frontier shipments of hazardous waste. This realisation raised a potential conflict between the objectives of the single market and environmental considerations. The chapter examines how legislative and judicial rule-making resolved this problematic policy interrelationship.

Our final case study, in Chapter 9, extends coverage to legislation introduced under the health and safety provisions incorporated in the SEA. Brought into the treaties with a view to ensuring that safe working conditions did not become a casualty of the competitiveness of the single market, Article 118a served as the legal base for the Maternity Directive. This legislation sought not only to protect pregnant workers at the workplace but also to strengthen their rights as workers and their entitlements in terms of maternity leave. In other words, it sought to secure progress in respect of the Social Charter and the Social Action Programme. These latter aspects brought about an early conflict between the British government and other governments about the legitimate boundaries of supranational social policy. This chapter therefore examines regulatory change brought about as part of the flanking measures for the SEM programme.

The SEM was a multi-faceted programme. We cannot claim to cover all the different dimensions, for example the efforts to remove fiscal barriers to trade. On the other hand, we have sought to take account of a 'real' single market by examining some of the related issues like merger control and the interaction with related policies.

Notes

1   We are concerned here with the systemic properties of the EC or the EC pillar of the EU. As Helen Wallace has noted, the three-pillared structure of the post-Maastricht EU introduced competing policy methods (H. Wallace 1996a: 55–7).

2   The case for a *Kompetenzenkatalog* is most frequently made by the governments of the German *Länder* as a way of trying to restrict the EU further intruding upon what, within the Federal Republic of Germany, are their legislative responsibilities.

3   The definition of 'efficiently' is loose here, for we are not wishing to present the pooling of sovereignty as something driven exclusively by a rationalist set of calculations.

4   Joseph Weiler, in reviewing this constitutionalism, has raised questions as to whether its integrity can be maintained through a period where the legitimacy of the EU is under strain. The issue of differentiated integration may also chip away at its integrity (see Weiler 1997).

5   The term 'inter-governmental' is used in the sense of central–local relations here rather than in the sense of international relations.

6   That is not to say that the EP is lacking in legislative powers, for these have been increased successively by the SEA and the TEU (see below).

7   The most explicitly re-distributive policy is the Cohesion Fund, which was set up under the Maastricht Treaty to 'provide a financial contribution to projects in the field of environment and trans-European networks in the field of transport infrastructure' (Article 130d, EC). A protocol to the TEU restricted access to the Cohesion Fund to those states with a GDP below 90 per cent of the EU average. Access was thus restricted to Greece, Ireland, Spain and Portugal. The Cohesion Fund is therefore much more targeted in its re-distribution than the structural funds, which make up the other financial instrument with this function.

8   The largest body of his work is contained in Majone (1996); also see the review of his work generally in Caporaso (1996).

9   Our work on governance regimes connects in with two sets of American writings. One, on American political economy, uses the notion of governance regimes to capture the pattern of economic governance in individual economic sectors (Campbell, Hollingsworth and Lindberg 1991). The other work – by Oran Young (1989) – uses the international relations literature on regimes to explore different international regimes for managing natural resources. Young has a threefold conception of regimes; he sees them as having substantive, procedural and implementation components (1989: 15–21). These two sets of work are recommended to those interested in developing institutionalist accounts of policy sub-systems.

10 This section cannot provide all the necessary detail on each of the institutions and actors listed. For a guide to the institutions and actors, see Nugent (1994).

11 The different balances of power are given procedural expression: for an overview of comitology, see Docksey and Williams (1994). As they note, in 1993 there were 294 such committees, split between advisory, management and regulatory committees (Docksey and Williams 1994: 125).

12 The Council of Ministers adopted the title 'Council of the European Union' in the aftermath of the Maastricht Treaty. We use the old title – which in any case continues to be used – since it was the one relevant for the majority of the period under study.

13 For fuller details on the Council, see the accounts by Hayes-Renshaw and Wallace (1996) and Westlake (1995). The hierarchy is different for a number of policy areas not relevant to our cases: agriculture, monetary policy, external trade policy and the CFSP and JHA activities. Each departs from this committee structure.

14 On this subject-matter, which is of general significance rather than a concern in individual negotiations, see Hosli (1996).

15 The SEA also made it necessary to secure the assent of the EP for enlargement of the EC/EU and for certain types of association agreements.

16 One struggle occurred in the context of regulating standards for the titanium dioxide industry. The Commission sought to legislate on an internal market legal base (Article 100a), which would have been subject to both QMV and the cooperation procedure. The Council changed the legal base to Article 130s (environment), which was subject to unanimity and the consultation procedure. The ECJ ruled in favour of the Commission and the EP, who had challenged the Council's action.

17 The President of the Court is responsible for deciding on the form of hearing and on who will hear the case. The Administrative Meeting of the judges can decide that a case should be heard by the Full Court or that cases relating to the same issue be conjoined (Brown and Kennedy 1994: 253–4).

18 References for preliminary rulings under Article 177 are still only heard by the ECJ.

19 The phrase 'judicial architecture' comes from Jacqué and Weiler (1990).

20 As Weatherill and Beaumont note (1995: 188), the establishment of the CFI has in fact done little to reduce the workload of the ECJ.

21 For example, between 1988 and 1993, 202 preliminary rulings on questions relating to the free movement of goods were given, as compared with 66 direct actions (Brown and Kennedy 1994: Tables 7 and 9).

4

The regulation of mergers and acquisitions in the single market

Introduction

This case study, like those which follow, is concerned with illustrating the dynamic process of creating the SEM. In common with the other case-study chapters it deals with the following key issues. First, what were the origins of the SEM-related policy dynamics relating to the particular regulatory issue? In short, what triggered policy change? Secondly, what was the character of the changes brought about? Thirdly, what is the character of the resultant governance regime? Has it already been subject to evolution in the phase of putting policy into practice? Finally, and analytically, we are concerned with the role of institutions in the transformation of governance associated with the SEM and the SEA. This particular issue can be broken down further into more specialised questions. Did the supranational institutions have some kind of autonomy, perhaps facilitating policy change? Or were the national governments the key actors in policy change, through the Council of Ministers? What was the interaction between the judicial and legislative routes to regulation: was there a significant impact on policy dynamics deriving from the ECJ? What were the roles of institutional norms and ideas? Was change path-dependent or, alternatively, reflective of major change in the pattern of integration? We are concerned, then, with the different analytical insights which may be gained from the new institutionalist literature discussed in Chapter 2.

In line with each of the case studies, the chapter is structured in the following way. First, it looks at how the regulatory issue came to be constructed in the policy debate. How did the issue become salient to the SEM programme; how did the EC become involved in a regulatory capacity; and how was the policy agenda shaped? In a second part, the chapter looks at the rule-making process: how the European rules for regulating merger and acquisition (M&A) activity were formulated. Who were the key players? In the final part of the chapter we look at the regime created and its character.

Before addressing these issues, however, it is important to give some contextual information on the regulation of mergers and acquisitions. Why is the issue important? How does it relate to the single market programme? What is at stake?

The regulation of mergers and acquisitions is part of the armoury of competition policy. It is therefore amongst the policy instruments which are designed to ensure the existence of transparent, competitive market conditions. Thus, rules are established that delineate what activities are deemed incompatible with promoting the efficient working of the market mechanism. In short, competition policy is a classic example of government – here the EU – acting as a regulator.

In the EU context competition policy has been concerned with controlling several forms of market-distorting behaviour:

- agreements between undertakings that might impact upon the market in an anti-competitive manner (Article 85, EC);
- the abuse by one or more undertakings of a dominant position within the common market (Article 86, EC); and
- practices distorting the common market predominantly undertaken by national authorities, typically the payment of state aid to an undertaking operating within its borders.

It was to these policy instruments that the 1989 Merger Control Regulation (MCR), the subject of this chapter, was added.

The regulation of M&A activity, like the other competition policy instruments, has to be orientated around an understanding of competition. However, even before entering into the politics of this case study, we have to note that there are competing views amongst economists as to the nature of competition (see Young and Metcalfe 1994). The predominant understanding of competition has derived from neo-classical economics, which sees 'perfect competition' as a situation where economic resources are allocated optimally. Where firms secure significant market power – for instance through M&A activity – then perfect competition is undermined. From a neo-classical perspective, therefore, the role of competition policy is to combat the distorting effects of market power.

This neo-classical view is, however, contested – largely on the grounds of being too static and abstract. The Austrian School, for example, regards competition as part of a continuing process (see Young and Metcalfe 1994: 121). Thus, the higher profits secured by an enterprise from its market power may provide the basis for greater innovatory capacity, with beneficial effects in the longer term. The Chicago School also took a more tolerant view of market power, and this view became highly influential in the USA from the 1970s. This school holds that the market is resilient, and that regulation by the authorities may be counter-productive.

Taking these divergent views on the character of competition policy one stage further – into the realm of industrial politics – it can be seen that we are dealing with a critical issue concerning the character of state–market relations. Thus, given that there have been distinctive views amongst the Member States on the character of state–market relations, the character of merger control goes to the very heart of economic policy and its instruments. A number of discrete policy issues made up the particular policy 'mix' prevailing in the individual Member State on the eve of the SEM programme.

- In those states with a strong tradition of state ownership in the economy, competition policy tended to be quite restricted, perhaps excluding state-owned enterprises from its purview. In such states, typically France and the Mediterranean countries, industrial mergers were often encouraged by the state as part of the construction of 'national champions' in particular industrial sectors. Typically these states encouraged domestic *consolidation* with a view to strengthening national competitiveness abroad. Others, however, saw heightened domestic competition as spurring international competitiveness.
- A further issue concerned identifying the 'relevant' market for making competition policy judgments. Here, too, economists are divided. There is a political dimension too, since it is more difficult for smaller states to regulate to ensure the presence of competition. As the relevant geographical market is often beyond national borders, smaller states in general lack the regulatory powers of the larger ones.
- The mechanisms of competition policy also revealed significant differences. Two are particularly worthy of note. First, was competition largely regulated by legal process, i.e. through reference of practices to the court system for interpretation of the law? Or, was regulation largely undertaken through more political means? This contrast is inevitably compounded with a second area of difference, namely the extent of discretion in the hands of regulators (Wilks and McGowan 1994). British policy has traditionally been political rather than legal in character and has vested considerable discretion in the Secretary of State for Trade and Industry. By contrast, German policy has revealed greater reliance on the courts, with correspondingly less scope for discretion in response to lobbying.

If we move on to the question 'what was at stake' with the MCR, we are concerned with several potential challenges:

- a challenge to the existing balance of policy between the pursuit of domestic competition and the pursuit of international competitiveness;
- a challenge to existing national procedures of competition regulation;
- a challenge to the vested interests of national authorities through the transfer of some of their powers to the European Commission;

- a potentially major change to the regulatory framework for the business community; and
- a weakening – through the SEM programme – of the view that the national market was the 'relevant market' for competition policy decisions.

With the removal of national barriers to trade went much of the justification for regulation at the national level, except in very specific product markets or in the provision of local services. In short, what was envisaged was a further fundamental shift in the regulation of economic governance in the Member States. Thus, the proposal for supranational merger regulation exploited the logic of the SEM by removing regulatory powers from national authorities – at least, where they had such powers – and vesting them in the European Commission. A fundamental re-regulation of an important component of competition policy was proposed. This re-regulation entailed some loss of national sovereignty. It also raised the question of trust. Could an EC regime for regulating M&A activity be relied upon to give 'acceptable' results, given the diverse set of established national competitition norms?

But what had merger regulation to do with the SEM programme? On the face of it there was no link. Merger control was not one of the specific measures listed in the Commission White Paper on completing the internal market. However, as we emphasised earlier, it would be misleading to see the SEM programme as being synonymous with the Commission White Paper. As will be seen, the dynamics of the SEM created a new set of norms which spread more widely through the EC institutions. This point can be underlined by the fact that the heads of government first expressed a desire for the supranational regulation of mergers at the 1972 Paris summit, and the Commission first tabled proposals in 1973. Yet it was only in 1989, as part of the legislative momentum associated with the SEM, that legislation was agreed.

Constructing a regulatory framework for action

When it came to negotiating the Treaty of Rome no explicit reference was made within the competition policy provisions for the regulation of M&A activity.[1] The specific circumstances of heavy industry had already been addressed; and none of the Member States possessed at that time explicit national measures for regulating mergers.[2] The competition policy provisions of the Rome Treaty were designed to execute the spirit of its Article 3(f), which referred to the institution of 'a system ensuring that competition in the Common Market is not distorted'.[3] The two main instruments of EC competition policy are Articles 85 and 86, dealing with the behavioural and structural aspects of markets respectively. Their operationalisation was facilitated by Regulation 17/62, in which the Council of Ministers granted the Commission powers to implement and enforce the two articles.

In examining how a regulatory framework came to be constructed, we are concerned with the interaction of two separate processes: the legislative process initiated by the Commission in 1973; and judgments arising from the EC's judicial process. We need to be conscious of both legislative and judicial forms of regulation, for they both – cumulatively – shaped the eventual MCR.

The first development came in the mid-1960s, when the Commission concluded that some form of control of concentrations was necessary if mergers were not, in some instances, to hamper competition (Brittan 1991: 25). In 1966 the Commission published its 'Memorandum on the problem of concentration in the common market'. It took the view that Article 85 did not apply to 'agreements whose purpose is the acquisition of total or partial ownership of enterprises or the reorganization of the ownership of enterprises' (quoted in Green *et al.* 1991: 277). Thus it concluded that only Article 86 was capable of applying to mergers, although there was also a fear that effective control would only be achieved through a treaty amendment (Allen 1983: 225; Brittan 1991: 26).

Until 1972 the Commission had not operationalised this view. In initiating proceedings against the Continental Can Co., the Commission was not only taking action on the specific concentration but also seeking to develop the principle that it could regulate mergers through Article 86. The general principle was upheld, following appeal, by the ECJ in its February 1973 *Continental Can* judgment (*Europemballage Corporation and Continental Can Co. Inc.* v. *Commission*, Case 6/72). It established the principle that a company with a dominant position could be regarded as abusing its position by taking over a competitor. However, the specific case against Continental Can was dismissed on the grounds that the Commission had not satisfactorily identified the relevant market.

Despite the evolution of Article 86 into a legal tool capable of regulating mergers, it was evident even in 1973 that it was an inadequate policy instrument. Why?

- It only applied to a *strengthening* of a dominant position rather than to its creation. Hence the prior existence of a dominant position would have to be proven.
- It was necessary to prove an *abuse* of the dominant position, and the test for this was quite narrowly defined.
- If both the above difficulties could be overcome, it could only be applied formally on an *ex post facto* basis: a very messy arrangement for property rights.
- It was unclear where mergers would be subject to EC control, and where to national control such as existed. There was no guarantee of a 'one-stop shop'.

- Ultimately, the Commission failed to use Article 86 in a substantively successful decision against a merger, thus rendering any informal *ex ante* leverage weak.

The *Continental Can* ruling did, however, feed into the Commission's first attempt to provide for merger regulation through legislation (*Official Journal*, C92/1–7, 31 October 1973). Specifically, the Commission embodied some of the text from the judgment in its proposal. In the continuing absence of an agreement on its legislative proposal for controls (see below), it turned its attention, from the mid-1980s, to Article 85, which it had itself rejected as an appropriate merger control instrument in its 1966 memorandum.

This received wisdom was challenged when the ECJ gave its 1987 judgment in the *Philip Morris* case.[4] It ruled that Article 85 could apply if a concentration occurred as a result of *agreements* entered into by companies. In such cases M&A regulation would derive from the Rome Treaty's provisions relating to restrictive agreements and cartels. Just as the *Continental Can* case had opened up Article 86's applicability to regulating merger control, so the *Philip Morris* judgment did likewise as regards Article 85. But the judgment also failed to create a clearly defined regulatory regime for mergers. As Green *et al.* described the consequences: 'the law on take-overs and mergers was in disarray' (1991: 279). Why?

- There was no clear indication as to when an agreement tantamount to attaining control of a competitor needed to be notified.
- If such an agreement were found to be in breach of Article 85, it would be declared null and void (under the terms of Regulation 17/62): a situation which would create corporate confusion.
- Article 85 would only apply to mergers involving an agreement; a hostile takeover would not be covered since there would be no agreement. This situation clearly gave rise to issues of fairness, especially as different patterns of corporate governance in Member States meant that hostile takeovers were unevenly distributed through the EC.

With the exception of the coal and steel provisions, the situation prior to 1990 was a highly imperfect regime for merger control. Perhaps the most important attribute of the merger regime following the *Philip Morris* judgment was the resultant corporate uncertainty: a dynamic instability that could only be overcome by agreement to purpose-built arrangements. This instability became a useful instrument in the Commission's attempts to persuade the Member States to reach agreement. Contextually, it needs to be recalled that the SEM programme was envisaged to prompt corporate re-structuring in the EC. Thus increased M&A activity was envisaged at a time when the regulatory regime was at its most uncertain. Only two years were to elapse between the *Philip Morris* judgment and the passage of the MCR 4064/89. Progress on securing M&A regulation through legislative means was to be greater during this period than over the preceding fourteen years.

In order to understand the nature of what was at stake, we concentrate upon five key regulatory issues:

- The scope of the MCR: what should constitute a merger of 'European interest'?
- What should be the criteria according to which mergers would be judged?
- In particular, should it be possible to exempt a merger on 'public interest' or industrial policy grounds?
- What should be the relationship between the MCR and national merger regulation, where the latter existed?
- What should be the administrative agency for regulating mergers, and what should be its executive procedures?

Constructing the MCR

The Commission's recognition in the mid-1960s that some form of control over mergers was desirable found little support until the early 1970s when the heads of state or government, meeting in Paris in October 1972, indicated their support for regulation in their communiqué (*Bulletin of the EC* 10/1972). Their support was a compromise, however, illustrating the tension between seeing mergers in terms of industrial policy objectives or seeing them in terms of competition goals.

In its 1973 Draft Regulation the Commission sought to transfer the logic of its extensive powers in other aspects of competition policy into merger control, also incorporating parts of the *Continental Can* judgment to define some of the policy principles. It did this because the judgment formed the Commission's provisional licence to act.

How did the Draft Regulation measure up in terms of the five key issues identified earlier?

- Its scope was to be inclusive (see Article 1, *Official Journal*, C92/2, 31 October 1973).
- The criteria for regulating mergers built on those set out in the *Continental Can* judgment.
- Crucially, they included a public interest clause (in Article 1(3)), facilitating exclusions for 'concentrations which are indispensable to the attainment of an objective which is given priority treatment in the common interest of the Community'. The term 'common interest' appeared to permit industrial policy objectives (see Allen 1983: 228).
- The proposals would intrude upon existing national regulatory powers on mergers and did not offer a 'one-stop shop' for the corporate sector.

- Finally, the Draft Regulation proposed the Commission as the exclusive executive agency, with appeal to the ECJ. Companies involved in M&A operations would be obliged to give *ex ante* notification of large mergers (Article 4(1)) but the Commission could choose to investigate others *ex post*. The Commission would have a range of sanctions, including suspension of the merger and the imposition of fines.

The reaction of the Council was decisive to the fate of this proposal. It became bogged down as a result of fundamental disagreements: the scope of the proposal was too large, and the Commission would have too much executive authority (Allen 1983: 229–30). France, Italy and the UK preferred a process whereby the Council would decide on mergers, whereas the Commission was favoured by the Federal Republic of Germany, the Benelux states and, not surprisingly, the Commission itself. The UK and France favoured the inclusion of public interest criteria (including industrial, regional and social policy considerations). Germany favoured reference to competition criteria alone. The result of these differences of view was to create a decisional stalemate. The Commission's efforts to break the logjam in 1981, 1984 and 1986 were unsuccessful. With no real backing from interest groups, no enthusiasm for the principle of supranational regulation (never mind consensus on the procedures) within the Council, the Commission was unable single-handedly to maintain any momentum. However, the legislative process was about to enter a dynamic phase. The corporate uncertainty created by the November 1987 *Philip Morris* judgment; the Commission's ability to play upon corporate fears; and the Member States' endorsement of the SEM programme, with the associated reconstruction of industry: these factors ensured that developments took on much greater urgency. Hence we now focus on the regulatory environment and the positions of the principal policy-making 'players' on the eve of the critical phase of the legislative process.

The regulatory environment   Perhaps the main change in the regulatory environment derived from the increase in merger activity itself. Data collected at the time by the European Commission from the business press of M&A activity, and involving at least the 1,000 largest firms in the EC, show a clear increase in activity pre-dating the 1985 agreement on completing the internal market (see Table 4.1).[5] The higher rate of increase from 1986–87 to the end of the decade would appear to reflect the strong impulse given by the SEM programme to merger activity, although global trends and the economic cycle were other influences. Within the figures is concealed a further trend, namely a major shift to mergers with an international, cross-border dimension. Between 1987 and 1990 mergers at national level increased by 12.6 per cent, while Community mergers grew by 131.5 per cent and international mergers by 113.8 per cent.

Table 4.1: Number of mergers and acquisitions of majority stakes involving the 1,000 largest European firms, 1982/83–1990/91, in the industrial sector

Year	Number
1982/83	117
1983/84	155
1984/85	208
1985/86	227
1986/87	303
1987/88	383
1988/89	492
1989/90	622
1990/91	455

Source: EC Competition Reports.

Table 4.2: Numbers of Community majority acquisitions, i.e. cross-border operations (including mergers), in the industrial, distribution, banking and insurance sectors, broken down into size of combined turnover 1987/88–1990/91

ECUs	1987/88	1988/89	1989/90	1990/91
>1 bn	108	163	237	165
>2 bn	80	123	176	127
>5 bn	44	79	115	79
>10 bn	26	55	74	47

Source: Commission Annual Reports on Competition Policy.

A more differentiated set of data is to be found in Table 4.2. These give some idea of the size of mergers in the industrial and service sectors, as measured by the combined turnover of the firms concerned. These data, which by contrast with those in Table 4.1 relate only to cross-border acquisitions involving companies from Member States, give an indication of the increase in large-scale mergers: those which the Commission sought to regulate.

Cross-border mergers had increased at precisely the time when the predictability of supranational regulatory arrangements had decreased. Indicative of the challenges faced was the 1988 GEC/Siemens bid for Plessey: admittedly a slightly atypical case because of defence implications. The bid was notified – largely voluntarily – to the authorities in the UK, the Federal Republic of Germany, France and Italy as well as to the European Commission (Woolcock 1989: 1). It was considered by the Office of Fair Trading

(OFT) and the Monopolies and Mergers Commission (MMC) in the UK; by the Federal Cartel Office (Bundeskartellamt, BKartA) in Germany; by the European Commission; and there were also notifications to four national authorities outside the EC. Seven law firms were involved in the preparation of papers (Woolcock, Hodges and Schreiber 1991: 16). Little wonder, then, that companies began to see the prospect of notifying to one EC agency, the principle of the 'one-stop shop', as attractive.

Economic actors   The principal socio-economic actors concerned with lobbying on the EC regulation of merger control were groups in the business sector. At the Community level a major source of lobbying was UNICE. Other EC interest groups played a more limited role. At the national level, business interest organisations, such as in the UK the Confederation of British Industry (CBI) or the Institute of Directors, proved adept at expressing their views, as did their counterparts in the other Member States.

The original Commission proposals of 1973 had been viewed by industry without enthusiasm. However, changing corporate attitudes following agreement on the internal market programme and the *Philip Morris* judgment had a major impact. The destabilising effect of the latter for mergers with a European dimension was recorded by Woolcock, 'company lawyers now feel they have no option but to notify the Commission under Article 85 (EEC), as well as the national authorities' (Woolcock 1989: 18).

UNICE's November 1987 position paper recognised the deficiencies of exisiting EEC treaty provisions and the divergent practices in the Member States and, with the Federation of Danish Industries dissenting, drew the consequences. It supported supranational regulation subject to certain conditions.

They included (UNICE 1987):

- The establishment of 'pre-defined objective and transparent economic and legal criteria . . . which . . . should in particular favour cross-border mergers within the framework of the EEC Treaty. They should also be such as to enable industry to strengthen its competitive position on European and world markets'.
- Incorporation of the principle of the one-stop shop: mergers covered by the Regulation should not be subject to national controls.
- The decision-making procedure on mergers should be swift and efficient.
- The companies concerned should have a choice between *ex ante* control (i.e. when the proposed merger is notified) and *ex post* control (upon conclusion of the merger).
- 'A mechanism should be established to make it possible for mergers which cannot be approved by the Commission under the rules of competition to be authorised in the Community public interest.'
- Finally, the Regulation should be the only merger control instrument of the EC and, when implemented, should not be retrospective.

These were the basic principles which were to guide the UNICE position over the two years leading up to the MCR. The question of defining the MCR's thresholds scarcely featured in the UNICE position papers. The national industry federations had divergent views on the desirable levels, and UNICE largely skirted around this internally divisive issue.

The trade unions' principal concern was with regulating the impact of mergers and takeovers upon the labour force of the companies affected. However, the general line of the European Trade Union Confederation (ETUC) also favoured measures which would hinder cartelisation of the European economy.

The views of national governments Given the need for unanimity in constructing a regime for merger regulation, the role of national governments was extremely important. Their domestic circumstances differed in a number of respects. Member States like the UK and Germany, which had (by the late 1980s) well-established domestic merger control practices, had quite different interests from a state like the Netherlands, which had no legislation to prohibit mergers. The situation in Germany and the UK was characterised by the existence of parapublic agencies entrusted with domestic merger control activities: the MMC and the OFT in the UK, and the BKartA in Germany. For these two states there was a kind of double vested interest. First, both the governments and the national regulatory agencies had a vested interest in guarding their powers from predators. Secondly, they were unwilling to cede their powers to the supranational level without assurances that the new authorities would use them in an acceptable manner. Thus, the form of regulation was also crucial. We can illustrate the situation by reference to the four larger Member States, all of which held reservations when the Draft Regulation was proposed in 1973.

The French and Italian governments traditionally had more interventionist, *étatist* economic policies. Hence they held very serious concerns that the kind of industrial reconstruction they promoted, e.g. the creation of 'national champion' firms to facilitate international competitiveness, would fall under the EC's regulatory competence (Pearce and Sutton 1986). Even if such reconstruction were conducted within the national context, this was no guarantee that the mergers would not be of the necessary magnitude to interest the EC authorities, especially under the Commission's early proposals. In the changed circumstances generated by the SEM there was something of a 'U-turn'; both states transferred their wish for industrial competitiveness from the national to the European arena. The French in particular wanted 'European champions', and a strong national presence in such firms. It was recognised that the perception of issues in a European context meant that the national regulation of mergers was no longer sufficient. Moreover, there was a feeling that the German authorities in particular were pursuing national policies which discriminated against the strategy of French firms, particularly where these were located in the public sector. A classic case of this was the attempt by Thomson-Brandt, the large French public sector concern, to link up with Grundig in Germany with a view to achieving a more effective presence in the international consumer electronics industry. The BKartA blocked this proposal, and it was clear that appeal to the Federal Minister of Economics against the decision would also be unsuccessful due to political objections regarding French public sector involvement (Pearce and Sutton 1986: Ch. 12). Thus the French government came to see EC merger control as reducing, or eliminating, such discrimination. The logic of French strategy thus became one of supporting EC regulation but with a public interest clause to permit cross-border mergers in cases where Europe's competitiveness would be enhanced.

Traditionally Germany has been seen as the principal torch-bearer of market principles in the development of economic integration. In reality the Federal Economics Ministry's economic rhetoric has always been slightly misleading, not least given the Germany authorities' generosity with state aids.[6] The German government's position on merger control seemed unambiguous. Woolcock comments: 'Throughout the entire ... debate on EC merger control the Germans have pursued a consistent policy based on competition criteria alone' (1989: 21). Other aspects of German policy only emerged in the latter stages of negotiations, once the possibility of agreement emerged. At this stage the insistence on market principles from Bonn was reinforced by the representations from the BKartA in Berlin.[7] The BKartA's concerns were twofold. First, it shared Bonn's concern that the policy should use competition criteria alone, and not become a covert industrial policy instrument. Secondly, it was concerned that the EC legislation would exclude the possibility of German control over mergers which might limit competition in Germany whilst not doing so on the EC market. In consequence, it sought some form of dual control. It wanted both these criteria met before it could countenance a transfer of competence. As a fall-back position, therefore, it was prepared only to allow the EC to regulate very large mergers. The Federation of German Industry did not share the second of the BKartA's concerns; in line with UNICE, it favoured the 'one-stop shop' principle.

The position of the UK government was one of reservation concerning the need for EC-level control. By the time that momentum was regained in the negotiations, following the 1987 *Philip Morris* judgment, UK policy *practice* was very much in line with that of Germany.[8] Hence it too favoured competition criteria and a high threshold. One further element became part of the British government's position, and with support from industrialists, namely that the EC should take measures on corporate governance because it was felt that UK companies were more prone to hostile takeovers because of more transparent ownership structures. This view was triggered by the hostile bid for Rowntree by the Swiss company Nestlé (see Woolcock 1989: 26).

Merger control: making the rules

On the eve of the final phase in law-making, the situation was broadly as follows. The Commission sought to exploit the *Philip Morris* ruling to secure agreement on the then draft of the Regulation. UNICE and national industry associations supported the principle of EC regulation. However, no agreement could be reached in the Council of Internal Market Ministers. On 25 April 1988 the Commission submitted a significantly revised new proposal to the Council (*Official Journal*, C130/4–11, 19 May 1988). Key changes at this stage included:

- a higher threshold for denoting M&A activity of interest to the EC authorities (an aggregate turnover of ECU 1 bn but with some other qualifications);
- a strengthening of the public interest criteria in assessing M&A cases, thus moving away from the use of competition criteria; and
- a shortening of the periods during which the Commission would enquire into concentrations.

France, the UK and Germany held out against agreement (*Financial Times*, 3 June 1988: 2), for reasons discussed above. Agreement was blocked in the Council but the regulatory 'logic' of the situation was rather different. The Commission's Directorate General for Competition (DG IV) was reported to have given no less than twenty-five formal decisions on M&A activities, and thirty-six provisional clearances (*Financial Times*, 6 February 1989: 4). For example, it had made creative use of its competition policy powers to intervene in the British Airways/British Caledonian merger and in the Irish Distillers case: in the latter on an *ex ante* basis (*Financial Times*, 5 September 1988: 4). All this was happening despite the absence of legislation enabling such action! Equally, the evidence emerging from the business environment and the arguments presented by its representatives continued to suggest the logic of a transfer of powers to the supranational level. Thus, the Commission's Competition Report for 1987 indicated that speciality chemicals companies were involved in almost a quarter of cross-border concentrations. This prompted the European Council of Chemical Industry Federations to issue its support for EC regulation, calling particularly for a clear division of responsibilities between Member State and EC authorities, including the 'one-stop shop' principle (*Agence Europe*, 27/28 June 1988: 16).

The logic of the SEM and the political positions of the EP and Ecosoc also supported the principle of granting the Commission powers to regulate mergers.[9] However, as historical institutionalists emphasise, policies do not emerge simply on the basis of rational choice. Rather, the policy debate and the resultant policy outcome are shaped by their institutional context. In the case of the MCR the crucial context was that within the Council of Ministers. In that institution the UK government still appeared to be the principal obstacle to agreement, although the then draft of the Regulation was the version least suited to the German authorities' interests.

At its meeting on 21 December 1988 – and despite the best endeavours of both the Commission and the Greek presidency at mediation – the Council's deadlock persisted. The UK and German governments were demanding a threshold of no less than ECU 10 bn aggregate annual turnover of the parties to the concentration. This would have limited Commission authority drastically compared with the latter's ECU 1 bn proposal.[10]

There were, moreover, ominous signs of the German position becoming much more critical of the Draft Regulation as a result of lobbying by the BKartA. This situation was underpinned by a classic interaction between domestic politics and EC negotiations resulting from the proposed merger between Daimler-Benz and Messerschmitt-Bölkow-Blohm (MBB) affecting several engineering branches. The BKartA eventually ruled against the merger. Following deep divisions inside the German cabinet, and a resignation threat from the President of the BKartA, Professor Kartte, the new Federal Economics Minister, Herr Haussmann, overruled the BKartA and approved the deal. This domestic override merely reinforced the BKartA's fears: the proposed EC MCR, with its public interest provisions, would be subject to extensive lobbying and similar overrides. Thus, the BKartA did not feel able to place its trust in such arrangements. Hence it strongly articulated the wish to tie the policy to competition criteria, to raise the thresholds and, from April 1989, to press for an independent European Cartel Office along German lines. The last of these had already been recommended by the Chairman of the UK's MMC, Mr Sydney Lipworth, in January 1989.

Thus the incoming Commission, with Sir Leon Brittan holding the competition portfolio, was still faced with a major task, although there seemed to be an expectation on all sides of agreement. This marked the start of the final phase of negotiations, during which the position of the French government was to be decisive. The French government had moved to a position of support for the MCR but was concerned to maintain the public interest exceptions. The French Minister of European Affairs, Mme Cresson, emerged at the end of 1988 as a supporter of a quick agreement on the grounds that it would assist French (public-sector) companies to overcome national – especially German – objections to cross-border M&A activities (*Financial Times*, 22 November 1988).[11]

The decisive contribution of the French government was to be its tenure of the presidency of the Council in the second half of 1989. This required the government to make a delicate calculation of national interests. Was agreement on a regulation, even if substantively not entirely to French liking, preferable to no agreement? Would such a sub-optimal agreement nevertheless be compensated for by being able to take the presidential kudos, i.e. for successfully concluding the protracted negotiations?

What was to become the compromise agreement concerning the principal threshold for defining a European merger had already emerged in December 1988, when Peter Sutherland, the outgoing commissioner, floated a figure of ECU 5 bn (the qualifying aggregate worldwide turnover figure for Commission regulation). This was the threshold which Sir Leon Brittan proposed to the Council on 31 March 1989, and which Member States gradually agreed to (*Financial Times*, 1 April 1989: 1). Germany and France accepted this level in May, leaving only the UK favouring a much higher threshold of ECU 10 bn, although other governments wanted a lower one (see below). It is also worth mentioning that, whilst the larger states wanted a higher threshold to retain sovereignty, the logical interests of business were for a lower threshold, since this would increase the scope of the 'one-stop shop' approach.

Two further elements combined to make up the definition of a European merger: at least two of the undertakings concerned must achieve an aggregate Community-wide turnover of at least ECU 250 m; and, if the concentration clears this and the ECU 5 bn hurdle, it is still not deemed to fall within the Regulation if two-thirds of aggregate Community turnover is achieved within a single Member State.

Smaller states, such as the Netherlands, Belgium and Denmark, together with Italy, had wanted a lower threshold than ECU 5 bn to catch as many mergers as possible. What is crucial to understand is that the effect of the thresholds would be uneven according to the size of national economies. Mergers of importance to competition in the smaller economies might inevitably involve a smaller aggregate turnover. Further, there was much greater recognition in these states that the relevant market was the European one; in strategic industries it was impossible for each of these countries to sustain competition amongst home-based firms.

The tension with the smaller countries was eventually resolved in two ways. First, the agreed Regulation (Article 1) included a review of the thresholds four years after adoption (i.e. in 1993, see below). The Commission made clear that it favoured a reduction to ECU 2 bn at that point but the UK refused to allow this into the legislation. It was specifically entered in the Regulation, with the UK dissenting, that the thresholds revision would be subject only to QMV (contrary to the Treaty's prescription of unanimity). Secondly, the so-called 'Dutch clause' (Article 22(3–5)) was inserted. This permits a Member State to request the Commission to investigate a merger which falls below the thresholds to assess the impact of the concentration on the member concerned. This provision, initially to last until the four-year review of the MCR, would have the effect of inviting the Commission in to assess the impact of a concentration on the domestic market.[12]

The agreement on thresholds was highly complex, and sought to satisfy the preferences of a number of member governments with differing views. The thresholds decisions were by no means the product of a debate aimed at rational identification of what constituted a 'European' merger. They were, rather, the product of how particular interests were mediated by the institutional dynamics of the Council.

The criteria for judging what amounted to a concentration were not especially contentious during the final negotiations. However, the question of permitting a public interest defence of a merger was much more problematic. France was particularly insistent on this (on industrial policy grounds), with some support from Italy, Spain and Portugal (chiefly on regional policy grounds). Germany, with support from the UK, wanted competition criteria alone to be utilised. With a public interest clause in the successive drafts over a sixteen-year period, it was a considerable surprise when, in the final weeks of negotiations, it was dropped in favour of a competition criterion alone. In its Article 2, the MCR only permits taking into account 'the development of technical and economic progress *provided that it is to consumers' advantage and does not form an obstacle to competition*' (our emphasis) (*Official Journal*, L395/3, 30 December 1989). Straightforward textual analysis suggests there is no public interest defence. The MCR in fact seems to be the most competition-orientated mergers policy in Europe, for in Germany even the BKartA may be overruled, and UK legislation provides a public interest defence. However, we need to look at how policy has operated in practice (see below).

What of the relationship provided for between national and Community authorities? The wish on the part of UNICE and other industrial interest groups had been to ensure that 'European' mergers, whatever the thresholds, could not be considered by the national authorities as well (the 'one-stop shop' principle). This wish came into conflict with German concerns, as a large economy, that a 'European' concentration might create oligopolistic conditions on the German market but the German authorities would lack the legal competence to act. The concerns of the BKartA related to a lack of trust in supranational regulation. The result is that Article 9 permits national authorities to make a case that there is a 'distinct market' within a single Member State. This issue became salient in the final stages of negotiation. Both the CBI and UNICE (amongst others) opposed this development precisely because it appeared to undermine the 'one-stop shop' principle (UNICE 1989a; *Financial Times*, 23 November 1989: 26). UNICE, in a final position paper, offered its support for the German clause on very clear conditions (UNICE 1989b). The 'German clause', like the virtual exclusion of a public interest defence, was a prerequisite for German agreement to the MCR, and was only agreed at the final session of the Council on 21 December 1989.

The fifth regulatory issue identified above relates to the administrative arrangements for regulating concentrations falling within the MCR. The Commission was agreed as the regulatory agency. Suggestions of involving the Council of Ministers had been abandoned in 1986. Moreover, the German government had already achieved major concessions; its insistence on a European Cartel Office had to be ceded. However, the right balance still had to be found between the wishes of the corporate sector for speedy decisions to facilitate corporate certainty and the administrative resources of the Commission. Under the compromise agreed, the Commission has one month to decide whether a merger is compatible with the common market. Should its decision be negative, it has four months to conduct a full investigation. The potential workload for the Commission was determined by the threshold levels, thus meaning fewer referrals than under its own preferred lower thresholds.

Historical institutionalist appraisal In Chapter 2 we outlined historical institutionalism and the different aspects of European governance that it could illuminate. In taking stock of the emergence of the MCR, what conclusions can we make regarding the contribution of historical institutionalism?

- The legislation agreed did not reflect a rational outcome of the bargaining process; it did not represent the rational outcome of state preferences. With the Dutch and German clauses, the MCR looked 'designed by a committee', and it was. The institutional context left its imprint upon the legislation.
- In terms of *systemic change*, it is clear that governments only advocated supranational merger regulation in an explicit form at a summit meeting in 1972, when there were only six Member States. They had given no explicit treaty competence for such regulation except in the special cases of coal and steel. Eventually, the French, German and British governments had to recognise the need to have regulation because of corporate interests' pressure, the jurisprudence of the ECJ and the 'logic' of the SEM. There is little evidence of the MCR 'strengthening the state', since Member States could have opted to retain national controls rather than to cede regulatory powers for large-scale mergers to the Commission. Regulatory authority was ceded to the Commission, and the governments were quite clear that this process was happening, for it lay at the heart of their hesitancy to agree until a trustworthy system was in place. The story of the MCR also reminds us clearly that the process of economic and political integration is not just a story of grand bargains. It must also include the developments these bargains unleash, the separate dynamics in the EC's judicial process,

and underlying developments outside governmental control (in this case, corporate behaviour).

- That being said, the *governance structure* prevailing for deciding competition legislation was crucial. The need for unanimity affected the pattern of bargaining between the governments, with the positions of the French, British and German governments being crucial. The French decision to embrace supranational regulation – even without the desired public interest component – was facilitated by its brokering role as president of the Council but, ultimately, it was the German/British positions that influenced the content of the MCR. Why? These two countries each held veto powers; their wishes had to be accommodated. Moreover, these countries had formal institutions with responsibility and established practices for regulating mergers. Their governments were bolstered by the influence of domestic regulatory agencies.

- *Policy evolution* was cumulative and iterative. From the Commission's initial attempts in 1973 to draw upon practice in other parts of competition policy to the utilisation of the ECJ's judgments, policy options evolved in a manner which was 'sticky' and lacked rationality. The interaction between the legislative and judicial processes was particularly striking. Thus, we may fruitfully be able to trace decision-making processes backwards, identifying continuities on the way. However, without adding additional ingredients, such as the increase in M&A activity, SEM-related dynamics and the lobbying of the business community, path-dependency leads into a cul-de-sac. It was the critical conjucture of the various factors in 1987–89 which resulted in the MCR.

- As regards the *norms of governance*, we can record that the dynamics of the SEM influenced business behaviour and contributed to the need to regulate. Ultimately, governments could not block legislation which followed the logic of the SEM. Thus, the French government fundamentally re-thought its policy in the light of the logic of the SEM. It was also influenced by the raised expectations surrounding the Council presidency during a time of accelerated integration. Static notions of the 'national interest' do not help here. The British and German governments were also able to draw on their experience and domestic knowledge of merger regulation to shape the debate about the form of the legislation, especially the reliance on competition criteria. Their values also fed into the consequent regulatory regime and its institutions, to which we now turn.

The regulatory regime for merger control

In examining the regime's operation within the space constraints here, we will focus only on the following aspects (which also aroused controversy when the Regulation was negotiated). These are:

- the administrative arrangements;
- the broad operationalisation of policy criteria; and
- the review of the MCR's regulatory thresholds.

Administering the MCR

After the MCR was agreed, some nine months were available to set up the administrative arrangements before the legislation took effect on 21 September 1990. The Commission's administrative performance in policing competition policy more generally had been criticised as slow. For merger control, it faced an exacting timetable. Moreover, any administrative deficiencies would rebound on the Commission at the four-year review of the thresholds.

The main responsibility for running the MCR rests with the Merger Task Force (MTF) in the Commission's DG IV, answerable to the commissioner (Sir Leon Brittan until the end of 1992 and, from then, Karel van Miert). The staff complement of the MTF is approximately fifty officials under a director. Within this grouping there are several case-handling teams, with about eight in each comprising a minimum of one economist and one lawyer plus support staff.[13] Staff have been drawn from three sources: inside DG IV itself, from elsewhere inside the Commission, and from the relevant national agencies within the Member States. This mix of sources, along with the Commission's usual nationality proportions, has ensured that a hybrid approach has developed rather than one based on a dominant national tradition. However, the resultant organisational sociology of the MTF is complex: bringing together secondees from Member States familiar with varying domestic merger practices; a mixture of these national secondees with permanent Commission staff; as well as a mixture of economists and lawyers.

The Commission appears to have coped reasonably well with the workload of cases which it has had to confront, although some aspects of the work has been subject to criticism (Neven, Nuttall and Seabright 1993). In the period from 21 September 1990, when the MCR came into force, until the end of 1995, 393 cases had been notified to the Commission. The lion's share of these cases had been declared as raising no serious concerns about compatibility with the common market (Article 6(1)(b), MCR).[14] Also part of the Merger Task Force's work are pre-notification enquiries which might reveal, for example, that a proposed concentration is not covered by the MCR. As illustration, in the two-year period up to September 1992, the MTF had had 137 informal, pre-notification enquiries.[15] In these 'pre-notifications' companies may seek to establish what information the Commission requires at the formal stage, prior to proceeding to a merger or takeover (or not, as the case may be).

In the case of formal notifications the MTF has one month to produce a decision in the first phase of MCR scrutiny. This first phase, although under the leadership of the MTF, is by no means confined to that unit. The MTF has to consult the Commission's Legal Service, which is involved because it might subsequently have to defend actions before the ECJ; DG III for its industrial policy advice or another Directorate General if transport (DG VII) or financial services (DG XV) are concerned; and DG II (Economic Affairs) when important general economic questions are raised. All this is in addition to internal consultation of other parts of DG IV, as well as referral of preliminary findings to the Director-General, and the commissioner's *cabinet*.

By the end of the month one of three decisions is possible: a decision that the merger falls outside the MCR's scope; clearance of the merger; or a decision to open proceedings by moving on to the second stage. In the case of the first two, the commissioner has a *habilitation* power, i.e. delegated authority to act on behalf of the Commission as a whole. In the case of opening proceedings, the competition commissioner must consult the Commission president.

Throughout this first phase the national authorities in the Member States are kept informed of developments but they do not participate in the decision-making. However, it is during the first three weeks following notification of the merger that a national authority must indicate whether it potentially creates a distinct market problem (under Article 9). Ironically, the first country to be able to utilise the 'German clause' proved to be the UK (on *Steetley/Tarmac*).[16]

Where mergers or acquisitions are referred to the full proceedings of phase 2, the Commission has four months to reach its decision. During this period the MTF's function is to draw up its objections, and this entails consultation with other parts of the Commission, as in the first phase. However, it also entails hearings and consultation of the Advisory Committee on Concentrations, which is composed of representatives of the authorities of the Member States. Moreover, the MTF may be involved in negotiations with the parties to agree conditions, on the basis of which the merger may proceed. Hearings of affected parties serve to supplement written submissions. However, it is also possible for third parties to lobby the MTF, provided that they have followed the *Official Journal*'s announcement of the opening of phase 2 proceedings. The third parties may include competitors or even representatives of the workforce: the latter having been a particular concern of the EP at the negotiation stage. In the de Havilland case, for example, British Aerospace and Fokker were given a platform for their views on the proposed concentration of their competitors.

Following inter-service consultation, the MTF draws up a preliminary draft report, and it is this which is submitted to the Advisory Committee. The committee's decision, whether in support, in opposition or split, is only advisory but the Commission is expected to take account of it in the draft decision.

The draft decision is considered at an inter-service meeting and is then referred to the competition commissioner. If it is deemed satisfactory the commissioner then presents it to the College of Commissioners. It is worth noting that this function places the commissioner in a role demanding particular oral skills. Sir Leon Brittan's background as a barrister and as a former MP at Westminster were valuable assets in putting cases to the College, which votes by simple majority. In the de Havilland case, the most controversial hitherto, the College voted by the narrowest of majorities (9–8) in favour of Sir Leon's recommendation. It is indicative of the time constraints faced by the MTF that it must allow sufficient time within the four-month period to accommodate the consequences of an adverse decision by the College.

The involvement of the College is the most overtly politicised stage. It would therefore be naive to assume that it is devoid of lobbying: far from it! In the controversial de Havilland case, parties and third parties to the proposed merger engaged in intense lobbying. This went as far as the *cabinets* of all the EC commissioners (see Ross 1995: 177–9). However, it is likely to be relatively rare that overt politicisation reaches the extent seen in that particular instance. Nevertheless, in a major review of the MCR, Neven *et al.* (1993) argued that the lack of transparency in the existing procedures may permit regulatory capture, whether by national government interests or by industry. Their findings also suggest that firms and their legal advisers are confident of being able to gain concessions from the Commission during negotiations on concentrations.

There are three possible outcomes of phase 2. One is that the concentration may, after enquiry, prove to be compatible with the common market. At the other extreme is the opposite finding, with a decision to prohibit. The majority of cases, however, have been conditional clearances. These typically entail agreement to a divestiture on the part of one of the parties, or some other form of condition. Such conditions are set down in the decision so as to be binding.

During the negotiation of the MCR, the German government advocated that case-investigation and decision-making should be located in an autonomous regulatory agency so that a clearer distinction could be drawn between the detailed investigation and the political review stage (see Ehlermann 1995; Neven *et al.* 1993: Ch. 8; Wilks and McGowan 1995). At present, the Commission's regulatory role combines that of 'police officer, prosecutor, judge and jury', a combination which many see as undesirable (Wilks and McGowan 1995: 267). However strong the merits of the argument for an autonomous cartel office may be – and Germany is the leading advocate – the nature of such institutional reform will at least require it to be part of a larger bargain, perhaps even of a wider reform of the Commission's structure. Nevertheless, the German government proposed such a reform in the context of the 1996/97 IGC, although it failed to secure adoption.[17]

Policy criteria

The Commission's concern in reviewing concentrations is to establish whether a dominant position has been created or strengthened that could impede effective competition in the EU market or a substantial part of it. Consideration of a public interest (or 'efficiency') defence to outweigh any negative consequences of a merger was excluded from the MCR. That is not to say that such a dimension has been wholly neglected. Neven *et al.* (1993) are of the view that efficiency arguments have had simply to be considered in an implicit manner rather than being given the appropriate evaluation, thus compounding the problems of (non-)transparency in the procedures. In addition, the issue is implicitly connected to technical debates about identifying the 'relevant market' when undertaking an appraisal.[18] In the de Havilland case it was precisely this issue which was the centre of the controversy, as reflected in the minority report of the Advisory Committee on Concentrations:

> A minority does not accept the Commission description and analysis of the market. The Commission has chosen a methodology that gives the highest market share possible to the parties. They consider that not only is the Commission's approach to statistical analysis of the market flawed, but the Commission has underestimated the strength of competitors and customers in the market, exaggerated the real strength of D[e]H[avilland]C[anada], ignored the history of competition in the market and the potential for new entrants. Further, this minority considers that the Commission is not so much protecting competition but rather protecting the competitors of the parties to the proposed concentration. (Hawkes 1992: 34)

Despite this critical minority report, and the slender majority in the College of Commissioners, the principle of a competition-orientated policy appeared to be upheld. Some of the criticism was directed at an overlegalistic appraisal of the market and a failure to take into account the more dynamic assessments of markets of the Chicago School of economics.[19] This appraisal may in part have been due to the organisational sociology of the investigating team. The broader point illustrated by the de Havilland case is that any attempt to justify a concentration on efficiency grounds has to be presented in the narrow terms of market definition if it is to stand any chance of success.

The main concession in the general direction of public interest considerations is the significant number of conditional approvals of concentrations reviewed in phase 2 proceedings (by the end of 1995, 13 out of 24 cases – see Box 4.1). Of course, these decisions are taken entirely according to

Box 4.1: Statistics on Commission decisions taken under the MCR, 1990–95

Total no. of notifications to Commission which led to a decision	379
No. deemed not in scope of MCR	34
No. deemed not to raise serious doubts about compatibility with common market	324
Total of cases where final decision taken in phase 1	358
No. where proceedings to phase 2 initiated	24
No. where conditions attached	13
No. where concentration approved without conditions	7
Prohibition	4
Total of cases where final decision taken in phase 2	24

Note: Figures do not summate exactly because of withdrawn notifications and other statistical factors.
Source: Commission of the EC, DG IV, Merger Task Force Registry.

the provisions of the MCR and associated implementing legislation. However, the willingness of the MTF to help companies meet its competition-orientated criteria may be some gesture in the direction of assisting the creation of greater economic efficiency.

One final aspect of the criteria for appraisal is worthy of observation here. This relates to a concern that the MCR is not sufficiently orientated towards oligopoly situations because of its market-share criteria. This was one of the factors which prompted the BKartA to insist on the 'German clause', for it felt its domestic legislation to be more rigorous in this regard. In *AEG Kabel/Alcatel* the BKartA sought Commission approval to put the German clause into effect on just such grounds. The Commission, however, had to be convinced of the risk of *dominance*, and it was not. As a result the German request was refused. The issue arose again in the context of *Nestlé-Perrier*.[20] The MTF took the view that after the acquisition, Nestlé and BSN (which was not party to the acquisition) would hold *joint market dominance*. Its conclusion was to approve the acquisition but to make it conditional on Nestlé disposing of five brands of bottled water to a single customer. This new customer was to be debarred from selling them back to Perrier for ten years.

Bright summarises this development thus:

> The Commission was clearly waiting for the right case to come along before flexing its muscle and adopting the collective dominance concept. *Nestlé-Perrier* was that case and the Commission seized the opportunity, in effect, to add to

the text of the Regulation so that it now applies to the creation or strengthening of either a single or a joint dominant position which significantly impedes effective competition. (Bright 1992: 23)

The Commission had effectively changed the law through an administrative decision. The cumulative development of policy norms, as emphasised by historical institutionalism, is emphasised by the contribution of such decisions.

The 1993 review of the MCR

What of the 1993 review of the MCR? On the face of it, the review was supposed to be about thresholds. The Commission's well-publicised wish for a reduction of the principal threshold to ECU 2,000 m was a 'marker' placed in 1989. The review, however, took place within a slightly different context from that prevailing in 1989. Normatively, and in terms of the Maastricht Treaty, the subsidiarity principle had come to be a major preoccupation in the activities of the Community. Within the Commission, there was public confidence that merger control regulation – including a lowering of the thresholds – was compatible with this principle.[21] However, the governments of France, Germany and the UK indicated to the Commission that they did not favour a lowering of the threshold, the British government invoking the subsidiarity principle as support (*Financial Times*, 1 March 1993: 16).[22] Bowing to political reality and the new context of only taking on powers where supranational control promised better results, the Commission announced in July 1993 that it was deferring revision of the thresholds until 1996 and merely introducing some procedural innovations (CEC 1993a).[23]

In 1996 the Commission produced a Green Paper in which it proposed lowering the aggregate worldwide turnover thresholds to ECU 2 bn (1990 ECU 5 bn) and the aggregate EU-wide threshold of at least two of the parties to ECU 100 m (250 m). As an alternative it sought to regulate all mergers requiring multiple referral, i.e. to more than one national authority in the EU. Following further efforts by some national governments to invoke subsidiarity as a way of stopping more encompassing supranational regulation, the Commission formally proposed thresholds of ECU 3 bn and ECU 150m respectively as well as the right to review cases where three or more national authorities would have to be involved in regulating a cross-border merger (CEC 1996b). On 24 April 1997 the Council of Industry Ministers reached unanimous political agreement on a revision to the MCR but with final ministerial adoption deferred to enable the UK House of Commons to conduct its formal scrutiny once re-convened following the general election. The complex terms of the agreement, entailing no less than four different thresholds, was designed to bring in a 'one-stop shop' in those mergers where multiple referral – to the authorities of three or more Member States – would otherwise take place (Council of the EU 1997). Underlining the iterative nature of policy-making, this arrangement was to be reviewed three years after formal adoption.

Conclusion

The MCR was an important accompanying measure to the SEM pro-gramme. It complemented the existing supranational powers in competition policy, providing competences which the Commission had been seeking unsuc-cessfully for over a decade. The Regulation was an essential instrument in the move towards a single market and away from economic fragmentation. In terms of multi-level governance, the character of this development was essentially re-regulatory, transferring some existing powers from the national to the supranational level. It was certainly not de-regulatory, since certain Member States lacked domestic powers for the control of concentrations.

Looking at the pattern of economic governance more widely, the MCR entailed a more competition-orientated view of state–market relations. National regulators would no longer be able to act in a discriminatory way concerning foreign takeovers, at least where these exceeded the MCR thresholds. Equally, large-scale state-led industrial reconstruction – as had been promoted particularly by France – could not be carried out without regard for the consequences upon competition. While both these changes related only to concentrations of such magnitude as to be within the MCR's scope, they entailed a shift in the state–market balance of eco-nomic governance in the EU.

It might be argued that the MCR lacks teeth since only a small number of proposed concentrations have been prohibited by the Commission (see Box 4.1 for statistics on Commission decisions). Neven *et al.* argue against this point:

> the smaller number of merger refusals by the EC authorities compared to those by the German, British or US authorities cannot be used to infer that EC merger control is less restrictive than that of the other jurisdictions; by itself it could just as well indicate that the EC has been more successful in dissuad-ing firms from putting forward anti-competitive proposals. (1993: 152)

What is striking, however, is that there seems to have been some creeping departure from the text of the MCR.[24] Although the Regulation relies on competition criteria, efficiency arguments for a concentration – which are not provided for in the legislation – are seen to have entered into the negotiations on individual concentrations.

Two points are relevant here. First, through such developments an institutional memory is built up that may depart in subtle ways from what was agreed in the Council. The MTF decision on collective dominance was another example of this: a minority of the Advisory Committee had argued unsuccessfully that this situation was not even provided for in the MCR.

Such departures from the formal provisions can become part of the regulators' *acquis* or become institutional norms. Analytically, this situation may be accounted for by historical institutionalism and its emphasis on path-dependency. Secondly, whilst Britain and Germany – arguably the two most influential governments in the negotiation of the MCR – had sought to minimise the discretionary powers of the Commission by the emphasis on competition criteria, it is clear that they were not completely successful in achieving this goal.

The MCR strengthened the competition policy of the EC/EU and it strengthened the powers of supranational regulators. However, the regulation of concentrations is one small part of a wider picture. In order to transform economic governance, developments consistent with this one would be necessary across competition policy as a whole, including the regulation of state subsidies to industry, not to mention in the SEM domain. Our attention now turns to an area where the SEM programme sought to liberalise protectionist tendencies, namely in the award of public procurement contracts.

Notes

1 Separate legislation was established for the coal and steel industries in the European Coal and Steel Community (ECSC), and continues to this day. For examination of how that regulatory regime fits into the wider picture discussed in this chapter, see Bulmer (1994).

2 In fact, of the EC Member States at the time of the negotiation of the MCR, the UK had been the first to introduce merger control in its 1965 Monopolies and Mergers Act. In 1973 Germany also adopted merger control legislation under an amendment to the 1958 *Gesetz gegen Wettbewerbsbeschränkungen*.

3 This is now Article 3(g) of the EC Treaty, and the term 'internal market' substitutes for the original version's 'common market'.

4 *British American Tobacco Co. Ltd* v. *Commission* and *R. J. Reynolds Industries Inc.* v. *Commission* (joined cases 142/84 and 156/84). The applicants were complaining against agreements between Philip Morris and Rembrandt Group Ltd. For full details, see Fine (1987).

5 See CEC (1992a: Annex IV) for further details of the sample, and for further data and analysis relating to 1990/91.

6 A European Commission survey of patterns of state aid, published in 1988, placed Germany second in a league table of members giving state aid, although when weighted for Gross Domestic Product, the Federal German Republic occupied the middle range (Bulmer 1992). The level of aid subsequently increased sharply due to the industrial support afforded to the former state concerns of East Germany.

7 For a more detailed assessment of the German position, see Woolcock 1989: 21–4, and Woolcock *et al.* 1991.

8 This situation had been given greater force by the adoption of the 1984 Tebbit Doctrine, which set down in a parliamentary answer of 5 July 1984 that references to the MMC would primarily be on competition grounds.

 9   For the position of Ecosoc, see OJ C208 (8.8.88), 11–17; for that of the EP, see OJ C309 (5.12.88), 49–54.

10   See Table 4.2 for the number of mergers above the two negotiating thresholds.

11   As a Commission official reported to the *Financial Times*, 31.7.89, 2, 'a number of them [French companies] have told us they have come across obstacles in other member states. They don't like it and they think they might get a better deal from the Community.'

12   The existing Dutch Merger Code lacked the power to block concentrations. Instead, it was designed to ensure a tripartite information process. Through this clause in the MCR, it became possible for the Dutch or others to utilise the MCR as a tool of *domestic* regulation. This compromise solution was reportedly a British proposal, tabled by Corporate Affairs Minister John Redwood at the Council of Ministers on 10 October 1989 (*Financial Times*, 10.10.89, 2).

13   This section draws on interviews in DG IV and the MTF. Also see Cook and Kerse (1991: 89–90).

14   Data supplied to the authors by the Merger Task Force Registry, 19 January 1996.

15   Data based on interview information from the MTF, October 1992.

16   In 1993 the German authorities secured the right to examine *CPC/McCormick/ Rabobank/Ostmann* but only because the Commission forfeited the right to examine it because of a miscalculation of the deadlines (see Wilks and McGowan 1995: 266).

17   The Reflection Group preparing for the 1996/97 IGC on treaty reform did not propose such a reform, although that did not preclude its emergence in the IGC proper.

18   This is an area where economists have differing perceptions of how to implement the MCR. For an explanation of the method used by the Commission, see CEC (1993b: 138–40).

19   Comments made by the French member of the Advisory Committee to one of the authors.

20   This case involved Nestlé taking over Perrier but, anticipating objections from the MTF, Nestlé indicated that upon completion of the deal, one of Perrier's brands, Volvic, would be sold to another competitor in the bottled water sector, BSN. This would have resulted in the 'new' Nestlé holding some 36.8 per cent of the market in bottled water, BSN holding 30.9 per cent and others holding 32.3 per cent. See Bright (1992) for full details of the case.

21   See, for instance, Sir Leon Brittan's address 'Subsidiarity in the Constitution of the European Community', *Agence Europe*, 18.6.92.

22   The French government's reluctance to lower thresholds was influenced by dissatisfaction with the outcome of the de Havilland case. This decision thus appeared to reverse the logic behind French agreement to the MCR in 1989.

23   The amended procedures are set out in Commission Regulation 3384/94, in OJ L377 (31.12.94), 1.

24   It is difficult to substantiate this argument with specific illustrations – as Neven *et al.* (1993) found in undertaking their research – precisely because the Commission's procedures are less than transparent, and because of corporate secrecy on certain data.

5

Regulating public procurement contracts in the utilities sectors

Introduction

The deepening and widening of the EU's procurement regime formed a key component of the Commission's 1985 White Paper on *Completing the Internal Market* (CEC 1985a). Our study of the development of the procurement regime is important in shedding light on the nature of the White Paper exercise; on linkages with the wider development of the SEM; and on the norms and values which have become institutional features of the SEM.

It is not difficult to understand why the liberalisation of procurement practices should play such an important role in the completion of the internal market. At a very basic level, the foundation of the SEM is the non-discrimination principle. Procurement practices which discriminate on grounds of nationality cannot, therefore, be accepted within a single market. Further (and as we note in Chapter 10), it is not just directly discriminatory measures which segment the SEM. National rules which, while applicable to national and non-national suppliers, none the less, make it harder for the non-national to supply goods or services also run counter to the logic and values of the SEM. Procurement practices which mandate the use of national technical standards, for example, fall into this category of indirectly discriminatory measures.

Nationalistic procurement practices also insulate contracting entities from forces of competition by locking them in to national suppliers (especially if R&D is also developed within that relationship). These national networks make it harder for competition to emerge between, for example, telecommunications companies if the technical networks that have been created are purely national and prevent market entry (or make the costs of market entry prohibitively high). In this way, nationalistic procurement in the utilities sectors does not fit within the EU's sectoral ambitions of liberalised telecommunications and energy supply.

In short, procurement practices which directly or indirectly discriminate on grounds of nationality, and which insulate contracting entities from the forces of competition run counter to the logic and values which have become institutionalised in the creation of the SEM.

The 1985 White Paper contained proposals for the revision of existing procurement directives (the Supplies and Works Directives of the 1970s) and for the extension of the procurement regime to the so-called 'excluded sectors' (the utilities). The White Paper also proposed the adoption of a directive to provide remedies for breach of the procurement rules. Thus, the White Paper was central to the completion of the legal framework for liberalised procurement. In this chapter we trace the development of the EU procurement regime, focusing specifically on the extension of the regime to the utilities sector. Directive 90/531/EEC[1] formally brought the utilities sectors within the EU procurement regime and it is the institutional environment surrounding the negotiation of this Directive which forms our focus. Directive 90/531/EEC has been superseded by Directive 93/38/EC[2] which consolidates (but does not alter) EU procurement rules on works, supplies and services in the utilities sectors.

The extension of the procurement regime to the utilities sectors was important (but also politically sensitive) because it sought to apply rules generated in the context of *public* procurement to contracting entities which, as a result of the forces of privatisation, were increasingly in the *private* sector. Indeed, the difficulty in applying common rules to both public and private undertakings had been the justification for the previous exclusion of the utilities sector from the procurement regime. As we indicate, this 'difficulty' continued to be a force which shaped the outcome of the negotiation process.

In the first part of this chapter we explore the construction of the policy problem of nationalistic procurement. We highlight the nature and scale of the problem and note the earliest legislative attempts to deal with the issue at EU level. Importantly, we examine the way in which the economic construction of the problem by the Commission was used in the context of the SEM programme in order to push forward a number of Commission agendas, which included not only the extension of the procurement regime to the utilities but also European standardisation and sectoral policies. We also note the increasing global pressure for liberalised trade in the area of procurement.

In the second part of the chapter we examine the negotiation of the Utilities Directive. While the Commission may have succeeded in placing the extension of the procurement regime on the Council agenda, within the arena of the Council important exemptions and exclusions were negotiated for certain industrial sectors. But it was not only the influence of the Council which was brought to bear on the Draft Directive. Key decisions of the ECJ were reflected in the Draft Directive.

In the final part of the chapter we explore continuing developments at the international level and examine the extent to which the completion of the SEM has influenced global trade liberalisation initiatives. We also highlight the Commission's desire to ensure proper enforcement of the procurement rules by seeking to provide EC remedies for breaches of the rules. We conclude with an analysis of the changing structure of the procurement market and its implications for the procurement regime and the application of EC competition rules.

Our aim is to underline the policy linkages between the development of the procurement regime and other policy areas such as technical harmonisation, sectoral liberalisation and competition policy. In this way, we highlight the extent to which the problem of procurement has been constructed within norms and values which have become institutionalised features of EU policy-making. We also suggest that the inclusion of procurement policy within the White Paper, together with the construction of an economic 'case' for liberalised procurement, can be viewed as an agenda-setting exercise by the Commission. However, given the inter-institutional nature of EU rule-making we also examine the relative roles of the Council, the EP and the ECJ in shaping the procurement regime.

Constructing the problem

In this part we set the scene for the extension of the EU's procurement regime to the utilities sector. Four aspects are highlighted:

- the problem of nationalistic procurement;
- the establishment of an EU procurement regime;
- the drive to complete the internal market; and
- the emergence of global procurement rules.

The problem of nationalistic procurement

Our aim in this section is not to give a country-by-country analysis of procurement practices but rather to indicate the ways in which national practices may segment the SEM. Discrimination against non-national suppliers of goods and services can arise in three ways.

First, *public* procurement by state entities can be used to promote national economic and social policies. The insulation of national supplier companies from competition may serve to promote the development of (national) technologies and may protect national job opportunities. Even in the absence of deliberate manipulation, as Cox notes (1993: 30), favourable post-war economic conditions did not require contracting entities to pay an overly close attention to cost-considerations in their purchasing decisions. Yet, even during the recession of the 1970s, nationalistic procurement was defended on the grounds of protection of employment, especially in vulnerable regional economies. Politically, government officials have tended to present nationalistic purchasing as a vote-winning

strategy, while the national media has often viewed the award of government contracts to 'foreign' suppliers as verging on a treasonous betrayal
of the electorate. The Charpentier and Clark report (1975) on public purchasing found

> a deep-rooted feeling, common to politicians, officials and industry, and invari-
> ably supported by organs of public opinion, that the taxpayer's money should
> be used to purchase domestic goods and not foreign goods. (quoted in Sohrab
> 1990)

Secondly, the development of close relationships between contracting
entities and their suppliers can *de facto* discriminate against non-national
suppliers. That is to say, industry standards and technical specifications have
often been created as a consequence of these close relationships. Indeed,
the costs of R&D of new technologies have often been subsidised by the
inflated costs of nationalistic procurement. Two types of problem may
then emerge. The first problem is that competitive tendering may discriminate against non-national suppliers where the terms of the contract require
the use of products which conform to national technical specifications. This
may introduce unacceptably high adaptation costs for non-national suppliers.
The second problem is that the creation of national technical specifications
and standards may segment the market for the service provided by the contracting entity (e.g. the provision of telecommunications services). In this
way, the vertical (or quasi-vertical) integration of the relationship between
contractor and supplier may stifle competition in the service provided by
the contracting entity (and further exclude the export potential of non-
national supplier companies).

Thirdly, discriminatory procurement may arise where public authorities
directly regulate or grant special or exclusive rights to private undertakings. Nationalistic procurement may arise either as a result of direct influence from the state, or from a feeling within the private undertaking itself
that nationalistic purchasing is important to the ongoing relationship with
government.

It is significant that the second and third types of problem can arise in
the context of the purchasing activities of private entities. While the original EU procurement regime (discussed in the next section) focused upon
public procurement, the Commission's desire to extend the procurement
regime to the utilities can be seen as an attempt to deal with the market-
segmentation problems of *private* purchasing. Thus, the extension of the
procurement regime to the utilities can be seen as an extension of the non-
discrimination principle to include the activities of private entities.

Some examples may help to indicate the ways in which close and
dependent relationships between contracting entities and their suppliers have
segmented the SEM. One way in which close and dependent relationships
have been formed is through R&D practices. Historically, the high cost of

R&D has bound national utilities to particular suppliers. This could take the form of complete vertical integration or quasi-vertical integration in the form of cooperative R&D. Within the telecommunications sector, for example, very close relationships between national suppliers and the procuring utilities were exhibited (between British Telecom and GEC and Plessey; between the Direction Générale des Télécommunications and Alcatel; between Deutsche Bundespost and Siemens) (CEC 1988a). In the UK, British Telecom was involved in close cooperation with GEC, Plessey and STC in the development of the System X switching system.

National utilities have both directly subsidised (often in pursuit of national industrial policy objectives) or indirectly subsidised R&D by permitting suppliers to inflate the cost of contracts to reflect ongoing R&D projects (see Schnöring 1991). Thus, the development of new technologies in the context of close and dependent relationships between purchaser and supplier tended to increase market closure. Allied to the foregoing is the role of national technical standards in contributing towards market closure. Especially where new technologies have been developed within individual Member States, the use of national standards has created barriers to trade between states. Even if there was a willingness to open up markets to competition, insofar as a potential supplier's products did not conform to the national standard, the market effectively remained closed.

Thus, through the development of national technical networks and the multiplication of R&D costs, the EU of the twelve produced twelve different telecommunications systems (at a cost of some ECU 11 bn) in a market which the Commission estimated could only support three systems while Japan had spent only ECU 2 bn on a single system. If procurement was open on an EU basis (and providing that European or international technical standards were available) then the anticipated supply-side concentration would achieve economies of scale. This theme of achieving economies of scale and reducing supply-side overcapacity (see below) would, according to the Commission, reap savings not only in the telecommunications equipment sector, but also in the boiler-making, railway locomotive manufacturing, turbine generator and switchgear industries.

As we indicate below, the presentation of the economic case for liberalised procurement was important to the Commission's attempts to widen and deepen the EU's embryonic procurement regime, in the context of the drive to complete the internal market. It is to that embryonic regime that we now turn.

The establishment of the procurement regime
We noted in the introduction to this chapter that the principle of non-discrimination between national and non-national suppliers of goods and services is at the heart of the SEM. It is this principle which underlies the strategy of negative integration pursued by the Treaty rules on free

movement. It also follows that the competence of the EC to adopt positive harmonisation measures for procurement could not be questioned in that national procurement practices had a direct impact upon the functioning of the common market (justifying the use of Article 100 for the adoption of such measures).

As Winter notes (1991), the earliest EC directives on procurement did little more than highlight the application of the principle of non-discrimination to national public procurement practices. It was in the early 1970s that the EC established a more regulatory system for the coordination of contract-awarding procedures. In 1971, the Council adopted the Works Directive,[3] followed in 1976 by the Supplies Directive.[4] The objective of these Directives was to open up government contracts to competitive tendering and to ensure the application of non-discriminatory criteria for the qualification of an entity to tender for such contracts. The Directives required the publication of potential contracts in the *Official Journal* of the EC; the application of non-discriminatory criteria in the procedures for the tender and award of contracts; prohibitions on the specification of discriminatory technical standards; and the award of contracts according to three different types of procedures ('open', 'negotiated' or 'restricted'[5]).

The Supplies and Works Directives only applied to contracts to be awarded by *public* authorities and where the contracts had a value of more than ECU 1,000,000 (public works) or ECU 200,000 (public supplies). The utilities sectors were directly excluded from the ambit of the Directives (with the exception of public works contracts in the area of telecommunications which were subject to the Works Directive).

Thus, these early Directives provided the foundation and the model for the development of the EU's procurement regime. They embodied the values of non-discrimination and competition provided for in the Treaty and established a regulatory system of contract-notification to give effect to these values.

However, as the Commission noted in its review of the procurement regime in 1986 (CEC 1986), these Directives were 'inadequate to ensure the achievement of their objectives'. The Commission found that contract-splitting (to bring contracts below the thresholds in the Directives); extensive use of the restricted and negotiated procedures for awarding contracts rather than the competitive open procedure; and wide interpretation of exemptions within the Directives had resulted in their minimal application. There was also outright defiance through the use of discriminatory technical standards and disqualification of potential tenderers. The Commission found that less than a quarter of public expenditure in the areas governed by the Directives had been advertised in the *Official Journal* (let alone actually spent on intra-EC trade).

Therefore, by the time of the launch of the SEM programme, it was apparent that the existing procurement rules were not working. Moreover, it was evident that the exclusion of the utilities sectors left an important area of procurement outside EU control.

Completing the internal market

It may seem paradoxical that a governance regime which had so clearly failed to live up to expectations should become such an important aspect of the White Paper on the *Completing the Internal Market*. We argue that agenda-setting by the Commission helps to explain this apparent paradox. As we suggested in the introduction to this chapter, discriminatory procurement cannot be reconciled with the idea of an internal market in which goods, services, workers and capital move freely regardless of nationality. Nor can discriminatory procurement be reconciled with a market in which distortions to competition are to be removed. Insofar as the Member States were prepared to accept the SEM programme (underpinned by these values), it would be difficult, if not impossible, for them to resist the Commission's demands for a tightening up of the Supplies and Works Directives.

Not only did the Commission propose revisions to the Supplies and Works Directives (in particular to limit the use of the 'restricted' and 'negotiated' award procedures), it also sought to extend the regime to include the former excluded sectors – the utilities. This proposal was sensitive because of the historic protection afforded to these sectors by Member States (protection in the form of state ownership, control or regulation), and because of the potential inclusion of private entities. However, by presenting the review of the procurement regime as a 'package' of proposals, the Commission sought to apply an irresistible logical force to a previously immovable object. In this way we can see that the White Paper was not simply a *description* of the measures necessary to complete the internal market, but also a mechanism through which the adoption of individual proposals could be justified according to an internal market logic.

In order for the Commission to support its logic, it sought to develop a clear economic rationale for liberalised procurement and harnessed expert reports in order to make its case for the extension of the regime to the utilities, namely the Cecchini report (Cecchini, Catinat and Jacquemin 1988) and the study by W. S. Atkins on *The 'Cost of Non-Europe' in Public Sector Procurement* (Atkins 1988). According to the Atkins report, the estimated annual savings in public expenditure of non-discriminatory and competitive procurement were in the region of ECU 8–20 bn. This was an attractive prospect for Member States under increasing budgetary pressures (or those, like the UK, that had elevated the reduction of the public sector borrowing requirement to the status of ideological imperative).

As Cox has noted (1993), the economic rationale for regime change was premised around the savings which would follow from the (assumed) changes in procurement practice. These could be categorised under three 'effects':

- *the static effect*: contracting entities would reap savings from the ability to purchase from the cheapest supplier in the market.
- *the competitive effect*: if the insulation of purchasers from competition had given rise to inflated prices, then the introduction of competition should ensure that prices reverted to their 'real' level.
- *the restructuring effect*: in many ways, this could be seen as a key source of savings. In short, the anticipated consequence of competitive procurement was a restructuring of supply-side industries leading to the creation of European companies of sufficient size to compete within both the European and the global markets.

Thus, the economic case for liberalised procurement fell within a classic economic paradigm of the benefits of competition within a single market. As one Commission official noted to us in interview, the Member States could hardly extol the benefits of competition within the SEM for private industry while not applying the same logic to public purchasing or to the purchasing activities of utilities owned, controlled or regulated by the state.

The Commission relied extensively on the *Cost of Non-Europe* report. A senior Commission official indicated to us that the ability to present the proposals for the revision and extension of the procurement regime along-side the studies which had been undertaken by Atkins had made it much more difficult for the Member States to resist change. And as Margue suggests (1991), the studies helped to remove some of the pressure exerted by industrial lobbies opposed to the Utilities Directive. Thus, the Commission harnessed the flow of information and the economic logic of competition to make its case for an extension of the procurement regime to the utilities.

One should not, however, get too carried away with the role of the Commission. We attach significance and explanatory value to it, but by no means reduce the agreement of the Utilities Directive to the skill of the Commission. Domestic political and economic forces were also at play. Politically, the role of the public sector was changing whether in the form of privatisation policies or in the form of the introduction of competitive tendering practices nationally. And, as we indicate below, supplier companies began to wake up to a new economic environment in which national markets were no longer safe. None the less, the assertion of these political and economic realities no more explain by themselves the development of EU procurement policy than agenda-setting by the Commission does. Rather, it is the mix of political forces, and their translation through the institutional structure of EU governance that is important.

We noted above the changing behaviour of supplier companies. There is evidence that supplier companies sensed a change in the economic environment (at least nationally, but also in anticipation of the SEM), and sought to engage in mergers and cooperative ventures, first, at the national level,

and later at the European level. Budgetary pressures on national governments meant that procurement policies could not ignore questions of price.
Further the privatisation of contracting entities (e.g. in the UK, British
Telecom, British Gas, British Airways) and indeed the privatisation of
publicly owned supplier companies (e.g. in France, Compagnie Générale
d'Electricité, Compagnie de Constructions Téléphoniques) made clear that
competition on price would become an ever-dominant feature of the utilities sectors. Long-term 'safe' contracts with government were set to give way
to short-term considerations of price. In anticipation of this, a rationalisation of supplier companies (through mergers and joint ventures) emerged.

An example from the energy sector is illustrative. Close relationships
between suppliers and purchasers were prevalent in the power equipment
sector up until the late 1970s when falling demand, budgetary constraints
and inflationary pressures resulted in a reduction of power plant orders.
Suppliers to national utilities – traditionally only required to compete on
price in the international market – became aware that the national market
was no longer as 'safe' an environment, especially in view of overcapacity
in the provision of the utility service. The result was an increase in national
merger activity and the creation of national champion power suppliers
(GEC in the UK, Alsthom in France, Siemens in Germany and Ansaldo in
Italy) (see Ninni 1990).

Concentration at the national level was followed by international merger
activity. The merger of Sweden's ASEA with Switzerland's Brown Boveri
was indicative of this trend and was followed by that of GEC with Alsthom,
and Ansaldo with ASEA-Brown Boveri.

Equally, the internationalisation of markets had an impact on traditional R&D patterns. As Schnöring notes (Schnöring 1991), the vertical
or quasi-vertical integration between telecommunications companies (like
British Telecom or Deutsche Telekom) and their traditional suppliers has
now all but gone.

In view of these dynamics one might have a certain sympathy with the
view expressed by a writer in *The Economist* (1989) that, 'It is the combination of global business ambition, spreading privatisation and greater
budgetary rigour that will drive Euro-procurement, not the other way
round.' However, that view might be seen as both overestimating the degree
of market-driven change, and underestimating the heterogeneity both of
different product markets and of the pace of change in different Member
States. Certainly, at the time of the negotiation of the Utilities Directive,
it would have been premature to conclude that changes to government
policies and the behaviour of private undertakings would result in an
increase in cross-border trade.

There is, however, one important issue raised by increased merger and
joint venture activities of supplier companies. It would be ironic if the
anticipated savings to be reaped from the removal of *public* barriers to free

movement were to be offset by increases in prices charged by dominant private supplier companies. In this way, the drive to complete the internal market cannot be divorced from the application of EU competition policy. Therefore, there is an important policy linkage between the deepening and widening of the procurement regime and the creation of an instrument of merger control (see Chapter 4).

Global procurement

One outcome of the Tokyo Round of General Agreement on Tariffs and Trade (GATT) negotiations in 1979 was the agreement of a government procurement code. The aim of the code was to promote access to government contracts among the negotiating countries. In the context of the EU, one immediate consequence was that for supply contracts governed by the code, the contract threshold level was lowered to ECU 130,000.

However, and as we shall discuss more fully below, the liberalisation of procurement has become an enduring feature of subsequent GATT (and now WTO) negotiations, with an increasing attention towards the utilities sectors. In the 1980 GATT talks, the USA made known its wish for US telecommunications and electrical suppliers to be permitted to tender for contracts (amid fears of the creation of a 'fortress Europe'). This international pressure for trade liberalisation did, however, create something of a dilemma for the Commission as it presented its case for liberalised *European* procurement. The logic of free trade and open borders would suggest the need for greater access to international contract markets. None the less, the fear of a 'fortress Europe' and the protection of European markets could be used a negotiating position with which to bargain for the liberalisation of US contracts. Moreover, the protection of the European market would be a potential precondition to persuading (at least some) Member States to open up *national* markets.

One can see, therefore, that not only did the Commission have a role to play in persuading Member States to agree to liberalise procurement, it also had a role to play in international negotiations which would itself be affected by developments within the single market. This highlights Scott's insight that there is a need to avoid the mistaken tendency to view the single market and the EU's external trade policy as distinct spheres of study (Scott 1995: 155).

Reconstructing the governance regime for procurement

The deepening and widening of the procurement regime in the context of the 1985 White Paper can be seen as a reconstruction of that regime. While the liberalisation of *public* procurement remained the key objective, the extension of the regime to the utilities sectors also entailed the application of the logic and values of the internal market to *private* undertakings.

Before we turn to the negotiation of the Utilities Directive itself, we indicate the actors involved in the decision-making and lobbying processes.

Actors within the governance regime
As we suggested above, the Commission played an important role in preparing a package of procurement measures which were included in the 1985 White Paper. Policy responsibility for procurement was, at the time, held by DG III (though along with other internal market policy sub-sectors, DG XV has now assumed responsibility). The ambition to include the utilities within the procurement regime was, however, barely matched by the human resources necessary within the Commission to bring this about. Indeed, one reason why the utilities remained excluded in the 1970s was the lack of staff to provide the groundwork for their inclusion. Even in 1987, the Public Procurement Unit within DG III consisted of only one head of department and five staff. However, the heightened significance attached to procurement resulted in organisational changes. In the late 1980s, the Procurement Unit was split into two, with one half (3(b)(3)) dealing with policy-making, and the other (3(b)(4)) concentrating on enforcement. A new head of department was appointed to lead policy-making and staff were seconded from other parts of the Commission.

The Commission was assisted in its work by two Advisory Committees, one of which pre-dated the work on the utilities and was composed of representatives of the Member States. The other Committee was established specifically to advise on the utilities and was composed of approximately 25 representatives of major contractors and suppliers (e.g. EdF, Babcock Engineering, Alsthom). Further the Commission held 'sectoral hearings' to seek the views of the actors in each of the specific sectors to be covered by the Directive.

The Commission is not, of course, a monolithic structure. As we have identified, the extension of the procurement regime was also closely linked to other policy areas such as competition policy and sectoral policies (e.g. telecoms liberalisation). DG III, therefore, had to coordinate its activities with DG IV (competition), DG XVII (energy), DG XIII (telecoms) and DG VII (transport). For those external trade aspects of the Directive, DG I also had to be consulted.

This differentiated organisational structure had a very immediate impact upon the desire to extend the procurement regime to the utilities. Originally, the Commission submitted two proposals to the Council: one on the energy, transport and water sectors[6] and the other on telecommunications alone.[7] The justification given by the Commission for this bifurcated approach was the distinct history of telecommunications procurement and the role of procurement as part of the package of measures for the development of an EU telecommunications policy (CEC 1988a; para. 439). This distinctive approach to telecoms was also evidenced by the establishment of a new DG to handle telecoms policy (anecdotal evidence suggests that it was the head of this new DG that wanted a distinct telecoms directive). One saw, therefore, a tension between the construction of telecommunications procurement as a matter of procurement policy and as a matter of the sectoral ambitions of DG XIII. At the insistence of the EP, the Commission merged the two proposals into a single proposal.

The Commission based its legislative proposal on the internal market legal basis, Article 100a. At the time, this called for the use of the co-operation procedure and thus the EP (and the Economic and Social Committee) was involved in the decision-making process. The lead committee within the EP was the Economic and Monetary Affairs Committee. But, given that the Directive also covered specific sectors, the Transport and Energy Committees were among the committees that were also consulted. As we indicate below, the view from these sectoral committees was coloured by their construction of the role of liberalised procurement in these sectors.

While the use of the cooperation procedure certainly provided opportunities for the EP to make its views known, we recognise that the Commission–Council dialogue was perhaps more crucial in shaping the Directive. We discuss this more fully below.

Decisions of the ECJ were important both in shaping the content of the Directive (in respect of the illegality of regional preference schemes) and in elaborating upon the application of the Treaty rules on free movement to procurement practices more generally. Further, the ECJ has continued to play an important role in power disputes between the EU institutions. As we note in the final part of this chapter, the EP brought legal proceedings before the ECJ to challenge the legal basis of measures adopted in implementation of a procurement agreement between the EU and the USA. Once again, the ECJ must be recognised as occupying a central position as the other institutions play for rules and play for power through the medium of EC law.

Although not involved in the legislative process, the adoption of the Utilities Directive had clear implications for the European standards agencies: CEN, CENELEC and ETSI (see Chapter 6). The Directive's requirement that European standards be specified in contract notices was part of the Commission's policy on increased development of European standards (to overcome technical barriers to trade), and can be seen to have placed increased pressure on these agencies to deliver standards.

Not surprisingly, the legislative institutions of the EU were subject to lobbying from a number of sources. National sectoral interests (e.g. in the area of telecoms manufacturers, the Association of the Electronics, Telecommunications and Business Equipment Manufacturers in the UK; the Zentralverband der Elektrotechnischen Industrie in Germany; and the Federation of Electrical and Electronic Industry in France: Schneider 1992) were represented through their national industry representatives (the CBI in the UK; the Bundesverband der Deutschen Industrie in Germany; and the Conseil National du Patronat Français in France), and also at the European level through UNICE. However, as well as being represented through 'horizontal' lobby groups, sectoral lobby groups also emerged at the European level such as the European Telecommunications and Professional Electronics Industry (ECTEL) and the European Confederation of Associations of Manufacturers of Insulated Wires and Cables (EUROPACABLE). Moreover, round table meetings of significant European manufacturers also took place which, as Schneider argues, 'may even outweigh the position of traditional European business associations in the shaping of EC industrial policy' (1992). Membership of such round table groups included important electronics manufacturers like Philips, Siemens, GEC and Plessey.

One should not ignore the role of the utilities themselves in the lobbying process. As we noted above, the Commission held meetings with utility companies while the Directive was being drafted (though British Gas declined to be involved). UK utilities were also represented through the UK Institute of Purchasing and Supply, or for those utilities still in public hands, through the Nationalised Industries Chairmen's Group.

In summary, the breadth of the Directive had the consequence of bringing a large number of interested parties (national and European, sectoral or horizontal) into the lobbying process. Our focus, however, is upon the inter-institutional interaction in the legislative process and it is to this that we now turn.

Negotiating the Utilities Directive

The original Supplies and Works Directives had been agreed on the basis of unanimous voting in the Council using the consultation procedure. The reconstruction of the procurement regime took place against the backdrop of the institutional changes made by the SEA, in particular, the introduction of Article 100a, EC and the cooperation procedure. Thus, the institutional dynamics of decision-making were different in that QMV was possible in the Council, and the EP had a greater involvement in the legislative process.

The Supplies and Works Directives provided the model for the extension of the procurement regime to the utilities. Thus, the Utilities Directives also provided for the publication of proposed contracts in the *Official Journal*; the application of non-discriminatory qualification criteria; and the award of contracts according to the 'open', 'negotiated' or 'restricted' procedures.

As we noted above, the Commission's original proposal was to have two directives (one specifically covering telecoms). However, at the request of the Economic and Monetary Affairs Committee of the EP,[8] the two proposals were merged into one.[9] Our analysis of the negotiation of the Utilities

Directive is, therefore, based on the merged proposal. We focus on the following key issues:

- the entities to be subject to the procurement rules;
- the exclusion and exemption of certain activities;
- the 'flexibility' of the contract-award procedures;
- the contract-value thresholds above which the rules would apply;
- the role of technical standards;
- the exclusion of regional preference schemes; and
- the 'buy Europe' clause.

The entities covered by the Directive   The procurement regime established in the 1970s simply covered state or public entities. However, the Utilities Directive had a wider ambition than the liberalisation of public procurement. As one Commission official put it, the issue was no longer one of *public* procurement, rather, 'It is about breaking long-standing incestuous relationships between national monopolies and their client suppliers.'[10] The scope of the Utilities Directive is wider in that it includes private-sector undertakings operating under 'special or exclusive rights'. The term 'special and exclusive rights' is itself derived from Article 90, EC (though an attempt is given to define the term more specifically in relation to the utilities in Article 2(3) of the Directive). In pursuit of its sectoral policies, the Commission has sought to ensure that special and exclusive rights do not operate to prevent the liberalisation of key markets like telecommunications. Thus, it is no accident that the terminology used in relation to procurement is traceable to the wider ambitions of the Commission to liberalise the provision of utility services.

Specific entities covered by the Directive are listed in Annexes I to X of the Directive (following the approach adopted in the GATT code). Thus, both public and private entities are brought within the regime. This had important implications for the 'strength' of the regime in that interest groups like UNICE made clear that if private undertakings were to be subject to procurement rules, the rules had to be 'flexible' enough to allow for the operation of 'proper' commercial judgment. This we shall examine further below.

Excluded and exempted activities   The Directive applies to undertakings which carry out 'relevant activities' (defined in Article 2(2) of the Directive). Notwithstanding the Commission's desire to bring the previously 'excluded' sectors within the procurement regime, the result of negotiations was the non-inclusion, the exclusion and the conditional exemption of certain activities. Thus, the structure of the Directive provides an interesting narrative of its negotiation. The different dynamics of each sector and sub-sector are played out in the different means (and different reasons) by which certain activities fell outside the scope of the Directive.

For example, the recitals to the Directive indicate that the procurement practices of airlines are to remain outside the scope of the legislation, notwithstanding the high level of national control and regulation exhibited in this sector. Two different types of justification can be discerned. First, in the Communication which accompanied the proposed Directive (CEC 1988a), the Commission pointed to the high level of supply-side concentration in aircraft manufacture (e.g. the main suppliers of aircraft being Boeing, McDonnell Douglas and Airbus). On this account, one of the stated aims of the procurement legislation (supply-side concentration) was already in evidence. However, this does not itself justify the exclusion of other types of procurement by airlines (e.g. procurement of electrical equipment or on-board entertainment or food and drink supplies). Neither the Economic and Monetary Affairs Committee of the EP nor Ecosoc were happy with the generality of the exclusion of airlines.

The second rationale for the non-inclusion of the airlines rested with the Commission's policy of a gradual liberalisation of this sector. In other words, the non-inclusion of airline procurement owed more to the inappropriateness of the timing of the Directive than to the inappropriateness of the idea of competitive procurement in this area. This may also help to explain why the EP Transport Committee was in favour of the non-inclusion of airline procurement, in the sense that the Committee conceptualised the problem as being connected to the liberalisation of the airline industry generally rather than as a specific procurement issue.

This highlights an important point. Notwithstanding that the Commission had clearly marked out procurement in the utilities as an important area to be targeted in the context both of the SEM programme as a whole and as part of its sectoral strategies, none the less it had to work with the Council to ensure the agreement of the Directive. As we discuss in our chapter on airline liberalisation (see Chapter 7), the policy has been one of slow, negotiated change. One can compare this with telecommunications where the Commission has adopted a sometimes cavalier approach to its sectoral policy (e.g. in the use of Article 90 Commission directives rather than using Article 169 infringement proceedings). As Cox has noted, the need to keep the Council 'on-side' not only had the effect of empowering the Member States in a number of instances, but also had the effect of disempowering the EP and Ecosoc in the negotiating process (Cox 1993; 173–8).

The idea of not including or excluding activities because of their relationship with other EU policies can also be seen in the non-inclusion of shipping (the key problem here being state aid to the shipping industry[11]) and the exclusion of purchases of energy and fuels for the production of energy (to be dealt with instead in the context of the creation of a single energy market). However, it should be pointed out that the extension of the procurement regime to the purchase of fuels would have been politically problematic because of the operation of subsidies for coal production in Germany and the then contractual arrangements between British coal and the UK electricity generators.

Another politically problematic area was the Commission's desire to include within the regime companies operating in the oil and gas exploration market. One study of the UK sector of the North Sea estimated that approximately 80 per cent of contracts were awarded to UK suppliers.[12] The Commission was particularly concerned that the UK Offshore Supply Office might seek to influence companies to 'buy British' through its control of production and export licences. The UK opposed the application of the procurement regime in these sectors and deadlock within the Council prevented Ministers from adopting a common position on the Directive in December 1989. However, a common position was reached in February 1990 which provided for Member States to seek exemption for their oil and gas exploration industries. Article 3 of the Directive allows Member States to apply to the Commission for exemption if they can show that exploration licences are granted on the basis of objective and non-discriminatory criteria; that other entities are free to seek authorisations to exploit areas on the same terms; and that national rules (formal or informal) do no require undertakings to disclose to national authorities the nature of their procurement practices. As Cox has noted (1994), this procedure raises the fear that discriminatory procurement practices will be maintained unless the Commission is able adequately to scrutinise the enforcement of national provisions notified to it.

One can read the story of the scope of the Directive in two ways. Upon one reading, the Member States successfully drove a coach and horses through the Commission's proposal. On another reading, the fact that the Member States were prepared to extend the procurement regime to the utilities at all created a foothold for the Commission from which to move forward in the future. These two readings are not mutually exclusive.

The contract-award procedures   The Utilities Directive follows the model of the Supplies and Works Directives in placing an obligation upon contracting entities to publish their proposed contracts in the *Official Journal* (the proposed contracts also being reproduced in the Tenders Electronic Daily (TEDs) database). The same rules also apply in respect of the application of non-discriminatory qualification and award criteria. However, the Utilities Directive departs from the revised Supplies and Works Directives in an important respect. The revised Directives limit the scope for the use of the 'negotiated' and 'restricted' contract award procedures, making the use of the 'open' procedure the norm. The Commission was forced to concede that a more 'flexible' approach be taken to the utilities in the light of the application of the rules to private companies. As the Commission argued (CEC 1988b),

> The requirements should not be conceived as a comprehensive regulation of the procurement function, but as the minimum safeguards needed to permit the entities concerned to secure the best offer from all Community firms that are in a position to compete.

Thus, provided a 'call for competition' is made *any* of the three contract-awarding procedures can be used. However, the procedures for making a 'call for competition' are themselves subject to exemptions, and a call for competition can be made simply by publishing (annually) a 'periodic indicative notice'.

Ecosoc took a rather dim view of these flexible procedures and in suggesting that they undermined the regulatory goal, said that the rules on calls for competition were 'so elastic as to render the requirements meaningless'.[13]

The level of thresholds The Utilities Directive also departed from the Supplies Directive in applying different (higher) thresholds for supplies. Under the Supplies Directive, the procurement rules come in to play for contracts over ECU 200,000 (or ECU 134,000 for those covered by the GATT code). However, notwithstanding that the Commission proposed the same thresholds for utilities supplies, the Council set a higher threshold of ECU 400,000.

A different threshold was also set for telecoms supplies. The Economic and Monetary Affairs Committee of the EP suggested a threshold of ECU 800,000 (though this proposal was not accepted by the EP itself which preferred a uniform threshold for all supplies). The Council agreed upon a threshold of ECU 600,000 (it is understood that French telecoms suppliers had lobbied for a higher figure).

The problem which this all presents is that depending upon the categorisation of the contract, four different thresholds will apply: ECU 200,000 for non-utilities supplies; ECU 134,000 for contracts covered by the GATT code; ECU 600,000 for telecoms supplies; and ECU 400,000 for all other utilities supplies. This does little to aid the transparency of the rules.

As for works contracts, the Utilities Directive adopts the uniform threshold of ECU 5 m.

Technical standards In its case law, the ECJ found that the specification of a national technical standard in a procurement contract constituted an illegal barrier to trade where equivalent materials not certified under the national standard were capable of being used.[14] The Directive goes a stage further in mandating the use of European standards (where they exist) in contract documents or, if such standards do not exist, requiring reference to 'other standards having currency within the Community'. This mandating of European standards provoked some resistance from purchasers and national governments. Even within the Commission there is a belief that the compulsory use of European standards may not be compatible with EC competition law. It will be recalled that European standards are produced by private agencies and their function is to provide a voluntary means of promoting price and quality competitiveness. To require compliance with standards not only changes the character of these standards, but may also have the effect of institutionalising dominant technologies and restricting market entry of new technologies.

The UK Institute of Purchasing and Supply argued for a more flexible approach and noted that manufacturers had complied with standards where they felt it was in their interest to do so.[15] However, it is evident that the policy linkage which the Commission made between non-discriminatory procurement and the pursuit of increased European standardisation ensured the compulsory reference to European standards provided for in Article 13 of the Directive.[16]

Regional preference schemes We suggested at the outset that the values which underpin the internal market (free movement and the removal of distortions to competition) are reflected in the goals of procurement policy. However, if we take the single market as including not simply the internal market but also flanking policy areas such as regional policy, a tension begins to emerge. On the one hand, national schemes which seek, through discriminatory rules, to protect regional economies are inconsistent with Treaty rules on free movement. On the other hand, the kind of supply-side rationalisation envisaged by introducing competition could be expected to have a negative impact on regional and local economies. How then should the institutional contradiction between the goals and values of internal market and regional policies be reconciled?

For the Commission, regional preference schemes (which preserved a certain percentage of government contracts to disadvantaged regions) were incompatible with the internal market, and it proposed that they be brought to an end by December 1992. It suggested that any negative impact upon regional economies should be dealt with through the allocation of structural funds and funds from the European Investment Bank. In this way, the regional policy aspects of procurement were constructed within the context of the broader SEM/SEA deal in which the potential 'losers' would be financially compensated.

The EP, however, sought to remove the 1992 deadline for the cessation of these schemes. The Commission and the Council both resisted the EP's demands and found support in a decision of the ECJ issued on the same day as the Council adopted its common position. In its *Du Pont de Nemours*[17] decision, the ECJ found that a regional preference scheme which preserved 30 per cent of government contracts for the Mezzogiorno region of Italy was contrary to Treaty rules on free movement. Thus, the Directive provided for the cessation of regional preference schemes by the end of 1992.

It is interesting that the ECJ, the Commission and the Council had little difficulty in applying the norms and values of the internal market to regional preference schemes (thereby categorising them as unlawful), but were able to reconcile this with the SEM by constructing such schemes within a flanking policy of the SEM in the form of regional policy. This illustrates our argument that not only are particular norms and values institutionalised in the governance of the SEM, but also that such institutional structures provide a mechanism by which actors construct and render meaningful policy problems and policy solutions.

The 'buy Europe' clause   The external trade dimension of procurement was also reflected in the Directive. The Commission proposed a system for preferring EU bids for contracts by allowing:

- the rejection of a tender where more than half of the value of the contract was represented in goods produced or services provided outside of the EU, and
- discrimination in favour of EU companies which submitted tenders for a price no greater than 3 per cent above that of a non-EU tender.

However, this EU preference would not apply to countries with which the EU had negotiated agreements, e.g. under the GATT (Article 6 of the GATT code provided for the reciprocal opening up of procurement markets).

There was disagreement among the Member States over whether the best mechanism for encouraging reciprocal liberalisation of procurement was to be found in a clause such as that proposed by the Commission. Germany, Denmark, the Netherlands and the UK were prepared to accept a more diluted clause in expectation of imminent agreements with third countries. However, France, Spain and Italy preferred a more stringent clause not only to protect EU markets but also as a tougher negotiation strategy. This division of views threatened the adoption of the Directive, and in particular, agreement could not be reached on whether the inclusion of the clause should be made conditional upon the outcome of ongoing GATT negotiations.[18] In the end the Council agreed to the Commission's original proposal. As we indicate below, the adoption of this clause had an important impact upon the conduct of international negotiations.

Summary
We suggested that the proposal of the Utilities Directive was an example of agenda-setting by the Commission. However, it is clear that it is one thing to put a proposal on the table and another to ensure that the directive adopted matches the original ambition. It is striking how far the

Commission was prepared to go to accommodate the wishes of the Member States (even against objections from the EP). The result was a Directive whose regulatory goal was compromised in both its scope and its intensity. At the same time, the Commission had brought about the widening of the procurement regime to include the former excluded sectors.

Our analysis suggests the importance of paying attention not only to the interaction between institutional actors (in particular the influence of decisions of the ECJ), but also to the role of institutional norms and values in the construction of policy problems and in the selection of policy solutions.

Reconstruction re-visited

In this final part we explore the external and internal development of the procurement regime. Externally, we highlight the effect of the 'buy Europe' clause of the Directive and the development of an increasingly international approach to procurement liberalisation. Internally, we examine the severe problem of non-transposition of the procurement directives and the implications for enforcement of EC law rights created by these directives. Finally, we note the intersection between the procurement rules and the application of merger policy.

Global procurement
The inclusion of the 'buy Europe' clause provoked a fierce reaction from the USA. Barely a month after the Directive came into force (1 January 1993 for nine of the then twelve Member States), the US government notified the EU that as of 22 March 1993 EU companies would be prohibited from bidding for federal government contracts. Three months of intense negotiation between the EU team (headed by Sir Leon Brittan) and the US team (led by Mickey Kantor) followed. Talks were also held on 18 March 1993 between then Commission President Delors and US President Clinton. It emerged that the main area of contention was access of US companies to European electricity and telecoms markets. During the course of negotiations, the deadline for the imposition of trade sanctions was extended and a partial agreement was reached on 21 April 1993 ('partial' because telecoms remained an unresolved aspect of the negotiations).

The agreement established the principle of reciprocal access to *public* procurement contracts in the areas of works, supplies and services. Thus, the benefit of the Utilities Directive was extended to US companies in return for a waiver of Article 3 of the Buy America Act. The EU and the USA also agreed to fund jointly a study on procurement opportunities, and upon completion of the study to begin negotiations on a self-contained telecoms agreement. It was also specified that the agreement would terminate in May 1995 or upon the conclusion of the Multilateral Agreement on Government Procurement (then being negotiated by the members of the WTO).

In order for the EU to implement the Memorandum of Understanding between the EU and the USA, legislative measures were required which, of course, require a legal basis within the Treaty. Once again, the legal framework of EU governance imprinted itself upon this implementation process. The Council adopted two Decisions to implement the Memorandum using Article 113, EC (the provision relating to the Common Commercial Policy) as the legal basis. Article 113 does not provide for even the consultation of the EP. The EP brought legal action before the ECJ challenging the legal basis of these Decisions.

The case brought by the EP was important not only as another example of the EP seeking to play for rules and to improve its power position through litigation, but also because the ECJ's decision would have consequences for the future conduct of international trade negotiations. At stake was whether the EU had exclusive competence to negotiate and conclude international trade agreements. If so, Member States would no longer be free to adopt bilateral agreements. The point was not merely moot. In March 1994, the Commission announced that it was investigating a report that Germany and the USA had entered into an agreement whereby Germany undertook not to apply the 'buy Europe' preference (thereby undermining the negotiation strategy on which the clause was premised ahead of crucial WTO talks). The Commission was less than happy with this state of affairs and argued that this matter was within the exclusive competence of the EU which prevented the adoption of bilateral measures.

The outcome of the EP's litigation was effectively decided by the ECJ's Opinion 1/94[19] which concerned a separate legal action brought to determine the respective competences of the EU and the Member States in the conclusion of the World Trade Agreements. The rather unsatisfactory Opinion given by the Court was that only the free movement of goods and certain aspects of services fell within Article 113 and the exclusive competence of the EU. Applied to the Memorandum of Understanding this meant that not all aspects of the agreement fell within Article 113. Thus, the ECJ upheld the EP's view that Article 113 could not be the sole legal basis of the Council Decisions.[20] There is, therefore, no single legal basis and no single decision-making procedure for the implementation of international trade agreements. And, once again, the decisions of the ECJ can be seen to frame the EU decision-making process.

It is important not to lose sight of the important international developments among the questions of legal competence. A new Multilateral Procurement Agreement was agreed and annexed to the 1994 WTO Agreement. The Agreement not only covered central and local government procurement but also extended to the utilities at least as regards the electricity sector and ports and airports. The key battleground of telecoms was, however, left outside of the scope of the Agreement.

Transposition and enforcement

The transposition of all the procurement directives into national law has emerged as a key problem with the regime. Infringement proceedings were brought by the Commission against all the Member States (barring those with derogations) for non-implementation of the Utilities Directive. The production of a consolidated Utilities Directive (covering services contracts as well as supplies and works) appears to have been used a justification for transposition delays.

Failure to transpose directives seriously impedes the operation of the procurement regime. The ECJ has sought to overcome the problem of non-transposed directives through the application of the doctrines of direct effect and state liability. Non-transposed, but directly effective directives can be enforced against *the state* or an emanation thereof. A potential problem, therefore, is whether *private* utility companies can escape attempts to enforce unimplemented directives against them. The ECJ made clear in its *Beentjes* decision[21] that 'the state' is not to be identified in narrow formal terms but in functional terms. Further after the ECJ's decision in *Foster*, it is arguable that unimplemented directives could be enforced against a privatised utility where that utility performed functions granted under special or exclusive rights.[22]

Another route open to potential contract tenderers is to seek damages for losses arising from the failure of a Member State to transpose the procurement directives. The ECJ made clear initially in its *Francovich* decision[23] and more specifically in its *Factortame (III)/Brasserie du Pêcheur* judgment[24] that states can be liable in damages for losses suffered as a result of breaches of EU obligations. Under the preconditions established by the ECJ, failure to transpose a directive on time meets the preconditions for state liability. However, the ECJ found that the UK's erroneous transposition of one of the clauses of the Utilities Directive was a genuine mistake and did not meet the preconditions for state liability.[25]

It has not only been the ECJ that has created EC remedies for breaches of obligations. The procurement regime is innovative in the use of Remedies Directives. Directive 92/13/EC[26] establishes the remedies and review procedures for the utilities. The Directive seeks to ensure that appropriate national enforcement mechanisms are in place (traditionally a matter for the national legal orders). However, the Member States still retain discretion as to how this system will operate. For example, Member States may choose whether to provide a remedy at the pre-contractual stage (e.g. interim measures to suspend the contract-awarding procedure), or after the contract has been awarded. Further, although it must be possible to seek an award of damages, whether one can seek damages for the loss of the value of the contract as well as the costs of tendering appears to be left to the Member States to decide. The Commission has noted its concern that the application of the Remedies Directive may in fact vary between the Member State (thus undermining its original goal) (CEC 1996c).

The Remedies Directive also provides for the establishment of an attestation system whereby contracting entities can have their procedures assessed for conformity to the Utilities Directive. From the perspective of industry, attestation procedures are a less invasive approach which emphasise good procurement practice (rather than the punishment of infringement). However, and much to the irritation of UNICE, the Directive did not make the attestation procedure an alternative to the court-model of remedies. Both are to be made available. From UNICE's perspective,[27] the potential benefits of attestation can only be reaped if attestation is an alternative to traditional legal remedies (though both its French and Italian delegations supported the Commission strategy of the availability of both types of procedure). In June 1995 CEN and CENELEC adopted European standards for attestation.[28]

It is, of course, still open for aggrieved parties to complain to the Commission and for the Commission to bring infringement proceedings under Article 169. The Commission's right to seek interim measures (including the suspension of a contract either before or after a contract has been awarded) has been recognised by the ECJ.[29] Even the threat of litigation may be sufficient to ensure compliance with the procurement rules. As Trepte notes (Trepte 1993: 207), one of the most notable examples was the 'Danish bridge' case where an aggrieved contractor complained to the Commission and ultimately received compensation from the Danish government.

The Commission has also sought to ensure that where projects are in receipt of EU funding, the contracting entities comply with the procurement rules. A review in 1988 suggested that preferential allocation of European Regional Development Funds could be given where there was compliance with the procurement rules. However, this enforcement mechanism is obviously limited to those projects (and those states) in receipt of EU funding. Moreover, funds have tended to be paid out on the basis of a presumption that the rules are being followed. To be sure, final tranches of funding can be withheld, but for some contractors this may be a premium worth paying for the award of the contract. Further, it was suggested to us by Commission officials that DG III's desire to ensure proper enforcement of the procurement rules was in conflict with DG XVI's wish to be seen to be funding projects.

In summary, it is apparent that the system of regulation through directives has created significant transposition problems. Some of these problems may be obviated by the application of the doctrines of direct effect and state liability. The procurement regime is innovatory in its use of Remedies Directives, but it appears to be the case that these Directives may fall short of the achievement of uniform remedies in the Member States. Indeed, the traditional route of complaining to the Commission may yet be the most fruitful strategy for aggrieved companies.

Supply-side concentration
One goal of the procurement regime is the promotion of supply-side concentration. However, if the supply side of a market becomes too concentrated then the potential benefits of open competition may be offset. Thus, an effective system of competition control is the necessary corollary to the application of the procurement regime. The Merger Task Force considered two mergers which raised questions as to the degree of supply-side concentration in the telecommunications sector. In the case of the concentration between Alcatel Alsthom and Telettra, the Commission cleared the merger (after the initial one-month inquiry) on the basis of potential competition from new entrants and undertakings given by the companies.

A full investigation was, however, launched into the proposed joint venture between Italtel and Siemens Telecomunicazioni (Siemens Italian subsidiary). In particular, there was concern that the procurement rules would be undermined by such a concentration. But, in February 1995, the merger was approved despite the high market share (over 50 per cent) of the proposed joint venture. The Commission took the view that dominance would not be created given the initiatives that were under way to liberalise the telecommunications sector.

Unless the procurement regime is to create a paradox of replacing one set of costs (market closure) with another (the costs of monopoly), it is important that DG IV undertakes rigorous economic analysis to determine the effect of a concentration on competition. In this way, the procurement regime is not inconsistent with the economic logic of the SEM in the sense that the competition rules will play an important part in the regulation of the SEM.

Conclusions

The Commission estimates that the EU procurement market is worth some ECU 720 bn a year, constituting 11 per cent of EU GDP (CEC 1996c). Thus, not only is liberalised procurement a key symbolic aspect of the internal market (in terms of its reflection of the principles of free movement and undistorted competition), but there are also very valuable contracts at stake for EU companies. It is clear from our analysis that the EU's procurement regime has failed to live up to the expectations which drove the decision to include the deepening and widening of the procurement regime within the 1985 White Paper.

Our interest has been in the construction and reconstruction of the procurement regime. We have suggested that the Commission played an important agenda-setting role in its inclusion of the utilities within a package of procurement measures attached to the White Paper. In this way, the extension of the procurement regime to the utilities was brought within the logic and values of the internal market, making it harder for Member States to resist this widening of the procurement regime. We have argued that the logic and values which brought procurement within the internal market also served to locate regional preference schemes outside the internal market and subject to the norms, values and policy instruments of regional policy. This point illustrates well the light which a historical institutionalist approach sheds on the roles of norms and values in the construction of policy problems and the identification of policy solutions.

A historical institutionalist approach also draws attention to issues of organisational structure and organisational linkages. At a very basic level, we noted the impact of the differentiated structure of the Commission upon the initial decision to propose a distinct procurement directive for telecoms. We also suggested that there may be tensions between the different directorates of the Commission in that each directorate constructs the policy problem of procurement according to its own norms and imperatives.

Our discussion of the external trade aspects of procurement highlighted the contentious issue of EU competence and the relative roles of the Member States, the Commission and the EP in decision-making processes. In common with our other case studies, we argued that the ECJ continues to play an important role in policing the boundaries of power between national and EU levels and between EC institutions. The legal system of the EC is also important to the issues of the non-transposition of procurement directives and the availability of remedies for breach of the procurement rules.

In conclusion, the institutional structure of EU governance – organisationally, procedurally and normatively – can be seen to have left its imprint upon the development of the procurement regime. The regime has evolved over time to both deepen and widen. However, the regime is clearly not effective enough to ensure fully open procurement practices. Given the importance of this area to the internal market, this may be a warning that the legal foundations of the SEM more generally may be more symbolic than real and that if the SEM is to have a real presence, the implementation and enforcement of SEM rules will need to be taken more seriously.

Notes

1   OJ L297 (29.10.90), 1.
2   OJ L199 (9.8.93), 85.

3   JO L185 (16.8.71), 5.
4   OJ L13 (15.1.77), 1.
5   • 'Open': as the name suggests, this procedure provides for competition among any tenderers who wish to apply. The full terms of the contract to be awarded are advertised in advance.
    • 'Restricted': this procedure may take the form of an invitation to express interest from which certain tenderers may be asked to formally apply, or may take the form of requesting tenders from an agreed list of suppliers.
    • 'Negotiated': under this procedure exclusive contracts are negotiated with contractors, often leading to the awarding of continuous and long-term contracts.
6   OJ C319 (12.12.88), 2.
7   OJ C40 (17.2.89), 5.
8   PE DOC. A2-75/89 (Rapporteur Mr Fernand H. J. Herman).
9   OJ C264 (16.10.89), 22; COM(89) 380 final.
10 L. Kellaway, 'Brussels Attempts to Stamp Out Nationalistic Buying', *Financial Times*, 26.2.90, 4.
11 See Directive 87/167/EEC on state aid in the shipping industry; OJ L69 (12.3.87).
12 W. Dawkins, 'Tighter EC Policy on Contracts Planned', *Financial Times*, 28.3.89.
13 OJ C139 (5.6.89), 25, para. 2.6.
14 Case 45/87, *Commission* v. *Ireland (Dundalk Water Scheme)* [1988] ECR 4929.
15 Institute of Purchasing and Supply, Internal Magazine (quoted in Sohrab 1990).
16 It is evident from the Council Resolution on European standardisation that procurement policy is an important driving force for standardisation policy: OJ C173 (9.7.92), 1.
17 Case 21/88, *Du Pont de Nemours Italiana SpA* v. *Unità Sanitaria Locale no. 2 di Carrare* [1990] ECR I-889.
18 L. Kellaway, 'Public Procurement Pact Eludes EC', *Financial Times*, 23.12.89, 3.
19 Opinion 1/94 [1994] ECR I-5267.
20 Case C-360/93, *European Parliament* v. *Council* [1996] ECR I-1195.
21 Case 31/87, *Gebroeders Beentjes BV* v. *Netherlands* [1988] ECR 4635.
22 Case C-188/89, *Foster and Others* v. *British Gas plc* [1990] ECR I-3313. In 1995, the English High Court applied the ECJ's decision in *Foster* to conclude that the provisions of Directive 75/129/EEC (collective redundancies) could be enforced against a privatised water authority: *Griffin* v. *South West Water Services Ltd* [1995] IRLR 15.
23 Cases C-6, C-9/90, *Francovich and Bonifaci* v. *Italy* [1991] ECR I-5753.
24 Cases C-46/93, C-48/93, *Brasserie du Pêcheur SA* v. *Germany, R* v. *Secretary of State for Transport* ex p. *Factortame* [1996] ECR I-1029.
25 Case C-392/93, *R* v. *HM Treasury* ex p. *British Telecommunications plc* [1996] ECR I-1631.
26 OJ L76 (23.3.92), 14.
27 UNICE position papers of 20.2.90, 29.11.90 and 21.5.90.
28 EN 45503 (24.1.96).

29 Case C-87/94R, *Commission* v. *Belgium* [1994] ECR I-3595. The case concerned the award of a bus contract by the Walloon Regional Transport Association. The Commission delayed for three months after notification of the complaint before it sought the suspension of the contract. On the facts, the President of the Court refused to grant interim relief on the ground that the delay did not satisfy the requirement of urgency necessary before the Court would grant interim relief.

6

The removal of technical barriers to trade

Introduction

The elimination of technical barriers to trade is a core aspect of the SEM. Together with the removal of physical and fiscal barriers to trade, technical harmonisation formed a major component of the 1985 White Paper on *Completing the Internal Market* (CEC 1985a). Yet, the removal of technical barriers both pre-dates and post-dates the SEM programme. Our aim in this chapter is to examine the evolution of technical harmonisation and to place the White Paper programme within a broader history of decision-making.

We suggest that three phases in the evolution of the governance regime can be identified. In the first phase, a highly jurisdictional approach to the removal of technical trade barriers was taken. That is to say, by using both negative integration (through the courts) and positive integration (through the adoption of EC legislation) an attempt was made to wrest regulatory policy out of the hands of the nation states and into the control of EC institutions. However, we explore the difficulties which attended this model of governance and the displacement of this model with a new approach to technical harmonisation.

The second phase in the evolution of the regime was the development of the new approach to technical harmonisation. The new approach altered the manner of EU governance. That is to say, while the courts maintained a highly jurisdictional approach to the scope of free movement rules, a regulatory space was opened up for the Member States to occupy in the form of the *Cassis de Dijon* 'mandatory requirements' exception to the principle of free movement. None the less, this regulatory space was one policed within a framework of EC law by the ECJ. Within the legislative arena, a less regulatory approach to technical harmonisation emerged, in part as a response to the introduction of the principle of 'mutual recognition' by the ECJ in *Cassis*. The ECJ had signalled in *Cassis* that national rules which, although they diverged in detail, none the less converged in terms of their regulatory goal, need not be harmonised if the principle of mutual recognition was applied. This would, therefore, limit the task of EC legislation to the harmonisation of 'essential requirements'. It was also apparent in the second phase of development that the traditional approach to harmonisation (Pelkmans and Vollebergh 1986) which required total and vertical harmonisation (discussed below) was over-regulatory. The detailed nature of technical harmonisation did not lend itself to the legislative procedures of the EC, resulting in a poor level of production of harmonisation instruments. To use Sunstein's terminology a regulatory paradox emerged of attempted over-regulation leading to under-regulation (1990). Institutional reform to EC legislative procedures took place in the form of the SEA. However, the new approach also resulted in an increased reliance upon (private) European standards agencies to develop European standards as a mechanism of technical harmonisation.

The third phase of the regime is characterised by an extension of the regime to the problems posed by national standards themselves and attempts to reform the system of European standardisation to improve upon the delivery of European standards. We also note the deepening of the regime to include the mutual recognition of certification and testing practice.

This study differs from our other case studies in that we do not select a single piece of legislation and examine the influence of organisational structures, rule-making procedures, norms and values in shaping the legislation. Rather, we take a more meso-level approach and explore the evolution of the governance regime through the phases noted above. We aim to highlight the path-dependent nature of change and the important organisational and procedural linkages between actors involved in decision-making. In this way we bring to light the role of European standards agencies in decision-making as well as the role of the formal EC legislative institutions. We also note the way in which consumers' groups have sought to institutionalise practices of consultation with European standards agencies in recognition of the increased role played by these agencies. Further, we draw a connection between sectoral policies being pursued by the Commission (e.g. telecommunications liberalisation) and the development of new institutional forms (e.g. the European Telecommunications Standards Institute). In this way, we not only reflect upon the path-dependent evolution of technical harmonisation, but also indicate policy linkages between standardisation policy and sectoral policies.

Constructing the problem

At the heart of any discussion of technical harmonisation lies the need to reconcile the demands of the free movement of goods with the need to ensure that valued regulatory objectives (e.g. the protection of public safety, consumer and environmental protection) are also safeguarded. Traditionally, regulatory policy has been determined at the level of the nation state.

However, divergent national rules which require product adaptation restrict free movement and competition, while preventing manufacturers from taking advantages of economies of scale in production. On this basis, the 1957 Treaty of Rome established two key policy instruments for the removal of technical barriers to trade: negative integration through the application of Treaty rules on free movement, and positive integration through the adoption of EC laws approximating national rules.

However, the simple establishment of these two policy instruments tells us little about their use, significance or interrelationship. Rather, we need to look to the development of norms and values which have emerged to structure the use of these instruments. Of importance is the extent to which such norms and values push in favour of EC control over regulatory policy or pull back in favour of control at the level of the nation state. In this part of the chapter we examine the initial approach taken by the Commission and the ECJ to technical harmonisation.

The 'traditional approach' to rule-making

The Commission's traditional approach to technical harmonisation has been described by Dashwood as 'total harmonisation' (1983). The essence of this approach was a desire to remove all disparities between national rules through the harmonisation of all technical aspects of products and their components. This required the adoption of directives covering specific products, and indeed covering individual components of products. This approach can be described as *vertical harmonisation*. A good example of this approach is the technical harmonisation of motor vehicles. The Commission's goal has been to establish a set of common rules conformity to which permits vehicles to be issued with a single certificate of conformity. Thus, rules have been adopted in relation to particular types of vehicles (e.g. tractors) and for specific components (e.g. lighting devices).

Vertical harmonisation constitutes a highly jurisdictional approach to rule-making in the sense that it identifies any disparity between national rules as a potential trade barrier. This broad identification of trade barriers can be seen in the Commission's definition of 'measures having equivalent effect to quantitative restrictions' in Directive 70/50/EEC.[1] As Craig and de Búrca note (1995: 611), Article 3 of that Directive clearly envisaged that technical rules governing such features as product composition and weight – regardless of whether these requirements also applied to domestic products ('indistinctly applicable' measures) – could constitute trade barriers under Article 30, EC.

The total, vertical harmonisation approach proved to be problematic. As a matter of principle, the identification of *any* disparity between national laws as a potential trade barrier would seem to suggest that the SEM could only be regulated by a set of uniform EC rules. Politically, this was unlikely to be acceptable. In more practical terms, such an approach places enormous strain on the legislative capacities of the EC, as soon became evident. In 1968 (with the imminent deadline of the end of the transitional period by which time the central elements of the common market were due to be in place) the Commission launched its *General Programme for the Elimination of Technical Barriers to Intra-Community Trade* (CEC 1968). As Pelkmans and Vollebergh note (1986), the Programme involved a three-stage package of measures to be completed by 1 January 1970. In all, some 100 directives were to be adopted. However, by the end of 1969, the timetable for completion had slipped to the end of 1970, with proposed directives shunted to the second and third stages of the programme. By 1973 only 35 directives had been adopted – 12 being put through the Council as a single 'package' – and the deadline for the completion of the Programme had been revised once again.

A number of factors can be noted for this poor start to legislative harmonisation. First, it has to be recognised that technical harmonisation is a difficult task – especially against a background of different national regulatory traditions. While France and the UK have tended to formalise technical regulations in national laws (and especially through the use of delegated legislation), the German approach has been to rely on standards set by the Deutsches Institut für Normung (DIN). Under legislation adopted in 1968 (the *Gerätesicherheitsgesetz*), such standards may become *de jure* legal requirements in that products manufactured in accordance with DIN standards are taken to comply with the legislation.

Secondly, during the 1970s national technical regulations continued to be produced which not only increased the scale of the EC's harmonisation task, but also indicated the lack of willingness to shift technical regulation to the EC level. Thirdly, the total harmonisation approach placed unacceptable burdens on an EC legislative process already burdened by the need for unanimity in the Council.

In order to stem the tide of national technical regulations (and in addition to changes to the Commission's internal procedures to speed up Article 169 infringement proceedings against Member States), a 'Gentleman's Agreement' was signed in 1969. Under the Agreement, Member States undertook to notify the Commission of any draft technical regulations which they intended to adopt. A five-month standstill would then operate during which the Commission or other Member States could raise objections to potential technical trade barriers which might be created by the national measure. However, it has been observed (McMillan 1985: 94) that the Agreement was honoured more in its breach than in its observance.

Negative integration

The jurisdictional approach to legislative harmonisation taken by the Commission was supported by the equally jurisdictional approach to the scope of Article 30, EC taken by the ECJ (see also Chapter 10). In *Dassonville* the ECJ described a trade barrier as a national measure which 'actually or potentially, directly or indirectly' hindered inter-state trade.[2]

For our purposes, what is significant is the interrelationship between negative and positive integration. A jurisdictional approach to negative integration necessarily has the effect of limiting the scope for the application of national regulatory policy unless Member States are also given the regulatory space to seek to justify national rules. If the effect of such a jurisdictional approach is the finding of national laws to be incompatible with Treaty rules on free movement then *either* Member States must find a way of protecting valued regulatory objectives without creating trade barriers *or* technical regulation must be shifted to the EC level in order to allow valued regulatory objectives to be reconciled with the requirements of economic integration. In the latter case, judicial policy on negative integration increased pressure for EC legislation.

The ECJ compounded its pressure on the EC legislative institutions through its rulings on 'preemption'. The ECJ found that where common rules had been adopted within the EC for the common organisation of a market or in order to exhaustively regulate an area then the Member States correspondingly lost regulatory competence in the same area.[3] As Waelbrock observed (1982), the Court took a 'conceptualist-federalist' approach to preemption in the sense that it was assumed that as the EC adopted more and more legislative rules, the concurrent competence of the Member States to adopt national rules would gradually be replaced by an exclusive EC competence to regulate. Clearly, this approach was consistent with the positive harmonisation strategy of total and vertical harmonisation.

Reconstructing the governance regime

The first phase of technical harmonisation was characterised by the desire to produce uniform, technical EC rules which eliminated disparities between national technical regulations. While that may have been the ambition, the failures of the legislative institutions left it as a largely unrealised ambition.

In this part, we examine a shift in the harmonisation regime characterised, particularly, by a changed role for EC legislation. We analyse the development of a new approach to harmonisation in which much of the detailed work of technical harmonisation passed from the legislative institutions to private standards-setting agencies (see generally Schreiber 1991; Pelkmans 1987). This 'reference to standards' approach empowered a new set of actors: the Comité Européen de Normalisation (CEN), the Comité Européen de Normalisation Électrotechnique (CENELEC) and later the European Telecommunications Standards Institute (ETSI). The new approach also resulted in an increased use of mutual recognition as an alternative integration strategy, together with a more effective mechanism to stem the growth of national technical regulations (the 'Information Procedure Directive').

What is significant about the development of the new approach to technical harmonisation is the extent to which the most important elements of institutional change were brought about without Treaty revision. We suggest that given the importance of the new approach, it is mistaken to view Treaty alterations as necessarily *the* most significant form of institutional change.

Cassis de Dijon, *negative integration and mutual recognition*

The ECJ's decision in *Cassis de Dijon*[4] has proved to be something of a *cause célèbre* for integration studies, not least in terms of providing a crossing-point for legal academics and political scientists to talk to one another. The decision is generally referred to as introducing the principle of mutual recognition; a principle taken up by the Commission and applied to develop a new approach to technical harmonisation.

The decision in *Cassis* pulls in a number of different directions. On the one hand, it continued the jurisdictional approach to Article 30 by making clear that its scope extended to indistinctly applicable measures. On the other hand, and in recognition of the absence of common EC rules, the ECJ left open a space for national rules which were, 'necessary in order to satisfy mandatory requirements relating in particular to the effectiveness of fiscal supervision, the protection of public health, the fairness of commercial transactions and the defence of the consumer'. The ECJ, recognising that harmonisation had not progressed to the extent of replacing national rules, and recognising the danger of regulatory gaps emerging, levered open a space for the Member States. At the same time the space was only a space within a framework of EC law controlled by the national courts and the ECJ (see Alter and Meunier-Aitsahalia 1994).

The pursuit of negative integration through the courts creates a somewhat uncertain environment for manufacturers (Burrows 1990). Will a court consider a particular national measure to be a trade barrier? Are the costs of legal actions smaller than any potential adaptation costs? Is the Commission likely to bring legal proceedings (thus saving on the use of the manufacturer's own resources in litigating)? While negative integration may be necessary, compared with the certainty of compliance with a set of harmonised rules, it is by no means a panacea.

Given the problems associated with both positive and negative integration, the ECJ's establishment of the principle of mutual recognition was understandable. The Court established that – in principle – where goods are lawfully placed on the market in one Member State, there is a rebuttable presumption that the goods also comply with technical rules in the importing state (Burrows 1990). This idea of the functional equivalence of different national rules removes the need to harmonise to remove all disparities between national rules. Rather, the harmonisation function can be limited to the establishment of essential requirements.

In one sense, the introduction of mutual recognition did mark a departure from a model of governance in which technical regulation was understood as increasingly a task for EC legislative institutions. However, we should not get too carried away. First, mutual recognition is very much an *additional* tool of integration (indeed its strength is in its complementarity to harmonisation through rule-making – see Majone 1992). Secondly, mutual recognition is contingent on the existence of institutional structures through which technical equivalences can be recognised, and also on different national rules actually pursuing equivalent strategies.

As we saw from *Cassis* one important institutional forum for mutual recognition consists of the courts. In other words, economic actors may litigate to place their products on markets where they believe that rules in the importing state are equivalent to those in the exporting state. However, mutual recognition may therefore simply replicate the problems associated with the judicial reconciliation of integration and regulation insofar as it is the courts that are the institutional focus for mutual recognition. If mutual recognition is to be operational, it would seem more important that administrative bodies which routinely handle imports should give effect to mutual recognition. For this to function, it is apparent that structures of cooperation, information exchange and mutual confidence need to be built. In short, mutual recognition – like the Treaty-based tools of integration – is nothing without the institutional structures through which it is operationalised.

In respect of the 'equivalence' of national regulations, this cannot be simply presupposed. Clearly, where national rules pursue the same goals and the differences between them are matters of detail rather than policy, there is the potential for an effective operationalisation of mutual recognition. That is not the case where there is a clash in regulatory traditions between Member States. A good example here relates to product safety. Should a manufacturer be liable for all defects in products (including latent defects which were not identified or identifiable having regard to the state of scientific knowledge at the time) or only those defects which were apparent or foreseeable?

The decision in *Cassis*, none the less, was important not only in establishing a potential new solution to the problem of technical barriers, but also, as Alter and Meunier-Aitsahalia have argued (1994), in providing a catalyst for a political debate about the development of strategies for technical integration. The decision can be seen as marking a turning-point which led to the Commission's new approach to technical harmonisation.

The development of harmonisation policy

Alter and Meunier-Aitsahalia (1994) rightly caution against assuming that decisions of the ECJ have *direct* policy effects (in the sense of changing policy in and of themselves). Rather, and consistent with the approach we have adopted, decisions of the Court can provide solutions, ideas, or simple pressure for policy change. Court decisions have no quality independent of the settings in which they are invoked. In an unprecedented step, the Commission issued a Communication 'concerning the consequences of the judgment' in *Cassis*.[5] As Alter and Meunier-Aitsahalia argue (1994), the debate which followed the Commission's broad interpretation of the consequences of the judgment set in train a process by which a new approach to harmonisation emerged.

Defining the scope of this new approach is not unlike defining the scope of the single market. One can take a narrow definition or a broad one. Narrowly defined, the 'new approach' – identified in a 1985 Commission Communication (CEC 1985b) – concerned the limitation of EC harmonisation to the establishment of the 'essential requirements' of products, with conformity to European technical standards harnessed as one technical means by which to conform to these essential requirements. Broadly, however, the new approach also encompassed a change in the institutional structure of governance to ensure a more effective delivery of harmonised EC laws and standards. In this broad sense, one also needs to consider the institutional reforms brought about by the SEA; reform of the formal relationship between the EC and the European standards-setters, together with internal reform of the processes of standardisation; and the attempt to stem the tide of national technical regulations and standards through the 1983 Information Procedure Directive. For the sake of simplicity, we will use the term 'new approach' to identify the Commission's reference to standards strategy. However, it should be borne in mind that this strategy is intrinsically linked to the general reform of harmonisation policy.

The new approach
In 1985 the Commission produced a Communication on its new approach to technical harmonisation in which it set out the principle of the 'reference to standards' (CEC 1985b). The elements of this new approach are as follows:

- EC legislation should only harmonise essential requirements (the move from total harmonisation to minimal harmonisation).
- European technical standards should be promulgated to meet the technical needs of conforming to the essential requirements.
- Conformity to a European standard raises a presumption of conformity to EC law and gives rise to the right of access to the EC market provided the product is accompanied by an appropriate means of attestation. A product otherwise complying with the essential requirements must be accompanied by an attestation of an independent body before having the right of free access to the market.
- In the absence of European standards, products manufactured in accordance with national standards (which must be notified to the Commission

as being considered to meet the essential requirements) are entitled to the presumption of conformity.

The effect of the new approach was not only to limit the legislative role but also to change the orientation of harmonisation away from product-by-product regulation (vertical harmonisation) towards the harmonisation of groups of products (horizontal harmonisation). In this way, the scope of harmonisation could be expanded without incurring further risks of over-regulation.

The new approach entailed the use of the reference-to-standards approach in new priority areas – mechanical engineering, building materials and electrical appliances. No attempt was made to undo the harmonisation work already achieved, e.g. in the area of motor vehicles. Further, it was recognised that the new approach could not be applied in areas where, for example, national rules did not pursue equivalent objectives, or the area did not lend itself to standardisation. In short, it is important to view the new approach as an additional harmonisation tool and not as a replacement of the traditional approach to harmonisation. Indeed, many of the SEM measures (identified in the White Paper) followed the traditional approach to harmonisation.

The reference-to-standards approach raised issues of both principle and efficacy: would it result in the privatisation of regulatory policy (see McGee and Weatherill 1990) and would it be any more effective?

The new approach began a process of re-defining the role of formal EC institutions and their relationship with the European standards-setters. Egan has described this process of harnessing private agencies for public ends as 'associative regulation' (Egan 1991: 39):

> Associative regulation is based on accommodation, public concertation and partnership. It reflects a new public-private dimension by adopting a partnership arrangement between the private European standardisation bodies and the European Community institutions.

The extent to which this partnership constitutes a privatisation of rule-making is dependent upon how far the essential requirements of regulatory policy are set down in EC legislative instruments. Strictly speaking, any delegation of this function to the standards agencies would constitute an unlawful delegation of power. But it is clearly the case that the kinds of choices made by standards agencies have an impact upon the nature of regulatory policy. What is important, then, is the level of public interest and consumer representation in standards-setting. The example of Germany is apposite.

The German approach has been that products manufactured in accordance with DIN standards and approved by the Ministry of Labour are deemed to satisfy German product safety law and have access to the market (Joerges 1988; Micklitz 1986). This might therefore be viewed as a private setting of safety standards. However, as Joerges points out, DIN must take into account the public interest and accept consumer representation in standardisation. Moreover, the Ministry of Labour must consult with consumers, trade unions and others represented in an Advisory Committee before approving of a standard. One cannot adopt too simplistic or binary a division between public and private. For instance, even those states like the UK and France which have traditionally used 'public' forms of regulation of technical products none the less consult and rely on information provided by private industry. The point, therefore, is not so much the existence of the private standards-setters but how that power is exercised and what forms of public representation are allowed in standardisation. We return to this in our discussion of the third phase of regime evolution.

It is worth examining why the Commission opted for the reference-to-standards approach at all, given that in the 1980s it was apparent that European standardisation was not capable of delivering harmonised European standards at anything like the rate that new national standards were emerging. Indeed, worried by the threat of market segmentation through national standards, the Commission, in a 1980 Communication (CEC 1980), highlighted that,

> After fifteen years in existence . . . neither the CEN nor CENELEC have altogether lived up to the hopes that were placed in them: the number of European standards produced each year falls well short of requirements, and they sometimes incorporate 'national deviations' that greatly lessen their impact.

On this account, it would seem surprising that the Commission should invest such hope in its new approach. How does one make sense of this?

The Commission had few choices open to it. Its pre-existing legislative strategy was failing and much of the Commission's time was spent adapting existing directives to technical change. Further, by 1980 the Commission was pursuing some 250 infringement actions against Member States for non-implementation of the directives already adopted. A new strategy was required if the Commission was ever to move on from existing initiatives to broaden its scope and give effect to the single market. In other words, the *status quo* was not really an option.

Moreover, as it became more apparent that technical barriers arose equally through national standards as through national technical regulations, the whole issue of the reform of European standardisation came on to the agenda. In this sense, the new approach was connected not merely to the *harnessing* of European standardisation, but also to the *reform* of European standardisation.

In 1984, prior to the adoption of the new approach, the Commission, together with CEN and CENELEC, agreed on a new formalised relationship. 'General Guidelines for Cooperation' were established and the financing of work undertaken on behalf of the EC was agreed in a Framework Contract in 1985 (which has subsequently been revised) (CEC 1990a). Reform to the internal voting procedures of the European standards bodies was also undertaken in 1986. The 1984 General Guidelines also involved a greater commitment in principle to the consultation of consumers in standardisation (Farquhar 1995).

Other institutional changes occurred to meet the demands of the new approach and Community policies towards standardisation generally. Staff numbers at CEN increased from 10 in 1983 to 75 in 1992 and to 110 at the beginning of 1996. CENELEC staffing also increased from 13 to 35 in 1992 and to 42 at the beginning of 1996. The secretariats of both bodies were fused into one. Of some significance is the increase in the number of the Technical Committees (TCs) and working groups which undertake the work necessary to produce a draft European standard (prEN). Thus, whereas for CEN, in 1983 there were 53 TCs, this figure had grown to 269 by 1996, supported by 126 sub-committees and 1,298 working groups. CENELEC's TCs (including sub-committees) grew to 75 by 1996 supported by 247 working groups.

It is not only the TCs and working groups which bring standards work to the stage of the preparation of a prEN. Associated Standardisation Bodies (ASBs) have approached CEN with drafts in specific sectors. Thus, the European Committee on Iron and Steel Standardisation (ECISS), the Association Européene des Constructeurs de Matériel Aérospatial (AECMA) and the European Workshop for Open Systems (EWOS) have helped in the preparation of approximately 100 European standards (Kendall 1991). For its part, CENELEC has concluded five Cooperation Agreements to take draft work from the following organisations with a view to the production of European standards: the International Association of Electrical Contractors (AIE); the European Computer Manufacturers' Association (ECMA); the European Confederation of Associations of Manufacturers of Insulated Wires and Cables (EUROPACABLE); the International Organisation of Legal Metrology (OIML); and the International Union of Producers and Distributors of Electrical Energy (UNIPEDE).[6]

We examine below whether these organisational developments have succeeded in improving the delivery of European standards. For the moment, we can conclude that despite action to place an increased emphasis on European standardisation, none the less, the Commission's decision to pursue the new approach must be seen as something of an article of faith. We would, however, emphasise that the new approach not only harnessed the activities of standards agencies, it also had an impact upon their institutional structure and their development.

Institutional reform and the SEA
The introduction of Article 100a by the SEA as the legal basis for internal market measures changed the legislative procedural framework in which harmonisation directives were to be agreed. The cooperation procedure and the possibility for QMV in the Council would henceforth apply (now, of course, the co-decision procedure applies to Article 100a). However, the

quid pro quo for the loss of the national veto was the introduction of Article 100a(4) which permits Member States to apply to the Commission to maintain in force a national rule of a more stringent standard than a Community harmonised directive. On the face of it, this would seem to undermine the point of harmonisation in that it extends the possibility of permissible diversity between national rules. However, in only one case has the Commission actually permitted a country (Germany) to continue to apply its national laws (on pentachlorophenol), which itself resulted in litigation by France against the Commission.[7]

The importance of the SEA lies, however, in its connection to the SEM programme. As we noted at the outset, the removal of technical barriers to trade formed an important part of the White Paper on *Completing the Internal Market*. Despite the introduction of the new approach, it would not be suitable for all legislative action. Thus, the institutional reforms to the legislative process were a necessary corollary to the SEM programme and the development of technical harmonisation within that programme.

The Information Procedure Directive

As we noted above, the 1969 Gentleman's Agreement on the notification of national technical regulations failed to stem the tide of market-segmenting technical rules. Moreover, the problem of national technical barriers increasingly lay with technical *standards* rather than with technical *regulations*. It is against this background that the Community adopted Council Directive 83/189/EEC.[8]

The Directive turned the 1969 Agreement's requirement to notify the Commission of draft national technical regulations into a matter of legal obligation. The Directive also extended the scope of the Agreement to cover draft national technical standards. The Directive has been amended on subsequent occasions to broaden its scope and now covers not simply rules governing the access of products to markets, but also rules governing the whole 'life-cycle' of products (e.g. rules on disposal or re-use).[9]

Under the Directive, draft technical regulations must be notified to the Commission and are subject to a 'standstill' period of three months from the date of notification. If the Commission or a Member State gives a detailed opinion that a measure may create obstacles to the free movement of goods, the standstill is extended to a total of six months (or four months for voluntary agreements). The Commission – in consultation with the Standing Committee established under the Directive – may decide that the appropriate course of action is for it to propose a harmonisation directive (in which case the standstill extends to twelve months). Otherwise political pressure is applied to amend the draft to remove trade barriers, always with the threat of legal action in the background.

Draft technical standards (comprising new work rather than the implementation without modification of European or international standards) must also be notified to the Commission, the Standing Committee and the

European standards bodies. The Standing Committee may recommend that mandates be agreed between the Commission and the European standards bodies to develop European standards. Or it may recommend that the national draft be amended.

What significance can be attached to this Directive? First, the Directive establishes an alternative mechanism to the tools established in the Treaty for the control of national technical trade barriers. Once again this indicates the manner in which the search for a more operationally-effective governance regime has been carried out without recourse to Treaty reform. Secondly, in its application to draft technical *standards* the Directive is indicative of the increased attention in the second phase of the regime's evolution with the problem posed by national standards. Thirdly, the Directive is concerned with the establishment of new standard operating procedures through which organisational linkages and information flows between national governments, the Commission, national and European standards bodies are created. We would suggest that one consequence of these linkages is the 'Europeanisation' of standardisation through the interaction of national and European-level actors.

Summary

The second phase of the evolution of the governance regime is marked principally by the development of the new approach to technical harmonisation and the increased emphasis on the need to tackle the problem of national technical standards. In consequence, organisational linkages between Community institutions, national and European standards-setters assumed a greater importance and intensity. At the level of law-making, institutional reform brought about by the SEA can also be seen as part of the package of measures by which the harmonisation regime was to be rendered more effective. Notwithstanding the SEA, the extent to which reform of institutional procedures has been effected without Treaty revision is striking.

Within the judicial arena, while the ECJ continued its jurisdictional approach to the regulation of free movement, it did open up a regulatory space for national regulatory policy (in the absence of common EC rules). None the less, this space existed within a framework of ECJ supervision. Finally, the ECJ introduced the principle of mutual recognition: harnessed by the Commission to limit the legislative role of EC institutions to the establishment of essential requirements.

Reconstruction re-visited

In this final section, we explore two aspects of the continued evolution of the governance regime: the attempt to enhance the effective delivery of

European standards, and the need for improved testing and certification procedures. Our principal focus shall be on the first of these issues for the hallmark of this third phase of evolution is the importance attached to European standardisation. In examining European standardisation we return to the issues previously raised about this form of associative regulation, in particular, the relationship between EC institutions and European standards-setters, and the need to incorporate the desires and values of consumers within the process of standardisation.

Standardisation: meeting supply with demand

Increasing demands It is important to bear in mind that the work of CEN and CENELEC pre-dates EU mandated standards. CEN was established in 1962 to carry out – at the European level – a similar function to that of the International Standardisation Organization (ISO), Similarly, CENELEC – founded in 1962 as CENELCOM and changing its name to CENELEC in 1973 – paralleled the work of the International Electrotechnical Commission (IEC).

Standardisation has traditionally been, and still remains, an industry-driven mechanism for producing voluntary technical standards, conformity to which is a badge of quality. None the less, the share of work undertaken on behalf of the Community has increased. By the early 1990s, approximately one-fifth of European standardisation work was mandated by the Community. By the mid-1990s, this had risen to one-third. The increase in the demand for standards lies less with the extension of the new approach and more with the request for standards in pursuit of broadly defined policy ambitions. For example, we noted in our chapter on public procurement (Chapter 5) that there was a close policy linkage between the liberalisation of procurement, the liberalisation of telecommunications and European standardisation policy.

As the Commission's Green Paper on Telecommunications indicates (CEC 1987a), the key to the Commission's policy is the creation of a common market in the provision of terminal equipment, network equipment and telecommunications services. Over the years – according to Commission estimates – the EU has spent ECU 11 bn on the development of national technical networks with distinctive standards. For an EU market to develop, harmonised technical standards for telecommunications must be adopted.

On 12 February 1988, ETSI came into formal existence with the aim of creating European standards for telecommunications. Unlike CEN/CENELEC in which the national delegations are the primary participants, the ETSI has direct participation from network operators, users, manufacturers, research bodies and service providers (decisions are made by the national delegations). In its resolution on standardisation in the field of information technology and telecommunications,[10] the Council indicated its support for ETSI and invited the Commission to forge links with it. Mandates have been agreed between the Commission and ETSI in support of a new approach directive (the Telecommunications Terminal Equipment Directive), as well as in support of legislation for the creation of an internal market in telecommunications (e.g. Directive 90/387/EEC[11]).

In summary, we suggest that increased demands for European standards came not only from the extension of the new approach, but also from other policy developments within the EU including the pursuit of sectoral policies. All of which again raised the question of whether the European system for standardisation was capable of meeting the demands placed upon it.

Institutional reform? While demand for European standards has increased, the ability of European standards-setters to deliver standards has traditionally been outpaced by *national* standards bodies. Whereas in 1989 CEN and CENELEC promulgated some 150 European standards in 1989, the comparable national figures were approximately 400 in the UK, 350 in France and 650 in Germany (Schreiber 1991).

In 1990 the Commission produced a Green Paper on Standardization in which it sought to address the need for a more effective delivery of European standards (CEC 1990a). The Commission pointed to the delays involved in the TCs in reaching consensus on drafts, compounded by a six-month public enquiry stage. It also noted the delays involved in the transposition of European standards into national standards. Fundamentally, the Commission highlighted the need for greater support from industry for the standardisation programme, as well as the need to set priorities within that programme to avoid standardisation becoming too little, too late.

The mechanism suggested by the Commission for improving the efficiency of standardisation was institutional reform – the establishment of a 'European standardisation system'. Its aim was the promotion of sectoral standardisation, subject to a set of common rules of action developed by a central European Standardisation Council supported by a European Standardisation Board.

While welcoming the attention being paid to standardisation, the response from the European and national standards bodies to the Green Paper presented some common criticisms. The adoption of the European standardisation system was felt to create new levels of bureaucracy which would themselves create inefficiency in standardisation. Moreover, it was argued that increased sectoralisation – outside the distinctions between CEN, CENCELEC and ETSI – would give rise to problems concerning coordination of work, create duplication of effort, and result in further waste of time and resources. The British Standards Institute, in its response, favoured better management techniques and work allocation within the existing European bodies, rather than the addition of a new institutional structure.[12]

CEN was particularly keen to highlight the traditionally private and consensual nature of European standardisation. In its view, industry would only be prepared to allocate the time and resources it felt was necessary for the long-term development of markets. The pace at which industry was prepared to move would not necessarily be the same as the pace at which the Commission might wish to see change.

A common theme of criticism was that the Green Paper underplayed the importance of international standardisation, particularly in terms of where industry was prepared to see resources targeted. In some areas, industry wanted to look beyond the single market, to the challenges of global competition. The majority of CENELEC's standards are direct translations of internationally agreed standards. As the British Standards Institute pointed out in its response, 'The increased adoption of international standards as European standards is an obvious means of improving efficiency and conserving scarce resources for other necessary work.' Indeed, it might be said that the importance of international standards was underplayed, while the value of sectoralisation – an EU preoccupation – was overplayed. CEN contended that the benefits of sectoralisation (the focus of attention on standardisation in a given sector) had to be balanced against the disadvantages in terms of fragmentation and duplication.

Despite the criticisms made of the Green Paper, there was no denial that the system needed to improve its rate of delivery of standards. It was also recognised that there was a greater need to agree 'horizontal' standards covering a range of products, rather than highly descriptive 'vertical' standards limited to particular products. In turn, the need for horizontal standards required greater coordination between the TCs to avoid the duplication of work. For example, TC 207 (furniture) and TC 252 (child safety) both developed distinct standards for children's furniture.

The radical institutional reform proposed in the Green Paper has not transpired. What then should we make of the significance of the Green Paper to the evolution of the harmonisation of standards? It has been described as being both badly timed (in terms of distracting the standards bodies from their work in order to respond to the paper) and a bridge too far. From the Commission's perspective, while the solution proposed by the Green Paper was misconceived, none the less the dialogue prompted by it was necessary and useful. It challenged standards bodies to justify their practices. It brought standardisation into the open, emphasising the salience of standardisation for future economic integration. In this respect, the Commission drew support from the Council's Resolution of 18 June 1992 on the Role of European Standardization in the European Economy.[13] The resolution repeated the need for European standards in the creation of trans-European networks and in support of the procurement regime.

However, the Green Paper has had repercussions for European standardssetters. A limited level of sectoralisation has been created, but *within* CEN.

Table 6.1: Total published European documents at the beginning of 1996[14]

Documents	CEN	CENELEC
ENs[1]	2,167	1,440
HDs[2]	9	574
ENVs[3]	197	23
Reports	30	19
Guides	–	2

Notes:
1 European Standards.
2 Harmonised Documents.
3 European Prestandards.

In order to coordinate work across the TCs more effectively, Technical Sector Boards (BTSs) have been established. This step formed part of a more wide-ranging review of CEN's handling of work contained in a document approved by CEN's administrative board on 25 April 1991 entitled *Strategy for the Development of European Standardisation*. Similarly, CENELEC's General Assembly ratified *The Way Forward: CENELEC Strategic Plan '92-'96* on 29 October 1991. This document sets down the principles and priorities for the development of standardisation.

Further, there have been clear improvements in the rate of delivery of standards documents. In 1991, CEN produced 322 documents, rising to 710 in 1995. CENELEC produced 243 documents in 1991, increasing to 444 in 1995. The total number of documents as at the beginning of 1996 are represented in Table 6.1.

Yet, concerns as to the effective delivery of European standards remain. In October 1995, the Commission produced a new Communication on *The Broader Use of Standardization in Community Policy* (CEC 1995a). While reinforcing the importance of standardisation,[15] the Communication clearly recognises that standardisation still has its problems. The Commission itself acknowledges its need to programmatise its harmonisation strategy (thereby prioritising certain standardisation work over others), and to recognise that mandates must take into account the voluntary nature of standardisation (therefore mandates must not be too restrictively drawn). However, the Communication also strikes a note of mild irritation that the European standards agencies have not fully recognised the role they play in pursuit of EU policies (especially as regards the setting of priorities, the management of mandates and the monitoring of delays). This highlights the potential tension between formal EC institutions and agencies which, while outside of the formal structure of the EU, none the less, perform functions which are central to EU policies.

In conclusion, it is evident that many of the problems associated with the traditional approach to legislative harmonisation have been repeated in the area of standardisation. For example, as the demand for standards has grown it has become necessary to engage more in horizontal standardisation than in the traditional vertical approach. Similarly, if the demand for harmonised legislation created a need for institutional reform of the EU, so too has the demand for standards required institutional reform of the European standards-setters.

However, there is a danger that in seeking to improve the efficiency of standardisation, the openness and transparency of decision-making will be sacrificed. At the very least, concerns must be raised as to a heightened role for private agencies in operationalising EU policy in the absence of institutionalised structures which ensure the representation of consumer interests. We return to the representation of interests below.

Testing and certification

The removal of technical barriers to trade through harmonised rules and standards is a necessary but not a sufficient condition for a barrier-free SEM. It is apparent that if each Member State insisted upon the application of its own systems to test and certify that products conform to harmonised rules, trade barriers would re-emerge at the level of testing and certification. At the same time, it is important that products do in fact comply with EC rules and standards in order to be legitimately placed on the market. Accordingly, products governed by new approach directives must be accompanied by an appropriate means of attestation in order to create a presumption of conformity (safeguard clauses are written in to the directives to permit Member States to block the placing of a product on the market where it can be shown that a product has not in fact been produced in conformity with the necessary rules).

In its 1985 Resolution on Technical Harmonization and Standardization,[16] the Council established two approaches to conformity attestation. Either a product can be tested and certified by a third party, or self-certification can be carried out by the manufacturer. The resolution envisaged that each new approach directive would specify which type of attestation was required (Farr 1992).

However, unless there is mutual confidence between Member States that products do in fact comply with all the relevant EC rules, and that attestation procedures have been properly carried out, trade barriers may re-emerge. Accordingly, the issue of conformity assessment has been tackled in three principal ways:

- the development of the 'CE' mark;
- the 'global approach' to conformity assessment; and
- the creation of the European Organization for Testing and Certification.

The CE mark was introduced as an indicator that a product was entitled to free movement with the SEM. Only where a product was in fact unsafe or the CE mark had been illegally affixed could it be denied free movement. But what does the CE mark actually indicate? Under some directives it implied conformity to the essential requirements, but, for example, under the Simple Pressure Vessels Directives it implied conformity to national standards implementing European standards (Farr 1992: 63). Further, in some cases the CE mark may be affixed by the manufacturer (a form of self-certification) but in others, third-party testing is required. In consequence, the CE mark did not emerge as an indicator of quality but merely as a description of a product's conformity with individual directives. One obvious problem this creates is where a product is covered by more than one directive. In this case, the CE mark is ambiguous.

Obviously, if the CE mark is not a clear indicator of the compliance of a product with the relevant rules, there is the danger that further testing and certification will be required each time a product crosses boundaries. Thus, the CE mark debate has been subsumed into the broader debate about testing and certification.

In seeking to improve testing and certification, the Commission proposed a *Global Approach to Certification and Testing* (CEC 1989a). This was approved by the Council on 21 December 1989 in its Resolution on a Global Approach to Conformity Assessment.[17] The 'global approach' attempts to give some consistency in the testing and certification procedures across the directives. It provides a choice of 'modules', each of which establishes the rigour of the testing and certification procedures. Each directive will then specify which modes of testing and certification (defined in relation to these modules) can be used. In this way, although the EU is not engaging in the formal harmonisation of testing and certification, none the less the global approach is indicative of some degree of EU colonisation of this area in support of its overall harmonisation goals.

The global approach to conformity assessment has been formalised in a Council Decision[18] which also establishes the rules under which the CE mark may be affixed. A Council Directive has been agreed to harmonise the meaning of the CE mark across all the new approach Directives.[19] Thus, the CE mark now indicates that a product is presumed to comply with the provisions of all directives which apply to it, including provisions covering conformity assessment.[20] However, there is a danger that the damage has already been done. For example, the extension of the CE mark – even in its harmonised form – to the Low Voltage Directive was reported to have encountered resistance from industry and consumers. It was felt that the existing system of third-party certification had provided a good guarantee of quality, and that the introduction of the CE mark would erode that guarantee of quality.

The fear of the operation of inadequate systems of testing and certification also gave rise to the creation of a new European-level organisation: the European Organization for Testing and Certification (EOTC). The EOTC came into being formally in 1993 after a three-year pilot period. In its 'Mission Statement' it described its goal as 'establishing mutual confidence between all parties concerned with conformity assessment issues, so as to facilitate the free circulation throughout Europe of goods and services that have demonstrated conformity with technical specifications'. Thus, the *modus operandi* of the EOTC is the encouragement of mutual confidence and mutual recognition of testing and certification between national bodies. In theory, this function is to be carried out outside of any other structures established by EC directives or national laws regarding the mutual recognition of testing and certification (the 'regulated spheres'). However, the distinction between regulated and non-regulated spheres may be illusory or indeed blurred where a product is only partially covered by a directive. Thus it seems clear that if duplication of testing and certification is to be avoided, the scope of the EOTC cannot fall into simple categories. That said, the primary restriction on its reach rests with the resources available to it (the Commission has made clear that any future funding from it is dependent upon matching funds from the membership of the EOTC).

The primary function of the EOTC, therefore, appears to be that of a structure through which information can flow and trust and confidence be developed: there is no attempt to develop a bureaucratic response by creating a uniform European system of testing and certification. Rather, through EOTC Agreement Groups and Sectoral Committees mutual recognition is to be pursued.

Standardisation and the representation of consumer interests
Insofar as the reconciliation of the objectives of integration and regulation takes place within the traditional – and formally constituted – institutional structures of the EC, the legitimacy of harmonisation draws upon the constitutional pedigree of the institutional actors carrying out their mandated tasks. With the increased role of private European agencies in the harmonisation process, concerns have been raised as to the privatisation of regulatory policy and, therefore, the legitimacy of the actions of CEN, CENELEC and ETSI has been questioned. One response to this potential problem of legitimacy has been a call for the increased representation of consumer interests in the standardisation work undertaken by these agencies.

Consumer interests have found representation both within the institutional structure of the Commission (the Consumer Consultative Council (EC-CCC)) and outside (principally through the Bureau Européen des

Unions des Consommateurs (BEUC), but also through the Confederation of Family Organisations in the EC (COFACE), the European Community of Consumers Cooperatives (EUROCOOP), and the European Trade Union Confederation (ETUC)). It is also worth remembering that consumer interests may be represented in the national standards agencies and by their representatives within the European standards agencies.

As part of the 1980s reforms to the relationship between the EC and CEN/CENELEC, consumer representation in standardisation was to be enhanced through the attendance of members of the EC-CCC as observers of the work of the European standards bodies. Further, as Farquhar details (1995), BEUC was to act as the central point for the development of a consumer information network regarding European standardisation. This entailed the establishment within BEUC in 1985 of a standardisation secretariat (Secrétariat Européen de Coordination pour la Normalisation (SECO)), acting as a sub-committee of the EC-CCC. Thus, the SECO emerged to support the lobbying of the EC legislative process when new approach directives were under discussion; to provide a mechanism for the reaching of common agreement among consumers groups to be advanced within CEN and CENELEC meetings; and to coordinate an information network.

A more radical plan was outlined in the 1984 Bosma Report (quoted in Farquhar 1995) for the establishment of a Consumer Advisory Committee to advise the standing committee established under the Information Procedure Directive. Importantly, this Advisory Committee would seek to enhance the access of consumers' representatives to the technical knowledge necessary for them to articulate their concerns to the standards agencies. The plan was not implemented, and for another ten years the commitment to increased representation of consumer interest was ritually repeated in Commission Communications and Council Resolutions, but without institutional change. Indeed, the launch of the Commission's Green Paper on Standardization held up movements put forward by CEN for an EC/EFTA consumer standardisation committee to be based within CEN, as the Commission wanted to wait for responses to its paper before contemplating change (Farquhar 1995: 62).

One can see the drive for enhanced consumer representation on standardisation being pulled in two different directions. On the one hand, agencies like CEN sought to internalise and therefore to control the management of representation by suggesting the establishment of a consumers' standardisation committee within CEN. This, of course not only threatened the potential independence of such a representative body but also split consumer representation across each of the standards agencies. On the other hand, the EC-CCC has sought to be the controlling influence on the development of interest representation, in partnership with the EFTA-CCC. The 'winner' in this battle has been the EC/EFTA-CCCs in that in

1992 agreement was reached on the establishment of a new structure for the representation of consumer interests in standardisation (the European Association for the Co-ordination of Consumer Representation in Standardisation (ANEC)), independent of the European standards agencies and with strong representation from both the EC-CCC and the EFTA-CCC.

The simple creation of the ANEC is far from sufficient. As Farquhar highlights (1995), problems remain in terms of the access of the ANEC to the CEN technical board, to the ETSI decision-making structure, and to the Commission's own standing committee. To be sure, observers now sit on 52 TCs and working groups shadow the work of the TCs. However, access is also needed to the policy-making structures of the European standards agencies and the Commission. The resourcing of representation has also not been resolved by the creation of the ANEC. The SECO, as the secretariat for the ANEC, provides one full-time member of staff – an assistant and a secretary. While funding from the Commission has increased from an annual ECU 200,000 to ECU 350,000 these are none the less limited resources.

It is evident that the drive towards European standardisation has necessitated a change in the institutional structures through which consumers interests are represented. To expand Egan's notion of 'associative regulation', the representation of consumer interests provides the third and linking part of the triangle between public legislative institutions on the one side and private standards-setters on the other. Whether that side of the triangle will serve to legitimate the actions of the other two sides will depend not only on its ability to harness technical resources, but also on its ability to increase its human and financial resources to enable it effectively to represent the consumer interest.

Summary

In the third phase of the regime discussed above, issues of effectiveness and institutional design have been central issues. We noted the (abandoned) proposal for a European standardisation system. Instead, more incremental institutional reform has taken place. Further, new institutions have emerged to deal with issues of testing and certification.

It is clear that as the regime has evolved new problems and issues have emerged which have created their own internal pressures for reform. We find, then, both a widening and a deepening of the harmonisation regime, accompanied by institutional change that not only reflects the values of efficiency, but also attempts to reflect values of consumer participation. It is striking that these not inconsiderable developments have taken place without Treaty revision. Further, in the case of consumer representation in standardisation, change has been brought about through the activities of European-level lobby groups in dialogue with the Commission and the standards bodies themselves.

Conclusions

We started our story of technical harmonisation with a tale of two policy instruments (negative and positive integration) and two key actors (the ECJ and the Commission). What emerged was a more complex narrative with numerous sub-plots and a much larger cast.

Technical harmonisation has evolved in organisational, procedural and normative terms. It is clear that the inter-organisational linkages between the Commission and the European standards agencies is a defining characteristic of this governance regime. As the importance of standardisation has increased and as sectoral policies have been pursued by the Commission, organisational change has been required to keep up with the demand for European standards. Equally, as the supply of standards has increased, consumer representatives have sought to have their voices heard in decision-making processes not only within the EC institutions but within standards agencies themselves. In this way new operating procedures of consultation, as well as new organisational structures, have emerged.

While the SEA introduced importance changes to the legislative process, it is striking how little of these profound changes to the governance structure have been brought about through Treaty revision. Rather, what this case study illustrates is the need to analyse the *operationalisation of EU governance*. That is to say, if we are to understand the nature of EU governance we need to engage in the kind of detailed policy analysis that we have sought to present in a case study like this. It is not enough to assume that Treaty revisions are the most significant form of change and therefore seek to reduce European integration to these high-profile events. What matters is how policy actors actually interpret and develop their mandates or roles. In this way, it is necessary to contextualise significant moments (which may or may not include Treaty revisions) within broader histories of decision-making, thereby exposing path-dependent elements.

Applied to our case study on technical harmonisation, we can understand the evolution of this regime in terms of *institutional exploration*. The transition from one phase of the regime to another has been a process of seeking to remedy the problems of past approaches. As new policy instruments (mutual recognition, European standards) have emerged to deal with policy problems, limitations and new problems have been exposed. However, the consequence has not been a radical re-structuring but an incremental process of increasing institutional complexity: the addition of new approaches rather than the replacement or removal of past strategies. This is clearest in the Commission's failed attempt to radically overhaul the European standardisation system.

In one sense, however, there has been a fundamental change, and that has been at the level of the norms which guide the governance regime. The sort of jurisdictional approach taken both by the Commission and the ECJ in the early phase of the regime sought to transfer regulatory policy-making away from the nation state to the EC level. Carried to its logical conclusion, the EEC Treaty would have become less of a framework for action and more of a dense code of rules fleshed out by legislative provisions. Our study indicates that even in an area that is central to the functioning of the internal market, the EC institutions have stopped short of such a wholesale transfer of power. Disparities between national rules remain and Member States have retained some level of control over regulatory policy. However, the space which is occupied by Member States is one which is supervised within the framework of the EU. Thus, the technical harmonisation regime has evolved from one imbued by the norm of direct EU control to one imbued by ideas of EU supervision and surveillance. We conclude with the suggestion that this normative evolution has arisen as a consequence of institutional learning and exploration.

Notes

1   JO L13 (19.1.70), 29. 'Measures having equivalent effect to quantitative restrictions' is the terminology used in Article 30, EC to describe barriers to the free movement of goods.
2   Case 8/74, *Procureur du Roi* v. *Dassonville* [1974] ECR 837.
3   For example, in Case 60/86, *Commission* v. *United Kingdom (Dim-Dip)* [1988] ECR 3921, the ECJ held that the Community's approach to the technical harmonisation of motor vehicles preempted the adoption of the 'dim-dip' lighting system by the UK.
4   Case 120/78, *Rewe-Zentral AC* v. *Bundesmonopolverwaltung für Branntwein* [1979] ECR 649.
5   OJ C256 (3.10.80), 2.
6   Sources are CEN and CENELEC Annual Reports.
7   In Case C-41/93, *France* v. *Commission* [1994] ECR I-1829, France successfully challenged the Commission decision permitting the continued application of the German law. It was argued that the Commission had failed in its obligation to give sufficient reasons for its decision. However, the Commission reconsidered the German request and it is understood that the Commission has now given a reasoned explanation for its decision to permit Germany to continue to apply its national law.
8   OJ L109 (26.4.83), 8 (subsequently amended).
9   Directive 94/10/EC amending Directive 83/189/EEC, OJ L100 (19.4.94), 30.
10 OJ C117 (11.5.89), 1.
11 Council Directive 90/387/EEC on the establishment of the internal market for telecommunications services through the implementation of open network provision: OJ L192 (24.7.90), 1.
12 *The Future of European Standardization*: the British Standards Institute's response to the European Commission Green Paper.
13 OJ C173 (9.7.92), 1–2.

14   The figures for CEN are those at the end of 1995, whereas those for CENELEC are from January 1996.
15   It is interesting that the Commission identifies European standards as an 'alternative to regulation' as a means of connecting its standardisation policy with the application of the subsidiarity debate. Further, it also connects standardisation with the promotion of a 'European Quality Policy', responding to the White Paper on *Growth, Competitiveness, Employment* (CEC 1993c).
16   OJ C136 (4.6.85), 1.
17   OJ C10 (16.1.90), 1.
18   Council Decision 93/465/EEC, OJ L220 (30.8.93), 23.
19   Council Directive 93/68/EEC, OJ L220 (30.8.93), 1.
20   Originally, the Commission had proposed a Regulation concerning the affixing of the CE mark. This proposal met with an objection from the Council which pointed to the Declaration annexed to the SEA which states that in the use of Article 100a, preference is to be given to the instrument of the directive. Accordingly, the Commission withdrew its proposed Regulation and replaced this with a Directive and Decision.

7

Air transport liberalisation

Introduction

This chapter is concerned with the liberalisation of air transport within the EU. Until the end of the 1970s the EC had played no role in the regulation of air transport, and its initial efforts in the early 1980s were very modest. On 1 April 1997, however, a fully liberalised set of European rules on access, fares and airline competition was in operation, with the Commission playing a key regulatory role. How this dramatic transformation came about is the subject of this chapter. Initially we look at how the problem was constructed: institutionally and in terms of global developments in the airline industry. In the second part of the chapter, we undertake an analysis of the politics of negotiating the three packages of liberalisation. Negotiation of the packages brought about the construction of a governance regime for air transport liberalisation out of three theretofore disconnected parts of EC activity: EC transport policy; the single market initiative; and competition policy. In the final part of the chapter we examine the character of the governance regime, and how it has developed since the passage of the legislation.

On the face of it, an alliance of liberalisers 'won' in the negotiations but the political and regulatory struggle has now moved to other issues, most notably competition policy: the possible subversion of a single aviation market through state subsidies, and the need to regulate against the emergence of airlines with a dominant position in the EU market-place. In addition, airport and air traffic congestion threaten to restrict the benefits of liberalisation.

Identifying the regulatory issue

There are at least three plausible ways of understanding regulatory change in the context of EC air transport.

- A functionalist explanation based on the international dynamics of the *air transport sector* would emphasise a sectoral 'logic' to integration. It would see European liberalisation as part of a pattern originating with the Airline Deregulation Act of 1978 in the USA. Although of limited direct impact upon the European aviation scene, US de-regulation influenced the UK government's national civil aviation policy during the 1980s. Moreover, the UK was a prime mover in the negotiation of bilateral liberalising agreements with a number of fellow Member States that, in turn, paved the way for subsequent EC-wide regulatory change.

- A second perspective would be to examine liberalisation in the context of *EC transport policy*. Despite its prominence in the 1957 Treaty of Rome, transport was very much a cinderella policy. By the early 1980s the policy had produced few concrete results due to Member State resistance. However, pressures gradually began to build up to develop transport policy. Not least amongst these were the decisions of the ECJ that clarified the application of competition policy rules to air transport.

- A third approach to air transport liberalisation is to interpret it as part of the single market package. At first sight this might appear somewhat perverse. Why should air transport – the responsibility of DG VII – be connected with a programme centred on a quite separate part of the Commission, namely DG III (as was then the case)? One important factor was that air transport regulation became part of the broader neo-liberal developments that influenced certain member governments, most notably Mrs Thatcher's in the UK and its support for the internal market initiative. At the level of economic ideas, therefore, regulatory change in air transport was seen as having the same objectives as the internal market programme more widely: with opening up market access; removing regulatory burdens; and increasing welfare through more competitive markets. Further, the Commission saw these developments as fitting its institutional 'mission': of breathing life into a moribund part of the Rome Treaty; of enhancing the EC's internal transport and communications network; and of extending its own regulatory authority.

It is this third interpretation which is offered here, although not to the exclusion of global developments in air transport. It recognises the fact that air transport liberalisation was subject to many of the same dynamics and thinking which were behind the internal market programme. It also takes into account the fact that air transport regulation was mentioned, albeit weakly, in the White Paper (CEC 1985a: paras 109–111).

The chapter deals with the liberalisation of access and fares in intra-EC passenger air transport, as well as the progressive application of EC competition rules. There are various other policy issues related to airline regulation which we cannot place at the centre of the case study, although they are closely related.

- The internal market in air transport has an external counterpart: the regulatory arrangements for EC–third country air transport, including with key markets, such as the USA, and near-neighbours, such as the central and eastern European countries, the Member States of the EEA and Switzerland. Global airlines like British Airways and Lufthansa are naturally as interested in international rules on air transport as in the European ones.

- The progressive application of the competition rules outlined here chiefly concerns the regulation of inter-airline cooperation on fares, capacity-sharing and ticketing. However, there are other important competition issues which are not central to liberalisation or only became so after agreement on the third package in 1992. These are: regulating the fair provision of information (schedules and fares) to travel agents through Computer Reservation Systems; regulating the ownership of precious take-off and landing slots at congested airports; ensuring that airline restructuring does not create dominant airlines through M&A activity (governed by the MCR discussed in Chapter 4); and ensuring that government aid to airlines does not distort competition.

Air transport liberalisation is thus located in a wider set of industry dynamics and regulatory issues. What, then, was the shape of European airline regulation prior to liberalisation?

Structure of the European airline industry prior to liberalisation
Until liberalisation gained momentum in the 1980s the EC was virtually irrelevant to regulating air transport. Regulation was achieved internationally under the auspices of the International Civil Aviation Organisation (ICAO) and bilaterally between pairs of states. Within the European context the appropriate agency was the European Civil Aviation Conference (ECAC), comprising twenty-two countries until recent expansion following the end of the Cold War. The ECAC's membership seemed more appropriate for overseeing European air transport regulation.

The European air transport market predominantly comprises international traffic, the core of which is intra-European. Domestic air transport is of less importance and in some Member States, such as Belgium, non-existent for geographical reasons. As a consequence of this situation there was little scope for individual states to obtain significant benefits from domestic liberalisation. Indeed, the domestic arrangements were themselves quite closely controlled because of intermodal considerations, chiefly the protection of national, state-owned railway networks. Intra-European air transport was subject to bilateral regulation: between Member States and between pairs of airlines. Thus, both domestic and intra-European air transport were highly regulated. There was one area of the industry where greater liberalisation was in operation, namely in respect of charter flights, chiefly to help the tourist industry. In 1985 international non-scheduled flights between ECAC member countries amounted to no less than 42 per cent of the total passenger-kilometres flown (see OECD 1988).[1]

The character of the European air transport sector was quite different from that prevailing in the USA, whether before or after de-regulation.[2] There, the vast majority of airline flights are domestic. Accordingly, sovereignty is not at stake. Furthermore, intermodal competition is limited in the USA and is thus not a regulatory consideration. Moreover, on domestic services the USA had nothing to compare with the European state-owned and sub-sidised 'flag-carrier'. Finally, there was negligible charter traffic. The more straightforward character of the US airline sector enabled the Carter Administration to liberalise domestic air transport in 1978 at one fell swoop.

With its greater complexity, and greater international character, the European air transport industry was more difficult to liberalise. An entrenched regime of international and bilateral regulation had to be reformed. The origins of international civil aviation regulation lie in the 1944 Chicago Convention, which created the ICAO to monitor the technical, legal and operational aspects of international air transport. The pattern for regulating international air services bilaterally was through agreements modelled on the one agreed between the USA and the UK in 1946, known as the Bermuda Agreement.

This regulatory framework gave rise to the so-called five 'freedoms of the skies', based upon the assumption that a nation state has sovereignty over its airspace.[3] The first four freedoms have formed the basis of international air transport in Europe and elsewhere; only with fifth freedom rights do circumstances go beyond bilateralism. They involve an airline having the right to convey paying passengers from a second to a third country but were exceptional prior to liberalisation.

The basic method of developing these freedoms was on a bilateral basis between governments. Issues such as fares and capacity were largely determined by the pair of airlines concerned. The inter-airline bilateral conferences were held under the auspices of the International Air Transport Association (IATA), to which the flag-carriers and other major international airlines have traditionally belonged. The IATA has acted largely as a self-regulatory agency under the supervision of national authorities.

The structure of the European airline industry was very much the product of these regulatory arrangements. Each state had an airline which performed the role of 'preferred vehicle' of national air transport policy (Button and Swann 1989: 265); it was almost invariably in state ownership and in receipt of state subsidies. During the period of liberalisation, British Airways was the only such EC 'flag-carrier' wholly in private ownership (privatisation in 1987), while a majority of the Dutch flag-carrier, KLM, was in private ownership. All other flag-carriers were in some form of state ownership. These airlines were very influential insiders in national air transport policy-making.

Of course, the airline industry did not merely consist of such flag-carriers. Three other types of passenger carrier may be mentioned:

- A second group of smaller airlines offered predominantly domestic but in some instances also international services. In the former category were Air Inter (France) or ATI (Italy). In the latter category was UTA (France), whilst British Caledonian (UK) had a mix of both. Although France and the UK had more than one carrier, there was scarcely any competition between them on individual routes.
- A third category of airlines was largely confined to charter operations, such as Britannia Airways (UK), Condor (Germany) or Sobelair (Belgium): the last two of these being wholly-owned subsidiaries of the respective national flag-carrier.
- A fourth category of regional airline was emerging, chiefly operating turboprop airliners of up to 50/60 seat capacity, such as Loganair (UK), Netherlines (Holland) and Delta Air (Germany). These airlines overwhelmingly flew domestic or 'thin', often inter-regional, routes.

In short, prior to EC liberalisation the European airline industry was characterised by nine factors (see Box 7.1). One commentator summarised

Box 7.1: The key characteristics of intra-EC international air transport in the preliberalisation period

---

- Member states licensed airlines owned and controlled by their nationals.
- Member states licensed international air services bilaterally.
- Only one airline from each state was permitted to fly each international route (and the points that could be served were specified in the bilateral agreements). Commission data indicate that of 988 intra-EC airline routes only 48 had multiple designation, i.e. beyond the two airlines (CEC 1988c). The same data indicate that only 88 of those routes permitted fifth freedom rights.
- Capacity was usually split on as close to a 50/50 basis as the two airline fleets permitted.
- There was a 50/50 revenue split between the two airlines regardless of the pattern of revenue receipts. This meant that improvements in in-flight service would not benefit the airline concerned.
- Fares were decided on a bilateral basis by the airlines, subject only to ratification by the national regulatory authorities.
- Normally, designated airlines were partially or wholly under state ownership.
- State-owned airlines were in many cases in receipt of state subsidies of various types and/or had their operating losses written off.
- Bilateral agreements between states authorised non-scheduled flights catering for the tourist trade.

---

the situation thus: 'probably no other worldwide economic activity of importance is more thoroughly regulated, less free of official restraint and guidance, than is air transport' (Lisstzyn, quoted by Barrett 1987: 6). This begs the question: why was the situation thus? In essence, governments had a tight control over 'their' airlines, and for a range of reasons: the national flag-carrying airline as symbol of national pride and identity; the consumer interest; public-service obligations; industrial policy interests; tourism or employment (Wheatcroft and Lipman 1986: 36).

To market economists this state of affairs clearly resulted in a poor allocation of resources on three counts:

- collusion between carriers resulted in limited consumer choice;
- non-price competition meant that advertising wasted resources, a factor encouraged by widespread revenue-sharing between airlines; and
- the limits on market access facilitated rent-seeking behavior on the parts of suppliers of labour and of services, such as ground handling (Barrett 1987: 11).

Doubtless these were important factors leading to the Commission's conclusion in 1979 that those costs under enterprises' control were some 20 per cent higher than in the USA (CEC 1979). Nevertheless, the deficiencies of the existing system were not recognised universally. The director general of civil aviation in France commented that 'the cooperative aspects of regulation have fostered an efficient air transport system, ensured that safety is not jeopardised and allowed complementary services to be set up amongst various categories of carriers' (quoted in Wheatcroft and Lipman 1986: 38).

This broad pattern of regulatory arrangements and consequent poor resource allocation prevailed on an EC-wide basis until 1988. However, some significant developments did begin to take place both bilaterally and multilaterally, and these were important to the gathering momentum within the EC context. The American domestic experience had repercussions in a quintessentially international industry. In the late-1970s Sir Freddie Laker launched an assault on the regulation of transatlantic travel with his low walk-on 'Skytrain' fares from the UK.[4] This high-profile venture alerted British consumers to the potential benefits of liberalisation.

The British Conservative government was a prime mover in developments. In its 1984 White Paper on Competition in Air Transport it removed legislative barriers to entry and to the setting of fares in domestic air transport.[5] It then shifted attention to efforts at bilateral liberalisation. The result was a set of limited liberalising measures agreed between 1984 and 1987, commencing with an Anglo-Dutch agreement but leading on to agreements with Germany, Belgium, Luxembourg and Ireland. In these cases barriers to entry were lowered and greater flexibility on tariffs was permitted, albeit with varying degrees of success (Doganis 1991: 79–82; McGowan and Seabright 1989: 298–99).

There was one other source of pressure for liberalisation and, crucially, it was multilateral and European: namely the ECAC (see Wheatcroft and Lipman 1986: 45–8). The ECAC investigated the character of European air transport, and the resultant 1982 report on Competition in Air Services – the COMPAS report – recommended the adoption of measures to open up route entry, reduce capacity constraints and liberalise pricing. This report shaped the European agenda and helped make the Member States more receptive to the liberalisation policies which had already taken hold in the UK. Hence, although it received a mixed response, it was an important source of ideas for the Commission's 1984 proposals which were taken up in the Cockfield White Paper.

The emergence of regulation by the EC

Title IV of the Treaty of Rome was dedicated to transport policy. Its Article 84 stated that 'The Council may, acting unanimously, decide whether, to what extent and by what procedure appropriate provisions may be laid down for sea and air transport.' This article provided a very limited legal base for air transport regulation: there was not even an invitation for the Commission to submit proposals.

During the negotiation of the Treaty of Rome the Transport Title had been extremely contentious, the provisions being hotly contested between liberal and interventionist states (Abbati 1987: 29–41). The result was a hurriedly drafted set of articles with a lack of clarity as to their meaning. Experts on air and sea transport had not been involved in negotiations. So, when agreement was finally reached on how to cover other modes of transport, and with a pressing need to conclude negotiations, air and sea transport were excluded from the general provisions of Title IV. Article 84 resembles an afterthought (Abbati 1987: 31, 38). Thus it was in part a product of the institutional profile of the negotiating teams that air transport was in this weak situation.

The situation was exacerbated by the limited European legislation on transport policy generally. In 1962 the Council of Ministers specifically *exempted* air and sea transport from the competition rules, through Regulation 141/62, pending the development of an air transport policy (Argyris 1989: 6). The situation was 'the Rome Treaty at bay' (Button and Swann 1989: 269). However, in a 1974 ruling the ECJ began to chip away at the notion that the two modes were excluded from the general rules of the Treaty.[6] This development led the Commission to reconsider matters and, in 1979, it set out its broad objectives for air transport policy in what is known as Memorandum No. 1 (CEC 1979). It was only at this time (1979) that the Commission established an air transport policy unit within DG VII.

Memorandum No. 1 contained some fairly modest suggestions relating to liberalisation of services: for instance, to encourage cheaper fares and better service provision between the regional airports of the EC. The suggestions were low-key but did stimulate three items of proposed legislation: on promoting inter-regional air services; applying the competition rules to air transport; and liberalising the bilateral system of approving fares.[7] None of these was immediately to lead to legislation because Member States questioned both whether the EC should regulate air transport and the substance of the (very modest) moves to liberalise the sector. However, for a historical institutionalist analysis the important factor was that the Commission had placed a marker: it wished to initiate policy in the area. Essentially, this phase of policy development, lasting from 1979 to 1986, was concerned with agenda-setting.

Setting the agenda
Guy Peters has pointed out that 'the exact social and political construction of the issue is as important to the final determination of how the issue will be processed and decided as is the initial decision to consider it at all' (1994: 10). In this sense the character of the first items of agreed legislation was unilluminating. The first piece of legislation agreed – in 1983 on inter-regional air services – was very weak.[8] It was only of minor significance, for the possibilities of generating economic benefits on international routes between regional airports was very limited. However, on a symbolic level it represented the first departure on the part of the EC from the traditional bilateral/international regulatory approach.

Having achieved this first step, and with the COMPAS report's findings available, the Commission produced Memorandum No. 2 on Air Transport (CEC 1984). This document was a much more ambitious statement of Commission intentions to create a single market in air transport. It was a clear statement that the route ahead was towards liberalisation, albeit not towards American-style de-regulation. The approach would be progressive so as to achieve the twin long-term goals of market liberalisation and market integration. Three areas were given particular emphasis, namely tariffs, capacity and competition. On the first it was proposed to loosen regulatory arrangements and enable greater flexibility by ending the situation whereby fares were subject to the approval of both sets of national authorities. Secondly, on capacity, it was proposed to end the predominant pattern of the 50/50 split by creating greater flexibility. Thirdly, there was legislation for introducing the EEC Treaty's competition rules to the air transport sector.

The Commission had made its contribution to the 'social and political construction of the issue', at least within the transport policy context. What were the sources of other inputs into the agenda-setting phase? We can divide these sources into two categories: those exogenous and those endogenous to the EC institutional structure.

The exogenous influences derived from:

- increasing awareness of the ideas behind, and character of reform relating to, US de-regulation;
- the domestic and then bilateral reforms introduced by the UK government, 1984–87; and
- the impact of the COMPAS report within the framework of the ECAC.

There were five endogenous influences, as follows:

- The EP had provided some limited publicity to the possibilities of liberalisation. Lord Bethell, the British MEP, led a campaign for the 'freedom of the skies'. In 1981 he sought to have the Commission take action against a number of European airlines for anti-competitive behaviour.[9] This action was disallowed, but only on procedural grounds. Sir Freddie Laker, with characteristic flamboyance, took advantage of the campaign to press for the right to operate services to no less than 666 points in Europe!
- A much more important development was the incorporation of aviation liberalisation measures in the Cockfield White Paper (CEC 1985a), adopted at the June 1985 European Council. By taking up the proposals of Memorandum No. 2 (and some relating to other aspects of transport policy), the Commission gave them greater importance and the stronger idea of a single aviation market came about. In consequence, it would thenceforth be very difficult for the opponents of liberalisation. Obstructionism might be feasible if air transport could be 'ring-fenced' as transport policy. However, once absorbed into the broader dynamics of the single market, with the 1992 deadline, the internal market 'logic' to liberalising air transport was a major factor in assisting reform.
- An important development was the ECJ's ruling in *Nouvelles Frontières* that the competition rules should in fact apply to air transport.[10] The case was of considerable importance in further developing a twin-track approach towards liberalisation. The first track consisted of establishing a new set of rules on market access and behaviour. The second track centred on whether the existing, bilateral regulatory arrangements outlined above were contrary to European competition policy. The importance of the April 1986 *Nouvelles Frontières* judgment was that it provided just such a decision. The judgment fitted in with the evolving jurisprudence of the ECJ, building upon its 1974 judgment in the 'French merchant seamen' case and on its 1986 ruling in *European Parliament* v. *Council* that the latter had failed to carry out its transport policy treaty obligations in certain respects.[11]

  The impact of the ruling was similar to the situation regarding merger control after the *Philip Morris* case (see Chapter 4): there was a regulatory vacuum which could only be clarified by filling the void through legislation. For those Member States which had hoped that Memorandum No. 2 might take many years to implement, if at all, this new situation came as a rude awakening, for the procedural arrangements had been reversed. Legislation was now necessary *to restrict* the applicability of the competition rules. Tactically, this gave the initiative to the protagonists of liberalisation, namely the governments favouring such a step, the Commission, some elements within the EP and consumers (see below). The Commission was quick to try to test its new powers confirmed in the *Nouvelles Frontières* judgment. As Nicholas Argyris, the former Head of Division for Transport and Tourism in DG IV, points out, as early as June 1986 the Commission had charged ten airlines with infringements of the competition rules. These proceedings under Article 89 were not formally dropped until legislation came into effect at the start of 1988 (see Argyris 1989; Naveau 1992: 41–2). The interaction between the legal process and policy-making was of crucial importance to the construction of the policy agenda.

- The SEA had been signed in February 1986 and came into effect from July 1987. Under Article 16 of the SEA, Article 84 of the Treaty of Rome was amended, moving from unanimity to QMV in the Council on air and maritime transport policy. This development would make it more difficult for one or two governments to block liberalising legislation.
- Finally, the UK government was keen to promote liberalisation of the industry and gave this goal strong emphasis at a critical stage, during its presidency in the second half of 1986. The UK presidency was followed conveniently by that of the Netherlands, the other main government advocating liberalisation. Liberalisation had gained such momentum that the first package could be agreed in 1987, albeit under the Belgian presidency following a dispute over whether the legislation should include Gibraltar.

It was against this background, therefore, that the Commission developed its programme of legislation to liberalise air transport. This programme culminated in three packages, agreed in 1987, 1990 and 1992 respectively.

Constructing the rules for a single aviation market

Despite the exogenous and endogenous dynamics towards liberalisation, there were many vested interests sustaining the existing arrangements: vested interests on the part of the industry organisations, individual airlines, national governments, trade unions, outlying regional communities of Member States and so on. Hence the elaboration of the legislation was to be highly politicised.

Economic actors

Three principal categories of non-governmental actors can be identified: airlines, consumers and employee representatives. Several European-level interest organisations within each category as well as individual airlines were acting as lobbies.

The airlines are represented in three interest groups. The major group is the Association of European Airlines (AEA), traditionally comprising the European flag-carriers although its membership is not confined to the EC/EU Member States.[12] The AEA had to reconcile a spectrum of views from state-owned airlines resistant to liberalisation (for example, Olympic of Greece) to those more favourably disposed (such as British Airways or KLM). The second major group is ACE, l'Association des Compagnies Aériennes de la Communauté Européenne, representing the important European charter airline sector (ACE 1991; 1992). This group included both private airlines and the charter subsidiaries of flag-carriers. The third group, the least significant of the three, was the European Regional Airlines Association (ERA). As its title indicated, it represented around 20 smaller regional carriers: a growth sector but one especially susceptible to volatility (new carriers, bankruptcies). The ERA seeks to remind the Commission of the importance of European inter-regional services.

Finally, it is worth mentioning that one or two airlines were outside any interest group – at least at the time the legislation was being agreed. Perhaps the most important of these was the UK carrier, British Midland. It has been prominent in seeking to capitalise on European liberalisation through offering competitive service and fares, having developed this approach by entering into competition with British Airways on key domestic routes following UK domestic liberalisation in 1984. It sought membership of the AEA but was refused admission until 1993 (*European Report*, No. 1873, 7 July 1993: III/1). Neither a charter nor a regional airline, it had to operate as lobbyist in Brussels in its own right during the negotiations on liberalisation. Since its track-record was identified with the kinds of benefits that the Commission hoped for on a Europe-wide basis, namely increased choice and price-competition, its views were listened to in the Commission. This situation ran counter to the Commission's usual practice of preferring to consult transnational interest groups. Individual flag-carrying airlines, such as British Airways, also sought to present their views to the Commission, British Airways being concerned that its views were diluted within the AEA. Air France was another airline with its own representative in Brussels (Kassim 1995: 199).

Two groups of consumer interests were active in negotiations, and were supportive of liberalisation: the Bureau Européen des Unions des Consommateurs, BEUC (the most active), and the International Organisation of Consumers' Unions (IOCU), based in The Hague. The UK Consumers' Association was prominent in the work of both.

A different form of European lobby group developed during the 1980s, based around the interests of air transport users, and with strong British input. Distinctively in the EC, the UK possessed a relatively autonous regulatory agency for aviation policy: the Civil Aviation Authority (CAA). The CAA had sponsored the Air Transport Users' Committee, created in 1973 to represent users' views. In 1982 a similar interest group was set up at supranational level: the Federation of Air Transport Users' Representatives in the EC (FATUREC). Based in London, it shares organisational resources with its UK counterpart.

Finally, in the realm of ideas rather than interest groups, two British 'think tanks' – the Trade Policy Research Centre and the Adam Smith Institute – produced reports supporting liberalisation (discussed in Wheatcroft and Lipman 1986: 76–7; also Barrett 1987). These reports, together with the work of Lord Bethell's 'Freedom of the Skies' campaign and the pressure for lower airfares in *Business Traveller* magazine, helped promote the ideas of liberalisation.

On the employees' side, two bodies were involved in a limited way on the liberalisation issue: the European Cockpit Association, representing senior flight crew; and the trade union body, the Committee of Transport Workers' Unions. These and other groups are more prominent on matters relating to working conditions in the industry. Nevertheless, they regarded as unwelcome within the EC context the way US de-regulation had lowered both wage rates and levels of unionisation in the airline industry.

It can be seen that the issue of air transport liberalisation was quite heavily populated by interest groups. However, it must be recalled that these groups were still at the initial stages of building contacts with the EC, since the latter had no real history of regulating the sector. Hence relations between groups and the EC institutions were very much in flux. It must also be recalled that lobbying at the national level remained important. In the overwhelming majority of Member States the state-owned flag-carrier had insider status in the national transport ministry. It was chiefly in the UK that the consumer interest and the views of scheduled airlines competing with the flag-carrier were listened to by government and the CAA.

The views of national governments
The UK government was the foremost supporter of liberalisation: reflecting the importance of the sector in the UK; the vibrance of its airline industry; the importance of London Heathrow as a transatlantic 'gateway' to Europe; the domestic attention given to the consumer lobby (see Wheatcroft and Lipman 1986: Ch. 6); and the Conservative government's ideological sympathy to airline de-regulation. The CAA was particularly exposed to the ideas of its main counterpart body, the US Federal Aviation Authority. Within the UK Nicholas Ridley's period as Secretary of State for Transport from 1983 to 1986 witnessed strong political emphasis upon

liberalisation, and this momentum helped pave the way for the Dutch and British presidencies of 1986, when the issue was actively pursued on the Council agenda (see Stevens 1997).

A grouping of other states – led by Germany and France – was prepared to entertain liberalisation but wanted it to be limited in nature. Until unification and the end of the Cold War there were limitations on Germany's air transport potential. Transport was regarded as a 'protected sector', exempt from competitive pressures (Esser 1995). The 'Iron Curtain' impeded the development of Frankfurt, the Federal Republic of Germany's principal airport, into a European gateway to the east. Moreover, the four-power agreements (between the USA, USSR, UK and France) determining Berlin's constitutional-legal status excluded Lufthansa from serving a major city in its potential network, Berlin. Independent airlines, such as German Wings, had failed to compete in the domestic market because of an inability to obtain prime-time take-off and landing slots and, with them, lucrative business patronage. Smaller scheduled airlines have, in consequence, operated from regional airports such as Nuremburg, Hamburg and so on. A conservative policy prevailed.

France had been an exponent of the 'preferred vehicle' approach, with Air Inter filling this role on domestic services, Air France on most international routes, and the private airline UTA operating to a smaller range of extra-European destinations, particularly in Africa.[13] Despite this apparent plurality of airlines, the principle of French aviation policy was one French carrier per route. A group of regional operators, such as TAT and Air Littoral, largely operated short-range services on behalf of Air France or Air Inter. Liberalisation would potentially present a radical challenge to the French industry; accordingly, the government was more conservative than its German counterpart.

Also falling into this group of (very) cautious supporters of liberalisation were the Belgians, Luxembourg and the Republic of Ireland. The UK government negotiated bilateral liberalisation agreements with each of these states in the mid-1980s. The Anglo-Irish market has been cited as one where clear and tangible benefits arose from liberalisation (McGowan and Seabright 1989: 299). The emergence of Ryanair as a competitor to Aer Lingus in the Anglo-Irish market in 1986 gave the Irish industry a foretaste of European liberalisation.

The third category comprised those countries opposed to liberalisation. These were the Mediterranean states (Greece, Spain and Italy) along with Portugal and Denmark. The Danish case was somewhat distinctive. It arose out of concern that Scandinavia's peripheral location would limit possible benefits, and of fears about the impact of EC regulation on the status of Scandinavian Airlines System (SAS) as a tri-national flag-carrier with Sweden and Norway. For the southern states, the situation was fairly clear. They had state-owned flag-carriers which were in some cases much less efficient than their northern counterparts. In addition, they had a number of public service obligations which were seen as warranting special arrangements: the Greek islands; the Balearics and Canaries (Spain); and Madeira and the Azores (Portugal). Routes to these communities either were cross-subsidised or losses were underwritten. The perceived threat to both of these practices discouraged the governments and flag-carriers from favouring liberalisation.

Behind the different national positions lay a set of domestic preferences influenced by interest groups and corporate actors. However, the EC's liberalisation policy was not simply the rational outcome of these national preferences along the lines set out by Moravcsik (1993). The autonomy of EC institutions played an important role too.

EC institutions, rules and norms
What is most surprising about this case study is that the Commission, supported by the rulings of the ECJ and by the British and Dutch governments, was able to completely transform the regulatory legislation well within a decade. The main challenge to an inter-governmentalist account, therefore, is: explaining the impact of the Commission and the ECJ upon the policy agenda; and explaining how the Commission saw the legislation through despite having the active support of only two governments (the British and Dutch). Moreover, most of the sector-specific interest groups resisted change as well!

The jurisprudence of the ECJ and the inclusion of air transport in the SEM programme had a catalysing effect, and the SEA's introduction of QMV provisions transformed the institutional rules and policy norms. The Commission shifted from hesitance to becoming a true initiator in the vanguard of European integration. DG VII drafted legislation proposing the regulatory arrangements for setting tariffs and so on. Meanwhile DG IV was engaged in drafting block exemptions from the competition rules to cover those areas of inter-airline cooperation that were seen in a positive light; everything else would be deemed 'suspect' and thus subject to action by the Commission under its competition powers. It is important to note the way in which the commissioner for competition, Peter Sutherland, reacted to the *Nouvelles Frontières* ruling and challenged the EC flag-cariers to prove their activities were not anti-competitive, e.g. by threats of legal action. Without any substantive change to its powers in the air transport sector, the whole 'culture' of the Commission was transformed into one of dynamism.

The shift from unanimity to QMV on air and maritime transport policy was important for thinking in the Council. Whilst provision for QMV does not always translate into its utilisation, for the convention in the Council is to seek consensus wherever possible, the effect was to weaken the position of the opponents of liberalisation. The procedural changes

Box 7.2: The principal legislation in the three packages of air transport liberalisation

---

Package 1 (14 December 1987)
Council Decision 602/87/EEC on capacity-sharing between carriers on scheduled air services between Member States and access for air carriers to scheduled intra-Community air service routes
Council Directive 601/87/EEC on fares for scheduled air services between Member States
Council Regulation 3975/87/EEC determining the application of EEC competition rules to undertakings in the air transport sector
Council Regulation 3976/87/EEC further concerning the application of EEC competition rules to certain categories of agreements and concerted practices in the air transport sector

Package 2 (24 July 1990)
Council Regulation 2342/90/EEC on fares for scheduled air services
Council Regulation 2343/90/EEC on access for air carriers to scheduled intra-Community air service routes and capacity-sharing between carriers on scheduled air services between Member States
Council Regulation 2344/90/EEC amending the application of EEC competition rules to certain categories of agreements and concerted practices in the air transport sector

Package 3 (23 July 1992)
Council Regulation 2407/92/EEC on licensing air carriers
Council Regulation 2408/92/EEC on access for EC air carriers to intra-Community air routes
Council Regulation 2409/92/EEC on fares and rates for air services
Council Regulation 2410/92/EEC amending the application of EEC competition rules to undertakings in the air transport sector
Council Regulation 2411/92/EEC further amending the application of EEC competition rules to certain categories of agreements and concerted practices in the air transport sector

---

under the SEA did not apply the cooperation procedure to air transport policy, so the EP was confined to giving its opinion on the legislation.

Negotiating the three packages
In broad terms there are features common to each of the three packages – summarised in Box 7.2 – and it is worth mentioning these at the outset. Each package has been based broadly on a three-pillar approach. The first

pillar concerned the regulation of tariffs; the second addressed bilateral arrangements on market access and capacity-sharing; and the third related to the application of EC competition rules to air transport. As the liberalisation process developed, so the scope and impact of the measures widened. Thus the first package (1987) set out the principles and the foundations for EC liberalisation. The second package (1990) extended these through a set of interim arrangements. And finally, the third package (1992) embodied the positive law of the single market in air transport (Naveau 1992: 52). A change in the scope of the legislation occurred as the packages evolved. Originally aimed at liberalising *international* passenger air transport within the EC, by the end of the process legislation related to *all* passenger air transport within the EC: whether international or domestic. The principal explanation for this extension of scope derived from a further major judgment of the ECJ, in the *Ahmed Saeed* case (see below).

The first package   The origin of the first package lay in the proposals contained in the Commission's 1984 Memorandum No. 2 on air transport (CEC 1984). As Box 7.2 indicates, the package comprised four measures, of which two related to competition policy aspects. These measures were agreed by the Council of Transport Ministers on 14 December 1987, and took effect at the start of the following year. What were the main features of the first package?

- The Fares Directive reduced national/bilateral regulatory procedures for fares, facilitating the introduction of lower tariffs.
- The Capacity-sharing and Access Decision ended the traditional pattern whereby national authorities presided over the 50/50 sharing of route capacity between one airline from each pair of states. A phased widening of the share, to 60/40, was permitted. At the same time, the principle of multi-designation was introduced, enabling routes to be flown by more than one airline from each of the pair of states. The Decision also enabled some limited extension of fifth freedom rights but restricted through regional airports. On this basis, Aer Lingus routed some of its 'thinner' services through Manchester, enabling it to pick up passengers for Paris, Zürich and other continental destinations.
- The two Council Regulations determined what practices should be exempt from EC competition policy, for instance to enable passengers to re-book between airlines and to enable airlines to share scheduling information between reservation systems. Anti-competitive behaviour not covered by block exemptions would be subject to the full rigour of competition policy, with fines of up to 10 per cent of company turnover (see Green *et al.* 1991: Part III).[14]

Bargaining within the Council largely corresponded to the national governments' positions outlined earlier. Specific sticking-points arose in two areas. Some Member States were reluctant to proceed to opening up fifth freedom rights. This issue was resolved by confining such rights to regional airports rather than through 'Category 1' airports.[15] Special deals on fifth freedom access were secured by Spain, Ireland and Portugal. A further area of controversy concerned the status of Gibraltar Airport. Sovereignty is disputed over the territory where Gibraltar Airport is located and, despite bilateral Anglo-Spanish efforts to find a *modus vivendi*, the package was only able to proceed on the basis that Gibraltar Airport was considered to be outside the scope of the legislation. This situation continued to prevail in 1992, when the third package was agreed. The package was adopted on the basis of consensus despite the formal provision for QMV.

Before the second package was agreed, a further major ECJ ruling affected the liberalisation process, namely the *Ahmed Saeed* judgment of April 1989. EC competition rules were held additionally to relate to international air transport *between EC members and non-Member States* as well as to *domestic travel within Member States*. This judgment clearly paved the way for increased supranational regulation just as earlier ECJ rulings had done.[16]

The second package   The second package, comprising three Council Regulations, was a modest, interim step in the liberalisation process (see Naveau 1992: 71–4; van de Voorde 1992: 518–19). Conditions for the setting of tariffs were relaxed in the Fares Regulation; capacity-sharing was further relaxed, with both fifth freedom and multi-designation rights being extended; finally, block exemptions from competition policy were continued but in modified form. One new feature introduced in the second package was the possibility for a Member State to declare a regional route to be subject to a public-service obligation. The Azores, the Greek Islands and Porto continued to enjoy temporary exemptions from the access and capacity-sharing legislation. The legislation included a clear commitment that cabotage rights were to be an integral part of liberalisation . . . but not until the next package! Under cabotage, it becomes possible for British Airways to convey fare-paying passengers between two points in another Member State, say between Paris and Lyon. The second package was modest but maintained the momentum towards liberalisation.

The third package   The third package was to be the final stage towards creating a single market in air transport. The package comprised five measures (see Box 7.2), agreed from Commission proposals. All five included the regulation of domestic travel within Member States, following the logic of the *Ahmed Saeed* judgment and logic of the goal of a single market. However, the regulation of international air transport between the EC Member States and non-Member States was not incorporated in the third package and has still not been agreed.

- The Licensing Regulation of the third package was important because it also reflected the logic of an internal market. It represented re-regulation at the supranational level to bring about the freedoms of establishment and to provide services. Thus the measure was designed to provide a common standard for issuing an operator's licence EC-wide; to allow unrestricted, cross-border, intra-EC investment; and to enable an airline controlled by EC nationals the freedom to provide services anywhere in the Community. Operating requirements – for instance, the demonstration of financial fitness – would be subject to uniform regulation across the Member States.

  The other four legislative drafts were essentially concerned with how to regulate air transport from 1993. Should fares and access be left to market forces, as overwhelmingly had been the case with US deregulation? Or should a more cautious approach be adopted, as suggested by the trade unions and some flag-carriers? Further, should the competition rules be applied more rigorously, and should the Commission have greater discretion in implementing them? These positions were articulated by consumer interests: by the International Organisation of Consumers' Unions (IOCU) and the UK Consumers' Associations (IOCU 1991; Consumers' Association 1991). They were also advanced by the users' group FATUREC (FATUREC 1991).

- The Fares Regulation established a regime that was based on the principle of automatic approval of fares, but with safeguards against excessively high prices as well as against a ruinous downward spiral (see Articles 6 and 7 of Regulation 2409/92/EEC for details). The Council overturned the Commission's original proposals for regulating fares on the grounds that they were excessively bureaucratic and that there were doubts about the Commission's ability to resolve disputes. The Fares Regulation subjected charter carriers to EC legislation for the first time, enabling their rates to be set freely and with all restictions on their sale being removed. ACE, the non-scheduled carriers' group, had lobbied to ensure that its member airlines would not be disadvantaged (ACE 1991; 1992).

- The Access Regulation abolished capacity-sharing, a feature of bilateral airline regulation that had no place in a fully liberalised regime. The Commission's starting position in the negotiations had been to press for total liberalisation of access (see Article 3 of its proposed Regulation in CEC 1991a: 45). In this aspiration it was supported by consumer interests (IOCU 1991; Consumers' Association 1991). The aim was to include 'seventh freedom' and cabotage rights. The seventh freedom right refers to the right for an airline registered in country A to fly passengers between countries B and C. Thus, British Airways, for instance, could run free-standing, commercial services between Stuttgart and Thessaloniki (as it now does). Cabotage relates to an airline from country A flying *domestic* services within country B. Thus, British Airways could run free-standing, commercial services between Paris and Lyon.

This proposal was at once radical but merely consistent with a single market in air transport. However, it was not favourably received by all the flag-carriers represented in the AEA, where the majority position favoured a transition period of two–three years (AEA 1991). Given the flag-carriers' access to 'their' governments, the support for phased introduction was reflected in the member governments too: even though they had agreed to the principle of full liberalisation in the Access Regulation in the second package. Only six states were prepared to accept seventh freedom services (the UK, Germany, Ireland, Belgium, Luxembourg and the Netherlands). On cabotage rights, the same protagonists existed with the exception of Germany. Greece, Spain and Portugal were quick to point out that their geographical circumstances necessitated special arrangements. Council negotiations sought to find a consensus between the various national positions. The following compromise solution was arrived at: First, fifth freedom rights were fully liberalised. Secondly, seventh freedom rights were to be introduced from 1993. Thirdly, 'add-on' cabotage would be possible from the same date. Thus Lufthansa currently operates a domestic British service between Birmingham and Newcastle as an additional leg of a flight to and from Germany. To achieve this agreement the principal opponents of full liberalisation received concessions. Full, 'free-standing' cabotage was postponed until April 1997. Greece and Portugal were given five-year exemptions from some of the rules.

A further area of debate concerned making certain routes subject to a public-service obligation (PSO) to mitigate the effects of full liberalisation. This was permitted for routes to airports in a peripheral region but subject to a clear set of procedures. These included the need to advertise for tenders in the *Official Journal*, as well as ensuring that subsidies on such routes were transparent and in accordance with state aid rules (Articles 92 and 93). This step represented a tightening of the operating conditions of a PSO route compared to the second package.

Two other specific arrangements in the Access Regulation are worth mentioning. First, charter services were included in the access legislation for the first time. Secondly, certain safeguard measures were built in, for instance to restrict traffic for environmental or congestion reasons, provided this is done in a non-discriminatory way.[17]

- The Commission had several objectives in its proposed Regulations on competition rules. First, and consistent with the *Ahmed Saeed* judgment, it wished to extend the purview of the competition rules to domestic air transport.[18] A second objective was to increase the extent to which the competition rules applied to the EC airline industry. The effect of the legislation was to enable Article 86 to be used by the Commission to regulate the abuse of dominant positions, whilst also permitting Article 85 to be used against anti-competitive agreements between companies. The consumers' and users' organisations wanted to ensure that the competition rules would be utilised vigorously so as to avoid the emergence of 'mega-carriers', such as had happened in the USA (Consumers' Association 1991). The national flag-carriers took the opposite view. They wanted the greater stability of block exemptions being granted for an indefinite period rather than the Commission's proposal of renewable short-term arrangements. The compromise was a long-term agreement on more narrowly defined principles for block exemptions. However, the Commission secured its third objective, namely to have increased freedom to legislate on the precise form of the exemptions, using its important regulatory powers in the competition policy domain.

The third package was the culmination of a liberalisation process which went much further than had been anticipated when it was included in the internal market White Paper. That this was so is testimony to the interaction of the legal and policy-making processes, and to the ability of the Commission to use its slender resources. The supranational institutions (the Commission and the ECJ) played a central role in securing major regulatory change. They ensured something approaching *de*-regulation in respect of access and fare-setting on intra-EC and domestic air transport. Moreover, the EC emerged to regulate the policy area from a situation where it previously had no authority whatsoever. In that sense the reforms led to major *re*-regulation at the supranational level. This development was perhaps the most dramatic amongst our case studies, representing a complete turnaround in a ten-year period.

Historical institutionalist analysis
What specific insights may be obtained from new institutionalism?

* How did air transport liberalisation fit in with *systemic change*? Did the member governments willingly authorise, by treaty, what actually happened? The answer is: emphatically, no. The circumstances in aviation policy in 1957 were completely different, and the references to liberalisation in the internal market White Paper were modest and quite vague. The only specific agreement was in the SEA, namely to introduce QMV for Article 84, but it is unclear how far all governments had thought through the potential ramifications of this step. Were the governments happy none the less with the liberalisation as proposed? Even here, the conclusion is that, on balance, they were very reluctant. Only the British and Dutch governments were emphatic

protagonists of liberalisation. The others only came into line reluctantly when ECJ jurisprudence and Commission threats of legal action
against flag-carriers made liberalisation inevitable. This was not a story
of a strengthening of state power or Member States being 'rescued'.
Rather, liberalisation 'deprived the Member States of the powers by
means of which they were previously able to practise policies of patriotic interventionism' (Kassim 1995: 198). In short, the EU institutions
utilised their autonomous power resources to go beyond what most
member governments wanted.

- The *governance structure* of the policy areas (transport and competition) was crucial. The provision for QMV changed the calculations of
Member States. And the Commission's strong regulatory powers in
competition policy enabled it to follow up on the *Nouvelles Frontières*
ruling. These two features of the governance regime were decisive in
securing the liberalisation legislation. It is also worth noting that only
a small minority of the airline industry advocated liberalisation; the trade
unions were opposed; and only weak consumer groups were supportive.

- *Policy evolution* was iterative. Once the momentum developed in the
mid-1980s, the interaction between the judicial and legislative processes
was crucial. The 'construction of the policy problem' – an important
aspect of agenda-setting (Peters 1994) – was undertaken by the Commission in the aftermath of *Nouvelles Frontières*. The Commission set
the terms of the policy debate, eliminating blocking strategies. Thereafter the successive packages were cumulative in effect, reflecting a
phased introduction rather than a 'big-bang' de-regulation of the type
brought about in the USA.

- Finally, we can see that *policy norms* were transformed in the Commission by the *Nouvelles Frontières* ruling and the link with the SEM,
reinforcing the 'mission' of DGs IV and VII. However, there were
distinctions between the approaches of the two DGs. DG IV officials
were much more competition-orientated than the more industry-friendly
officials of DG VII. This contrast was best encapsulated in interview
with an AEA official, who unfavourably described DG IV as 'the
ayatollahs of competition'. The significance of these different intra-
institutional values is not without continuing importance, given that
DG VII retains responsibility for regulating state aids to the airline
industry. The Commission's liberalisation policy was bolstered by ideas
emanating from British and Dutch governmental circles. With London
Heathrow as the main transatlantic gateway to Europe, and Schipol
seeking to emulate that position, national officials were exposed to US
policy ideas. Both the British and Dutch airline industries – by virtue
of being wholly or largely in private hands – were seeking to increase
their competitive positions. The significance of this situation was that
these two countries were well placed, on the basis of their experience,

to 'punch above their weight' in Council negotiations and to offer the Commission evidence of how liberalisation might work. The institutional transmission of policy ideas on liberalisation was important.

By 1992 a supranational 'governance regime' for air transport had evolved. It was defined by: emergent institutional roles, rules and norms; a set of transnational interest groups and corporate actors which had come to focus their activities on the supranational institutions on this issue; and a corpus of legislation and jurisprudence which regulated the policy issues. This regime has developed in the subsequent period, and we now consider that aspect.

Evaluating the governance regime for air transport

The third package of air transport liberalisation measures took effect at the start of 1993 but full liberalisation only took effect on 1 April 1997. This staged process of liberalisation has meant that the airline industry and the national authorities have been in a gradual process of adaptation. What regulatory issues have resulted from the three packages of legislation?

Regulating the liberalisation legislation

The legislation that has been agreed vests significant regulatory powers in the Commission: to deal with disputes over fares and access matters, as well as with the application of the competition rules. This continues a division of labour between DG VII, which is responsible for most air transport matters, and DG IV, which deals with the competition policy aspects including, in the MTF, M&A activity in the sector. DG VII has had to deal with a number of disputes concerning putting the legislation into practice and with state aids for certain flag-carriers. It should be underlined that all the legislation in the third package took the form of Regulations, so there was no need to wait for the national parliaments to transpose the legislation into national law: a stage of implementation that has proved problematic in some areas of SEM legislation.

The most noteworthy challenge to the access legislation came with the so-called 'Battle of Orly', Paris's second airport, where domestic flights are concentrated. Two factors were relevant: the opening of the rail link to the UK via the Channel Tunnel, creating new, intermodal competition on the Paris–London route; and the French authorities' discriminatory attempt to stop British Airways flying to Orly on the grounds of capacity constraints. Air France sought to move some of its Paris–London flights from Charles de Gaulle to Orly Airport, for the latter is more rapidly accessible from central Paris, and thus more competitive with the Eurostar train to the UK in terms of journey times. When British Airways and Air UK sought to do likewise, the French authorities blocked the flights on infrastructural grounds. British Airways had other reasons for wanting to fly to Orly: in 1993 it had acquired a 49.9 per cent stake in the French carrier TAT, historically an affiliate of Air France, to enable it to compete with Air Inter on domestic French routes out of Orly. It therefore wanted to integrate services. The French authorities had also initially refused permission for new services by TAT; had then been instructed by the Commission to remove obstacles; and had finally appealed – unsuccessfully – to the ECJ against the Commission's ruling.

Developments in May 1994 thus represented the culmination of a French challenge to the liberalisation legislation and of a British challenge to the French airline industry's structure. In what the French media dubbed 'la guerre du ciel', and the British media 'sky wars', British Airways threatened to ignore the French authorities' ban and arrive in Orly with a plane-load of politicians, MEPs, the media and senior management of the airline. In the event a one-month 'ceasefire' was called following bilateral talks between British and French ministers, after which services were allowed to commence. It should be emphasised that the French authorities' measures cannot be seen simply as opposition to foreign carriers, since the private French airlines AOM and Air Liberté were also obliged to resort to the courts to secure access to Orly, in order to compete alongside Air Inter on domestic routes (see *Financial Times*, 10 May 1995: 2).[19]

The power of the Commission to adjudicate in such disputes over access, with only subsequent *appeal* going through the more protracted legal process, ensured that blatantly discriminatory attempts to circumvent the legislation have been shortlived. The Commission's decision to dismiss the French authorities' efforts to interpret the legislation in a protectionist manner was important. It indicated that these provisions could only be used in very limited circumstances (see *Flight International*, No. 4430, 20 July 1994). The 'sky wars' episode was played out when an aid plan for Air France (see below) was being considered by the Commission and scarcely seemed likely to help the French government's case for obtaining approval.

The competition rules and the airline industry

Regulating the application of the competition rules to the airline industry requires a delicate balancing act. Where does inter-airline cooperation promote competition and where does it have an anti-competitive effect? One illustration will suffice to show the kind of problem that arises. Business travellers are as much concerned with convenience of service as with price. For their part, airlines wish to have high-yield business travellers, because they boost profit margins and cross-subsidise less profitable leisure fares. When a new entrant onto a route commences business it often wants to offer lower prices. However, the more established airlines on the route may refuse to allow passengers to transfer from the new entrant to their own services because its prices are lower. Ticket interchangeability may be

Table 7.1: Profitability of flag-carrying airlines of the present EU (15) in 1992 (US$000)

Airline	Net profit or loss (–)	Turnover
Aer Lingus	–195,600	1,381,000
Air France	–617,000	10,769,400
Alitalia	–11,900	5,510,700
Austrian	100	1,003,800
British Airways	297,700	9,307,700
Finnair	–16,800	1,132,200
Iberia	–339,800	4,136,700
KLM	–319,900	4,666,300
Lufthansa	–250,400	11,036,500
Luxair	600	252,600
Olympic	–224,800	922,500
Sabena	11,700	1,708,300
SAS (Denmark, Norway and Sweden)	–127,400	5,908,200
TAP-Air Portugal	–199,800	1,110,100

Source: CEC 1994a: 52.

denied. This action may in turn deter business travellers from using the new airline, for being able to 'inter-line' is an important convenience factor.[20] The European Commission has ruled that states must cooperate to the extent of offering inter-lining facilities (and the associated revenue-pooling) but this cooperation must not be taken to the extent of the old cartel-like arrangements of revenue-sharing that characterised the pre-liberalisation period.[21]

The liberalisation process has brought about considerable re-structuring in the industry. For DG IV the challenge is one of regulating market power. First, we illustrate the re-structuring:

- British Airways, consistently profitable in recent times (see Table 7.1 for 1992 comparisons), has acquired TAT and Air Liberté in France, bought the German airline Delta Air out of which grew Deutsche BA as domestic competitor to Lufthansa, and has developed a system of airline franchises. These franchisees may utilise the marketing and patronage benefits of association with British Airways, fly in British Airways livery but retain separate ownership.[22] The use of the British Airways flight code ('code-sharing') enables a more integrated service to passengers. It also reinforces the strategic importance of frequent-flyer programmes as a means of securing customer loyalty. British Airways' core business has been broken up into cost centres as a way of reducing labour costs and securing improvements of productivity. But British Airways' restructuring has not been confined to a European strategy. It bought a stake in US Air to develop a foothold in North America, although it withdrew from this arrangement in 1997 in favour of a marketing and code-share alliance with American Airlines. A stake in the Australian airline, Qantas, has also been acquired.

- KLM has progressively increased its holding in the carrier Air UK, which provides feeder services for KLM in Amsterdam from regional airports in Britain, to full ownership in 1997. KLM has forged an alliance with the American carrier North West Airlines.

- Lufthansa rapidly re-structured, as a late convert to liberalisation. German unification and the end of the Cold War opened up Berlin and new markets, progressive privatisation commenced, and competition from Deutsche BA began on core domestic routes. Lufthansa also engaged in creating distinct internal operating divisions as well as franchises in 'TEAM Lufthansa'. It bought a stake in the Austrian airline Lauda Air and a European marketing alliance has been developed with SAS. The latter has a 40 per cent stake in British Midland, which has lower operating costs, and some of the less economic SAS routes to the UK have been transferred to the UK carrier. Lufthansa may follow this move. Lufthansa has built a transatlantic marketing strategy with the US 'mega-carrier' United.

- Group Air France has been preoccupied with sorting out its financial problems (see below), a situation applicable to the other southern European flag-carriers, Olympic (Greece), Alitalia (Italy), Iberia (Spain) and TAP (Portugal). Air France has contracted the British carrier, Jersey European Airlines, to fly some of its Anglo-French services as a cost-cutting measure. The Belgian flag-carrier, Sabena, has had a series of financial difficulties. It was first invested in by Air France with a 37.5 per cent stake in 1992. However, the latter's own financial difficulties resulted in the stake being sold, and Swissair taking a 49 per cent stake in 1995 to avoid its marginalisation from new market opportunities as an EU and EEA non-member.

- Finally, it is worth noting that some really low-cost, 'no-frills' operators have begun to enter the market: for example, from the UK, easyJet and Debonair; from Belgium, Virgin Express. These developments are as much a part of the picture as the re-structuring of the flag-carriers.

Not surprisingly, these and other deals have kept the Commission's DG IV busy. Even before the MCR was agreed, the Commission used its (problematic) Article 86 powers to regulate British Airways' takeover of British Caledonian and the Air France–Air Inter–UTA concentration. Once the MCR came into effect, several concentrations in the European airline industry were handled by the Merger Task Force: Air France's 1992 purchase of a stake in Sabena; British Airways' 1992 stake in the French airline TAT (which it now wholly owns); British Airways' 1992 acquisition of Dan-Air; and Swissair's 1995 purchase of a 49 per cent stake in Sabena. Each of these concentrations was approved, sometimes subject to conditions, on the grounds that consolidation of the industry was inevitable as an accompaniment to the liberalisation process. Informal consultations with the Merger Task Force were held on mergers not pursued, including the aborted BA–KLM–Sabena consolidation. These proposals could have involved major objections from the Commission but were abandoned for commercial reasons.

In recent times the Commission has had to deal with the question of airline alliances and code-sharing where there is not necessarily a transfer of ownership amongst the partners. This issue was highlighted by the proposed alliance between British Airways and American Airlines (AA) in 1996, but the Commission had already started examining others from July 1996, including Lufthansa–SAS–United Airlines. The British Airways–AA alliance raised other concerns, namely about the market power of the alliance regarding flights between Heathrow and the USA. The proposed solution, namely the giving up of valuable take-off and landing slots at Heathrow, raised further competition policy issues. British Airways wanted to sell these slots (which would command a high price), whereas the Commission argued that it would be illegal to sell them because they were not owned by the carrier. This whole issue was still 'in the air' in March 1997, but with DG IV under Commissioner Karel van Miert appearing to take a stronger line than DG VII under Neil Kinnock.

Regulating state aids

The most significant intersection between air transport and the competition rules has come about in respect of state aid. The concern here is that subsidies distort competition, are unfair to privately-owned carriers, and may ultimately lead to descent into a 'subsidy war'. Such aid had been made available to virtually all the flag-carriers in some form or other, whether by writing off debts, overt subsidies, tax-breaks, exemptions from air traffic charges, offering monopoly concessions over prime duty-free shopping outlets or similar measures. Prior to the liberalisation process, EC regulation of state aid to airlines was scarcely relevant, given the assumption that air transport was not covered by the competition rules of the EC. Hence the Commission had to change gear from its earlier, more permissive approach to state aids (set out in CEC 1984) to more restrictive ones (see CEC 1992b; also *Official Journal* C350, 10, December 1994).

Prior to 1993, when the third package came into effect, the permissive approach tended to be based on an examination of whether the aid represented a viable way of putting the flag-carrier concerned onto a 'sound footing' (Balfour 1994; Kassim 1995: 201). Aid to Iberia and Sabena was approved on this basis. Aid to Aer Lingus, Sabena (for a second time!) and Olympic Airways brought matters to a head in 1993, as it coincided with a cyclical downturn in the industry. The Belgian presidency of the Council convened a crisis meeting of transport ministers in September 1993, and a committee of wise men (*Comité des Sages*) was set up to report on the industry's problems (CEC 1994a). Consequently, in December 1994, the Commission's position hardened: henceforth concessions were to be sought in return for its agreement to aid which, moreover, would be given on a 'last time' basis (*Official Journal* C350, 10, December 1994). There are still doubts about how rigorous a line the Commission is taking. Certainly, the approval of a state aid package to Air France of some FF 20 bn ($ 3.6 bn) did not augur well for a strict policy but it did entail the imposition of many conditions (see *Flight International*, No. 4432, 3 August 1994: 4–5).[23] In Summer 1995 an aid package for Iberia was submitted for consideration by Transport Commissioner Neil Kinnock. In this instance Iberia was seeking approval of a second aid package of Ptas 120 bn after having lost large sums of money through unsound investments in South American airlines. Aid was in fact permitted but scaled down (to Ptas 87 bn) and with conditions. However, the 'last time' principle was breached. As one German observer wittily put it, alluding to the practices in British public houses: 'last orders' are followed by 'very last orders' and then one may be invited to stay behind for a drink 'after hours' (Hein Vogel in *Luftfahrt*, July 1994: 53). There appeared to be a severe danger of this practice developing in respect of state aid, thereby undermining the achievements of liberalisation.

Conclusion

It is clear that the regulation of air transport has undergone radical transformation over the last decade. The rules for a single market have become reality. As we have argued, the role and configuration of institutions was crucial to regulatory reconstruction. The regulatory debate has now moved on to four issues:

- capacity constraints (access to 'slots' at key airports and problems of air traffic management over Europe);
- the impact of alliances, code-sharing and national bilateral agreements with the USA for market access within the EU;
- high infrastructure costs arising from ground handling and airport charges; and
- the extreme complexity of rules for cheap fares, on the one hand, and the inexorable increase in fully flexible airfares, on the other.

Together with state aids these represent the key regulatory issues for DGs IV and VII. How these are addressed will have a major impact on economic governance because of the pervasive impact of rules on property rights. The present re-structuring in the industry bears testimony to the dynamic that liberalisation has triggered. How long will it be before the first flag-carrier symbolically goes into liquidation to underline the end of the national carrier's status as the beneficiary of patriotic state interventionism? After all, member governments no longer have sufficient resources to prop up ailing flag-carriers, especially with the public debt targets set in the Maastricht Treaty for those apiring to join EMU. This situation has been recognised in both France and Italy, where governments have announced their intentions to privatise their flag-carriers.

The 'battle' for European skies is far from over but the Commission has secured the main powers to regulate the sector.

Notes

1   The situation was (and remains) quite different for charter flights for holiday-makers. The main charter airlines are owned by tour operators and the latter are concerned to offer good value to consumers in the competitive domestic holiday markets of northern Europe. Any attempt by one recipient government to impose regulatory burdens relating to price or access would be likely to lead to tour operators taking their business to another Mediterranean state.

2   For comparisons with the USA, see Pelkmans (1991); Button and Swann (1992); and McGowan and Seabright (1989).

3   The first freedom is the right to overfly; the second to make a 'technical' stop, e.g. to refuel; the third freedom is the right to set down passengers from the home state; and the fourth freedom is the right to pick up passengers to convey them back to the home state.

4   The demise of Skytrain in 1982 led – eventually – to Laker being awarded damages in the US courts on the grounds that the actions of some of the major transatlantic carriers had been in breach of US competition law. It is instructive that, at this time, similar activities between European flag-carriers were specifically excluded from EEC competition rules.

5   Limited British steps towards liberalisation and a multi-airline policy can be traced back to the 1960s.

6   For instance, on 4 April 1974 the ECJ gave its ruling on Case 167/73, *Commission* v. *France (Re French Merchant Seaman)* [1974] ECR 359. This applied rules on free movement of persons to maritime transport, which had been bracketed together with air transport in Article 84(2) (Balfour 1989: 37).

7   The three proposals are to be found respectively in: COM(80) final, 27 November 1980; COM(81) 396 final, in OJ C317 (3.10.82), 3ff.; and COM(81) 590 final, in OJ C78 (30.3.82), 6ff.

8   Directive 83/416/EEC of 25 July 1983, OJ L 237 (26.8.93).

9   Case 246/81, *Bethell* v. *Commission*.

10   Joined cases 209–213/84, *Ministère Public* v. *Asjes and Others* [1986] ECR 1425.

11   On the last of these, case 13/83, see Steiner (1990: 304) and Balfour (1989: 39).

12   Since the end of the Cold War membership has expanded to include some of the national airlines of central Europe, such as LOT of Poland and MALEV of Hungary.

13 Air France bought out UTA in 1990 and indirectly added to its stake in Air Inter in the process. The resultant Groupe Air France comprised the three scheduled airlines, although UTA lost its separate identity, plus the charter carrier, Air Charter.

14 The block exemptions entailed subsequent implementing legislation in the form of Commission Regulations. In 1989, in the *London European Airways* v. *Sabena* case, the Commission made first use of competition policy powers, imposing a fine of ECU 100,000 on Sabena: see Steiner 1990: 106.

15 For the list of Category 1 airports, see the Annex to Decision 602/87/EEC. The list of airports varied from one item of legislation to another but, in general terms, the capital city airport(s) of the Member States are included as Category 1.

16 *Ahmed Saeed Flugreisen and Silver Line Reisebüro* v. *Zentrale zur Bekämpfung unlauteren Wettbewerbs e.V.* For a fuller analysis of the *Ahmed Saeed* ruling, see Naveau (1992: 65–8); Case 66/86 [1989] ECR 803.

17 As will be seen below, the French authorities' attempts to use these provisions to block British and other carriers from using Paris-Orly Airport led to a bilateral dispute and legal action in 1994.

18 Indeed, Regulation 2411/92's substantive content quite simply boiled down to removing the word 'international' from the existing legislation (OJ L240 (23.7.92), 19)!

19 AOM had applied to fly Orly–Heathrow but had been denied landing slots at Heathrow. There was no suggestion that this denial was for reasons other than congestion at Heathrow. Due to congestion, availability of slots for new entrants is largely dependent upon other carriers giving up Heathrow services: a rarity. Air Liberté entered into financial difficulties in 1996 and was acquired by British Airways.

20 This situation proved a major handicap to the UK airline Air Europe when it moved into the scheduled market, and contributed to its demise.

21 This issue arose in a dispute about the acceptability of British Midland tickets on Aer Lingus services between Dublin and London and the Commission had to act.

22 Examples include Maersk Air Limited from Birmingham, Manx Airlines Europe and Loganair – both owned by British Airways' competitor, British Midland! – from UK regional airports, and Sun-Air in Denmark.

23 This approval drew criticism from British Airways, British Midland, KLM, SAS and private French airlines. Sir Michael Bishop of British Midland said, 'I find it extraordinary that the Commission can allow Air France to receive a sum almost equal to the total losses made by the world's airlines in 1993' (*Flight International*, No. 4432, 3 August 1994: 4–5). Sir Colin Marshall, British Airway's Chairman, pointed out that the aid to Air France amounted to about 60 per cent of BA's annual earnings (quoted in *Luftfahrt*, October 1994: 27). Seven European airlines and the UK government initiated an unprecedented legal challenge through a number of actions over the legality of the aid to Air France (*Flight International*, No. 4442, 12 October 1994: 4).

8

Regulating transfrontier shipments of waste

Introduction

A study of the shipment of waste may appear to lack appeal to anyone other than the most studious of environmental policy scholars. It may also seem a rather strange subject of study for a book on the SEM; after all, the regulation of waste shipments (and indeed the environmental impact of the SEM in general) was not dealt with by the 1985 White Paper on *Completing the Internal Market* (CEC 1985a). None the less, there is good reason to study the shipment of waste. In a very clear way, the regulation of waste shipments raises the issue of 'policy integration'. That is to say, to what extent was the environmental impact of the completion of the SEM integrated into the construction of the SEM? More particularly, to what extent can waste as an environmental externality be reconciled with waste as a commodity that can be traded and in respect of which services (disposal or recycling) can be provided? This relationship between, on the one hand, free movement within the internal market and, on the other hand, the objectives of a flanking policy area like environmental policy, forms a key theme to this study.

This chapter focuses upon the negotiation of Regulation 259/93/EEC on the supervision and control of shipments of waste within, into, and out of the EC.[1] This Regulation applies to movements of waste within the EU. But, it also incorporates (and to some extent goes further than) international obligations entered into by the EU in the context of the Basle Convention on the Control of Transboundary Movements of Hazardous Wastes and Their Disposal. As we highlight, the development of environmental policy at the international level has played an important role in shaping EU environmental policy.

In the first part of the chapter we examine the policy problem of waste generation and movement. Our attention then turns towards the emergence of an EU environmental policy competence. The 1957 Rome Treaty made no mention of EEC competence in environmental policy. However, through a connection with the impact of environmental measures on the functioning of the common market, an environmental policy competence was fashioned. We suggest that this informal competence masked tensions between the integration of the common (internal) market and the policy objectives of environmental policy. It was not until the creation of an express environmental policy competence by the SEA that these tensions became more visible. These institutional contradictions have been significant in shaping waste policy and form an important aspect of our study. The first part of this chapter concludes with a discussion of the emerging international response to movements of waste, particularly hazardous waste.

The second part of the chapter focuses more specifically on the institutional dynamics that surrounded the negotiation of Regulation 259/93/EEC. We explore the role of, and interaction between, different policy actors within the waste regime. Particular attention is paid to the impact of decisions of the ECJ regarding the correct legal basis for waste policy measures. It is against these background factors that we explore the negotiation of the Regulation, highlighting controversies over the legal basis of the measure and the right of Member States to ban imports of waste. The impact of international agreements is also noted.

In the final part of the chapter we focus on the difficulties that have been encountered in defining 'hazardous' waste and therefore the problems that have attached to the operation and extension of the Basle Convention. As with other case studies, the interaction between EU governance and international negotiations is an important feature of our study.

Our aim in this chapter is to interrogate the extent to which waste policy has emerged as a distinctive policy area with its own institutional norms and values which are different from those which exist within the internal market, and thereby to explore whether the goals of the internal market can be reconciled with those of environmental policy.

Constructing the problem

The problem of waste

Waste production is an externality of the manufacture, distribution and consumption of goods. Waste can take a number of different forms. One can, for example, distinguish between industrial waste and household waste. A distinction can also be drawn between hazardous and non-hazardous waste. Finally, waste can be for disposal or waste can be for recovery.[2]

Some indication of the scale of waste generation can be gleaned from the Commission's Environmental Action Programmes (EAPs). In its fourth EAP (CEC 1987b), the Commission estimated that over 2,000 million tonnes of waste are generated annually within the EU. The fifth EAP provided some country-by-country statistics (CEC 1992c): at one end of the spectrum Germany was found to produce approximately 61 million tonnes of industrial waste per year compared with 50 million tonnes each by the UK and France, 2 million tonnes by Denmark, and a mere 662,000 tonnes by Portugal.

However, the 'problem' of waste is not simply its generation, but what happens to it once it is generated. According to Commission estimates (CEC 1989b), over 60 per cent of household waste is simply dumped, while over 60 per cent of industrial waste is re-used. The process of disposal or recycling may also entail the transfrontier movement of waste either because the state in question does not possess sufficient or adequate disposal or treatment facilities or simply because disposal or treatment services can be more cheaply provided in another state. For example, until the unification of Germany, East Germany served as a dumping ground for West Germany's waste.[3]

Movements of hazardous waste have, not surprisingly, caused the most concern. The Commission has estimated that approximately 3 million tonnes of hazardous waste are subject to transboundary movements every year. Germany for example, has been estimated to export 700,000 tonnes of hazardous waste; the Netherlands 160,000 tonnes and France 25,000 tonnes (Task Force EC 1990). In terms of the international movement of hazardous waste, the United Nations Environment Protectional (UNEP) estimates that 500 million tonnes of hazardous waste are produced worldwide. The Organisation for Economic Cooperation and Development (OECD) has suggested that 80 per cent of hazardous waste travels to western Europe; 15 per cent to eastern Europe and 5 per cent to developing countries (figures quoted in Huntoon 1989: 247–8).

In summary the generation of waste poses three distinct types of policy problem depending upon whether:

1   waste is for disposal or re-use;
2   waste is subject to transfrontier shipment or not; and
3   waste is hazardous or not.

The development of EU environmental policy
The EEC Treaty contained no competence for the Community to enact environmental policy measures. In one sense this is not surprising given that the Treaty focused upon the establishment of policy measures for economic integration. None the less, it is interesting that no connection was drawn between economic integration and its environmental consequences. As we argue below, even in the context of the SEM very little connection was made between the SEM and environmental policy.

A brief history of the development of EU environmental policy is necessary to indicate some of the path-dependencies that have been created (see also Hildebrand 1993; Rehbinder and Stewart 1985; Wurzel 1993). The first recognition of environmental policy as a matter of EU interest came with the meeting of Heads of State and Government of the Member States at the 1972 Paris Summit[4] (following the United Nations Conference on the Human Environment, meeting in Stockholm in 1970 (Wurzel 1993: 180)). At point 3 of the Declaration of the Paris Summit, in recognising that economic expansion was not an 'end in itself', the Declaration continued, 'In the European spirit special attention will be paid to non-material values and wealth and to protection of the environment so that progress shall serve mankind.' More specifically, the Summit requested that the Commission draw up an action programme before 31 July 1973. On 31 October 1972, the Ministers of the Member States responsible for the environment met in Bonn to establish a basis for implementing this political commitment. In November of the following year the Council of Ministers adopted a Declaration including the first EAP.[5]

As Rehbinder and Stewart (1985: 17) have noted, the earliest 'environmental' measures adopted were concerned with the elimination of trade barriers (e.g. Directive 70/157/EEC on the approximation of national laws relating to the permissible sound level and exhaust systems of motor vehicles; Directive 78/1015/EEC on the approximation of national laws on the permissible sound level and exhaust systems of motorcycles). In each of these examples, the legal basis for the measure was Article 100 – the legal basis used for the adoption of legislation relating to the common market. This indicates that – especially in the absence of a specific environmental policy competence – environmental issues tended to be constructed within the rules and norms of the free movement of goods.

However, throughout the 1980s, and by means of successive EAPs, the principles which now guide Community environmental policy have been formed. These principles find expression in the environment policy title added in the SEA in Article 130r (but also to a lesser extent under Article 100a(3) in relation to single market legislation):

- the need for *preventive* action;
- the *proximity* principle: rectification of environmental damage at source;
- the *polluter pays* principle;
- the allocation of regulatory competence according to the *subsidiarity* principle;
- the need for a high level of environment protection (where necessary Member States being able to adopt more stringent standards than those at Community level); and
- the need to integrate principles of environmental protection into other policy areas.

We suggest that the history of EU environmental policy indicates that two parallel paths developed. One path connected environmental policy to trade barriers and distortions to competition and therefore attempted to construct environmental measures within the norms and values of the internal market. The other path sought to construct environmental policy according to its own norms and values and, in many ways, as an explicit counterpoint to the economic concerns of the internal market. This second path emerged later in the history of the EU decision-making and, as we argue, exposed institutional contradictions and tensions between the internal market and environmental policy. We can illustrate our point by reference to the emergence of EU waste policy.

The emergence of EU waste policy

The first directives adopted to regulate waste appeared in the mid-1970s. Two concerns motivated the appearance (and timing) of these directives. The first concerned a reaction to the 1973 oil crisis which, as Schmidt argues (1992), 'made Member States sensitive to the issue of recovering raw material through recycling of wastes'. In its March 1975 Resolution on Energy and the Environment,[6] the Council noted the need to recycle and re-use waste to conserve energy. Further, Directive 75/439/EEC on waste oils had the explicit goal of encouraging the recycling of waste oil to improve fuel supply.

The second motivation for the development of waste policy was the more general concern with the barriers to trade and distortions to competition that might arise from different national rules on waste disposal or treatment. This is evident from the rhetoric of the first EAP which pointed to the implications for the common market and international trade of national environmental rules affecting the production or distribution of goods. This motivation is also evident in one of the earliest (and important) directives adopted, namely Directive 75/442/EEC on waste.[7] As the first recital to the 1975 Directive states,

> Whereas any disparity between the provisions on waste disposal ... in the various Member States may create unequal conditions of competition and thus directly affect the functioning of the common market ...

Three years later, a complementary directive on *toxic* waste was adopted – Directive 78/319/EEC.[8]

The connection between environmental policy and the internal market was hardly surprising given that the Community lacked express legal competence to enact environmental measures. None the less, it was also apparent that the measures adopted went beyond the simple removal of trade barriers and distortions to competition. Thus, up until 1985, the principal waste measures had a dual legal basis of Article 100 (common market) and Article 235 (the residual legal basis for measures that pursue an objective of the Community but for which no more express legal competence exists). This use of Article 235 was a recognition (although not formally) of an emerging environmental policy competence.

Legally, waste measures could be adopted using this dual legal basis approach because both Articles 100 and 235 required unanimity within the Council and involved the consultation of the EP. Thus, at least procedurally, there was no tension between the common market competence and the emerging environmental policy competence (even if normatively such tensions might have existed). However, following the creation of an express environmental policy competence in the SEA (Article 130s), this dual legal basis approach could not be sustained given that Article 100a provided for QMV in the Council and the use of the cooperation procedure, while Article 130s required unanimity within the Council and only gave the EP the more limited right to be consulted. Accordingly, a choice had to be made between these legal bases; a choice which not only had procedural consequences, but also implied different normative constructions of the issue. We return to this theme in the second part of the chapter.

Another important aspect of the emergence of a waste regime is its extension to hazardous waste. In 1984 the Council adopted Directive 84/631/EEC on the supervision and control of the transfrontier shipment of hazardous waste.[9] This Directive was significant in establishing the policy approach to waste movements. The aim of the Directive was not to ban movements of hazardous waste (defined by reference to Directive 78/319/EEC) but rather to control such movements through a system of notification. Transfrontier movements of hazardous waste could not be executed until the competent authority of destination (or in the case of movements outside the Community, the final Member State through which the waste passed) had acknowledged receipt of the notification. Waste could then be shipped unless objections had been raised by Member States (based on environmental laws that are consistent with Community and international obligations).

The Directive did not directly deal with shipments of hazardous waste for disposal *outside* the EU. It is in this area that the major policy developments have occurred, triggered by an increasing concern at the international level with hazardous waste shipments to developing countries. Both the OECD and UNEP established formal and informal control mechanisms which have influenced the development of the EU's regulatory strategies. One example of this is apposite here. Directive 84/631/EEC was amended in July 1986 by Directive 86/279/EEC.[10] The Communication which accompanied the original Commission proposal[11] referred to the work of the OECD and UNEP and, in particular, to the OECD Council Recommendation on Transfrontier Movements of Hazardous Waste agreed in March 1985. In the OECD's Decision and Recommendation on Exports of Hazardous Waste adopted in the following year,[12] the members of the OECD committed themselves in a binding decision not to permit the export of hazardous waste to non-OECD countries without the prior informed consent (PIC) of the state of import and only then if the state of import possessed adequate waste management facilities. With this work in mind,

Directive 84/631/EEC was amended to first make provision for the regulation of exports of hazardous waste out of the Community, and second, to require the prior agreement of the state of import before waste could be shipped. This model of regulated waste shipment has been characteristic of international and EU waste shipment policy.

Environmental policy and the SEM

In the previous sections we noted the apparent lack of connection between the development of environmental policy (and waste policy, in particular) and economic integration. The fourth EAP (launched after the 1985 White Paper) highlighted the need for greater policy integration, but it is apparent that very little was done prior to the launch of the SEM programme to calculate the effects of the SEM on the environment or to suggest areas or mechanisms for integrating environmental policy into the SEM. While it is understandable that ideas of 'ecological modernisation' (an approach to economic and environmental policy that emphasises the need to ensure that the costs of environmental degradation are not simply displaced across time: see Weale and Williams 1993) were not prevalent when the EEC was established, there is less justification for the SEM programme's failure to deal with the environmental consequences of economic integration.

We can illustrate this problem of policy integration by reference to the importance of the *Cost of Non-Europe* study and the Cecchini report in coalescing support around the SEM programme (primarily through the expectation of public expenditure and efficiency savings). The studies undertaken took into account neither the sustainability of economic development nor the future costs of environmental degradation. Rather, as Weale and Williams have noted (1993), the Cecchini approach (Cecchini *et al.* 1988) was pervaded by a concern with the costs of national government regulation rather than the costs of the failure of markets to internalise the future costs of environmental degradation. In short, environmental concerns were constructed as being outside the SEM programme.

An attempt was made to address this deficit when the Council of Ministers in October 1988 requested the Commission to report to the Council on the environmental dimension of the internal market. The result was the convening of a Task Force on the environment, chaired by a Commission official, and composed of twelve members (the majority of whom were self-described as 'environmental economists'). The report of the Task Force, '1992' – *The Environmental Dimension* (Task Force EC 1990), while critical of the limited analysis paid to the environmental consequences of the completion of the internal market, none the less viewed this as the unavoidable consequence of the central economic goals pursued by the White Paper.

However, the report of the Task Force did little to remedy the White Paper's failure to integrate the environmental dimension. Notwithstanding the ethos of ecological modernisation which imbued the document, the Task Force simply did not possess the resources to engage in the type of modelling work which the Cecchini report had undertaken. The Task Force's report could not then be considered to be the environmental chapter of the *Cost of Non-Europe*. Moreover, coming some five years after the *Completing the Internal Market* White Paper, it could hardly be claimed that environmental considerations had been significant in shaping the SEM programme.

Thus, we suggest that the belated attempt to examine the connection between environmental policy and the SEM was more a case of the Commission wanting to be seen to be doing something about policy integration rather than a positive achievement of policy integration. The simple fact that the Task Force's report has rarely been referred to (and is quite difficult to get hold of) is indicative of its relative unimportance to the content of the SEM programme.

International waste regulation

While the 1972 UN Stockholm Conference began a process of international environmental awareness, it was not until the 1980s that more concrete steps were taken in relation to waste shipments. Initially, this took the form of the 1987 Cairo Guidelines and Principles for the Environmentally Sound Management of Hazardous Wastes. However, and in response to increasing claims that developing countries were serving as the dumping ground for the industrialised states,[13] joint action by the UNEP and the OECD resulted in the Basle Convention on the Control of Transboundary Movements of Hazardous Wastes and Their Disposal in 1989 (see Kummer 1992). The terms of this Convention were incorporated (and to a certain extent expanded upon) in Regulation 259/93/EEC on the transfrontier shipment of waste.

Regulation 259/93 also incorporated the results of negotiations between the EU and the African, Caribbean and Pacific (ACP) countries in the context of the Lomé Convention. Initially, trade cooperation between the EU and the ACP states did not contain an environmental dimension. But the Lomé IV Convention required that future cooperation be guided by principles of sustainable development and respect for the environment.

However, it is the work of the Basle Convention and the OECD which has had enduring repercussions. To a large degree, the work undertaken within the context of the Basle Convention built upon earlier action by the OECD. Thus, the decisions of the OECD are an important source of international rules insofar as they affect members of the OECD 'club' (including all EU states). Notwithstanding that much of the more recent work has been undertaken in conjunction with the UNEP and supported by individual states through the Basle Convention system, the OECD continues to operate independently of these systems. Of greatest significance here is the regulation of waste according to the OECD list system. Thus, the extent to which waste is harmful is graded under three headings: green, amber or red waste. In turn, this categorisation affects the regulatory treatment.

The problem that arises is that of overlapping regimes. Waste which is considered hazardous by non-OECD states which are parties to the Basle Convention may not be hazardous under the OECD classification (or vice versa). As we note below, the EU position is compounded by its own internal definitions of when waste is 'hazardous'. This lack of uniformity in the definition of hazardous waste resulted in a search for a more global solution (something which we highlight in the final part of this chapter).

Evaluation and summary
By the mid-1980s, the EU had enacted legislation establishing a structure for the management of non-hazardous and hazardous waste organised around the principles of prevention, re-use and safe disposal. In relation to movements of hazardous waste between Member States, a solution of notification and controlled movement had been established.

However, a severe implementation deficit became apparent. There was widespread non-implementation of directives (e.g. infringement proceedings were brought against Belgium for its failure to transpose the 1975 Waste and the 1978 Hazardous Waste Directives[14]). As Krämer has noted (1992: 198), two years after the deadline for the implementation of the 1984 Directive on shipments of hazardous waste, only Denmark and Belgium had transposed the Directive.

Environment legislation, unlike sex discrimination legislation, does not tend to create directly effective Community law rights which can be enforced by individuals against Member States in national courts. It has, therefore, been left to the Commission to bring actions against Member States before the ECJ. Thus, an important institutional feature of environmental policy is the existence of weak mechanisms for decentralised enforcement of Community law.

In relation to waste movements within the EU, it was clear that illegal waste shipments were continuing. Waste will move to where it can be disposed of or treated more cheaply. The failure by Member States to establish waste management plans to give effect to the principles of proximity and self-sufficiency resulted in continued waste movements. Further, given that waste movements were permitted rather than banned, illegal shipments were not as easy to detect. In the context of international waste movements, while the system of PIC provided some form of regulation for OECD countries, none the less this did not amount to the global 'solution' that developing states were looking for. The Basle Convention, however, provided a new and important basis for the development of a system of international control of waste shipments.

Accordingly, by the late 1980s there was a need to reconstruct the emerging waste regime to give full effect to the environmental principles which had been distilled through successive action programmes and formalised in the SEA. This involved a package of measures including revisions to the 1975 framework directive, the 1978 toxic waste directive and the 1984 shipment of waste directive. We now turn to the reconstruction of this regime.

Reconstructing the waste regime

In the first part of this chapter we explored the evolution of EU environmental policy and the development of particular measures in relation to waste. We noted that these measures pursued environmental policy goals while also seeking to remove barriers to trade and distortions to competition. We suggested that the introduction of an environment title into the Treaties by the SEA created procedural and normative difficulties in terms of the choice of legal basis of environmental measures. We also indicated that policy limitations in the operation of the EU waste regime, together with international developments, were significant in pressing for a reconstruction of the EU waste regime. It is to that reconstruction and the negotiation of Regulation 259/93/EEC that we now turn.

In this part of the chapter we indicate the actors involved in the decision-making and lobbying processes. We also pay specific attention to the choice of legal basis for waste measures. The legal basis of a measure is crucial to the procedures and values through which a Commission proposal become legislation. Disputes over legal bases are, therefore, disputes over the standard operating procedures and values which structure decision-making. Accordingly, legal basis litigation constitutes an attempt to change the institutional context of decision-making. Of course, this type of dispute is itself institutionally framed in the sense that the dispute is juridified and, therefore, shaped by the organisational structure, procedures and norms for judicial dispute-settlement in the EU. Finally, attention will be turned to the negotiation of Regulation 259/93/EEC.

Actors within the governance regime

With the incremental establishment of the EU's environmental policy competence came organisational change in the form of the establishment of a distinct environment policy Directorate General (DG XI: Environment, Consumer Protection and Nuclear Safety) in the early 1980s. This development might be seen as a constructive step in creating a new institutional actor to bring together the Community's environmental dimension. However, the creation of a distinct DG is problematic. Given the historic tendency to construct environmental policy in terms of the economic norms

and values of the internal market, it can come as little surprise that the
economic DGs (DG I, DG III and DG XV) have tended to dominate intra-
Commission power disputes (Weale and Williams, 1992: 58–9). Further,
the horizontal fragmentation of the Commission's bureaucracy is a symbol
of the traditional isolation of environmental policy within the EU's policy-
making process. Environmental issues can be more easily constructed as
distinct from rather than linked to the processes of economic integration
being pursued by other DGs.

The inter-DG bureaucratic power struggles also manifest themselves in
relation to external waste shipments given that such shipments necessarily
require coordination of activities between DG I (external affairs), DG III
(industrial policy) and DG XI. Thus, DG I and DG III have shown themselves to be more accepting of some level of 'waste tourism' out of the
Community, while DG XI (in implementing the principle of Community self-sufficiency in waste management) has been far less inclined to such
a trade.

From these observations we can suggest that DG XI as an institutional
actor has tended not to occupy the kind of position which other DGs do,
e.g. in relation to competition policy or the internal market more generally. The relative weakness of DG XI is due to (1) the functionally differentiated structure of the Commission; (2) the historic centrality of economic
integration; (3) the pre-SEA fragile legal basis for the development of a
Commission-inspired environmental policy; and (4) the post-SEA express
environmental competence which is, however, shared with the Member
States and subject to the subsidiarity principle.

Given the institutional background noted above, it is not surprising that
EU environmental policy has tended to be reactive to events (nationally
and internationally) rather than programmatic. For example, the Directive
on packaging and packaging waste adopted in 1994 (Directive 94/62/EC[15])
was a direct response to the adoption in Germany of the Töpfer ordinance
requiring manufacturers to reclaim waste packaging. While the ordinance
applied to national and non-national manufacturers alike, it clearly made
it more expensive for non-national manufacturers to reclaim packaging
because of the transportation costs involved. The Commission, therefore,
proposed the Packaging Directive in order to prevent distortions to competition within the SEM.

As we have noted already, international pressures have been significant in the development of EU policy. The spirit of the 1970 Stockholm
Declaration imbued the first EAP, while the influential 1987 Brundtland
Report of the World Commission on the Environment and Development
provided the language of 'sustainable development' which informed much
of the thinking behind the fifth EAP.

That said, the Commission did develop a more programmatic approach
to waste management with its 1989 *Strategy for Waste Management* (CEC

1989b). This document is significant in drawing together the EU's collective experience of waste regulation and providing a framework for re-establishing waste management as a priority area of EU environmental policy based on the principles of prevention, re-use and safe disposal. Whereas Cecchini failed to address environmental issues and the Task Force report failed to fill the policy vacuum, the strategy document provided an impetus for institutional change (especially in relation to revisions of the 1975 framework directive and the 1978 directive on hazardous waste). The strategy document can be said to have moved the Commission from a largely reactive role to a more proactive one.

The difficulty which has remained for the Commission has been to turn the principles of environmental policy and waste management policy into adequate proposals. At the very point at which environmental policy began truly to emerge as a legitimate area of EU regulation, the Member States reasserted control over this policy area. The SEA's creation of an express environmental policy competence was, none the less, conditioned by the operation of the subsidiarity principle (indeed it was through environmental policy that the subsidiarity principle first became formalised within the Treaty). Further (but prior to the changes made by the TEU), this competence was to be subject to unanimous voting within the Council. This enabled Member States to control the regulatory space in which environmental policy would be determined. Thus, the manner in which environmental policy was institutionalised within the Treaty affected the scope for its development.

We turn, then, to the role of the Member States. It is not necessarily the case that those Member States with records of high levels of environmental protection will be supportive of EU action if they fear that the decision-making process will create unnecessary delays and/or the adoption of a lowest common denominator decision that is less stringent than national standards.[16] The difficulty, however, with unilateral action by Member States is not only the potential distortion to competition within the SEM, but also the probability that waste will flow from countries having high levels of protection to those countries with lower levels (where waste can be dumped or re-used more cheaply).

This tension between national and EU levels of policy-making is well illustrated by the example of the Packaging Directive noted above. On the one hand, the adoption of the Töpfer ordinance in Germany was viewed by industry, other Member States and by the Commission as creating a barrier to trade and distorting competition, and thus the Packaging Directive was proposed. On the other hand, Germany, the Netherlands and Denmark voted against the adoption of the Directive on the ground that it was insufficiently stringent.

There can be little argument that the Member States have tended to be the dominant policy actors in EU environmental policy (although with the

TEU there has been a move to increased QMV in the Council, and thus a weakening of the individual and collective control of Member States). This strong role for the Member States does not undermine the institutionalist approach that we have adopted. There is nothing in this approach which privileges the role of the EU institutions at the expense of the role of the Member States. Rather, we argue that the relative role of the Member States and the EU institutions varies from regime to regime. Further, we would also make an important institutionalist claim – and it is one which is well demonstrated by this case study – that how policy approaches are institutionalised and how policy problems are institutionally constructed play powerful functions in decision-making processes and the construction of preferences.

The role of the EP in the policy process is of particular interest in relation to European environmental policy given the general perception (noted by Judge, Earnshaw and Cowan, 1994) that the EP has been an influential force. However, we share the same concern of these authors that such influence should not merely be presupposed. Indeed, influence over the policy process is invariably a matter of struggle. The choice of the legal basis of measures (which conditions which type of legislative procedure will be used) is clearly an important determinant of the EP's ability to influence the legislative process. Not surprisingly, this has been an area of struggle as the EP has sought to ensure its fullest participation in decision-making. The result has been inter-institutional legal basis litigation (which we consider in detail below).

The EP has sought to shape not only the content of specific directives but also the broader policy agenda through the use of its own rules of procedure in order to adopt 'own-initiative' reports. As Judge and Earnshaw note (1994), the EP sought to influence the Commission's Waste Strategy Communication through the adoption of an 'own-initiative' report while the Commission's document was being drawn up.

Moving beyond the formal institutional actors, a number of different European bodies exist to lobby on environmental matters, representing the interests of industry and environmental interests. At a horizontal level, these include Greenpeace (which engaged in extensive lobbying of the Basle Convention signatories), the European Environmental Bureau (EEB) and UNICE. At the more specific level of waste policy, a number of specific bodies representing the interests of industries engaged in waste management have emerged, such as the European Federation of Waste Management (Fédération Européenne des Activités du Déchet: FEAD), the European Recovery and Recycling Association (ERRA) and the European Organisation for Packaging and the Environment (EUROPEN). These bodies, together with nineteen others, were brought together through UNICE to form a 'Communication Network' (Collie 1993), the function of which was to coordinate responses to the proposed Packaging Directive. However, no such grouping was established in relation to the shipment of waste regulation and, indeed, one Commission official noted that UNICE had been less vocal on this issue than on others.

Lobbying on environmental issues is difficult because of the functionally differentiated structure of the Commission. Environmental groups are represented through the EEB. However, research has indicated that this body has tended to be reactive to Commission initiatives rather than having a more proactive role in agenda-setting (Mazey and Richardson 1993) and consultation by the Commission has become '*ad hoc*' and 'informal' (Krämer 1992: 128). The EEB certainly did not have a high profile in relation to the waste shipment regulation.

We turn to the interaction between policy actors in the decision-making process. Before we examine the negotiation of the waste shipment regulation, we explore the important issue of the legal construction of 'waste'.

The legal construction of 'waste'

In the first part of the chapter we noted that with the entry into force of the SEA and the creation of an express environmental policy competence, a choice emerged between basing environmental legislation on Article 130s (pre-TEU, necessitating only the consultation of the EP and requiring unanimity within the Council), or on Article 100a (involving the use of the cooperation procedure – pre-TEU – and permitting QMV in the Council). This choice of legal basis did not simply have implications for the role of the institutions in the decision-making process. It also had a bearing on which norms and values would guide the construction of the problem of waste. Was waste a commodity to be permitted free movement within the SEM and subject to the exclusive regulation of the EU, or was waste an environmental externality to be denied free movement according to the proximity principle and subject to the shared control of the Member States and the EU?

Not surprisingly, the ECJ was asked to rule on the appropriate legal basis for waste legislation in litigation brought by the Commission challenging the legal basis of the Council Directive on waste from the titanium dioxide industry.[17] The Commission had originally proposed the Titanium Dioxide Directive under Article 100a (internal market). However, the Council amended the legal basis to Article 130s (environmental policy). The Commission commenced legal action in 1989 challenging the use of Article 130s as the legal basis for the Directive. As a preliminary point, at this time the EP had not been granted *locus standi* by the Court to bring actions of this type, though it could intervene in the proceedings and comment on the action.

In his Opinion, Advocate General Tesauro saw the litigation as raising the choice between 'diametrically opposed philosophies'.[18] Unlike those previous directives that had been adopted on the dual legal bases of Articles

100 and 235, the procedural differences between Article 100a and 130s made it necessary to determine whether the Titanium Dioxide Directive fell under one legal basis rather than another. Both the Advocate General and the ECJ decided that while environmental concerns could be legally pursued by measures adopted under Article 100a, internal market goals could not be so pursued under Article 130s.[19] Thus, it was found that Article 100a was an appropriate legal basis for measures that pursued both internal market and environmental policy goals. Article 100a was the appropriate legal basis for the Titanium Dioxide Directive.

Interestingly, Advocate General Tesauro noted that the symbolic effect of Article 100a required that it be given an unrestricted interpretation because of its commitment to '. . . renewed integration through greater recourse to faster decision-making procedures and the enhancement of democratic guarantees . . .'.[20] In other words, there was an implicit recognition of the post-SEA enhanced status of the EP in the legislative process together with a limitation on the power of the Council. The expansive scope given to Article 100a is revealed as a political choice by the ECJ legitimating the enhanced role of supranational institutions in the decision-making process post-SEA.

Although the ECJ stated in the *Titanium Dioxide* case that environmental policy goals could be pursued by internal market measures, it was not clear what would happen if there was a clash between internal market policy and environmental policy. The point was raised in subsequent litigation brought by the Commission against Belgium in respect of a ban by the Wallonia region on the import of waste.[21] The issue before the ECJ was whether a ban such as this was contrary to Article 30, EC which prohibits restrictions on the free movement of goods. Clearly, the case raised the important question of whether waste was a 'good' and if so whether it ought to be treated according to the values of free movement or whether environmental policy could act as an exception to free movement. The ECJ concluded that waste was indeed a good and systematic bans on waste imports were contrary to Article 30. However, prohibitions on specific waste movements could be justified provided they were proportionate responses justifiable according to environmental principles such as the proximity principle.[22] The Court accepted that the Wallonia ban was justified because the anticipated waste flow was well beyond the treatment capacity of the region.

The *Wallonia Waste* decision was important in that although waste was constructed as a 'good', its regulatory treatment was informed through the incorporation of environmental principles that provided exceptions to the normal rules on free movement and, therefore, opened up an enhanced regulatory space for national authorities to occupy. In this sense, the Court was integrating environmental policy into the regulation of the internal market. The decision was significant in that the ECJ was seen to be taking environmental policy seriously. This focus upon environmental principles had consequences for how the ECJ would treat subsequent challenges to the legal basis of legislative measures. Put simply, given that the Member States had established an EU environmental policy competence, should not the rules and norms of environmental policy rather than the internal market provide the basis for environmental measures?

In 1991, the Commission brought an action challenging the Council's decision to amend the legal basis of Directive 91/156/EEC[23] (this Directive amended the 1975 Waste Directive and was part of a group of measures designed to implement the 1989 Waste Management Strategy).[24] The Commission proposed the Directive under Article 100a, but this was amended by the Council to Article 130s. The Council considered that the objective of the legislation was an environmental objective and not an internal market one.[25]

In concluding that Article 130s was the correct legal basis, the Advocate General stated that Article 100a was inapplicable where a measure falls within a distinct policy area (like environmental policy) even if the measure has ancillary effects on market conditions.[26] He distinguished the *Titanium Dioxide* decision on the basis *inter alia* that it was concerned with waste from a specific industry (the Directive could therefore be seen as addressing potential distortions to competition within that sector) whereas the Waste Directive was of general applicability and implemented the environmental principles contained in Article 130r. The Court followed the Advocate General's opinion and concluded that Article 130s was the correct legal basis.

The judgment is important in its recognition of environmental policy as a distinct policy area with its own rules, norms and values. It is also important in constructing waste within these rules, norms and values, rather than relying upon a connection with the internal market as a basis for EU competence. Given that Article 130s then required unanimity within the Council and only involved the consultation of the EP, the decision can be seen as less supportive of the supranational institutions than the *Titanium Dioxide* decision and, taken with the *Wallonia* case, can also be seen as accepting of Member States' control over EU environmental policy.

This story of litigation is important because it highlights the role played by the ECJ in holding the balance of power between the EU and the Member States, and also between EU institutions themselves. Inter-institutional litigation is an important mechanism by which institutional actors can seek to play for rules and to change the institutional context for decision-making by seeking to institutionalise one set of standard operating procedures and norms rather than another. As Majone argues (1989: 97–8):

> The main targets of institution-changing behaviour are procedural rules for debating issues, setting agendas, reaching decisions, and implementing them, rather than substantive rules prohibiting or commanding particular actions – for instance rules about how and by whom environmental standards should be set, rather than particular numerical values for those standards. Hence the

result of institutional change cannot be evaluated with reference to discrete, isolated decisions,[27] but must be assessed in terms of sequences of interdependent decisions taken by a variety of actors over a period of time. This assumption of continuing relationships among policy actors introduces a temporal dimension that is absent in the one-time choice situations usually considered in policy analysis.

In summary, the story of legal basis litigation is one of attempts by institutional actors to frame and re-frame their degree of participation in the policy process. The story also reveals the extent to which environmental policy had emerged as a distinct policy area governed by its own institutional rules, norms and procedures (see also Chalmers 1996). It was within this institutional context that Regulation 259/93/EEC was negotiated.

Negotiating the regulation

The Commission opted to use a 'regulation' rather than a 'directive' to establish a scheme for the controlled transfrontier movement of waste. Insofar as the measure also implemented binding international obligations entered into by the EU the use of a regulation was more appropriate than a directive. However, it was also clear that one of the difficulties attending Directive 84/531/EEC (which the Regulation also replaced) was that many of the Member States had failed to transpose the measure. By using the instrument of a regulation, at least the problem of non-transposition could be circumvented.

The Regulation contains an 'internal' section (dealing with waste movements within the EU) and an 'external' section (regulating movements of waste into and out of the EU). Different rules apply depending upon whether the waste is for disposal or is for recovery. The regime is further differentiated in terms of whether waste falls within different lists. 'Green' waste is subject to minimal controls (relating to the identification of the waste and the disclosure of information regarding the holder and consignee of the waste – Article 11). 'Amber' waste is subject to further controls (Articles 6–9), while 'Red' waste is subject to the most stringent controls. In particular, while amber waste may be shipped on the basis of tacit consent (i.e. where no objection is taken to the shipment), red waste may only be shipped upon the prior consent of the competent authorities concerned.

Our attention turns to some of the details of the Regulation. In this section we concern ourselves with a limited number of key issues, namely the legal basis of the Regulation; the ability of Member States to ban imports of waste from other Member States; and the external dimension of waste transfers.

Changing legal basis

The ECJ had not handed down its decision upon the legal basis of the 1991 Waste Directive prior to the proposal of the Regulation. The Regulation was proposed on the basis of Article 100a (for the internal aspects) and Article 113 (for the external aspects). For the Commission, the proposed Regulation was necessary as part of the completion of the internal market (given the removal of frontier controls and the need to ensure that national disparities in waste management be removed to ensure that conditions of competition were not distorted). The choice of Article 100a meant that the measure would be subject to the cooperation procedure (being prior to the shift to the co-decision procedure under the TEU).

In the October 1992 meetings of the Environment Council, the Member States indicated a clear preference for the use of Article 130s as the legal basis for the proposed measure. Belgium initially appeared to side with the Commission, though this perhaps owed much to Belgian attempts to require 'green waste' to be subject to controls. The Member States unanimously agreed to change the legal basis to Article 130s. In consequence, the EP would be denied its higher level of participation as provided for under the cooperation procedure. None the less, the change in legal basis could only be legally effected if the EP was re-consulted.[28] The EP, in its opinion on 20 January 1993,[29] stated that it would reluctantly accept the choice of legal basis because of its desire that the regulation be adopted timeously (the EP having indicated strong support for controls on waste movements out of the EU). However, given that the (then not in-force) TEU provided for the use of the cooperation procedure under Article 130s, the rapporteur made much play that had the TEU been in force, the EP would not find itself in the position that it did.

In summary, working within the institutional environment of the *legislative* process, the Parliament and the Commission lost the battle to maintain Article 100a as the choice of legal basis. However, having been granted a limited *locus standi* under Article 173,[30] the EP commenced *judicial* proceedings under Article 173, EC Treaty challenging the legal basis of the measure.

In view of the ECJ's previous decisions (discussed above), it was not surprising that Court concluded that Article 130s was the correct legal basis.[31] The Regulation was treated as 'part of the package of measures taken by the Council in relation to waste management, as laid down in particular in Directive 91/156'. The result of the litigation over that Directive provided the basis for the ECJ's decision on the shipment of waste Regulation. The waste shipment judgment is consistent with the emergence of waste policy as an area governed by a distinct set of norms and values as to the goals of policy and the relative exercise of power by policy actors.

Banning imports One of the most controversial aspects of the Regulation concerned whether Member States could exercise their regulatory competence to *systematically* object to the import of waste. The issue was particularly salient during the negotiations in the light of a bilateral Franco-German agreement in 1992 banning cross-border shipments of waste. This agreement followed on from the highly publicised discovery of imports into France of hazardous hospital waste from Germany.[32] The issue highlighted the tension between the principles of the free movement of goods on the one hand, and those of the principles of proximity and self-sufficiency in waste on the other.

For Member States with histories of waste management, the idea of self-sufficiency in waste is not necessarily problematic (even if it would be cheaper to export waste). However, for small Member States or states who have not invested in waste management technologies, the ability to export waste for treatment is important to ensure its proper, environmentally-sensitive treatment. Indeed, viewed from an EU level, provided there are adequate waste treatment centres within the EU, there is no reason why national borders should be important to waste policy[33] (the proper treatment of waste being the central objective).

However, and contrary to the wishes of both the Commission and the EP, the Regulation permits the Member States to provide for general, partial or systematic objections to shipments of waste for disposal within the EU. In a concession to the smaller states, the Regulation provides that Member States may not object to the import of hazardous waste (defined under Directive 91/689/EEC) if it is produced in such small quantities that it would be uneconomic to provide national disposal facilities.

The Member States were undoubtedly strengthened in their negotiating position by being able to draw on the idea of waste as an exception to the free movement of goods (as established in the ECJ's *Wallonia* decision). Once again, we would note the continuing influence of ECJ decisions in shaping policy-making.

Incorporating the Basle and Lomé IV Conventions   Developments at the international level have been significant in shaping EU environmental policy. In 1989, the Basle Convention on the Control of Transboundary Movements of Hazardous Wastes was signed by the EU and the Member States. In December of that year, the Fourth Lomé Convention was signed. Both of these Conventions provided new rules of international law regulating movements of waste. The goal of the Basle Convention, in particular, is to ensure the regulated movement of hazardous waste on the basis of the consent of the state of destination to the waste shipment and provided that adequate treatment facilities exist to deal with the waste. Therefore, the external dimension of waste policy was also reflected in the negotiation of the EU Regulation.

In Boxes 8.1 and 8.2 we outline the content of the Regulation insofar as it incorporates the provisions of the Basle and Lomé Conventions. We highlight three aspects of the Regulation:

Box 8.1: Waste for disposal

Exports of waste	Banned except to EFTA countries which are parties to the Basle Convention.
Imports of waste	Banned except from: – EFTA countries which are parties to the Basle Convention; – other countries which are parties to the Basle Convention; – countries with which the EU, or the EU and the Member States, have concluded bilateral or multilateral agreements; – countries with which the Member States have concluded bilateral agreements *prior* to the entry into force of the Regulation;[34] – countries with which the Member States have concluded bilateral agreements *after* the Regulation has come into force.

Box 8.2: Waste for recovery

Exports of waste	Banned except to: – countries that are parties to the Basle Convention; – countries which are signatories of the OECD Council Decision of 30.3.92 on the control of movements of waste for recovery; – countries with which the EU, or the EU and the Member States, have entered into bilateral agreements.
Imports of waste	Banned except from: – countries to which the OECD Decision applies; – countries which are parties to the Basle Convention; – countries with which the EU, or the EU and the Member States, have concluded bilateral or multilateral agreements; – countries with which the Member States have concluded bilateral agreements *prior* to the entry into force of the Regulation;[35] – countries with which the Member States have concluded bilateral agreements *after* the Regulation has come into force.

- the ban on exports of waste for disposal outside the EU;
- the different rules applying to waste for recovery and waste for disposal; and
- the relative roles of the EU and the Member States in the conclusion of international agreements.

The Regulation bans all exports of waste for disposal except to EFTA countries that are parties to the Basle Convention (Austria, Sweden and Finland – former EFTA states – are, of course, now members of the EU). This ban went beyond that provided for in the Convention which permitted exports for disposal if the state of export did not possess the necessary facilities to dispose of the waste in an environmentally sound and efficient manner. That the EU went further than the requirements of the Convention owed much to the attitude taken by African countries in the context of the Lomé IV Convention under which the EU agreed to ban all exports of waste (whether for disposal or for recovery).

This brings us to the different regulatory treatment of waste for recovery and waste for disposal. The distinction drawn in the Regulation between waste for disposal and waste for recovery is indicative of the tension between environment and trade policies. On the one hand, waste for recovery would appear to possess the quality of a 'commodity' more than waste for disposal. Indeed, one might say that its existence as a potential raw material is in tension with its construction as 'waste' at all. On the other hand, waste for recovery may still be hazardous and, ultimately, residues from recovery operations need to be disposed of. That the Regulation did not outrightly ban exports of waste for recovery (except to ACP states) indicated the extent to which the construction of waste as a 'good' maintained a powerful force over Member States' thinking. The EP was in favour of the export of waste for recovery provided the export was to OECD countries and only for a limited period of time (seven years) after which the position would be reviewed. In the final part of this chapter we will return to the issue of the export of waste for recovery to non-OECD countries.

As Boxes 8.1 and 8.2 indicate, the provisions of the Basle Convention regime are capable of being extended to states with which international agreements have been concluded. However, given, the thorny issue of the relative competences of the Member States and the EU in concluding international agreements, the Regulation identifies three negotiating possibilities:

- agreements concluded by the EU alone;
- agreements concluded by the EU and the Member States; and
- agreements concluded by the Member States.

How then is the question of who has competence to be decided? As is typically the case with questions concerning the division of power between the EU and the Member States, there is no simple answer. Once again, one has to look to the interpretation of the Treaty by the ECJ.

One answer might be that if waste is considered to be a 'good', then the external trade competence (Article 113) should form the legal basis for agreements concerning waste shipments into and out of the EU. If Article 113 is used, then the EU has exclusive competence to conclude the agreement. When the Commission proposed Regulation 259/93/EEC, it used Article 113 as the legal basis for the external aspects of the Regulation. However, with the change of legal basis to Article 130s, the use of Article 113 was dropped. Do the express Treaty provisions on environmental policy give a clear legal basis for the adoption of international agreements?

Article 130r(4) (Article 130r(5) pre-TEU) provides,

> Within their respective spheres of competence, the Community and the Member States shall cooperate with third countries and with the competent international organisations. The arrangements for cooperation may be the subject of agreements between the Community and the third parties concerned, which shall be negotiated and concluded in accordance with Article 228.
>
> The previous subparagraph shall be without prejudice to Member States' competence to negotiate in international bodies and to conclude international agreements.

But all this provision does is to say that the EU does have competence to enter into environmental agreements with third countries. It does not make clear when agreements can be entered into solely by the EU or jointly with the Member States.

If the failure of the Treaties to establish divisions of power between the EU and the Member States is typical, then so too is the resort to Protocols and Declarations annexed to the Treaties as a way of 'clarifying' what has been said (or left unsaid) in the Treaties. In a Protocol annexed to the SEA it was stated,

> The Conference considers that the provisions of Article 130r(5), second paragraph do not affect the principles resulting from the judgment handed down by the Court of Justice in the AETR case.

In the *AETR* case,[36] the ECJ concluded that the EU acquires *exclusive external competence* in an area where measures have been adopted within the EU covering the same area. Thus, where common environmental rules are laid down within the EU, then the EU has exclusive competence to enter into international agreements in areas covered by those rules.

The problem, however, in applying the *ERTA* doctrine is the degree of parallelism required between the adoption of internal EU rules on the one hand, and the subject-matter of the international agreement on the other.

In principle, if the international agreement is wider in scope than the internal rules then the agreement will have to be concluded by both the EU and the Member States. For the most part, international agreements will be tend to be 'mixed' agreements concluded by both the EU and the Member States.

It would be tempting to view this discussion as a technical matter divorced from the cut and thrust of politics. However, if a Member State finds that it is unable to table an amendment to a proposed international agreement because the issue falls within exclusive EU competence, then it is clear that issues of competence have a very real impact upon the decision-making process.

Summary

In this study we have highlighted the importance of the choice of legal basis of a measure. Given the historic link between the development of EU environmental policy and the common market, a path-dependency arose through which environmental policy remained connected to the internal market even after the SEA had introduced an express environmental policy competence (this we illustrated in our discussion of the *Titanium Dioxide* case). However, institutional change occurred. Although waste was constructed as a 'good', none the less, environmental principles served as a justification for limiting free movement. Once it was recognised that principles of environmental policy were distinct from the norms and values of internal market policy it became difficult to justify the continued use of Article 100a rather than Article 130s as the legal basis for waste measures. The effect of that decision was to place the Member States in a stronger position in the decision-making process (at the expense of the EP in particular).

We suggest that this story is a good example of the role of institutional structures not simply in terms of the division of power between the EU and the Member States (and between different EU institutions) but also in terms of the norms and values through which policy problems are constructed. Further, the story is indicative of the way in which policy actors seek to institutionalise one set of standard operating procedure, norms and values over another. Thus, it is necessary to view the institutionalist approach we have adopted as recognising the agency of actors, especially as they play for rules. What is important, however, is the relationship between agency and structure and the role of institutions in shaping not only strategic behaviour, but also expectations and preferences.

Our study also pointed to the interrelationship between international policy developments and EU rule-making (particularly through the incorporation and extension of the Basle Convention regime). In the final part of this chapter, we return to the ongoing influence of international developments.

Reconstruction re-visited

In this final part, we restrict our attention to the unanswered issues of the control of hazardous waste. We note the problems of defining 'waste' and 'hazardous waste' and of defining the scope of bans for the export of hazardous waste.

Regulation 259/93/EEC is part of a package of measures on waste, and it draws upon the definitions of 'waste' and 'hazardous waste' as provided in Directive 91/156/EEC and Directive 91/689/EEC, respectively. However, both within the EU and internationally, problems have been encountered in defining hazardous waste. In September 1993, the Environment Council tabled a proposal postponing the entry into force of the Hazardous Waste Directive because the committee established to draw up a list of hazardous waste had failed to reach agreement. Work recommenced in 1994, but the regulatory committee refused to endorse the Commission's draft list which meant that the Council had to vote on it. A Council Decision adopting the Commission's draft was adopted in December 1994. Similar problems were also encountered with regard to the lists of waste covered by the Waste Directive.

The definition of hazardous waste also became crucial to the development of international rules. As we noted above, there is a tension concerning the attempt to control shipments of hazardous waste while at the same time permitting waste for recovery (also potentially hazardous) to be used as a raw material. The Basle Convention parties met in 1994 to consider a ban on all exports of hazardous waste (including waste for recovery). Ahead of this meeting the Council of the EU considered a Danish proposal for a negotiating position that would provide a complete ban on exports of hazardous waste. France, Germany, the UK and the Netherlands did not, however, support this position, though later both France and Germany were reported to have dropped their reservations when it emerged that the east European countries were set to vote in favour of a complete ban on hazardous waste exports.[37]

The Convention parties agreed in Decision II/12 to a complete ban on all exports of hazardous waste from OECD to non-OECD countries with immediate effect in relation to hazardous waste for disposal, and from 1 January 1998 in relation to hazardous waste for recovery. The Decision itself did not formally amend the Basle Convention. Rather formal amendments had to be received by the Basle secretariat by 18 March 1995. In the period between Decision II/12 and the deadline for amendments, the debate over the export of hazardous waste for recovery was re-opened within the Council of the EU. Certain Member States were understood to be concerned that unless a global solution was found to the definition of hazardous waste then attempts to control its movement could either damage trade (if the definition of hazardous was over-inclusive) or damage the environment (if under-inclusive). A 'wait-and-see' approach began to emerge. However, the accession of Sweden, Finland and Austria to the EU did much to change the political dynamics.

Denmark, supported by its new-entrant allies, sought to propose its own amendment to the Basle Convention banning all exports of hazardous waste. Under the terms of the Convention either the Member States individually, or the EU and the Member States collectively, can propose amendments, but not concurrently. The Commission was alarmed at this preemptive move and dispatched an informal warning letter claiming that the issue required EU action. However, the Danish strategy forced the issue on to the Environment Council agenda in March 1995. The Council unanimously agreed to propose a Convention amendment that would implement the first part of Decision II/12 (banning the export of waste for disposal), while leaving the issue of waste for recovery till after the Global Workshop on the Implementation and the Applicability of Decision II/12 held in Dakar in mid-March 1995.

Politically, the initiative switched to the EP and the Commission. The EP voted overwhelmingly in favour of a resolution banning all hazardous waste exports to non-OECD countries.[38] For its part, the Commission proposed an amendment to Regulation 259/93 implementing the second part of Decision II/12 (banning exports of hazardous waste for recovery). Interestingly, the College of Commissioners agreed to the amendment by a majority with Commissioners Bangemann and Brittan voting against. This supports our contention that the 'economic DGs' have often appeared to be working to a different agenda from that of DG XI.

The Council, in June 1995, decided to authorise the Commission to negotiate within the Convention for the incorporation of the second part of Decision II/12.

Conclusions

Notwithstanding that the completion of the SEM would have consequences for environmental policy, it appears that little was done to integrate environmental policy into the programme for completing the internal market. To be sure, a new environmental policy competence was added by the SEA, but in many respects it introduced an institutional contradiction which opened up an opportunity for policy actors to play for rules. The ability to construct waste as both a commodity and an environmental externality exposed these tensions. On the one hand, a path-dependency had been created which constructed waste within the rules and norms of the common market (hence the historic use of Article 100 as a legal basis for waste measures). On the other hand, the principles of proximity of waste treatment and self-sufficiency in waste management suggested limits to the principles of free movement and re-introduced national boundaries as important. Ultimately, it was left to the ECJ to institutionalise the standard operating procedures, norms and values of environmental policy over those of the internal market.

Our study is also useful in highlighting the international dimension and its impact upon decision-making. Clearly, decisions made in the context of the OECD and the Basle Convention have had a direct influence upon the content of EU rules. International arenas add yet another layer of governance, the structure of which has an impact upon decision-making. As we noted above, it is evident that this additional layer of governance provides its own set of opportunities for strategic behaviour and preference-shaping.

Notes

1 OJ L30 (6.2.93), 1; CEC 1990b.
2 The idea of 'waste for recovery' poses a challenge to the idea of waste as being something without worth. It also raises the important issue of waste as a commodity.
3 After unification, approximately 700,000 tonnes of this waste found its way to France: France bans imports of household waste, *Financial Times* (21.8.92), 2.
4 *Bulletin of the EC* 10/72, 16–23.
5 OJ C112 (20.12.73), 1–51. The recitals of the declaration continue the theme of the necessity of environmental protection in pursuit of the spirit of Article 2 of the Treaty. In the fourth recital it states that the

> harmonious development of economic activities and a continuous and balanced expansion ... cannot now be imagined in the absence of an effective campaign to combat pollution and nuisances or of an improvement in the quality of life and the protection of the environment.

6 OJ C168 (25.7.75), 2.
7 OJ L194 (25.7.75), 39.
8 OJ L 84 (31.3.78), 43.
9 OJ L326 (13.12.84), 31.
10 OJ L181 (4.7.86), 13.
11 COM(85) 511 final.
12 Adopted on 5 June 1986, *International Legal Materials*, Vol. 25, No. 4, 1010–1012. This built upon an earlier Decision and Recommendation in which the system of controls agreed took the form of a non-binding set of principles – OECD Council Decision and Recommendation on Transfrontier Movements of Hazardous Waste, adopted 1 February 1984, *International Legal Materials*, Vol. 23, No. 1, 214–17.
13 For example, the Organization for African Unity passed a resolution on 25 May 1987 stating that the dumping of waste in Africa was a 'crime against Africa and the African people'.
14 Cases 65/81, 68/81 and 70–71/81 [1982] ECR 153, and Cases 227–230/85 [1988] ECR 1.
15 OJ L365 (31.12.94), 10.

16 Article 130r(2), EC states that the Community shall aim at a high level of environmental protection. Further, Article 100a(3) states that harmonisation measures concerning the environment shall take a high level of protection as their base.

17 Council Directive 89/428/EEC, OJ L201 (14.7.89), 56.

18 Case C-300/89, *Commission* v. *Council (Titanium Dioxide)* [1991] ECR I-2867.

19 The then Article 130r(2) provided that environmental concerns should form part of the Community's other policies. Further, Article 100a(3) provided that harmonisation measures should take as their base a high level of environmental protection. Thus, it was argued that environmental goals could be pursued under Article 100a, but that it was not possible for internal market goals to be pursued under Article 130s.

20 Note 18 above, at 2893.

21 Case C-2/90, *Commission* v. *Belgium (Wallonia Waste)* [1993] CMLR 365.

22 The Court's decision is somewhat difficult to reconcile with its previous jurisprudence. Where a measure directly discriminates against imports, it can only be justified under Community law if it falls within Article 36. This is notoriously difficult to achieve. Only where a measure is indistinctly applicable (i.e. it applies to national and imported products alike) can it be justified if it falls within the *Cassis de Dijon* 'mandatory requirements' exception (i.e. the measure will survive judicial scrutiny provided it pursues a legitimate regulatory goal and the means chosen is a proportionate response to the problem) (see Armstrong 1995). On this basis, given that the Wallonia ban appears to discriminate against imports, the mandatory requirements exception should have had no role to play. However, the Court concluded that the measure was not discriminatory because it implemented the environmental principle of 'proximity' which requires that waste be dealt with as close as possible to source (see also von Wilmowsky 1993).

23 OJ L78 (25.3.91), 32.

24 Case C-155/91, *Commission* v. *Council (Directive on Waste)* [1993] ECR I-939. The Commission argued that following the *Titanium Dioxide* decision, where a measure pursues both the objective of harmonising national laws (thereby seeking to prevent distortions to conditions of competition) and the protection of the environment, the appropriate legal basis is Article 100a. While the Directive aimed to reduce waste movements, none the less these were not prohibited and indeed waste for recovery was clearly treated as a tradable commodity.

25 The Council distinguished the situation from the *Titanium Dioxide* decision on the basis that in that case the legislation pursued two indissociable objectives. In the case at hand the Directive's primary objective was an environmental one with only an incidental impact on competition. It argued strongly that with the emergence of environmental policy as a distinct policy area with a distinct legislative competence attached to it, it was neither legally nor politically desirable that an expansive interpretation be given to Article 100a.

26 This followed the line of reasoning in Case C-70/88, *Parliament* v. *Council (Radioactive Contamination of Foodstuffs)* [1991] ECR I-4529, a decision of the full court.

27 We would suggest that the tendency to focus on high-profile Treaty change in isolation is an example of a discrete-decision approach to institutional change.

28 This point has been established in litigation by the EP (e.g. Case C-65/90, *European Parliament* v. *Council* [1992] ECR I-4593; Case C-388/92, *European Parliament* v. *Council* [1994] ECR I-2067).

29 OJ C42 (15.2.93), 82.

30 The EP had failed in a previous action to be granted standing under Article 173 to challenge the Council's comitology decision: Case 302/87, *Parliament* v. *Council (Comitology)* [1988] ECR 5615. It was not until 22 May 1990 that the Court partially reversed its decision and allowed the Parliament to bring actions under Article 173 to protect its prerogatives under the Treaty: Case C-70/88, *Parliament* v. *Council (Chernobyl)* [1990] ECR I-2041. Thus the Parliament's ability to challenge measures in the environmental sphere must be considered against the larger background of its persistent attempts to use litigation to enhance (or maintain) its position within the constitutional and institutional structure of the Community.

31 Case C–187/93, *European Parliament* v. *Council of the EU (Shipment of Waste)* [1994] ECR I-2857.

32 *Agence Europe* (3.9.92), 11.

33 As Advocate General Tesauro noted in his opinion in the *Wallonia* case, the adoption of unilateral bans by Member States on waste imports might well be inconsistent with the establishment of an integrated network of waste facilities for the EU.

34 Such agreements must be notified to the Commission and shall expire upon the conclusion of agreements by the EU, or by the EU and the Member States, with such countries.

35 Such agreements must be notified to the Commission and shall expire upon the conclusion of agreements by the EU, or by the EU and the Member States, with such countries.

36 Case 22/70, Commission v. Council (AETR/ERTA) [1971] ECR 263.

37 *Agence Europe* (15.3.94).

38 OJ C109 (1.5.95), 38.

9

The protection of pregnant women at the workplace[1]

Introduction

All of the case studies examined thus far have concerned issues with an economic focus, even if the transport of hazardous waste brought with it a strong environmental facet. This case study is different again. Like the regulation of mergers and the transport of hazardous waste, the protection of pregnant women at the workplace was not contained in the White Paper. However, more striking is the fact that the legislation is not obviously economic in character. Why, then, should it be the subject of attention in a study of the governance of the single market?

Two answers can be offered in response to this question. First, the legislation was agreed on the basis of Article 118a, which covers health and safety matters. This article was the product of the SEA, and was introduced as an adjunct to the single market. The connection with the SEM programme must be seen in the broad political context of the EC. Clearly, the White Paper was influenced strongly by neo-liberal economic ideology; indeed it represented neo-liberalism's high-point of influence in European integration thus far. Nevertheless, it was being introduced into a European Community with, in general terms, a strong commitment to social solidarity. Hence there was a desire to ensure that the economic liberalisation of the internal market programme went hand-in-hand with provision for a 'floor' of health and safety standards.[2] The new, more competitive single market was not to be achieved at the cost of conditions at the workplace.

A second justification for looking at this piece of legislation derives from our wish to give a true picture of the character and functioning of the single market. If we take our cues simply from what is in the White Paper, we omit from consideration some of the key factors which affect the competitiveness of (and between) European economies and companies. Differing national legislation affecting the workplace – for instance on working hours, sickness provision and part-time employment – are amongst these factors. Thus consideration of EC/EU measures affecting the workplace is important because they have a clear impact upon the European market. In particular, as labour practices change in the face of new competitive challenges, the growing percentage of women active in the labour-force heightens the salience of different national practices in the equal opportunities domain.

What, briefly, was the Maternity Directive about? In specific terms it had two aims: to provide a 'floor' of health and safety rules for working women; and to provide a minimum level of entitlement to maternity leave, pay and employment rights. More generally, the Directive aimed to be part of an emergent supranational social policy.

The structure of the chapter follows that familiar from the preceding case studies. We look, first of all, at the 'genealogy' of regulating the protection of pregnant women at the workplace. How did the proposal for the Maternity Directive emerge from the EC's insecure and disputed competence over equal opportunities and social policy legislation? How did the policy agenda come to be constructed in the way it was? In the second part of the chapter we are concerned with the politics of negotiating the Maternity Directive. Finally, the third part looks briefly at the resultant governance regime.

Constructing a regulatory framework for action

The construction of the EU's regulatory framework on maternity rights was protracted and fragmented. References to health and safety, social policy and equal opportunities were disorganised in the founding treaties; it took the momentum resulting from the SEM and SEA to pull the different strands together.

The founding treaties

The origins of supranational regulation of social policy matters lie in the Treaty of Paris. Treaty provisions were very fragmented but they were clear in respect of health and safety policy (Article 56, ECSC). Provisions in the EEC Treaty were diffuse and ambiguous. The most concentrated focus upon social policy comes in Articles 117–128 (Part Three, Title III of the Treaty).[3]

Quantitatively, twelve articles looked impressive; qualitatively they did not. Holloway (1981) has outlined the ambiguity and the resultant differences of legal interpretation of what was possible. One view was that the articles 'do nothing to restrict the autonomy of the Member States in the social field and do not establish a basis for a general Community social policy' (Holloway 1981: 32). Another interpretation was that the Commission was in fact entrusted with clear tasks but simply not given the necessary policy instruments except by utilising other articles in the Treaty.

However, virtually all these other articles – most notably Articles 100–102 or 235 – were concerned with achieving economic ends, thus undermining the notion of an EEC social policy at the operational stage. On both interpretations the EC's scope for action was weak. Article 119, concerning equal pay for equal work, deserves special mention. It set an important principle as well as containing some elaboration of how 'pay' is to be defined, and how the principle may be put into practice.

Why were these weak legal bases in the Treaty of Rome in the first place? The principal protagonists of a commitment to social policy provisions in the EEC Treaty had been the French government. It was concerned that its national legislation entailed higher social costs, thus representing a higher burden on *its* employers than was the case for those of the other five would-be EEC Member States. It therefore supported a harmonisation of social policy provision. The other Member States, however, were unconvinced of the need. The result was the confusion of Articles 117–122, in particular the contrast between the supportive rhetoric and the lack of policy instruments (Holloway 1981: 41–3).

Disagreement in the 1960s

Progress in operationalising the social policy provisions during the 1960s was largely limited to where economic motives predominated, chiefly on social security for migrant workers and the establishment of the European Social Fund (ESF). The disagreement over social provisions that had characterised the drafting of the Treaty was simply carried forward. In crude terms this disagreement was between a minority who wanted to see a harmonisation of social policy (France, the Commission and trade unions) and those who regarded that as unnecessary (crudely, the rest). This dispute went so far that social affairs ministers refused to meet in the Council: a kind of sectoral 'empty-chair crisis' which was eventually resolved in December 1966 by Mr Veldkamp, the Dutch Minister of Social Affairs (and president-in-office of the Council).[4]

The limited developments of the 1970s

In the 1970s two important strands of development emerged. The first arose from the 1972 Paris summit meeting and gave EC social policy a greater priority. The German Chancellor, Willy Brandt, was one of the proponents of invigorating the development of social policy and there was a more general view that the Community should be given a 'human face'. Thus, the Commission was encouraged by the Member States to produce a Social Action Programme (SAP) (*Bulletin of the EC*, 1974, supplement 2). It had three broad aims: full and better employment, improvement of working and living conditions, and greater participation on the part of the social partners in the economic and social decisions of the EC. On a more detailed level the Commission's action programme proposed thirty-six priority measures, aimed at developing, and providing coherence to, the EC's social policy activities. The real test, however, lay in the transformation of this programme into legislative reality. In this respect progress was very limited but it did entail the Commission conducting a lot of preparatory work for legislation, even if much of it did not bear fruit immediately.[5] In fact, we can identify four types of development. The first, and most basic, level of achievement took the form of proposals emanating from the Commission but which failed to gain the necessary support in the Council. The second level consisted of securing agreement for action programmes, including on health and safety (*Official Journal*, C1165, 11 July 1978). Such agreement lent a kind of legitimacy from the Member States for continuing Commission proposals. A third level of activity concerned securing Council Recommendations for action in the social policy field (for example that on positive action for women finally agreed in 1983: *Official Journal*, L331, 9 December 1983). Although having no formal status, these Recommendations may be regarded as 'soft law': ground-clearing declarations which can serve to 'soften up' a policy area for more concrete developments later (see Chapter 3). In the fourth category was the formal legislation itself; legislation on both equal opportunities and health and safety was adopted from the mid-1970s (see below).

The second development in the 1970s was the accumulation of case law relating to the social provisions of the EEC Treaty. The case law was particularly important concerning equal opportunities matters. Article 119 had established the principle of equal pay but also clarified that pay referred to any form of consideration, whether paid in cash or kind. In the absence of any subsequent legislation the three *Defrenne* cases were remarkable in testing the applicability and substance of the article.[6] In case no. 2 it was established that Article 119 was directly effective in the Member States; implementing legislation was not necessary. This was of profound importance. It meant that the principles embodied in Article 119 were directly enforceable in the national courts. Employers could not justify their actions on the grounds that they were acting in conformity with national law, for the principle of the supremacy of EC law had already been established.[7] These rulings contibuted strongly to equal opportunities subsequently being termed the 'flagship' of the EC's social provisions (Shaw 1993: 327).

New momentum from the mid-1980s

In the early 1980s developments continued in a piecemeal manner. In the political spotlight were disputes over attempts to strengthen industrial democracy through EC legislation. New momentum came with three developments in the mid-1980s: Delors' efforts to develop a social dialogue between the two sides of industry; the changes specifically introduced by the SEA; and the emergence of a 'social dimension' which in 1989 culminated in the European Community's Charter on the Fundamental Social Rights for Workers (henceforth the EC Social Charter). The last two are of most relevance here.

The SEA introduced Article 118a relating to health and safety matters. This gave the EC much clearer competence in the area and added a possibly wider remit by referring to the working environment. Moreover, it provided for the Council to vote on such matters by QMV, and further determined that this area should be one of ten to be subject to the co-operation procedure. This development strengthened the EP's role in such legislation, a factor of significance to this case study.

Article 118a embodies a number of regulatory tensions: the EC should provide a 'floor' of legislation on minimum requirements rather than *harmonising* national legislation; paragraph 2 is expressed in terms of *shared* competence. And whilst this may represent additional legislation, it should not represent an additional regulatory *burden*. Behind this compromise can be seen a variety of different national views: those supporting EC regulation as a means of ensuring that the single market did not lead to a 'rush to the bottom' in workplace conditions; those, such as the UK government, which did not want Article 118a to run against the de-regulatory thrust of the SEM; and those such as the Danish government, which did not want to have to reduce its relative high standard of workplace protection to an EC-average. Indeed, it had been the Danish government which had proposed EC regulation of health and safety standards at the IGC negotiating the SEA (Corbett 1987: 251). Limited though the developments arising from the SEA were, they were sufficient to sustain a momentum towards developing a 'social dimension' to the single market.

The evolution of the social dimension has been well charted (Leibfried and Pierson 1995; 1996; Rhodes 1991; Springer 1992; Teague 1989). The Commission sought to advance its 'protective' agenda for labour market and social policy. The broad aspirations of the social dimension – to enshrine a set of workers' rights – were to find reflection in the later Social Charter.[8] The form of the EC Social Charter was subject to considerable debate both before it was unveiled and then as it evolved into a final draft under the Commissioner for Social Affairs, Vasso Papandreou (CEC 1989c; discussed in Rhodes 1991: 260–4). It was finally submitted to the Council of Ministers by the French presidency in the Autumn of 1989, and placed on the agenda of the Strasbourg European Council meeting, held on 8–9 December. Final horse-trading took place in Strasbourg and agreement was achieved but between only eleven Member States. The UK government was unwilling to agree to the Charter, even after its contents had been diluted considerably.

The EC Social Charter set down a strong set of normative values to inform European social policy, albeit shared by only eleven Member States. In itself, however, it did not add any new EC competence. However, in the period running up to the Strasbourg summit, the attempt to transform the Charter into legislation had begun. The result was the second SAP. The SAP was submitted to the Council of Ministers at the end of 1989 (CEC 1989d). It contained a list of some 50 specific proposals for regulation. Some were relatively uncontentious, for instance those clearly concerning health and safety matters. Some were proposed Recommendations which would not be enforceable and, consequently, did not raise major problems. Others were more controversial, such as the proposal to regulate atypical work.

The SAP was a combination of new proposals, measures which had been submitted before, and new phases of existing programmes in sub-areas of social policy. This is evident in the section relating to equal treatment (CEC 1989d: 35–8). It included a proposed Directive on the protection of pregnant women at work. It also contained two proposed Recommendations, i.e. of a non-mandatory nature: one on child care, the other a code of conduct on the protection of pregnancy. Finally, it comprised the third Community programme on equal opportunities for women: the latest phase of measures which had started back in 1982. In other words the Commission, in seeking to construct an EC social policy, put together a diverse set of proposals around several policy issues, such as equal opportunities.

The final stage in this contextual outline of the evolution of the EC's social provisions came with the negotiation of the TEU, culminating in the Maastricht European Council in December 1991. Building on existing developments, a Social Chapter was negotiated for inclusion in the EC Treaty. However, under a Protocol attached to the TEU the British government availed itself of an opt-out from the Social Chapter.[9] The relevance of this episode to the Maternity Directive is limited, since the Directive was agreed before the TEU was implemented. However, it is clear that the British Conservative government held a restrictive view, at odds with the other governments, concerning the EU's regulation of social policy and of working practices. This position chimes with its position on the Maternity Directive.

How can all this material be organised coherently? In the absence of a coherent social policy provision, agreed to by all the Member States, we need to understand what the fragmented provisions amount to. Something loosely resembling a social policy is emerging, although its shape corresponds to a pattern of social *regulation* rather than to welfare provision, as Majone (1993) has made clear. The emergence of social regulation, rather than a conventional re-distributive, welfare-based social policy, is attributable to the EC's institutional characteristics, namely the absence of clear treaty authority and the Community's limited budgetary resources. Even the developing pattern of social regulation is contested, however, due to the British government's opt-out of the Social Chapter. At the level of policy issues it is possible to identify two areas under the umbrella of social regulation where rather greater (but certainly not complete) agreement exists. The two issue-areas are equal opportunities and health and safety. We look briefly at the trajectory of regulation in each of these issue-areas, with their own developmental logics which were brought together by the Maternity Directive.

Two issue-specific regulatory regimes

Equal opportunities policy is rooted in the Article 119 of the EC Treaty but was only really put into effect by the jurisprudence of the ECJ. The direct effect of Article 119, as established through the jurisprudence of the Court, was augmented by three important Directives agreed in the second half of the 1970s: on equal pay, equal treatment and social security matters (see Warner 1984: 150–6).

Subsequent institutional and policy steps have included:

- the Commission's establishment in 1981 of an Advisory Committee on Equal Opportunities, bringing together representatives from the statutory bodies monitoring the three directives of the 1970s (including the UK's Equal Opportunities Commission (EOC));
- from 1982 a succession of action programmes on equal opportunities;
- the establishment in 1977 of the Special Information Service for Women's Organizations and the Press;[10]
- the earmarking of funds for women within the framework of the ESF; and
- the creation of IRIS, an information network about women's training.

In addition to this, the Commission built up a range of contacts with interested parties as the three directives of the 1970s took shape. Interest groups responded by orientating themselves towards the Commission's Equal Opportunities Unit in DG V. These developments represented important steps in the construction of a regulatory regime for equal opportunities.

Health and safety matters featured most explicitly in the ECSC and Euratom treaties. However, during the 1970s a number of pieces of EEC legislation were passed, for instance in 1977 on safety signs. They had to pass two constitutional-legal 'tests'. First, they had to be essential to the economic goals of a common market, for the legislation had to be based on Articles 235 or 100, EEC. Second, both articles required unanimity in the Council of Ministers. Due to these two hurdles, the Council had adopted only six directives in the area over the period 1970–85 (Eberlie 1990: 89). However, as with equal opportunities policy, there were various other supportive activities undertaken by the Commission, notably two action programmes on safety and health at work. A third followed agreement on the SEA. In 1974 the Commission had established an Advisory Committee on Safety, Hygiene and Health Protection at Work. A newsletter called *Janus* served as a Commission information resource for health and safety policy.

The situation was transformed, however, with the new Article 118a; it alleviated both the aforementioned 'tests'. Now there was clearer competence, albeit shared with the Member States. Moreover, Council decision-making could be by QMV. Seizing the new opportunity, the Commission decided to press ahead with health and safety legislation. In 1987 Delors indicated that the Commission would advance on this front as the first step towards developing the social dimension (Eberlie 1990: 90). Tactically this was astute, for health and safety regulation was supported by all Member States, and responsibilities were now clear.

> It may be hazarded that the Commission formed a correct estimate of the implications of [its] proposals, while most of the Member States under-estimated them, quite simply because provision for safety and health has not been prominent on national agendas. (Eberlie 1990: 90)

The Commission's main thrust came with the third action programme, including 15 proposed new directives (CEC 1987c; Eberlie 1990: 90–1). A new approach was introduced with this programme, namely the adoption of a 'Framework Directive' which would establish a set of principles, for instance on the maintenance of health and safety records, the consultation of the workforce on such matters and so on (CEC 1989e). The Framework Directive set up an infrastructure for regulating health and safety provision, something important for those Member States which did not already have this.[11] Article 16 of the Framework Directive was especially significant in providing the framework for specialised 'daughter' Directives. Interestingly, no reference had been made in the 1989 action programme to such a 'daughter' Directive on maternity matters.

We have identified two issue-specific regimes awaiting a larger, agreed social policy framework within which they could be 'nested'. The conclusion to this section, therefore, is that the regulatory lineage of the Maternity Directive was threefold. Formally, its Article 118a basis placed its development within EC health and safety provision. And there was a legitimate health and safety dimension concerning the exposure of pregnant and breastfeeding women to hazardous agents at the workplace. In a political-ideological interpretation it was part of the protracted attempt to construct an EC social policy. Most accurately, however, the Maternity Directive was part of the EC's equal opportunities policy. It was in this context that parental leave originally had been proposed in 1983, and it was from DG V's Equal Opportunities Unit that the Maternity Directive emerged. The institutions and the actors involved took their cues overwhelmingly from equal opportunities considerations.

Constructing the Maternity Directive

Although we have presented the Maternity Directive as first mentioned in the 1989 SAP, it was not the first occasion that this issue was proposed for EC regulation. In 1983 the Commission had tabled a Directive on Parental Leave for Family Reasons, which had been blocked in the Council by a number of member governments including the British (Mazey 1988: 80; Vallance and Davies 1986). The proposal was deemed to be too radical for some. In particular, the Directive had proposed that *either* parent could take leave associated with the birth of a child: something which was not provided for at all in the legislation of Ireland, the UK, the Netherlands and Luxembourg (House of Lords Select Committee on the European Commities 1991: 7).[12] The proposed Maternity Directive was less ambitious but with a more secure legal footing.

The concerns of the proposed Directive were threefold: to protect pregnant or breastfeeding women at the workplace; to provide an EC-wide 'floor' of entitlement to maternity leave, pay and rights as a means towards eradicating barriers to the equal treatment of women at the workplace; and to make a contribution to the broad, socially protective objectives of the EC Social Charter and the SAP.

The first two concerns had been considered in a comparative EC study on the protection of working women during pregnancy and motherhood (summarised in *Social Europe* 1/86: 87–9). The study suggested a listing of certain kinds of work which should be prohibited for pregnant women. These included the handling of substances hazardous to the pregnant mother or the foetus, or work processes entailing physical strain. However, it noted that existing national prohibitions tended to be scattered across many pieces of domestic legislation. There were also significant national differences concerning what was prohibited. Thus the Maternity Directive attempted consolidation and codification, with a view to assuring more effective health and safety provision. However, the attempt to provide an EC-wide floor of maternity entitlements was of greatest controversy in the ensuing legislative process.

The legislation's context was the concern at overt and covert forms of discrimination against women at the workplace. In the age range 25–49 the activity rate of women in the labour market exceeded 60 per cent according to 1989 Eurostat figures. But women encounter a range of impediments to career development. Some are difficult to detect, for instance because of labour market segmentation. Thus, it may be difficult to prove discrimination against women in terms of pay, for some types of employment, such as nursing, have become 'women's work', and consequently lack amenable comparators for judging the presence of discrimination.[13] There is also an over-representation of women in part-time work, with its lower levels of entitlements (Rubery 1992). However, the immediate preoccupation was with the relationship of pregnancy to recruitment opportunities, job security, career development, retention of acquired rights, and general motivation.

The exact nature of the circumstances facing working women varied between Member States because of the differing forms and extents of protection assured under national law. Differences existed in respect of: the effect of pregnancy on employment rights; the length of maternity leave entitlement; the apportioning of this leave before and after the birth; the amount and duration of maternity pay; and the length of service required to qualify for maternity provisions. Box 9.1 illustrates the differences. Weighed against these considerations, of course, was concern on the part of both national governments and employers about how any increase in maternity provision should be financed, and about how maternity leave should be 'managed', especially since the absence of an employee from a small firm may have major disruptive effects.

The EC institutions
One of the characteristics of the Maternity Directive legislation is the prominent promotional role played by the supranational institutions. Of course, the Commission has the right of initiative. What is different in this case is that there was no powerful non-governmental lobby at the EC level, seeking to promote the legislation. And no individual national government had prioritised the strengthening of EC equal opportunities provision.

The European Commission's DG V (Employment, Industrial Relations and Social Affairs) is responsible for health and safety, equal opportunities and social policy more broadly. Equality matters are handled by DG V's Equal Opportunities Unit, which has acted as an important catalyst for improving the position of women. Interestingly, some of the staff of the Unit are seconded from national equal opportunities agencies responsible for policy implementation, thus reinforcing the Unit's 'mission'. Referring to the Unit, and its small group of civil servants, Springer comments that it has 'provided a center for contacts among interested national groups' (Springer 1992: 80; see also Barnard 1995).

Not only has the Unit been an important location for information-gathering and analysis, it has helped with the operations of the Centre for Research on European Women (CREW), based in Brussels, and with informal lobbying networks, such as the European Network of Women (ENOW) (Mazey 1988: 79). CREW provides valuable information on equal opportunities and is an important resource to policy-makers. Overall, the Unit has taken on an important sponsoring role that cannot be equated to conventional notions of agency capture. In fact, the situation is almost reversed for, as Mazey and Richardson observe, 'much of the work of DG V has been directed towards mobilising a constituency of support for policies which the Commission would like to pursue, but

Box 9.1: Maternity provision in the Member States

Member State	Maternity leave
Belgium	14 weeks altogether; 8 weeks must be taken after birth, the other 6 weeks can be taken before or after. 100 per cent of earnings first 4 weeks, 80 per cent thereafter.
Denmark	4 weeks before birth, 24 weeks after. 90 per cent of earnings (up to maximum level).
France	6 weeks before birth, 10 weeks after (longer for 3rd child and multiple births). 84 per cent of earnings.
Germany	6 weeks before birth, 8 weeks after (12 for multiple births). 100 per cent of earnings.
Greece	14 weeks altogether (16 for civil servants), 6 must be taken before birth. 100 per cent of earnings.
Ireland	14 weeks altogether, 4 weeks must be taken before the birth. 70 per cent of earnings. Mothers can request additional 4 weeks' unpaid leave.
Italy	20 weeks; 8 must be taken before the birth. 80 per cent of earnings.
Luxembourg	6 weeks before birth, 8 weeks after (12 for multiple births). 100 per cent of earnings.
Netherlands	12 weeks altogether; 6 weeks to be taken before birth. 100 per cent of earnings.
Portugal	90 days altogether; at least 60 to be taken after the birth. 100 per cent of earnings.
Spain	16 weeks altogether; at least 10 weeks after the birth. 75 per cent of earnings.
United Kingdom	11 weeks before birth, 29 weeks after. 90 per cent of earnings for 6 weeks, low flat-rate payment for 12 weeks, no payment for remaining weeks.
EC Maternity Directive, as proposed	At least 14 weeks, at least 2 weeks before birth. Full pay (or equivalent) for 14 weeks, at least 80 per cent if leave is longer.
Maternity Directive, as agreed (from October 1994)	14 weeks. Payment of allowance at least equivalent to what worker would receive if off work on health grounds. Non-regression clause: provision must not lower existing national arrangements.

Sources: House of Lords Select Committee on the European Communities 1991: 7; *Women of Europe*, Supplement No. 31, August 1990; *European Industrial Relations Review*, December 1990 and 1992.

which to date have been blocked by some national governments' (Mazey and Richardson 1994: 174).

Another of the Unit's roles has been to advise individuals, groups and agencies from the Member States on grievances concerning the implementation of EC law. The Commission has taken several Member States to the Court over what it has seen as national non-compliance, and has secured important victories (see Warner 1984).

There are two final remarks to make concerning the Commission. First, it should be noted that it was the Equal Opportunities Unit that was in charge of promoting the Directive rather than the separate Health and Safety Directorate of DG V, located in Luxembourg. Organisationally, the equal opportunities dimension took priority in the Commission's own handling of the Directive. Secondly, it was appropriate, given the under-representation of women in the College of Commissioners, that the Maternity Directive was proposed and agreed at a time when DG V was led by a woman commissioner, Vasso Papandreou.

The EP has also been prominent in promoting equal opportunities. This interest gathered momentum following the first direct elections in 1979: in October the EP established an *ad hoc* committee to examine the situation of women in Europe. Its work culminated in the Maij-Weggen report, debated in February 1981 (see Vallance and Davies 1986: 77–80). In December 1981 a Committee of Enquiry was established to continue this work. This committee work made the EP an important Commission ally and highly influential in the drafting of the latter's first action programme (1982–85). No less a participant than Ivor (now Lord) Richard, the Commissioner for Social Affairs, 1980–1984, conceded that 'the Action programme for Women, although emanating from the Commission, was largely based on Parliament's Resolution on the Status of Women passed in February 1981' (Vallance and Davies 1986: 86).

The Committee of Enquiry's 1984 report was influential in shaping the second Commission programme on equal opportunities, covering the period 1986–90. The EP's work was reinforced further in 1984, when its Committee on Women's Rights was created and entrusted with routinely reviewing draft EC legislation and policy, from an equal opportunities perspective. The Committee is an important influence upon the Commission and important to the governance of this policy area.

The ECJ is also an important institutional actor in equal opportunities, working in conjunction with the national court structures. Its concern is with the interpretation and implementation of existing EC law. It has contributed much to women's rights, both through the *Defrenne* judgments and subsequently through rulings on equal treatment in respect of retirement and pension rights. Further, the Court has ruled in two cases that dismissal or failure to employ on grounds of pregnancy constitutes direct discrimination which could not be justified on any grounds (*European Industrial Relations Review*, January 1991: 2–3; Shaw 1991).[14] These two rulings implied 'a positive obligation on Member States to construct systems of maternity and sick leave which allow women to be absent without suffering detriment to their careers': something the Maternity Directive was designed to provide (Shaw 1991: 318). Moreover, the rulings, based on interpretation of the 1976 Equal Treatment Directive, concerned some of the same issues as the Draft Maternity Directive. Because of the doctrines of direct and indirect effect, these rulings could be relied upon in the national courts to prohibit the dismissal of women during pregnancy. They had the effect of implementing the substance of Article 6 of the Draft Maternity Directive while it was still in its initial legislative stages![15]

Overall the ECJ has made a major judicial contribution to developing equal opportunities provision. According to Meehan, it 'has developed rigorous standards in equal treatment at work and in matters arising from pregnancy' (1993: 116).

Interest groups

Pressure group involvement in the Maternity Directive came from three types of group: employers, trade unions and women's or family groups. Employers and trade unions have well-established organisations, namely UNICE and the ETUC. This was not the case with women's and family interest groups. Women's groups lacked an effective lobby. In fact, it was not until the law-making process was under way that such a lobby was formed. This situation reflects the way in which transnational interest group formation tends to lag behind the EC's acquisition of new competences: socio-economic actors respond to the reallocation of institutional power.

During the passage of the Maternity Directive, women's interests were articulated more effectively by the EP's Women's Rights Committee than by interest groups. Only in 1990 did an EC-level interest group for women's affairs emerge, namely the European Women's Lobby (EWL). It comprises both national organisations and women's interests from other European interest groups (such as the ETUC). In July 1993 it only had two full-time executive staff and relied on part-time assistants. Unsurprisingly in the light of its slender resources, its organisational development has been slow. However, it is clear that this body came into existence to develop a more effective voice on precisely such issues as the Maternity Directive. Its own involvement in the Directive was confined to the latter stages of the law-making process.

Another interest group involved in lobbying, again at the end of the legislative process, was the Confederation of Family Organisations in the EC (COFACE), a group with origins dating from 1958. The prerequisite for membership of COFACE is an interest in family policy, broadly defined. The type of member organisations (in excess of 70 in mid-1993) differs from one country to another, and membership extends beyond the EC states. COFACE is a relatively small organisation, with only three policy staff to cover its wide range of concerns, which include consumer affairs, social policy and the CAP. In the context of DG V, its contacts up to 1992 had principally been with the Family Policy Unit. However, its member organisations are concerned with matters of pregnancy, motherhood and the role of the family. Consequently, it had some interest in the subject of the Directive. It happened to be holding its Administrative Council meeting in Vienna at the time the fate of the Maternity Directive hung in the balance. Alerted by a delegate to the importance of the issue, it issued a press release (COFACE 1992). This secured coverage in *Agence Europe* and resulted in the group becoming a more established participant in the equal opportunities policy area.

What is interesting in respect of the women's and family lobbies is not so much the influence they had upon the legislation as the influence the legislation had upon them! In both cases as the Maternity Directive took shape they became accepted policy-making participants on equal opportunities legislation.

The ETUC and UNICE clearly have major interests in workplace legislation. As will be seen, both organisations were much more fully associated with the Maternity Directive from its proposal through to its approval. The ETUC has a women's lobby to deal with legislation of this type, and from 1990 it had a close involvement with the EWL. UNICE's division for social affairs was responsible for formulating its position.

Member States

By contrast with the SEM programme in general, there was no member government making a major political stand by advocating the development of equal opportunities legislation. The closest to such a position came with the German government's unsuccessful attempt to have reference to 14 weeks' maternity leave and benefit inserted in the EC Social Charter, and the Danish wish to ensure non-regression from existing levels of health and safety provision. More broadly, there were, of course, protagonists for developing the social dimension of EC policy and there was widespread support for supranational health and safety legislation. On the other hand, all governments had a vested interest – in terms of the 'sunk costs' in a domestic consensus – in defending the status quo of existing national provision.

The UK government had the most distinctive position. It disputed the EC's competence to regulate maternity provision (although not the health and safety aspects), especially on the basis of Article 118a. It was also concerned about the costs of additional labour market regulation arising from the way in which British legislation for the protection of pregnant women would have to be upgraded. In one respect the government could claim Britain to have better provision, namely in the longer period of maternity *leave* provision (see Box 9.1). Altogether, the UK position confirmed Diana Kloss's conclusion that the UK government accepted the regulation of health and safety matters by the EC 'more readily than ... other areas of workers' rights' (Kloss 1992a; also see Kloss 1992b).

The UK's EOC has been one of the most active parapublic agencies with equality responsibilities in the EC (Barnard 1995). Kloss argues that the EOC has utilised the ECJ more to test cases in the equal treatment field than any of the other Member States (Kloss 1992b: 208). Many of the complaints received by the EOC relate to pregnancy and the workplace. Thus, there existed an apparent paradox. On the one hand, the British Conservative government acted as an 'outlier', resisting some aspects of the Maternity Directive in the Council of Ministers. On the other hand, the British regulatory agency – the EOC – was very proactive both as a participant in the network of women's agencies supporting stronger legislation and as an agent supporting UK citizens taking court action, sometimes against inadequacies of British governments' transposition of EC law.[16] The paradox is explained by the recognition that the government and the EOC were pursuing their distinct institutional roles. Barnard (1995) sees the role of the EOC as a facilitator of interest groups rather than as a government agency.

Negotiating the Maternity Directive

The Commission presented its draft of the Maternity Directive on 17 October 1990 (*Official Journal*, C281/3–8, 9 November 1990; see also EIRR, November 1990: 16–20; 28–31). It initiated what proved to be a tortuous passage through the cooperation procedure. The key legislative stages legislation are set out in Box 9.2. We use this case study to examine interinstitutional bargaining in some detail.

Box 9.2: The Maternity Directive: a chronology of the legislative process

Date	Stage of legislation
17 October 1990	Commission proposal
20 November 1990	Opinion of Ecosoc
12 December 1990	EP opinion, first reading
3 January 1991	Amended Commission proposal
19 December 1991	Council agreement on common position in meeting of Internal Market Ministers
13 May 1992	EP second reading
10 June 1992	Commission's re-examined document
17 September 1992	EP resolution pressing for adoption by Council
19 October 1992	Formal adoption of Maternity Directive in Council of Fisheries Ministers

The basic provisions of the Draft Maternity Directive were divided up into those relating to working conditions and those concerning maternity leave. There were four basic components to the former part (Articles 3 and 4):

- the undertaking of risk assessments of work activities to ensure pregnant women would not be at risk;
- where such a risk exists, a transfer to other duties/hours of work should be arranged without impact on employment rights;
- a guaranteed alternative to night work during specified periods of pregnancy; and
- the listing of specific agents and processes which pregnant or breast-feeding women should be excluded from without impact upon employment rights.

As regards maternity leave (Articles 5 and 6), the principal provisions were:

- a guarantee of fourteen weeks' leave on full pay or a corresponding allowance for all pregnant women (employed or unemployed) but with the possibility of a longer period of leave on 80 per cent of pay;
- detailed rules on eligibility;
- the right to attend for antenatal care without loss of pay; and
- the full guarantee of employment rights during the period of maternity leave (see also Box 9.1).

The eligibility arrangements would represent a significant improvement for some states, for it was proposed that employment or registered unemployment at the start of pregnancy was the only requirement for the benefits outlined.[17]

The Commission justified its proposal on the basis of divergencies and gaps in national provision concerning both workplace conditions and maternity provisions. The Commission was conscious of the need to seek slight upward movement toward good practice but without setting the regulatory hurdle so high that there would be disincentives for employers to hire women.

As is customary, the key interest groups published their reactions to the Draft Directive in line with views they had already been articulating. UNICE's view comprised a very detailed critique of both the health and safety issues and the maternity leave/payments issues (UNICE 1990). Its position was not too distant from that of the UK government in certain respects. For example, it regarded as highly questionable the regulation of the employment rights of pregnant women on the basis of Article 118a. It was critical of some of those health and safety aspects which would be burdensome on small- and medium-sized enterprises. It saw many of the proposed workplace prohibitions during pregnancy as being unnecessary if

a risk-assessment approach was being adopted. Moreover, on the bulk of
the issues concerning employment rights it simply took the view that these
were matters for the Member States to determine. On the maternity leave
and pay aspects, it was careful not to be critical of the equal opportunities
principles underlying the legislation (although it disputed the Article 118a
legal base) but it was critical of measures which would impose additional
costs on employers.

Of course, UNICE had to take into account the positions of different
national employers' organisations. Given the proposed Directive's particularly strong effect on existing maternity provision in the UK, the CBI had
particular concerns. For example, the proposal to abolish the existing
British qualification periods necessary to earn entitlement to maternity
leave was criticised because of the additional costs it would impose. The
CBI was also concerned that the burden of the increase in maternity pay
might be transferred to the employer rather than being provided for by
enhanced state provision through the Statutory Maternity Pay Scheme,
adminstered by the Department of Social Security.[18] The British government shared most of these views and represented them in the Council.

The ETUC was more positive in its appraisal of the Commission's proposals but it was critical of the Commission for not going far enough.[19]
For instance, it advocated maternity leave of 16 rather than 14 weeks. The
ETUC also convened a seminar comprising the ETUC Women's Committee, the Trade Union Bureau on Health and Safety, and other employee
representatives to draft detailed comments on health and safety issues for
pregnant workers.

The EP gave the Maternity Directive its first reading on 12 December
1990 following committee scrutiny, which the Women's Rights Committee was in charge of (*Official Journal*, C19/165–177, 28 January 1991).
The EP proposed a change to the title of the Directive, including reference
to breastfeeding women: a change which was reflected in the eventual
legislation. It also proposed substantive changes in order to to extend the
provision for breastfeeding women in the directive. It proposed greater
safeguards for the health and safety of pregnant women. It pressed for 16
weeks' maternity leave. It also pressed for the creation of a complaints
procedure for aggrieved parties under the legislation. The Commission
accepted the broad thrust of the EP's proposed amendments but by no
means all of its suggestions (CEC 1991b).

The most important reaction was that of the Council of Ministers, for
the Draft Directive had to secure ministers' approval to become law. It
quickly became clear that the UK government was unhappy at the Article
118a legal base for the part of the legislation that dealt with maternity
provisions. This was not just a matter of legalistic dispute; the Article 118a
base, allowing for QMV in the Council, had an important impact on the
strategy of the UK government. It meant that the UK government could

not rely on a lengthy rear-guard action against the proposal with the ultimate fall-back position of a veto, because the veto option did not exist in this case.

On 14 October 1991 the Council of Social and Labour Affairs Ministers discussed the proposal in detail. Michael Howard, the then UK Secretary of State for Employment, argued unsuccessfully that the Directive should be split into two, with only the health and safety component to be based on Article 118a (see *European Report*, 15 October 1991: IV/5). Although all Member States agreed on a ban on dismissal on the grounds of pregnancy – and the ECJ had already clarified the law – the UK and Irish governments suggested that this right should only be accorded to women with at least two years' service. The other major issue discussed was the matter of maternity payments. The Commission proposal of 100 per cent of pay came under attack, with several states favouring lower figures and some wishing this to be left to Member States' discretion. The meeting was inconclusive, however, owing to an industrial dispute amongst interpreters!

Eventually a text was approved on 19 December 1991 in a session of the Council of Internal Market Ministers. The governments of the Netherlands, holding the presidency, and of the UK were crucial to the agreement (*Financial Times*, 7 February 1992: 8). At the latter's insistence, the common position set the level of maternity benefit as at least equivalent to sickness pay: a level which would be cheaper for the UK to implement than the alternatives. The UK government was also keen to avoid associating the level of maternity payment with anything which *it* considered to be outside the EC's competence, namely *pay*, for fear that this would conflict with its opposition to the EC Social Charter. Procedurally, the decision was taken unanimously because it enabled ministers to get through all their departures from the Commission's proposed text. Having secured substantive changes reflecting its interests, the UK (and Ireland) nevertheless opted to abstain from the unanimous decision. This kept British options open, especially as the government still opposed the legal base of much of the Draft Directive.

Agreement on the common position triggered the second reading phase of the cooperation procedure, giving the EP a maximum of three (or by agreement, four) months to reach its view, once it formally declared the common position to have been received (namely 14 January 1992). The Council's common position was referred to the Women's Rights Committee, which adopted its report and presented it to the Plenum, which voted in favour of the Directive, but tabled no less than 17 amendments, on 13 May 1992.[20] The EP remained keen to see existing provision enhanced. Accordingly, it again called for 16 weeks' maternity leave rather than the 14 originally proposed by the Commission and accepted in the common position (EP 1992: 12–3). In addition, it was very unhappy about the Council equating maternity benefit with sickness benefit – the suggestion that pregnancy might be bracketed with sickness being particularly irk-some. The EP felt that any equation with sickness benefit should be accept-able *only* if this assured a benefit amounting to at least 80 per cent of salary. There was also a concern that the link with sickness pay might open the door to the already more generous Member States trimming back existing provision. These were the principal substantive amendments pro-posed by the EP but there were others.

The EP made two other proposals: that the Commission should review maternity provision in its three-yearly report on implementation; and that 'the Commission should consider resubmitting its proposal in 1993 under the new Protocol [i.e. of the Maastricht Treaty]' if the level of maternity pay could not be agreed at 80 per cent of salary or higher (EP 1992: 14).[21]

The Commission then took on its mediating function in the cooperation procedure under Article 149. It adopted eleven of the EP's amendments, either in part or entirely, and in June published a re-examined proposal (CEC 1992d). Concerning the main changes, the Commission turned down the EP's proposal for 16 weeks of maternity leave and reverted to its original proposal of 14 weeks. As regards the level of maternity pay, the Commission accepted the basis of the EP's views, and amended this to require at least 80 per cent of salary.

In considering how to respond to each of the EP's amendments at the second reading, the Commission had to bear in mind three things: one general, two specific. Its general consideration was the art of the possible: how far could it go – especially given the UK government's known reluct-ance to agree to the legislation and the Council's preference for acting consensually – without jeopardising the legislation as a whole? The two specific considerations concerned the voting rules at the second reading by the Council. The Council could adopt the Commission's revised proposal by QMV. However, if it wanted to change these, it needed to vote by unanimity. Hence, to press for an increase in the length of maternity leave, beyond what it had originally proposed, would have lacked credibility and could have precipitated the failure of the legislation. However, to reinstate the level of maternity pay at 80 per cent of pay was merely reiterating its earlier position, and could realistically secure a qualified majority in the Council.

The Council had three months in which to act. The Portuguese pres-idency placed the Maternity Directive on the agenda of the Council of Labour and Social Affairs Ministers, held in Luxembourg on 24 June. At this meeting the overwhelming majority of national governments indicated that they wanted largely to return to the common position agreed in December 1991. However, in order to do so, they needed unanimity. The Italian government, however, refused to agree to this. It wanted maternity pay to be at least 80 per cent of pay, thus demonstrating support for the views of the Commission and the EP. In consequence the meeting broke up with no agreement. There was neither the necessary unanimous support for reverting to the common position nor a qualified majority supporting the Commission's revised proposal (EIRR, July 1992: 2; *Women of Europe Newsletter*, June 1992).

To complicate matters further, the decisional delay deferred matters to the UK's presidency, commencing on 1 July 1992. As a firm opponent of increased social regulation, the British government assumed some control over the EC's agenda. Domestic British politics also came into play. Conservative 'Euro-sceptics' were in the ascendant, capitalising on the Danish rejection of the TEU in the referendum of 2 June. Would the government pursue the very critical line which had been followed by Mr Michael Howard when the common position was being negotiated? Or would his successor, Mrs Gillian Shephard, be more receptive to equal opportunities legislation? She had taken over not only the employment portfolio but also the coordination of women's policy, and the government had embarked upon increasing women's participation rates in senior civil service positions through a programme entitled Opportunity 2000. The Conservative Party had also put forward a commitment in its 1992 election manifesto to improve maternity leave entitlement for working women. In fact, the government remained opposed to the development of EC social policy.

The three-month deadline for the Council to adopt legislation – 12 September 1993 – looked increasingly likely to induce brinkmanship between the various actors. With time running out, the Council and the EP agreed under Article 149(2)(g) of the EEC Treaty to extend the deadline for Council adoption to 12 October.[22] The inter-institutional bargaining in the period that followed entailed the Commission, the EP and the Council all using the power resources available under the Treaty, but under strong pressure from groups on either side of the debate. How can the complex bargaining be summarised?

- Initially, pressure was put on the Italian government in the hope that there could be no unanimity amongst governments for returning to the weaker common position of December 1991 (EIRR, October 1992: 2). Attempts were made to sway other governments into supporting the Italian position.[23]
- In the EP itself a debate was called for the September plenary, with pressure placed on the British presidency.[24] Three areas were highlighted where there was scope for compromise. First, it was proposed that maternity pay should be at the level of 80 per cent of pay, and this should be achieved over a three-year transitional period. Secondly, a statement was desired stating that pregnancy was not to be considered a sickness. Finally, a non-regression clause was desired, to make explicit that no Member State could exploit less generous EC 'floor' provisions to lower existing arrangements.

- The British Council presidency sought to lobby the Italian government to stand by the agreement embodied in the common position (EIRR, October 1992: 2).
- Reversion to the common position came to be favoured by other actors as the October deadline approached, for the real prospect emerged of there being no agreement at all and of the proposal lapsing. COFACE (1992) and the EWL therefore moderated their positions.
- Inter-institutional negotiation took place between the Commission, the EP and the Council presidency on a triangular, bilateral basis. The bargaining was not simply inter-governmental; it involved a true inter-institutional dialogue.
- An informal ministerial meeting of Employment and Social Affairs Ministers was held in Chepstow on 13 October but again failed to reach agreement.[25] In the interim legal experts had found a way of gaining several extra days' leeway. The starting-point for the four-month period within which the Council had to act was now taken as the date on which its secretariat had received the Commission's revised proposal *in all the official languages*, giving a new deadline of 19 October (*Agence Europe*, 9 October 1992: 7–8).
- The Commission revised its proposals (requiring QMV), as did the Council presidency with its (requiring unanimity). Eventually agreement was reached in Coreper on 16 October, necessitating formal Council approval on the very last day, 19 October, at the Council of Fisheries Ministers.
- In the Council voting (on the Council's proposals, thus requiring unanimity) the Italian and British governments both abstained. The Italian government was unable to support the final text but was also unwilling to sabotage the legislation for it wanted to see progress on the SAP. The UK government abstained because it still disagreed with the legal base; there were even suggestions that it might challenge the legal base before the ECJ.[26] The final basis of agreement was achieved by means of three areas of compromise (see CEC 1992e; *Agence Europe* 19/20 October 1992: 8).
- A new recital was added, stating that the connection between the maternity allowance and sickness benefit 'should in no circumstances be interpreted as suggesting an analogy between pregnancy and illness'. This was further reinforced by a joint statement of the Council and the Commission that was entered in the minutes of the 19 October 1992 Council meeting. Unusually, this statement in the minutes was attached to the Directive itself in the *Official Journal* (L348/8, 28 November 1993).
- A non-regression clause was included, stating that the Directive 'may not have the effect of reducing the level of protection . . . as compared with the situation which exists in each Member State on the date on which this Directive is adopted' (Article 1.3).

- Two review clauses were incorporated to defer some issues of disagreement to later discussion. One required the Member States to report on the implementation of the Directive after four years; the other committed the Council to re-examine the Directive after five years (in 1997).

The Maternity Directive brought modest changes for all Member States and some more significant improvements for a small number (*Agence Europe*, 21 October 1992; *European Report*, 21 October 1992: IV/9). All Member States would have to make changes on evaluating risks on health and safety grounds and/or incorporate certain prohibitions on types of work. Several Member States (Greece, Ireland, France and Belgium) would have to formalise arrangements facilitating absence from work for antenatal examination. Workers' rights during pregnancy would be enhanced, especially in the UK. There would be a marginally longer period of maternity leave entitlement for Portuguese workers. UK maternity leave would be enhanced in three ways: through a reduction from two years to one year of service to obtain entitlement to maternity pay; an extension of the period of maternity pay to fourteen weeks (previously six); an increase from low flat-rate payments from the sixth to the fourteenth weeks). The Commission summed up on the outcome as follows:

> Although ... this directive is only an insufficient response to the Commission's proposals and the requirements laid down by MEPs, especially over night work and the level of maternity benefits, the Commission nevertheless considers that ... this text marks, for a certain number of workers and especially a certain number of Member States, an improvement compared to the present situation. (*Agence Europe*, 21 October 1992)

Historical institutionalist analysis
What conclusions can we reach concerning the role of institutions in this detailed account of EC rule-making? In essence, we feel that institutions played an important role in structuring the policy debate and that, in respect of the equal opportunities dimension, the supranational institutions developed autonomy and left their imprint upon the Maternity Directive.

If one takes an inter-governmentalist interpretation, namely that the national governments are the prime movers in the integration process, then one could justifiably argue that EC health and safety regulation was agreed to by all governments. Such an interpretation would see this regulation as a flanking measure for the supranational 'rescue' of sclerotic national European economies (that is, the SEM project). Regulation was needed to ensure that working conditions did not decline and to ensure that they were broadly comparable between the Member States. Following the analysis of Moravcsik (1993), the positions of the national governments could be seen as reflecting domestic preferences, as established nationally between governments and both sides of industry.

When it comes to the equal opportunities dimension to the legislation, it is much less clear that national governments were the prime movers. To be sure, the legislation was finally agreed on the basis of unanimity (albeit with abstentions). However, we need to bear in mind that the UK maintained opposition to the use of Article 118a as the legal base throughout the legislative process. Correspondingly, we must note that it was the Commission's decision to construct the regulatory issue in terms of health and safety legislation that enabled the Maternity Directive to take on a much wider remit of regulating maternity rights, pay and leave entitlement. These were precisely the kind of issues the British government sought to exclude from the EU's remit in the Maastricht negotiations culminating in the opt-out from the Social Chapter. The Commission exploited its autonomous power, supported by a network of equal opportunities agencies, and harnessed it to the knowledge that a decision could ultimately be reached by QMV in the Council.

In terms of of the particular governance structure for the policy issue, a much more persuasive case can be made to the effect that it left an indelible imprint upon the policy outcome. Three factors seem to be important. First, the Commission empowered the weak and poorly organised women's lobby: the Commission played an important role in acting as a kind of 'vanguard' for working women's interests. Secondly, the EP's Committee on Women's Rights played a supportive role in sustaining the Commission's support for equal opportunities. Thirdly, the procedural changes brought about by the SEA – the introduction of QMV and the cooperation procedure – changed the pattern of inter-institutional negotiations. Without these changes legislation may not have been agreed, for the UK government could have been more obstructionist. It might be speculated that, had the TEU been in force when the legislation was first proposed, the Directive might have been split into two, with the health and safety component being agreed under Article 188a, and the maternity pay and leave issues being agreed without UK participation under the Protocol and Agreement on Social Policy.

Women's interests suffer from the collective action problems of large unorganised groups of citizens: they lack the organisational ability to develop decisive influence on public policy. The Commission's empowerment of women's interest groups reveals the way in which partner interest groups emerged during the passage of the legislation. Thus, COFACE recognised the potential of the non-regression clause in social policy law, and pressed for its inclusion in subsequent legislation (COFACE 1993). The EWL was developing its policies through pressure for further regulation (EWL 1992). Such steps suggest that these groups will contribute to the future development of policy. Moreover, the Commission itself may well seek out these groups as partners in its advisory committees or funded activities so that they become institutionalised partners.[27] The emergence of such partners may be seen as an integral part of the construction of a *governance regime* for equal opportunities policy.

The final point on the governance structure concerns the changes brought about by the SEA. The interaction between the EP, the Commission and the Council became much more intricate, with a range of inter-institutional alliances being possible. Furthermore, the Commission's ability to revise its proposal right up to the last minute had the effect of making it difficult to predict whether the decision could *or would* be taken by QMV or by consensus. The institutional rules specific to the policy issue – i.e. defined *procedurally* as health and safety policy – played an important role in shaping the strategies of the UK and Italian governments in the final month of the legislative process. Further, the eventual shape of the Maternity Directive was the product of horse-trading within this context.

Emphasising once again the importance of policy evolution, we underline the importance of ECJ jurisprudence on equal opportunities and the way that rulings – for example, outlawing dismissal on the grounds of pregnancy – strengthened the Draft Directive and the Commission's hand in the legislative process. The interaction between law and politics was seen as central to the pattern of policy development. Specifically, the emergence of the Draft Maternity Directive was conditioned centrally by the way the Commission chose to construct maternity regulation, namely in substantive terms as equal opportunities and procedurally as a health and safety matter. The Commission was able to present the Draft Directive as a mere increment to two existing regulatory regimes and attenuate concerns about interference in matters of national sovereignty. An additional point concerns the interaction between legislation in this area and 'soft law'. Although EC declaratory statements are often perceived as unimportant 'Eurobabble', the numerous Declarations and Recommendations made in the area of equal opportunities do have a background effect in shaping policy norms, including DG V's 'mission'. Subtly, therefore, such soft law also contributes to the evolution of policy. Litigation by private parties drawing on the Maternity Directive, or upon domestic enabling legislation, may serve to expand the scope of the rules.

Finally, on the norms of governance our attention is drawn to institutional culture, the construction of meaning and the role of ideas. Certainly, DG V's Equal Opportunities Unit, the EP's Committee on Women's Rights and the various networks and statutory agencies associated with equal opportunities shared 'norms of appropriateness'. The presence of a network of contacts, for example through advisory committees or the ENOW, permitted the exchange of ideas on strengthening equal opportunities provision and on exploiting them before the courts. These shared norms were important to the sharing of knowledge and to facilitating the exchange of ideas for future policy development.

Evaluating the resultant governance regime

The experience of the Maternity Directive is entirely consistent with the pattern whereby the EC/EU has confined its action to social regulation rather than to social policy as defined in general terms (Majone 1993; also Cram 1993). A further point concerning the regulatory characterisitics of the EC is the reliance upon implementing measures by the Member States. This pervasive pattern – with the notable exception of competition policy – is confirmed with the Maternity Directive. The supranational authorities need to remain alive to the possibilities of accidental or deliberate subversion in the Member States at the enactment and subsequent enforcement stages. The equal opportunities governance regime is well organised in this respect. Agencies such as the UK's EOC are well versed in taking cases to court, utilising the possibilities of EC law. Interest groups at the national level, such as the UK's Maternity Alliance, offer advice to individuals with grievances on maternity rights concerning the possibilities for seeking legal redress through national and European law. The close connection between national groups, agencies, the European Commission, the EP's Women's Rights Committee, the EWL and the Advisory Committee on Equal Opportunities ensure that this governance regime operates at both the rule-making and the rule-implementation stages.

The Maternity Directive required Member States to enact domestic legislation within two years of the October 1992 agreement in the Council. Our research did not go on to a systematic examination of this important stage in the policy process. Thus, our observations on the regulatory regime will be confined to two matters: the continuing regulatory momentum within the EU; and the British case of enacting the Directive.

In the aftermath of agreement on the Maternity Directive the Commission pressed ahead with the regulation of equal opportunities matters. Apart from other matters contained in its third action programme, it sought to develop its policy further. In his presentation of DG V's 1993 work programme, the incoming Irish commissioner responsible for social affairs, Padraig Flynn, indicated that one key element was to re-start negotiations on the parental leave draft directive, originally tabled in 1983 (see *CREW Reports*, April 1993: 4). In the second half of 1993, the Council, under the Belgian presidency of Mrs Smet, proposed a regular annual meeting of the Council to be devoted to problems of equal opportunities, and this was agreed (*Agence Europe*, 25 September 1993: 8). Moreover, the wider context of the governance regime was cemented further by the convening of the Second European Summit of Women, held in September 1993, with support from the Commission and the Belgian presidency.

In its July 1994 White Paper *European Social Policy: A Way Forward for the Union*, the Commission included the following proposed policy developments for strengthening equal opportunities (CEC 1994b: 31–4):

- codes of practice to assure equal pay for work of equal value;
- the promotion of childcare arrangements;
- the publication, from 1996, of an annual 'equality report' on developments at the EU and Member State levels;
- pressure for passage of a directive on parental leave; and
- measures to facilitate access to justice in equal opportunities.

A new cycle of policy evolution appeared to commence, with a further SAP being launched in April 1995 to carry it through (see EIRR, June 1995: 12–19). By 1996/97, however, momentum in social policy legislation seemed to have petered out as a result of concerns about European competitiveness. In the meantime, however, an agreement on parental leave had been reached but amongst social partners – rather than by legislation – and under the Social Protocol, so not applicable in the UK (*Official Journal*, L145/96, 3 June 1996).

What, briefly, of the transposition of the Directive into UK law? The whole point of utilising a Directive as an instrument of EC law is to allow Member States some discretion as to *how*, but not as to whether, they put into effect EC legislation. During 1993 the UK government set about enacting the Maternity Directive. The EOC was highly critical of the form in which the legislation was transposed into UK law. Amongst its complaints were: the complexity of the procedures, the exclusion of women earning less than £56 per week, and the decision to pass the burden of additional maternity costs to employers (EOC 1993a; 1993b). The government's decision on this last point was taken as an alternative to increasing the statutory maternity pay scheme, funded by the state. The government's decision was seen as potentially discouraging employers from taking on women workers: precisely the opposite effect to that sought in the Directive! The key explanation for the government taking this line of transferring additional costs away from public expenditure lies in the Treasury rules which operate within British central government. Quite simply, the Treasury will not pay for additional public spending arising from EU policy commitments. Hence the domestic ministry concerned is confronted with funding the additional spending by making cuts elsewhere, in its domestic programme. Alternatively, it can transfer the additional expenditure out of the public sector altogether, as happened in this instance.[28] British employers were not happy at bearing both a financial burden and a complex legal-regulatory burden.

Transposition of legislation does not, of course, ensure enforcement or compliance. Certainly there is abundant evidence of deficiencies in this respect in health and safety legislation.[29] We may expect this situation to extend to the health and safety aspects of the Maternity Directive and beyond. Poor implementation of such legislation was one motivating factor behind the June 1994 establishment of a European Agency for Health and Safety at Work, based in Bilbao.

Although it is not possible to examine all aspects of the implementation of the Maternity Directive here, it should be clear that the manner in which it is undertaken is crucial. Where individuals feel that implementation has been inadequate, there may be ensuing (albeit protracted) litigation, complete with references to the ECJ for clarification. That litigation might feed back into the 1997 policy review, thus re-formulating the established rules and norms of the governance regime.

The passage of the Maternity Directive was thus but one stage in the iterative pattern of an evolving governance regime.

Notes

1 This chapter deals with Council Directive 92/85/EEC of 19 October 1992 (CEC 1992e). Its title is rather cumbersome, being the Directive on the Introduction of Measures to Encourage Improvements in the Safety and Health at Work of Pregnant Workers and Workers who Have Recently Given Birth or Are Breastfeeding (Tenth Individual Directive Within the Meaning of Article 16(1) of Directive 89/391/EEC). In what follows the legislation will be referred to as the Maternity Directive.

2 Indeed, the Commission's internal market White Paper makes a passing reference – in the section of the White Paper dealing with technical standards – to this connection by indicating that 'the interests of all sections [of the economy] . . . should be incorporated in the policy on the health and safety of workers' (CEC 1985a, para. 72).

3 All references here and in the accompanying text are to the unamended Treaty.

4 The resultant settlement, reached in the same year as the notorious Luxembourg Compromise, reasserted the Council's power by indicating that it, and not the Commission, should be responsible for initiatives on social policy. Just as resulted more generally from the Luxembourg Compromise, so in the specific social policy domain the Commission's authority was curtailed. And this from an initial position of some weakness!

5 Laura Cram's comments were helpful in sorting out some of the developments reported below.

6 *Defrenne* v. *Belgian State* (No. 1) (case 80/70); *Defrenne* v. *SABENA* (No. 2) (case 43/75) [1976] ECR 455; and *Defrenne* v. *SABENA* (No. 3) (case 149/77) [1979] 1365. On these, see Warner (1984: 148–50).

7 This principle was established in several well-known cases, most notably *Van Gend en Loos* (case 26/62) and *Costa* v. *ENEL* (case 6/64). For discussion, see Steiner (1990: 34–43).

8 The inspiration for this appears to have come from the Council of Europe's *European* Social Charter – as distinct from the later *EC* Social Charter. The former organisation's agreements or conventions do not have the binding and enforceable characteristics of EC law.

9 On the negotiation of the TEU, the social provisions contained in it, and the protocols attached to it, see Corbett (1992). On the resultant social policy confusion, see Shaw (1994) and Szysczak (1994). The Social Chapter must be distinguished from the earlier Social Charter.

10   Located within DG X (Information), this service publishes the newsletter *Women of Europe*, which is an important information source for those involved in equal opportunities work. Unlike most areas of SEM policy, there is not a plethora of competing (commercial) sources of information.

11   In the UK a general infrastructure existed as a result of the 1974 Health and Safety at Work Act. The Framework Directive still necessitated modification of some of its procedures. It turned into statutory obligations certain matters, e.g. consultation of the workforce, which had only been implicit previously (Eberlie 1990: 93–7). In the UK there was some consequent move away from the traditional self-regulatory approach towards a statutory pattern.

12   On this proposal see House of Lords Select Committee on the European Communities (1985).

13   Springer, quoting EC figures, states that 'ninety per cent of working women find their jobs in only twelve occupational categories' (1992: 66).

14   The two cases were: *Dekker* v. *Stichting Vormingscentrum voor Jong Volwassenen Plus*, case C-177/88; and *Handels-og Kontorfunktionærernes Forbund i Danmark, acting for Hertz* v. *Dansk Abrbeijdsgiverforening, acting for Aldi Marked K/S*, case 179/88.

15   This applied to those Member States where no adequate guarantees existed in national law. In a related development in the UK, the EOC backed two ex-servicewomen who had been dismissed when they became pregnant, as prescribed under their employment contracts. A court ruling found the contracts to be in breach of the 1976 Equal Treatment Directive. A succession of compensation claims was then filed by other ex-servicewomen dismissed on these grounds (see *Industrial Relations Legal Information Bulletin*, February 1992: 14–15).

16   The EOC also has *locus standi* to bring actions on its own.

17   For the UK, a continuous period of full-time employment for two years was required; five years, if part-time employment. For full details of the complex national arrangements prior to the Maternity Directive, see EIRR, December 1990: 18–19.

18   For full details of the positions of the CBI and other British organisations, see House of Lords Select Committee on the European Communities (1991). The House of Lords report includes the government's estimates of the costs of implementing the original proposals in the UK: £10 million for the health and safety provisions; between £400 million and £500 million per annum for the maternity pay provisions; and between £100 million and £150 million per annum in respect of extending employees' rights to return to their posts after pregnancy. These Department of Employment figures do not account for any benefits arising from the return to their posts of trained employees (i.e. as opposed to the costs of having to train new staff).

19   See the papers reproduced in House of Lords Select Committee on the European Communities (1991: 22–7).

20   There was also some additional consideration of the Directive in the EP's Committee on Social Affairs, Employment and the Working Environment.

21   This suggested utilisation of the Social Protocol was a risky strategy. To be sure, it might enable some of the UK's demands to be eliminated, thereby raising the general level of provision in the Directive. However, it would have

led to the UK being excluded and British working women being denied the benefits which the Maternity Directive, as shaped at the common position stage, would have brought about.

22   The substance of Article 149, EEC became Article 189c, EC following the treaty revision of the TEU.

23   On Belgium, see 'Les Écolos chargent Miet Smet de protéger la maternité', *Le Soir*, 10/11 October 1992: 2. Miet Smet was the Belgian Minister for Social Affairs.

24   Ten oral questions concerning the Directive were tabled for proceedings on 16 September 1992, and directed at the Council presidency or the Commission, followed by debate (*Official Journal*, Debates of the EP, No. 3–421, 16 September 1993: 132–42).

25   The Italian government was unable to negotiate as it was represented only at a junior level due to a governmental crisis.

26   In the event the UK government used an Article 173 action before the ECJ to challenge the Working Time Directive, also based on Article 118a, which provided for a 48-hour basic working week. The ECJ found that the legal base was correct in a November 1996 ruling.

27   We are grateful to Laura Cram for this point.

28   The impact of Treasury rules on European policy-making within Whitehall is being examined by Simon Bulmer and Martin Burch as part of a separate research project funded by the ESRC.

29   On this, see James (1993: 33–4).

10

The governance and regulation of the single market

Introduction

The preceding chapters have analysed the regulatory activities of the EU in terms of the adoption of legislative measures. Indeed, the centrality of legislative action to the completion of the internal market, in a sense, biases accounts of EU regulation in favour of a concern with legislative rule-making. In this chapter, our substantive focus is upon the judicial regulation of the SEM and the interrelationship between the Community and the national courts. Our conceptual focus is upon the linkage of an institutionalist approach to ideas of governance and regulation.

We develop our discussion in three parts. In the first part we analyse the significance of the language of 'governance' and its connection to the rise and transformation of the 'regulatory state'. As Rhodes has identified, 'the term "governance" is popular but imprecise' (1996: 652). The language of governance has become increasingly noticeable in academic discourse and has been deployed in a national context (e.g. Rhodes 1996), in a European context (e.g. Caporaso 1996; Jachtenfuchs 1995; Kohler-Koch 1996; Marks, Hooghe and Blank 1996) and in an international context (e.g. Rosenau 1992). We attach significance to this linguistic turn and suggest that the discourse of governance has emerged in order to conceptualise and, in a sense, to distance modern *governance* from traditional *government*. By 'modern governance' we refer to more complex, differentiated and diffuse systems of control than the more limited institutions and functions associated with the minimal, liberal state which we refer to as 'traditional government'. The language of governance brings to light the changing role and structure of the nation state and the emergence of the EC/EU can be seen as part of this process of transformation.

An important aspect of this shift from government to governance is the rise of the *regulatory* state. Indeed, the academic preoccupation with 'governance' is only matched by its concern with 'regulation'. We suggest that the language of regulation implies a qualitatively different role for modern governance in terms of the pervasiveness of systems of legal control, new functions for traditional institutions, and the development of new institutions and techniques of control. Viewed in this way, we can also move beyond the simple description of regulation as the EU's distinctive mode of governance, to highlight regulation as symbolic of a paradox of modern governance. We suggest that the resort to regulation amounts to both an assertion of governmental control and a simultaneous loss of control as power and authority becomes displaced from central governmental organs. Thus, regulation may be seen as increasingly concerned with governance without government, therefore highlighting problems of authority and legitimacy in the modern state and beyond.

In the second part, we apply a framework developed from this discussion to highlight the nature of the judicial regulation of the internal market. Analyses of the substantive regulatory activities of the ECJ have often been left out of accounts of the SEM. Our goal is not to provide an exhaustive analysis of the Court's free-movement jurisprudence but, rather, to highlight some of the institutional problems which the ECJ faces in seeking to reconcile the supply of integration with the demands of regulatory policy. A brief comparison is also made with the role of the Commission in competition policy.

In the final part we reflect upon different theoretical conceptualisations of the role of the ECJ and argue that an institutionalist approach captures the complex dynamics of a multi-level system of judicial regulation.

Governance and the modern state: beyond the state

The idea of the state conflates a number of different issues. The state is, at one level, a mythical beast: the embodiment of the nation and symbolic of social consensus. Moreover, the state attempts to reconcile the idea of a national identity with the identities of more discrete groupings (including the citizens of the state). But at another level, the state manifests itself more tangibly in the apparatus of government, in particular, in the traditional structures of government such as the legislature, executive and judiciary. One can, therefore, view the state as an institution with both normative and organisational features.

The emergence of a discourse of governance reflects a change to the institution of the state. These changes are both normative (in terms of the role and function of the state) and organisational (in terms of the changing organisational structure of government). The modern state has grown. The nineteenth century night-watchman state has been transformed by the emergence of the regulatory, welfare state. As the state has taken on increased functions of social and economic regulation, the apparatus of government has changed through:

- traditional institutions taking on new roles;
- the creation of new institutions to handle new tasks;
- the application of existing policy instruments to new ends; and
- the creation of new policy instruments.

The traditional roles of national government departments have changed to include tasks of economic management and the provision of social welfare. However, as the state has further evolved, increasingly the direct provision of public goods has been transferred to new institutions, with government departments seeking to steer the activities of these institutions. The growth of the state has also resulted in the increased use of legislation to regulate activities. Legislation has not simply created new prohibitions on activities, but has established, for example, whole frameworks for the notification and reporting of activities, the appointment of regulators and inspectors, and the periodic review of licences and permits (a classic example of this would be environmental policy). Legislation, therefore, can be seen as a trigger for a more significant system of regulation beyond the formal institutions of the state.

The role of national courts has also changed. Courts are no longer simply the arbiters of disputes between private individuals, applying a form of retrospective justice to an existing fact situation, but are increasingly involved in multi-party litigation involving the balancing of many competing interests (so-called 'polycentric problems'), the outcome of which will have enduring repercussions beyond the particular parties and the particular dispute in question (Chayes 1976). Further, the courts may also be involved in the review of specialised decision-making by new regulatory agencies or tribunals.

Our discussion above has sought to connect the discourse of governance with the changing institutions and practices (including legal institutions and practices) of the modern state. Even at the national level, governance is increasingly exercised 'beyond' the state insofar as we refer to governance beyond the traditional formal institutions of the state. The rise of the regulatory state disperses power to new inspectors and agencies. Further, as Rhodes' analysis of governance in Britain suggests (1996), fundamental change has taken place to governance within the traditional structures of the state. As Rhodes describes it, there has been a 'hollowing out of the state' through (1996: 661):

1 privatisation and limitations on public interventions;
2 transfer of functions from central and local government institutions to alternative delivery systems;
3 transfer of functions to the EU; and
4 introduction of new public management with a division of functions between policy and operational dimensions of public services.

Of course, our interest is in governance beyond the state in terms of the transfer of functions to the EU. The creation of the EEC and its evolution into the EU has brought with it a new set of institutions and instruments of governance. Indeed, the institutional structure of the EU is a prime example of the type of dispersal of power described by a discourse of governance. As we have highlighted in our case studies, the organisational structure of EU institutions distributes but also fragments power (e.g. between different Directorates General). Power is also distributed between institutions in the legislative process. Most importantly, power is divided between the EU and the national levels, often leaving it to the ECJ to police the boundaries of power (and through such adjudication, the Court also establishes its own domain of power and influence).

We are not alone in using the language of governance to conceptualise the EU. For Caporaso (1996), governance refers to the process of governing (by which he means 'collective problem solving in the public realm'), rather than to 'the institutions and agents which make up government'. For Jachtenfuchs (1995), the resort to the language of governance connotes a shift from 'the state' (as the fulcrum of political studies) to the 'political system', and is also suggestive of possible limits to the direct governance capacity of the political system (upon which we dwell further below).

As indeed we have suggested in Chapters 1 and 2, the emergence of the EU can be seen as part of a process of the transformation of the nation state. The EU represents a remarkable illustration of the creation of new institutions and policy instruments towards new goals (together with the adaptation of existing institutions, instruments and goals). But, as we argue below, we should not conflate this process of transforming the nation state with a process of governance wholly controlled by Member States (nor necessarily by EU institutions themselves).

We believe that there is a clear trend among analysts of the nation state and of the EU to adopt the discourse of governance as a means of describing governance beyond the state, by which we mean the dispersal of power beyond the traditional institutional structures of the nation state. However, if all this linguistic turn achieved was a focus upon a new set of actors then little would have changed. What is significant about this change of discourse (and this is crucial in respect of our analysis of the EU) is that it highlights governance as both differentiated and problematic. We have, in our adoption of distinct case studies, already highlighted the notion of differentiated governance through governance regimes.[1] Our interest here is in the idea of governance as problematic.

For Rhodes, modern governance is concerned with the steering of 'self-organizing networks' (1996: 658–60). However, one of the problems facing *government* is that '*integrated* networks resist government steering, develop their own policies and mould their environments' (1996: 659) (our emphasis). Three aspects of this insight are worth exploring. The first aspect is the idea of networks of actors. This idea draws on the insights of the policy network/community literature and points to the evolution of networks of decision-makers, experts and interest groups which increasingly operationalise public functions. Again, this approach reminds us of the need to identify accurately the complete set of actors engaged in EU decision-making processes. This insight alone does not takes us very far. It is the 'integration' of these networks of actors that is significant. We suggest that the term 'institutionalisation' can usefully be substituted for 'integration' to highlight the development of routines, standard operating procedures and normative structures through which policy problems are understood, managed and resolved. Finally, and consistent with our argument throughout the book, these processes of institutionalisation provide some autonomy for institutional actors in that direct forces attempting to steer such organisational networks may be resisted.

This leads us to an important conclusion. We view modern governance as the problematic attempt to reconcile a dualism of control/loss of control. That is to say, the emergence of governance beyond the state has been a response to the inability of traditional formal state institutions to manage the size and complexity of the regulatory tasks facing them. That governance is a pervasive feature of modern life none the less indicates that control or regulation has not disappeared, but rather that its institutional form has changed. However, in the process of changing, the control exercised by traditional governmental structures has weakened as power has been dispersed both internally within the nation state and externally to the structures of the EU. In this sense, the resort to national and EU regulation is simultaneously an act of control and a loss of control over decision-making. That is to say, national governments are only in control of both national and EU decision-making insofar as they can successfully steer the complex organisational networks which operationalise governance. Our belief is that national governments cannot always successfully steer such systems and that, at the EU level, explanatory power must be given to the role of supranational actors, interest groups, together with the rules and norms which shape their organisation and interaction. Thus, the discourse of governance is not merely a new way of describing government, but a discourse which problematises the control of national executive elites in steering both national and EU decision-making processes.

Specifically in the context of the EU, as Marks, Hooghe and Blank make clear (1996), the use of the discourse of governance reflects a particular theoretical position which challenges neo-realist or inter-governmentalist conceptions of state power as resting in the hands of national executives. We share such scepticism of neo-realist and inter-governmentalist accounts. Indeed, the tendency of such scholarship to provide a single narrative of the creation and exercise of EU governance attributes a degree of coherence and surrogate legitimacy to EU governance that we find hard to accept. Rather, we view the governance of the EU as not simply characterised by the dispersal of power and authority, but also as more fractured, potentially incoherent and tension-filled than inter-governmentalist or neo-functionalist perspectives would suggest. This implies that not only do national executives face problems of steering, but also the networks of actors at the EU level may face their own problems of organisation and policy coordination. Crucially, the discourse of governance requires us to problematise issues of control, accountability and legitimacy. The next wave of scholarship on the EU will be concerned not simply with the sort of exercise in which we have engaged (the mapping of governance), but with a more normative analysis of the type of polity which is emerging.

We have noted above the connection between the discourse of governance and the rise of the regulatory state. In the following section we reflect upon the regulatory nature of EU governance.

Regulation

Majone has remarked (1994: 78) that there is a tendency among European scholars to 'identify regulation with the whole realm of legislation, governance and social control' and therefore to conflate the specific issue of regulatory policy with more general issues of governance. By contrast, Majone, drawing on US experience, defines regulation as a distinctive mode of governance premised upon the promulgation and enforcement of rules (i.e. distinct from distributive or redistributive policies funded and controlled by budgetary and public expenditure considerations). Thus, Majone distinguishes between social regulation, on the one hand, and social policy on the other (Majone, 1993). Not only is regulation a distinctive mode of governance, for Majone regulation has the 'single normative justification' of the correction of market failure.

Majone has, thus, sought to describe the EU as a form of regulatory state (1994). Caporaso has also suggested that the imagery of the regulatory state is useful in analysing the EU (1996). But do we need to distinguish between governance as a broad issue of control and regulation as a specific mode of control?

One *can* distinguish between different modes of governance. To pick out governance through rules and to label this 'regulation' may be helpful, especially in the EU context where the EU possesses few policy instruments other than its rule-making powers. However, there may be good reasons for adopting a more inclusive definition of regulation. 'Regulation' connotes not just rule-making and rule-enforcement, but also broader processes of surveillance, inspection and control. Moreover, regulatory programmes do not always simply involve one mode of governance, but many. Only to focus upon one aspect as 'regulation' may be to artificially dissect a complex system of governance.

The real crux of Majone's claim to treat regulation as a distinctive mode of governance is his suggestion that regulation is underpinned by a single normative justification: the correction of market failure. The importance of this attempt to identify a single normative justification is that it places limits on regulatory policy – regulation as itself limited. Further, the source of this limitation is not mere arbitrary whim or political discretion, but is found within the science of economics. It is this theoretical position which justifies the discrete treatment of regulatory policy.

Three sorts of problems are associated with this image of regulatory policy. The first problem is its privileging of economic theory and the voice of the rational economist in the policy-making process. To be sure, economic knowledge is an important source of knowledge in the regulatory process, but neither does economics simply produce single true answers to policy problems, nor should economic knowledge be the sole reference point.

Secondly, in this process of privileging economic knowledge, the self-referential idea of regulation as itself regulated may give a mistaken perception of regulatory control as limited and therefore contained. The institutional processes of economic regulation may be anything but limited and controlled. Even attempts to apply, for example, a pure theory of competition may require far-reaching fact-finding investigations, hearings and analysis. In this way, the institutional form and context of regulation is highly significant to the extent of regulation.

Finally, there is a danger in shifting from a normative theory of regulation to a description of the EU as 'regulatory'. In short, we suggest that the 'oughtness' of Majone's approach is not borne out by the 'is' of EU governance. Rather, we agree with Caporaso (1996) and Wilks (1996) that the depiction of the EU as a form of regulatory state needs to be placed within the specific historical, social, political, economic and legal context of the EU. Looked at through the institutional lenses of EU governance, it becomes apparent that EU regulation does not possess a single normative justification of the correction of market failure.

It *is* possible to conceive of EU regulation as correcting market failure (e.g. competition policy corrects for inefficient allocation of goods and services as a result of restrictive agreements and the abuse of market power; social regulation corrects for the assumption of risks and employment conditions arising from asymmetric power relations between employers and employees; environmental regulation corrects for the failure to internalise environmental externalities arising from the production and consumption of goods and services). But, it is not necessarily the case that the correction of market failure is the only policy imperative being pursued.

Moreover, the conception of regulation as correcting market failures relates to the control of a market which is presupposed to be integrated. If one looks to the internal market (rather than the flanking policies which together with the internal market constitute the SEM), EU regulation is not concerned with market failure but with the barriers arising from divergent national regulation. One can construct an argument that EU regulation is correcting for the failure of the market in national public goods (i.e. national regulation), but that would be to put the cart before the horse. EU regulation exists precisely because of the historic lack of market or other mechanisms by which national regulations were exposed to one another.

For the reasons we highlight above we see no need at this stage to make the kind of distinction which Majone makes between regulatory policy as a mode of governance and other modes of governance except to admit that it is true that the primary policy instrument at the EU's disposal is control through legal rules. Rather, we talk of the governance of the EU when we talk in general terms about the governing capacity of the EU. We refer to regulation when we talk in more specific terms about the operationalisation of governance in discrete contexts. Indeed, we deploy the language of regulation to highlight the important institutional features of EU governance and their impact upon the style, content and efficacy of regulation.

Regulating the single market

We turn, now, to the application of the ideas developed above to the judicial regulation of the internal market. In our case studies, we noted the interaction between the legislative and judicial organs of the EU. Our concern here is more squarely with the role of the courts *per se*, and especially the interaction between the ECJ and the national courts. This focus is important because of the tendency to reduce the completion of the SEM to the enactment of White Paper legislative measures. As we have argued throughout, we need to look beyond the White Paper if our analysis of the SEM is to be adequate. Further, the judicial regulation of the internal market, in particular the significance to be attached to the ECJ's *Cassis de Dijon* decision, has been the battleground for different analyses and theorisations of the role of the ECJ in the integration process (see Alter and Meunier-Aitsahalia 1994; Burley and Mattli 1993; Garrett 1992; 1995; Mattli and Slaughter 1995; Moravcsik 1995; Wincott 1995). Therefore, it is appropriate that we consider this important aspect of internal market regulation, and that we seek to relate this to our general discussion of EU governance.

In our analysis we examine key features of EU governance and their impact upon the regulation of the internal market. An important aspect of study is the exercise of governance beyond the nation state in the form of transfers of power to EU institutions, but also the transformation of the roles of national institutions. We also analyse the problems attached to governance in terms of the ability of national and, indeed also, EU institutions to control the systems of regulation under their charge. These problems relate to (1) the establishment of limits to the scope of EC rules; (2) the role of national regulators; and (3) the difficulties in reconciling integration with regulation.

The judicial regulation of the internal market

Beyond the state

In addition to the provisions of the Treaty that provide for the adoption of internal market rules (positive integration), the Treaty also pursues negative integration through the prohibition on Member States from maintaining national rules which inhibit the free movement of goods (Article 30, EC); workers (Article 48, EC); services (Article 59, EC); capital (Article 67, EC). At a very basic level, regulatory policy is no longer simply a matter for the nation states to decide. Rather, the exercise of national regulatory policy is subject to EC control through the ECJ. Member States only retain regulatory competence to the extent that its exercise is compatible with EC law. In this way, governance extends beyond the nation state through the exercise of power by new, supranational institutional structures. These structures include not only the ECJ itself but also the Commission (which may enforce the provisions of the Treaty under Article 169, EC) and the legal services of the other institutions.

However, to focus simply on the supranational level would be to ignore the important transformation of the institutions of the Member States. Through the principles of direct effect and supremacy (and also through the ECJ's invocation of a duty of loyal cooperation arising from Article 5, EC), the ECJ has sought to transform national courts into Community courts (Maher 1994; Temple Lang 1997). Not only have national parliaments lost the sovereignty to enact rules incompatible with EC law, but the national courts have been placed in new roles with new duties *vis-à-vis* their national parliaments and the ECJ itself. This change to the roles of national courts is important. More legal actions are brought in the national courts challenging national laws which inhibit free movement than are instigated by the Commission using infringement proceedings. The litigation activities of private litigants are thus central to the system of judicial control over the Member States.

Controlling the regulatory system

We analyse three aspects of the problem of regulatory control: the limits of the rules on free movement; the relationship between the national courts and the ECJ in applying directly effective Treaty provisions; and the difficulties in reconciling the integration of the internal market with its regulation.

The scope of internal market rules on free movement: rendering 'suspect' national law The case law on free movement has been developed in the context of the Treaty rules on the free movement of goods (Article 30) and subsequently applied to the areas of workers and services.[2] The essence of the ECJ's approach has been a process of rendering national laws 'suspect' and then subjecting them to strict scrutiny. In particular, the ECJ has adopted:

- a broad jurisdictional approach to when national measures fall foul of the Treaty.[3] Thus, the scope of the Treaty is not limited to discriminatory measures but also includes measures which are 'indistinctly applicable' – they apply to national and non-national manufacturers, service providers or workers alike – if these measures make it harder or impossible to place products, services or workers on the Community market;
- in respect of *directly* discriminatory measures, a limited scope for the application of Treaty-provided exceptions to the free-movement principle (Article 36 on the free-movement of goods which permits exception to the free-movement principle on public policy grounds, e.g. protection of public health);
- a limited ability for states to argue that national rules which are indistinctly applicable none the less pursue valued regulatory objectives and do so without a disproportionate effect on inter-state trade (the *Cassis de Dijon* 'mandatory requirements' justification).

Our task here is not to engage in a detailed analysis of the case law of the internal market. Rather, we seek to indicate the problems encountered by the ECJ in establishing limits to the scope of its rules.

In respect of the free movement of goods, the ECJ extended its strict scrutiny of national laws beyond national rules on product composition, shape, packaging and labelling, to include challenges to national rules which in more general terms affected the sale of products, e.g. restrictions on shop opening hours. The extension of the Court's case law to general selling conditions became increasingly confused and many commentators noted the increasing difficulty in discerning the outer-limits of Article 30 (e.g. Gormley 1989; White 1989). In 1993 the ECJ, in its *Keck*[4] decision, redrew the boundaries of its regulatory control. It conditionally excluded from the scope of Article 30 national measures which related to 'selling arrangements' (i.e. not product-specific). Thus, the scope of Article 30 would no longer cover legislation such as the UK's Sunday trading legislation (which had previously been challenged in the national and the EC courts, and which had created much confusion among litigants, lawyers and courts alike).

The broad jurisdictional approach previously taken by the ECJ had created a framework in which undertakings could challenge a whole range of national laws, the impact of which on inter-state trade was largely speculative. The 'clarification' in *Keck* was an attempt to reassert control over the scope of Article 30 and to reduce the quantity of speculative litigation. However, the concept of 'selling arrangement' is itself somewhat ambiguous (and therefore subject to clarification through further litigation). As Weatherill has argued, it may be in the realm of the free movement of workers and freedom to provide services that the ECJ has begun more generally to refine the scope of its control over free movement (1996).

The ECJ has extended its approach to the free movement of goods into the areas of services and workers. It has, therefore, established an adaptable regulatory tool which it can routinely apply in cases coming before it. But as we discussed above, that tool has created problems of control for the ECJ. The ECJ appears to be refining that tool, but outside the area of goods. In its decision in *Alpine Investments*,[5] a Dutch law which prohibited telephone sales of financial services to customers in other Member States was found to violate Article 59 (even though it did not discriminate between Dutch service-providers or service-providers from other Member States established in the Netherlands). In its controversial *Bosman* decision[6] the ECJ also found that a rule which required the payment of transfer fees before players (whether nationals or not) could move between football clubs could constitute a barrier to the free movement of workers. Thus, if the effect of such a rule was to make it more difficult for a footballer in one Member State to seek employment in another, then this could constitute an infringement of the Treaty if it had a disproportionate impact on free movement.

The ECJ appears to be focusing more clearly on the issue of barriers to market access as the threshold for when measures may fall foul of the Treaty. Its approach is still highly jurisdictional and brings a broad range of national measures within the gaze of the ECJ. It is noteworthy that in *Bosman* the German government sought to rely on the subsidiarity principle in arguing that the ECJ should decline jurisdiction in the case. For the German government, what was at issue was a matter of national culture and identity (sport in general and football in particular), and therefore this was best dealt with nationally. This argument did not succeed and the ECJ therefore wrested this issue out of the hands of the national authorities and into the arena of the Court. It is not yet clear whether the German government's challenge to the jurisdiction of the ECJ is part of a wider discontent with the transfer of regulatory control away from the nation state.

We suggest that the evolution of the ECJ's case law is indicative of a process of seeking to maintain control over a system in which the ECJ is only partly in control. The Court cannot control the use which national litigants will seek to make of EC law. Thus, the boundaries of its jurisprudence are constantly tested by the ingenuity of litigants and their legal advisers. The result is not an incoherent system. But it is a system in which the coherence and function of regulation, and the control of the ECJ, is always in question.

The role of national courts The Treaty provisions which provide for the negative integration of the internal market are directly effective and therefore capable of being enforced in the national courts. To be sure, the Commission can bring infringement proceedings under Article 169, EC for breaches by Member States of these provisions. However, the majority of free movement cases emanate from the national courts. Two types of issue arise from this de-centralised enforcement of EC law. First, there is the organisational issue of the effectiveness of the connection between the national courts and the ECJ under Article 177, EC. Secondly, how capable are national courts of carrying out the tasks demanded of them by the ECJ?

Article 177, EC establishes a mechanism by which national courts may seek from the ECJ preliminary rulings regarding the correct interpretation of EC law. This is clearly an important connection between the national courts and the ECJ to ensure the uniform, but de-centralised, enforcement of EC law. For Burley and Mattli (1993), the Article 177 system is the centre-piece by which legal integration has been achieved and provides the focus for their attempt to apply a neo-functionalist analysis to EC law.

We suggest that the relationship between national courts and the ECJ is more problematic. The first problem is that of the success of the Article 177 system. After some encouragement by the ECJ, national courts became more than willing to seek preliminary rulings from the ECJ. The result has been an overloading of the EC judicial system and excessive delay for litigants. At one stage it was taking two years for preliminary rulings to be handed down. This delay has now dropped to eighteen months but that can hardly be considered to be satisfactory. Two solutions to this problem present themselves. Either the EC judicial branch expands to deal with the number of cases coming before it, or the national courts are encouraged to handle more cases on their own. The EC judicial branch has already expanded through the creation of the CFI. However, there is little evidence that this has significantly improved matters (it does not deal with Article 177 references at all). More radical reform may be required (especially in the light of the potential enlargement of the EU).

The ECJ has sought to encourage national courts to decide matters for themselves where possible either because there is a precedent in the ECJ's jurisprudence which can resolve the issue or because EC law is so clear that the national courts are able to deal with the issue (*CILFIT*[7]). The national courts themselves have sought to lay down guidelines on when national courts should seek rulings from the ECJ.[8] Yet, there is always a danger than national courts will not get things right, or will adopt a narrower perspective than the ECJ may have taken. This is something of which the national courts are also aware.[9] It is important, therefore, not to lapse into an assumption that the Article 177 procedure is a mechanism through which the collected wisdom of the ECJ simply flows down to the national legal orders. To be sure, it provides a connection between the national and legal orders. But there are problem attached to how that connection functions.

It is apparent that if national courts are to act as Community courts, they must know what it is they are supposed to do according to the case law established by the ECJ. This is all well and good if the ECJ gives judgments which are fully reasoned and transparent. But, if an Advocate General of the ECJ can describe the cases which have sought to clarify the scope of Article 30 as possessing 'scant and undoubtedly inadequate reasoning' (Tesauro 1996: 7), then there is little hope for the national courts. Not only may there be a problem of excessive demand for preliminary rulings, but the supply of rulings (both quantitatively and qualitatively) may be inadequate. Thus, the problem of making clear the boundaries of the free-movement rules is not just a problem for the ECJ, it is a problem for the national courts.

Even if the national courts get round the problem of knowing what to do, they may be faced with an equally large problem of doing what they are asked to do. In theory the ECJ identifies if a measure which applies to domestic and imported products constitutes a trade barrier, leaving it to the national courts to decide whether the measure has a disproportionate effect on inter-state trade. But how is a national court to assess the inter-state trade impacts? The English courts (from the top of the judicial hierarchy to the bottom) had enormous difficulty in assessing whether national rules which prohibited Sunday trading constituted disproportionate restrictions of inter-state trade (Hoffman 1997).

In summary, we can identify three types of problem which have emerged with regard to the relationship between the ECJ and the national courts in the regulation of the internal market: first, difficulties in defining the scope of the rules, leading to second, increased demand for Article 177 rulings from the national courts, but inadequate supply of rulings to allow national courts to carry out the tasks demanded of them, and third, the requirement that national courts assess the proportionality of trade barriers when they may be ill equipped to do so.

Reconciling integration with regulation   It is important to recognise that it is not simply within the political institutions that the goals of integration are reconciled with the need to give effect to valued regulatory objectives. It will be apparent from our discussion above that this task also falls to the national courts and to the ECJ. Whereas the political institutions can negotiate exceptions to and exclusions from rules, the courts have less room for manoeuvre. Either a measure falls foul of the Treaty or it does not.

Two types of issue arise here. The first concerns whether the demands of internal market integration can be reconciled with regulatory objectives expressed in national law. The second issue concerns whether integration within the internal market can be reconciled with regulatory objectives pursued by other EU policies.

In respect of the relationship between the internal market and national law, as Wils has noted (1993), over time the clearly discriminatory trade barriers have been removed, leaving the ECJ with the increasingly difficult task of reconciling the demands of integration with the desire to protect valued regulatory goals. A good illustration of the problems facing the ECJ was the question of whether Danish laws on re-usable drinks containers fell foul of Article 30. The Court found that in principle national rules designed to protect the environment (by requiring the supply of drinks in re-usable containers) could constitute proportionate and legitimate national rules, i.e. the valued regulatory goal might trump the free-movement principle. However, the Court found that a limitation on the quantity of non-approved containers which would be permitted to enter the Danish market was not proportionate (see also our discussion of the ECJ's decision on the Wallonia waste ban in Chapter 8).

In *Cinéthèque*,[10] the ECJ was asked to consider whether a French law which prevented the sale or hire of videos of films that were in their first year of release fell foul of Article 30. The Court found that the law did pursue a valued regulatory objective (the protection of cinema as a valued cultural good) without having a disproportionate effect on trade.

It is evident that not only does the ECJ have a difficult task in reconciling integration with regulation, but *how* it does so is shaped by the judicial tools it has fashioned (e.g. whether the regulatory objective falls within those recognised by the ECJ and whether there is a disproportionate impact on trade). Policy problems are, therefore, constructed within the language and logic of legal structures. The *Bosman* ruling discussed above not only raised the question of *how* the ECJ should reconcile the demands of integration with the regulation of football, but also *whether* this should be a task for the ECJ. As the ECJ itself stated in *Cassis*, its role in pursuing negative integration takes place 'in the absence of common rules'. In other words, in order for the Member States to wrest control away from the ECJ it is up to them to negotiate and agree EC rules (positive integration). However, the legislative arena is not one in which the Member States either collectively or individually have complete control. Not only must the Council increasingly cooperate with the EP as co-legislator, the extension of QMV has reduced individual veto possibilities. Therefore, the *judicial* reconciliation of integration and regulation is set to be a continuing feature of the governance of the SEM.

A different kind of issue relates to the relationship between internal market integration and the objectives of EU flanking policies. We have seen in the *Danish Bottles* example above that the goals of environmental policy are recognised as providing exceptions to the free movement of goods. But can integration within the internal market provide an exception to the operation of a flanking policy area? A good example is EC competition policy (albeit that our concern is not with judicial regulation but regulation by the Commission).

In its purest from, competition policy is based on a classical economic concern with the promotion of efficiency (or perhaps more accurately the avoidance of inefficiency which results from monopoly power). EC competition policy, while it has its roots in such classic concerns, may be said to be concerned more with the achievement of workable competition rather than with pure competition. The Commission's traditional approach to competition policy has also sought to prevent agreements between undertakings from partitioning the single market.

This need to accommodate the internal market goal has had a profound effect on the application of the competition rules. For example, the Commission has often been the object of criticism in its scrutiny of vertical agreements under Article 85, EC. The criticisms point to an overconcentration by the Commission on restrictions upon *intra*-brand competition (as where distribution agreements partition markets on national lines by preventing parallel imports) and an insufficient consideration of whether *inter*-brand competition has been affected.[11] Thus, the regulatory control over such agreements has tended to be premised upon their market-partitioning potential and not necessarily upon their impact on competition and economic efficiency.[12] Weatherill and Beaumont state the point nicely in their remark,

> the function of competition law in a common market extends beyond mere control of the anti-competitive consequences of collusion. It also looks to the objective of market integration, a matter of no concern within a national market. (1995: 667)

To be sure, the Commission has come under increasing pressure to engage in more rigorous economic analysis and to look more closely at whether agreements which appear to restrict intra-brand competition none the less stimulate inter-brand competition. In January 1997, the Commission adopted a Green Paper on *Vertical Restraints in EU Competition Policy* (CEC 1996g). Among the reasons the Commission cites for the necessity of this review are the virtual completion of the SEM and the trend in economic thinking towards a less regulatory approach to vertical agreements.

It may be that with the near completion of the SEM, competition policy will become more competition-minded and will conform to Majone's definition of regulation (see above). But, it must be stated that hitherto competition policy has sought to reconcile the operation of a regulatory policy which assumes an integrated market, with a market which was in the process of integrating.

Summary
We suggest that our analysis of the judicial regulation of the internal market highlights the usefulness of the language of governance. That language encapsulates the transfer of power to new institutions beyond the nation state, together with transformations to national institutions. The

scrutiny of national regulatory policy by EC and national courts is indicative of the shifting pattern of power which ideas of governance allude to. As we have also indicated, not only may there be a loss of control by national executives over national regulatory policy, but new structures of governance (like the ECJ) may find it difficult to control their own regulatory system. It is appropriate that we turn to a conceptualisation of the role of the ECJ in the light of these themes.

Governance and regulation: conceptualising the role of the ECJ

The role of the ECJ has been much debated in academic literature. In the following sections we explore the neo-rationalist and neo-functionalist images of the ECJ in the light of our analysis above. We suggest that an institutionalist conception of the ECJ is preferable.

Neo-rationalist and neo-functionalist images of the ECJ
There is a danger that we may overemphasise the controlling influences of actors like the ECJ and the problems which national executives encounter in attempting to steer the EU's governance structure. Two lines of argument present themselves. One line of argument would be that the actions of the ECJ do in fact correspond to the preferences of the Member States. What might pass for a loss of control is, none the less, part of the calculated trade-off for a system of supranational enforcement which ensures that all Member States respect the bargains they have struck (Garrett 1995; Moravcsik 1995). The second line of argument rejects the idea that the Court and the EC legal system reflects the preferences of the Member States, but notes that the ECJ may itself have problems in steering the system it has established.

The first line of argumentation – that the EC legal system conforms to the preferences of the Member States – is evident in Garrett's account of the role of the ECJ (1995). He presents a two-sided image of how the Member States and the ECJ interact. On one side, Member States will argue for upholding the compatibility of national law with EC law where the potential negative effects of a contrary ruling affect a clear and important national sectional interest. However, if the ECJ finds the national law to be incompatible with the Treaty there is, none the less, an incentive for the national government to comply with the ruling because of the benefit of supporting a legal system which enforces rules against all Member States and helps overcome problems of incomplete contracting. On the other side of the coin, the ECJ will tend to accept a government's argument for upholding national law where it is likely that the national government will not abide by its decision (calling into question the ECJ's authority and legitimacy). However, if the impact of a negative decision upon a Member State is diffuse, then this allows the ECJ to push forward a more integrative strategy. Together, these images present the Member States and the ECJ as being engaged in a game, each with a rational set of preferences, and the outcome of the game is referable to how these preferences are played out.

In our discussion of free movement (above) we gave a truncated overview of the case law in this area. Our aim was to highlight the extent to which the ECJ's case law opens and closes regulatory spaces. This contrasts markedly with the account of the judicial regulation of the internal market offered by Garrett which is an account wholly without law. As Mattli and Slaughter suggest in their critique of Garrett, it is almost as if, for Garrett, the ECJ's case law is so incoherent as to render it of no importance to adjudication (1995). We share Mattli and Slaughter's belief that to remove the law from the equation is unacceptable. The ECJ's currency is legal argumentation rather than precise calculations of costs and benefits. There may be incoherencies in the case law as we have noted, but that is hardly the same as saying that those incoherencies (and coherencies) are unimportant to decision-making.

Moreover, Garrett's position is not only empirically unsound; its own theoretical coherence is dubious. If the ECJ did decide cases in the light of the potential impact of rulings within Member States, then presumably this might give rise to different rulings on the same type of situation in different countries. How then is this to be squared with the benefits which Garrett claims Member States derive from having a legal system which ensures that all Member States are subject to the same system of enforcement? For Garrett (and also for Moravcsik who also applies a neo-rationalist analysis in an attempt to square 'judicial autonomy' with an inter-governmentalist approach: 1995), there is no such thing as irrational action on the part of the Member States. Whether Member States win or lose before the ECJ, their actions are rational. This is deeply uninspiring and amounts to a failure to get to grips with the legal dimension. Further, there is a danger in surrogately legitimating the actions of the ECJ by reference to the consent of the Member States. We prefer an image of judicial action which requires the ECJ itself to accept responsibility for its own actions.

We turn to what we consider to be the more problematic issue, namely that of system steering. We have argued that the system for the judicial regulation of the internal market is one which wrests control from the Member States who are unable then directly to steer the actions of the national and the EC courts. However, the ECJ may have its own difficulties in steering the judicial regulation of the internal market according to the regulatory tools it has created.

Mattli and Slaughter have placed the Article 177 system at the heart of their suggestion that a neo-functionalist analysis best captures this relationship between the national and the EC legal orders (Mattli and Slaughter

1995; see also Burley and Mattli 1993). While we do not doubt the importance of this mechanism, we do cast doubt on the claims that this mechanism is necessarily integrative (in the sense that Mattli and Slaughter use the term 'integration' to mean the penetration of the EC legal order into the domestic), and that the political effects of legal integration are masked. Rather, the excessive demand for preliminary rulings and the inadequate supply of such rulings indicates a more problematic relationship between national courts and the ECJ. Further, the types of cases which have increasingly come before the Court have, far from masking the political consequences of integration, raised the political consequences (whether in terms of national control of environmental policy or national control of sport – see above).

We do not disagree that litigants have increasingly transferred their expectations and activities to the EC level, in terms of their resort to EC law to seek to remove restrictions on trade. But we do not agree that this amounts to the integration of a legal community in neo-functionalist terms.[13] As we have highlighted, the ECJ has genuine difficulties in its relationship with the national courts (and vice versa).

Towards a reconceptualisation of the ECJ

We suggest that the evidence from the judicial regulation of the internal market justifies our use of the term 'governance' to analyse the regulatory activities of the ECJ. We find both a dispersal of power beyond the traditional institutions of the Member States and, indeed, a transformation in the role of national institutions such as the national courts. We also believe that this shift in control from the national to the EU level should not be thought of as a simple and linear transfer of control. As Wincott has argued, it may be a 'mistake to depict the Court as wholly in control of its environment' (1995: 583). We have suggested above that the ECJ encounters problems of steering both procedurally and substantively within the internal market.

Our position is neither that EC law is so incoherent or irrelevant that the actions of the ECJ can be reduced to games of preferences, nor that the ECJ is so clear about its vision of integration that a teleology of integration can be relied upon to explain ECJ action. Our view is that, as Wincott has suggested (1995), the ECJ has been able to act as a 'purposeful opportunist' seeking to explore the possibilities for expanding the scope and effectiveness of EC law.[14] The ECJ's abilities to act purposefully are, however, constrained. In particular, the legal formalism which Mattli and Slaughter highlight as important in masking and shielding the ECJ in its integrative endeavours, may actually be more significant at the more mundane level of locking in the ECJ to paths of action which bring to light unintended consequences and create problems of system-control. That is to say, the ECJ is like any court in that it must treat like cases alike unless it can find reasons for distinguishing or departing from what it has done in the past. As we noted with regard to 'selling arrangements' in respect of goods, the ECJ found itself in an area of legal control it did not want to be, yet found it hard to extricate itself until its decision in *Keck* in which the Court rather blandly announced it was acting 'contrary to what has previously been decided'. While the ECJ *can* extricate itself from its past decisions, it does so at risk to its authority and legitimacy.

Our image of the Court is also consistent with Wincott's identification of the ECJ as developing 'doctrines through an incremental and learning process' (1995: 586). There is a danger in Mattli and Slaughter's image of the ECJ which implies that it knows what it is doing and has the means at its disposal to bring its will about. Our belief is that the ECJ *explores*. It fashions policy tools and then seeks to explore their virtues and vices. But, through the very act of creating policy tools, the Court's act of control is also a loss of control. The ECJ, by following one route rather than another, denies itself the possibility of following the alternative path. Further, the choice of path itself may create unintended consequences, or the intended consequences may not create the desired effects. Thus, not only does the establishment of a system of EC courts (connected to national courts) create an organisational network which is beyond direct steering by the Member States, the institutionalisation of certain routines and standard operating procedures may make control of that regulatory system difficult for judicial actors themselves.

It is crucial to our image of the ECJ that it must accept responsibility for its policy choices. Thus, the legitimacy of its decision-making is reduced neither to the tacit consent of the Member States nor to a belief that it is conforming to a teleology of integration. The type of adjudication which the ECJ embarks upon has repercussions for the conduct of the activities of individuals, groups, national institutions and EU institutions. These repercussions reverberate beyond the specific facts of cases which come before the ECJ. It is important that we begin to interrogate more fully what type of order (what manner of governance and regulation) is created and institutionalised in law.

Conclusion

Descriptively, the discourse of governance is extremely useful in highlighting the differentiation of functions and dispersal of power beyond the formal institutions of the nation state. Further, it also averts to the transformation of national institutions as they engage in new regulatory tasks. These processes of power dispersal and of institutional transformation include the governance activities of the EU institutions. Modern governance is increasingly regulatory not simply in the sense of establishing new types of prohibitions, but also in terms of establishing whole regulatory systems of notification, surveillance and control.

Normatively, the discourse of governance problematises issues of control, particularly as regards the control of national executives over regulatory institutional structures. In our case studies we have examined the importance of the institutional structures of EU governance in shaping the policy process. In this chapter we highlighted the importance of the judicial regulation of the internal market in wresting control of national regulatory policy away from the nation state. But it is equally important to recognise that in the governance and regulation of the EU, the flow of policy problems and the institutionalisation of particular policy solutions may make it difficult for EU institutional actors themselves to control their own systems of governance and regulation.

We suggest that our approach to governance and regulation within the SEM sheds a theoretical light upon the activities of the ECJ which is different from that cast by neo-rationalist and neo-functionalist accounts of the Court. We believe that an institutionalist account of the ECJ is important in rendering contestable the governance capacity and legitimacy of ECJ decision-making.

Notes

1 Rhodes, in his analysis of national governance, also notes that 'Central government is no longer supreme. The political system is increasingly differentiated' (Rhodes 1996: 657).

2 There is evidence that the ECJ's approach to free movement is now being developed more in the context of workers and services (see Weatherill 1996).

3 In its decision in Case 8/74, *Procureur du Roi* v. *Dassonville* [1974] ECR 837, the ECJ adopted the highly jurisdictional approach to when measures had an impact on inter-state trade as had been developed earlier in respect of the competition rules (see Case 56/65, *Société Technique Minière* v. *Maschinenbau Ulm* [1966] ECR 235). Thus, a national measure had the necessary EC dimension when it 'actually or potentially, directly or indirectly' had an impact on inter-state trade. There are many close parallels between the development of the rules on free movement and those on the application of the competition rules. Many of the problems we discuss in relation to goods (especially in terms of an overloading of the EU institutional system) can also be found in the area of competition policy (e.g. the overloading of DG IV with notifications of agreements which companies are concerned may fall foul of Article 85(1). The Commission has sought to tackle these problems and its recent Green Paper on Vertical Restraints (CEC 1996g) is perhaps indicative of a less regulatory approach to these types of agreement. Further, the Commission has sought increasingly to rely on de-centralised enforcement of EC competition rules by the national courts (for a critique see Shaw 1995a). However, as we argue with regard to the de-centralised enforcement of the free-movement rules, there are problems attached to this.

4   Cases C-267, C-268/91 *Keck and Mithouard* [1993] ECR I-6097.
5   Case C-384/93 [1995] ECR I-1141.
6   Case C-415/93, *Union Royale Belge des Sociétés de Football Association* v. *Jean-Marc Bosman* [1995] ECR I-4921.
7   Case 283/81, *CILFIT* v. *Italian Ministry of Health* [1982] ECR 3415.
8   See the guidance which Lord Denning sought to provide for the English courts in *Bulmer* v. *Bollinger* [1974] Ch. 401.
9   See Justice Bingham's remarks in *Commissioners of Customs and Excise* v. *Samex ApS* [1983] 3 CMLR 194:

> Sitting as a judge in a national court, asked to decide questions of Community law, I am very conscious of the advantages enjoyed by the Court of Justice. It has a panoramic view of the Community and its institutions, a detailed knowledge of the Treaties and of much subordinate legislation made under them, and an intimate familiarity with the functioning of the Community market which no national judge denied the collective experience of the Court of Justice could hope to achieve. Where questions of administrative intention and practice arise the Court of Justice can receive submissions from the Community institutions, as also where relations between the Community and the Member States are in issue. Where the interests of Member States are affected they can intervene to make their views known ... Where comparison falls to be made between Community texts in different languages, all texts being equally authentic, the multinational Court of Justice is equipped to carry out the task in a way which no national judge, whatever his linguistic skills, could rival ...

10 Cases 60–61/84, *Cinéthèque SA* v. *Fédération Nationale des Cinémas Français* [1985] ECR 2605.
11 For example, Cases 56 and 58/64, *Consten and Grundig* v. *Commission* [1966] ECR 299.
12 It must be made clear, however, that the Commission has indicated a new awareness that vertical agreements do not necessarily restrict competition. That said, clauses in agreements which serve to partition markets will still run into difficulties: see Case 161/84, *Pronuptia* v. *Schillgalis* [1986] ECR 353.
13 It is also worth noting that this process of transferring expectations and activities to the supranational courts does not necessarily entail a transfer of 'loyalties' (to use Haas' definition of the creation of a political community; 1957: 16). It is, of course, possible, that individuals who successfully rely on EC law to win a case may feel more 'inclined' towards the EU, but then again their actions may be more instrumental. Mattli and Slaughter tend more towards Lindberg's definition of a political community which does not require a transfer of loyalties (Lindberg 1963: 6). But if this part of the definition is left out, one is left to ponder the predictive (rather than the descriptive) power of neo-functionalism.
14 Wincott borrows the idea of 'purposeful opportunist' from Cram's description of the Commission (Cram 1993).

11

The evolving single market

Introduction

We have sought throughout this book to explore the evolution of the SEM from its roots in the original conception of a common market, through to the White Paper on the internal market, and beyond to include policy linkages with such flanking policies as competition, social and environmental policy. Our aim has been to locate high-profile treaty revisions and particularised negotiations within broader histories of decision-making and the institutionalisation of organisational, procedural and normative structures which we view as shaping the outcome of the policy process.

In this chapter we shift focus to the time period following the expiry of the 1992 SEM deadline. The period has attracted the most public attention of any period in the integration story as a consequence of the difficulties associated with the negotiation and ratification of the TEU. It has also been a period in which the EU has enlarged from twelve Member States to its current fifteen with the accession of the former EFTA/EEA states of Austria, Sweden and Finland. The EU is also set to enlarge yet further to include the states of central and eastern Europe. Both the deepening of the EU in the form of the TEU and the widening in respect of the accession of new Member States have implications for the evolution of the SEM. The first part of this chapter, therefore, explores the potential impact of the TEU and of enlargement.

The second part of this chapter continues the analysis of the post-1992 period through an exploration of the EU's attempt to define a role for its governance structure in the wake of the near-completion of the White Paper legislative exercise. In this sense we are, as in the first part, analysing horizontal developments affecting all policy sectors associated with the SEM. However, our focus is more specifically located in the EU's self-conscious attempt to strategically develop the SEM in the light of considerations of subsidiarity, transparency and competitiveness.

Deepening and widening post-1992

In this part we analyse two very visible aspects of post-1992 development. In this first section, the impact of the TEU is explored, focusing on selective features of these treaty revisions. Our attention turns in the second section to the implications of an enlarged membership of the EU.

The TEU

In retrospect, the SEA can be seen as the beginning of a new cycle of Treaty revision which led to the signature of the TEU at Maastricht and leads to the further revision of the Treaties in 1997. In this section, we highlight:

- the emergence of the EU and 'flexible' decision-making;
- the introduction of the co-decision procedure;
- the provisions for economic and monetary union (EMU); and
- the conclusion of a Protocol and Agreement on Social Policy (PASP).

The impact of the subsidiarity principle is considered separately below.

From Community to Union: flexibility and decision-making The importance of the idea of the *acquis communautaire* to the building of a European *Community* might be considered to be threatened by the establishment of a European *Union* in which flexibility in the processes and outcomes of decision-making is introduced. Flexibility in EU regulatory decision-making may take three different forms:

- greater discretion for Member States within a framework of common rules;
- an inter-governmental rather than a Community process of decision-making, leading to common rules which are qualitatively different from EC law; and
- the adoption of rules or systems of regulatory control which apply to some Member States but not to others.

The first two of these forms of flexibility are not new and pre-date the TEU. Flexibility in the first of these senses can be seen with the development of the new approach to harmonisation, an increased sharing of competences and reliance on minimum harmonisation, mutual recognition (see Weatherill 1994) and the possibility of competition among rules (for an analysis see Sun and Pelkmans 1995). It can also be detected in the use of transitional periods and temporary derogations for some Member States.

The second sort of flexibility can be noted in the form of the inter-governmental pillars of the EU in the areas of Justice and Home Affairs, and Common Foreign and Security Policy. In these areas, an inter-governmental process of decision-making leads to the adoption of agreements and common positions which are generally not legally enforceable through the EC judicial system. Again, this form of flexibility pre-dates the TEU (though the establishment of the inter-governmental pillars render it more visible).

The third form of flexibility is different from the other two in that it implies differentiated integration (or variable geometry). It implies that some Member States will not be subject to certain rules or controls and will not, therefore, take part in their negotiation. It is this idea of flexibility which has been discussed in the context of the 1997 revisions to the Treaties to allow certain Member States to push forward a particular integration agenda while others will remain unaffected (at least not directly). This new form of flexibility can be seen in the TEU particularly in the form of the PASP (from which the UK is excluded). This example raises sharply issues as to the nature of EC law (are such directives *Community* law?); the erosion of the *acquis* (can one have an *acquis* '*communautaire*' where duties and rights are not the same across all Member States?); and the role of the ECJ in providing interpretations of EC law in the light of the objectives of the EU (which objectives?). This type of flexibility is new, and its more widespread utilisation would have profound consequences for the legal foundation of the SEM in particular and the EU in general. The politics of differentiated integration sit uneasily with a legal order influenced by the ideology of the *acquis communautaire*.

The co-decision procedure   The TEU amended Article 100a, EC to provide for the adoption of internal market legislation by the co-decision of the Council and the EP (the procedure provided for in Article 189b, EC). The significant changes which this procedure introduced include the greater involvement of the EP in the legislative process (including the ability to veto measures) and the convening of a Conciliation Committee in the event that the Council does not accept all of the EP's amendments. On the one hand, this might be considered something of a Pyrrhic victory for the Parliament in that the bulk of the White Paper measures had been adopted by the 1992 deadline. On the other hand, in looking beyond the White Paper we find that some thirty pieces of internal market legislation had been adopted by the Autumn of 1996 using co-decision. Moreover, if further treaty revisions go in the EP's desired direction, co-decision will become the norm for most types of decision-making.

The co-decision procedure has changed the institutional dynamics of legislating for the internal market. For the Commission, there has been something of a loss of control over legislative proposals while the EP has gained in power. This weakening of the Commission's control is clearest when the Council and the EP meet within the Concilliation Committee to agree a joint text (where previously they have failed to reach agreement).

It is the Commission's role to try and bring the Council and the EP together on a joint text. While this might be thought to give scope for tactical negotiation by the Commission, that the Committee is meeting at all is testament to the inability of one or both of the other institutions to agree on the Commission's original text. The best the Commission can hope for is damage limitation. Moreover, the normal rule that the Council can only adopt amendments not supported by the Commission by a unanimous vote does not apply to the agreement of a joint text. In this way, control shifts from the Commission to the Council and the EP.

The adoption of co-decision clearly strengthens the position of the EP to that of co-legislator. It now has the power to reject the Council's common position without the Council being able ultimately to adopt its own text (as is the case under the cooperation procedure). This 'veto' power was used to full effect when the EP voted to reject the proposed Directive on Open Network Provision (ONP) in the area of telecoms. The story of the fate of this proposed Directive displays well the new institutional dynamics of EU decision-making.

The introduction of co-decision created an anomaly. On the one hand, *legislation* adopted under Article 189b, EC procedure required the co-decision of the EP. However, if the legislation provided for delegated rule-making, the system of comitology provided no role for the EP. Detailed decision-making has been increasingly delegated to these committees. The EP has long complained of the unfairness of the comitology system (indeed it was the subject of its first attempt to use litigation under Article 173, EC), and the ONP Directive gave the EP the chance to use its enhanced post-TEU powers to raise the issue on to the agenda again. That this was a case of agenda-setting and playing for rules is indicated by the support that the EP had for the actual substance of the proposal. The EP rejected the proposal to bring the institutions round the table to try and reach an inter-institutional agreement to allow it some degree of supervision over texts agreed by these committees. The result was the agreement of a *modus vivendi* between the institutions giving the EP limited supervisory powers.[1] Morover, the EP had established a platform from which to argue for a review of the whole comitology system. Thus, the introduction of co-decision had the unintended consequence of bringing the comitology issue into the light, and opened a space in which the EP could seek to play for rules and institutionalise new standard operating procedures.

In general, the TEU added to the myriad of legislative procedures which exist for the adoption of EC legislation. The IGC considering revisions to the Treaties was asked to simplify the number of procedures, with the EP, not surprisingly, calling for an extension of co-decision to most policy areas, while retaining the assent and consulation procedures as the only two other rule-making procedures.

Economic and monetary union The TEU extended policy competences in a number of areas such as education; vocational training and youth; culture and public health; and consumer policy. The 'issue density' (Pierson 1996), therefore, of the EU has increased, raising issues as to the coherence and coordination of policy across these policy areas. However, it is the establishment of a timetable for EMU and the establishment of institutions (the European Monetary Institute and the European Central Bank) which stand out as the most significant extensions of EU competence.

As we noted above, the governance of the SEM has been characterised by the adoption of regulatory systems which to a greater or lesser extent apply to all the Member States. The provisions for EMU challenge that logic in two instances. The first instance is the UK and Danish opt-ins. Logically, if neither of these Member States opt in to EMU then the SEM will not be underpinned by a single currency applying to all the Member States. In the second instance, the TEU itself envisages that not all the Member States who wish to join a single currency will be in a position to do so according to the convergence criteria of Article 109j, EC Treaty. Regardless of how flexibly these criteria are interpreted, it is clearly possible that some Member States will be within a single currency and some will be outside it.

EMU, as provided for under the TEU, may also undermine the SEM itself. If distortions to competition can arise from national legislation, from national controls over regulated industries, from state aid, and from the behaviour of private undertakings in cartels or dominant positions, it is equally the case that distortions to competition can arise from national monetary controls. Further, if part of the logic of a single currency is that it will intensify cross-border trade and therefore promote the very economic integration that is supposed to be brought about by the SEM, then it is clear that the creation of differentiated integration in respect of a single currency ought to increase rather than decrease the divergences between those states inside or outside the single currency. Those Member States in favour of a single currency seem reluctant to consider whether it would be advisable to wait until the SEM is fully operational and economic convergence more tangible before proceeding to full EMU.

The problems associated with the ratification of the TEU highlighted the danger of European integration being seen to be simply a technical process of economic liberalisation divorced from the concerns of ordinary citizens. The move towards EMU also carries with it popular concerns as the drive to reduce inflation and public sector borrowing threatens to limit pay rises and public spending. The point is not unimportant if the future development of European integration can be blown off course by popular revolt. Thus, not only does EMU as provided for by the TEU threaten the coherence of the SEM, there is a danger that the domestic price of EMU may be greater than EU citizens are willing to pay, calling into question the already fragile popular support for the EU.

The Protocol and Agreement on Social Policy In the previous section we noted the danger of pursuing economic integration without due consideration of what integration may mean for the citizen. What citizenship of the Union actually amounts to is, of course, an important, but generally an open, question (e.g. Armstrong 1996; Closa 1994; de Búrca 1996; O'Keeffe 1994; Shaw 1996a). However, the 'citizen as worker' is an established identity within the governance of the SEM and, therefore, the idea of a European social space is inextricably linked to the idea of a citizen's Europe. Does, then, the PASP amount to a significant step towards the development of an SEM flanked by a strong committment to social regulation? Or has there been a weakening of social regulation post-TEU?

It will be recalled that as a consequence of the UK's unwillingness to amend the EC Treaty to establish a Social Chapter, the compromise solution of the PASP was devised. This allows the other Member States to either adopt legislative measures or to promote social dialogue between employers, employees and their representatives. On the one hand, the establishment of this institutional apparatus can be seen as an extension of social policy competence. On the other, it marks a significant departure from a model of governance based upon the adoption of rules common to all of the Member States: the *acquis communautaire*. Indeed, the PASP may be seen as an historical precursor to an increasingly *flexible* Europe (see above).

It is one thing to establish a legislative apparatus and another to provide for the conditions under which it can be operationalised. The concern of business, the Member States and the EU with improving the competitiveness of European business has resulted in an unwillingness to push forward an ambitious social policy programme. The Commission's White Paper on Social Policy (CEC 1994b) concluded that there was no 'need for a wide-ranging programme of new legislative proposals in the coming period'. Indeed, it is more accurate to say that the history of social policy since the early 1990s, particularly in the area of employment policy, has been a retreat from legislative measures and a move towards other policy instruments such as recommendations and social dialogue. For example, in 1990 the Commission submitted proposals for draft directives covering atypical work (e.g. part-time work and temporary or fixed term employment). In 1995, the Commission's Medium Term Social Action Programme (CEC 1995b) noted that these proposals would be withdrawn and consultations launched with the Social Partners under the PASP. These negotiations commenced in 1996 and have focused on part-time work alone.

Much faith is being placed on the use of the social dialogue as a mechanism for achieving a social Europe but without the need for legislative action. The social dialogue was utilised as a result of the withdrawal of the proposed Directive on parental leave, resulting in the conclusion between the Social Partners of a framework agreement in December 1995. The social dialogue is also to be considered in the context of a review of the Working Time Directive. It remains to be seen whether social dialogue agreements are indeed successfully implemented. A question mark also hangs over the representativeness of the Social Partners leading to the possible use of Court actions to challenge agreements.

That is not to say, however, that legislative action either within the context of existing legal bases or within the context of the PASP has not been forthcoming. The Commission withdrew its proposal on worker consultation and information, and its proposal on works councils, and instead submitted a single proposal under the PASP resulting in Directive 94/45[2] (the Works Council Directive). Further, the Council finally adopted a common position on the Commission's 1991 proposal for a Directive on the posting of workers (this time utilising the rule-making provisions which apply in respect of services – Articles 57(2) and 66, EC).

The SEA's creation of Article 118a, EC to allow for legislative action in the area of health and safety of workers had been a significant but limited extension of competence. It was not surprising in the light of Article 118a's use of QMV in the Council, and the UK's social policy opt-out, that the UK would insist on a restricted interpretation of the scope of Article 118a (preferring instead the use of the PASP, or legal bases which required unanimity within the Council, e.g. Article 100 or 235, EC). Thus, the UK challenged the legal basis of the Working Time Directive before the ECJ. However, the ECJ refused to give a restricted interpretation of the scope of Article 118a.[3]

In conclusion, the PASP enhances EU social competence but in a manner which introduces greater regulatory flexibility both in respect of instruments (the social dialogue) and obligated states (the UK's opt-out). In May 1997, the incoming Labour government of the UK announced its intention to sign up to the Social Chapter, ending its opt-out.

The enlargement of the EU

In the previous sections we examined the potential systemic impact of the TEU. In this section our attention turns towards another type of systemic change; the enlargement of the EU. From 1 January 1995, the EU of the twelve became the EU of the fifteen with the accession of Austria, Sweden and Finland. Negotiations may also lead to the accession of states from central and eastern Europe, creating an EU of twenty or more Member States.

Our goal in this section is to explore some of the implications of past and future enlargement for the governance of the SEM. In doing so, we highlight the central role that has already been played by the SEM in establishing an economic bridge for the integration of states into the EU. First, we examine the accession of Austria, Sweden and Finland. Second, we discuss the future enlargement of the EU.

The accession of Austria, Sweden and Finland   Preston has talked of a 'classic Community method' of accession by which he refers *inter alia* to the agreement of new Member States to be bound by the *acquis communitaire* from the date of accession without permanent derogation (Preston 1995). Transitional periods may be permitted, but the essence of the accession strategy has been not to permit 'flexibility'.

The difficulty with this strategy is that for each wave of new applicants there is a greater *acquis* to conform to. Thus, the UK, Denmark and Ireland acceded to a pre-SEM *acquis*, whereas Austria, Sweden and Finland had to adopt the much larger post-SEM *acquis*. However, this is not as problematic as it might seem given that as members of EFTA and the EEA these states had to a large extent already enjoyed liberalised trade in goods and services. Through a parallel process of creating the conditions of a single market, accession to the EU and agreement to be bound by the *acquis communautaire* was generally less problematic than would be the case for states which had not operated under conditions of free trade (for details of some of the particular difficulties see Granell 1995).

Politically, the accession of comparatively wealthy states was also significant in the sense that their absorption into the EU did not fundamentally challenge the SEM balance between economic integration (the internal market) and economic compensation (through Structural Funds).[4] Further, accession was not directly linked to institutional reform and therefore was not part of the revisions to the Treaties at Maastricht (Preston 1995: 455). Rather, the institutional implications of enlargement were dealt with outside of the context of Treaty revision.

Elections to the EP were held in the new Member States, enlarging the EP to its current 626 members. The College of Commissioners expanded to 20 members. However, the most significant institutional issue concerned the shift in the balance of power within the Council of the EU. Both Britain and Spain feared that an increase in the number of votes required to obtain a blocking minority in the Council would lead to increased possibilities for their being outvoted (Granell 1995: 133). With the accession of Austria, Sweden and Finland, a blocking minority of twenty-seven votes would be required (an increase from the then twenty-three votes). The solution to this problem – a mere three months short of the final conclusion of the acts of accession – was the Ioannina compromise. If it is likely that between twenty-three and twenty-seven votes may be cast against a proposal, the Member States will delay a vote on the proposal in order to seek greater consensus. Thus, although institutional change took place within the Council, it took place outside the context of Treaty revision, in particular, outside of the context of the building of the EU at Maastricht.

In summary, membership of EFTA and the EEA paved the way for the economic integration of Austria, Sweden and Finland into the EU through a process parallel to the SEM programme of removing trade barriers. The absorption of comparatively wealthy states did not fundamentally challenge the economic and political accommodation between the existing Member States. Finally, enlargement was not linked to the revisions of the Treaty at Maastricht.

It is against this background that we turn to an examination of the possible future enlargement of the EU to accommodate the states of central and eastern Europe.

The accession of central and eastern European countries   Assessed in the context of our previous discussion, the potential enlargement of the EU to central and eastern European countries (CEECs) displays some important differences. It is one thing to accommodate states which have been operating under conditions of liberalised trade and competition but it is quite another to attempt to accommodate states which have been subject to state control until comparatively recently. It also follows that if re-structuring is required – either before or after membership – the accession of the CEECs may have important financial consequences for existing members of the EU. Finally, the possible enlargement of the EU to twenty or more states raises in a very clear way the sort of political issues that were raised in the context of the previous enlargement: Can existing institutional arrangements be maintained for an enlarged EU?

Sedelmeier and Wallace (1996), in their excellent analysis of the EU's policy on central and eastern European enlargement, highlight the important institutional dynamics that have shaped EU policy. They argue that the fragmented structure of the Commission and the divergent interests of Member States (themselves subject to sectoral interest group lobbying) inhibited the development of an overarching accession policy framework. It was not until 1994 that the Commission and the European Council converged around a pre-accession strategy which first, politically accepted that economic relations between the EU and CEECs would lead to full membership and secondly, agreed that the mechanism for achieving integration was the extension of the SEM programme to such states.

As Sedelmeier and Wallace note (1996), relations between the EU and the CEECs had been conducted through programmes designed to aid economic restructuring (the Phare programme and the creation of the European Bank for Reconstruction and Development) and through the use of 'association agreements' (known as the 'Europe Agreements'). In this way, the EU was pursuing a strategy modelled on 'the paradigm of a classic trade agreement' (1996: 370). The development of what was to become the 1995 White Paper on the accession of the CEECs (CEC 1995d) marked a shift away from the trade agreement paradigm to embrace the idea of full membership of the EU through conformity to essential aspects of the SEM.

One sees then the shifting construction of the policy problem of enlargement in terms of two possible pre-formed paradigms. The first is the trade policy paradigm which has limited long-term political and institutional consequences and gives an important role to DG I, DG IA of the Commission and to the General Affairs Council. The other is the economic and political integration paradigm which does have long-term political and institutional consequences (arising from an enlarged EU) and which engages a larger set of policy actors (not only other Directorates of the Commission, but also the EP through its need to assent to any accession, the Internal Market Council and a broader set of social, economic and political actors).

Whereas for the former EFTA/EEA states membership of EFTA/EEA eased accession, for the CEECs, adjustment to the rules of the SEM is the core of the pre-accession strategy. The 1995 White Paper envisages a staggered process by which the CEECs will eventually put in place the *acquis* and therefore be able to seek full membership. Priority areas for action are highlighted. The core priority is the adoption of the internal market *acquis* (including both internal market legislation and competition policy). Areas of social and environmental policy which are directly linked to the internal market are included, but not all aspects of social and environmental policy are covered by the White Paper. However, the White Paper does state that full adoption of the *acquis* is a precondition of the conclusion of accession negotiations.

The accession of the CEECs will have an impact upon the political and economic bargain which supported the SEM/SEA package, and upon institutional reform more generally. For example, it is far less likely that regions of the present Member States which qualify for Objective 1 status under the Structural Funds (an important incentive for some Member States to agree to the SEM/SEA in the first place) will continue to do so if accession does indeed transpire. Moreover, it seems inevitable that this time the process of enlargement will be directly linked to institutional reform and Treaty revision. This was made clear in the Draft Treaty revising the EU Treaties presented to the European Council by the Irish Presidency in December 1996. However, as the Draft Treaty itself indicated, the issue of institutional reform is politically sensitive and would not be the subject of concrete proposals and agreement until the final stages of the IGC. Reform options included a limitation on the number of MEP's to 700; a reduction in the size of the College of Commissioners (or alternatively a limitation of one Commissioner per country); and, most controversially, a re-weighting of votes within the Council. In the event no agreement was reached on such reforms at the June 1997 Amsterdam summit.

In summary, relations between the EU and the CEECs are now constructed within the institutional paradigm of a pre-accession strategy in which gradual conformity to the SEM is to provide the bridge to membership. Unlike past accessions, institutional reform and Treaty revision became linked in the light of the need to have effective institutional arrangements for an enlarged EU.

Conceptualising change

In our final chapter we return to the theoretical issues raised in the earlier chapters. However, some brief comment on how we conceptualise the types of systemic change highlighted above is appropriate.

It is tempting in the light of the cycle of Treaty revisions instigated by the SEA to argue that Treaty revisions are *the* most significant moments in the integration process. Insofar as such revisions are viewed as purely inter-governmental bargains this would lead us to a privileging of an analysis of the preferences and power of Member States. However, we resist temptation. To be sure, Treaty revisions provide an important opportunity for political forces to be unleashed. Such forces may take as their object institutional change, calling into question the ability of an institutionalist analysis to conceptualise institutional change itself.

However, politics, as in physics, may display the effect of forces meeting immovable objects, or more commonly, of forces losing some of their kinetic energy through friction and resistance. In other words, we believe it is consistent with our approach to argue that institutions may shape political forces, even where the political force in question has institutional change as its object. Further, we take issue with a conceptualisation of Treaty revision in which the operationalisation of treaty competences is considered to be wholly constrained and referable to that bargain. This is not unlike arguing that governments once elected do exactly what the electorate want, or that the US Constitution can be understood in terms of the original intent of its authors. Worse than that, it reduces legal texts and institutional actors allocated tasks by such texts to the mere technical servants of those texts. Rather, political forces do not stop once the ink is dry on the treaty paper, nor do texts control their own interpretation. What is important is how the political forces which surround Treaty revisions are carried forward through time. Those political forces must also include those unleashed by EU institutions as well as Member States.

In conclusion, we agree with Pierson that a historical institutionalist analysis can be applied to systemic change such as Treaty revision (Pierson, 1996). We would also note that as Sedelmeier and Wallace's analysis of EU enlargement suggests (1996), institutional factors have a profound impact upon the construction of policy problems and their solutions.

The evolving governance of the single market

The first half of this chapter examined the impact of systemic changes such as Treaty revision and enlargement upon the governance of the SEM. Our focus turns from these general influences to more specific influences. The near completion of the 1985 White Paper programme by the 1992 dead-line raised the question of where this governance structure would and ought to go in the future. Reports and numerous principles have been produced in the attempt to define a strategy for the SEM. However, as we indicate, there has been no single dynamic and no uniform approach or programme around which the future development of the SEM could unite. In large measure this is due to the institutional system of governance which pertains in the EU and which makes reform of decision-making potentially as fragmented as decision-making itself.

Our focus is upon the evolution of rule-making. We explore three dimensions of this evolution. The first issue concerns the completion of the SEM legal framework. The second explores the transposition of SEM legislation and highlights the continuing role of the ECJ in seeking to ensure the effectiveness of EC law rights. Finally, reform of EU regulatory policy is analysed.

Completing the legal framework of the SEM

As successive Commission reports on the SEM post-1992 have noted (CEC 1994c; CEC 1995c; CEC 1996d), difficulties in the completion of the legal framework have been encountered in three policy areas: company law, taxation, and the free movement of persons.

The most visible symbol of failure in the area of company law is represented by the inability of the Member States to reach agreement on a European Company Statute (a proposal which has been around for decades). The approximation of company law is difficult given the quite different national structures and traditions of company law (e.g. as between preferences for private or public companies; the role of public regulation, private regulation or self-regulation of companies; and the scope for worker participation). A Commission proposal on the approximation of rules on takeovers has also encountered difficulties.[5] The opennness of the UK stock market means that hostile takeovers are not uncommon, whereas in other European countries they are virtually unheard-of. Further, the UK operates a system of self-regulation of takeovers policed by the City Panel on Takeovers using the non-statutory City Code of rules, norms and practices. Therefore, any proposal which seeks to approximate rules (even to a minimal degree) across the Member States is not only faced with differences in the experience of problems: for the UK it would mean the introduction of a legalisation and juridification of takeover regulation. Not surprisingly, the Commission proposal is being resisted and arguments have been made for the use of a non-binding Commission recommendation instead.

In the area of taxation, the Commission is seeking to complete the legal framework by removing the possibility of double taxation of companies; the possibility of tax evasion; and the possibility of the application of EU VAT legislation in different ways in different Member States.

The lack of EU progress in the elimination of controls on the free movement of persons is noteworthy. Member States have, historically, been less willing to create a frontier-free Europe for persons than they have for goods. Indeed, steps to remove frontier controls have taken place in the context of more flexible forms of inter-governmental cooperation among some, but not all, Member States of the EU (e.g. the 1985 Schengen Agreement and 1990 Schengen Convention[6]). However, the TEU does allow for inter-governmental cooperation to be brought within the framework of the EC pillar. Two EC regulations were adopted in 1995: one on the model visa for the EU[7] and the other establishing a list of those third country nationals that require visas to enter the EU.[8] Both these regulations are modelled on the Schengen visas. None the less, at time of writing, steps to remove *internal* frontier controls within the EU have made no progress within the Council.

Once again the contrast between economic liberalisation and the limited extension of the rights of citizens is apparent and serves to highlight the remoteness of the citizen from the core of the EU's activities. The Commission and the Parliament have few instruments at their disposal to push forward the free movement of persons (though legal pressure may be used by bringing an action under Article 175, EC for failure to act). In other areas where economic liberalisation has been less than the Commission would have liked (e.g. the creation of an internal market in energy) the Commission does at least have the scope to use other policy instruments (e.g. Article 30, EC or Article 90(3), EC).

Transposing SEM legislation
Given that SEM legislation tends to take the form of directives, gaps in the legal framework emerge where there is inadequate or inaccurate transposition, and most seriously, where there is a complete absence of transposition. Of course, transposition problems pre-date the SEM programme. Indeed, the judicial doctrines of the direct and indirect effect of directives (both of which pre-date the 1985 White Paper) can be seen as attempts to circumvent past failures by Member States to transpose directives. None the less, the sheer number of measures contained within the 1985 White Paper has rendered the problem of transposition more salient.

By December 1995, 93.4 per cent of White Paper measures had been transposed into national law (CEC 1996d). However, this figure masks differences in transposition rates between Member States (e.g. from 99.1 per cent in Denmark to 89.6 per cent in Greece) and between policy sectors (e.g. there are relatively poor transposition rates in the areas of public procurement, insurance and intellectual property). The enlargement of the EU has, of course, necessitated the transposition of legislation into the national legal systems of the new Member States. Austria, for example, is below the EU average in transposition rates, with 87.4 per cent of White Paper measures being implemented.

Transposition problems may take the form of either a failure to transpose or incorrent (or inadequate) transposition. As the Commission's report on the SEM in 1995 identifies (CEC 1996d), of the thirty infringement actions then pending against Member States, one half were failures to notify, whereas the other half concerned incorrect transposals. Monitoring transposal problems is problematic. Member States often simply fail to notify the Commission of the implementing measures. As well as seeking to improve notification procedures (through bilateral discussions with Member States), the Commission has hired consultants and contacted companies to try and analyse the implementation of directives.

An important mechanism by which transposition problems emerge is through national litigation in which companies and individuals seek to rely on unimplemented directives. Often they find that neither the doctrine of direct effect nor the doctrine of indirect effect provides an adequate legal remedy.[9] The ECJ's case law on the ability of legal persons to sue Member States for loss suffered as a consequence of a Member State's breach of its EU obligations therefore marks an important development in ECJ strategies to plug holes in the EU legal framework.

The ECJ first established the principle of state liability in its *Francovich* decision,[10] but it was not clear exactly on what basis the principle could be invoked, nor was the exact scope of its reach clear. Complete failure to adopt a directive was a fairly clear breach of obligations, but incorrect transposal or judicially determined breach of a Treaty obligation might be considered to fall outside the scope of the doctrine. In a series of cases in 1996 (*Factortame [III]*, *Brasserie de Pêcheur*,[11] *ex parte British Telecom*,[12] *ex parte Hedley Lomas*[13]), the ECJ elaborated on the conditions under which a state may be financially liable for a breach of its EU obligations (see Shaw 1996b: 291–4). In doing so, the Court has emulated its approach to the EU's own non-contractual liability under Article 215, EC. Thus, Member States will only be liable for loss if EC law confers rights on individuals and the loss is suffered as a consequence of a sufficiently serious breach of EC obligations. Where the breach concerns EC legislation, it must be shown that the Member States have manifestly and gravely disregarded the limits of their powers. Thus, while complete failure to transpose a directive will generally be such as to give rise to liability, misapplication or incorrect transposal of a directive may not do so (thus the UK escaped liability in respect of its erroneous interpretation of public procurement legislation in *ex parte British Telecom*).

It will be for national courts to apply the doctrine of state liability and to apply national rules on the award of damages (providing such rules are non-discriminatory and are effective). Once again, national courts are to be the enforcers of EC rights and EC remedies (see Maher 1994; Temple Lang 1997), albeit according to the rules and procedures of *national* law. Thus, while state liability may be an important new doctrine by which breaches of EC obligations can be monitored in the national courts, the application of the doctrine is set to highlight the tension between the effectiveness of EC law and its de-centralised application. The doctrine may indeed create 'an illlusion of remedies where few remedies are in practice found' (Harlow 1996: 222).

By way of conclusion, while we have concentrated on the mechanical problems of completing and transposing the legal framework, it is important to keep in mind that the reality of the legal framework of the SEM rests in its interpretation and application by national administrations. It is clear that the reception of EC legal norms, their interpretation and enforcement within national political and legal orders must itself be shaped through domestic institutional structures of governance. As we noted in respect of the doctrine of state liability, analysis of national *judicial* as well as *political* institutions is required.

Reform of EU regulatory policy

It is perhaps ironic that after years of legislative stagnation, the SEM programme resulted in the EU being construed as an over-eager regulator. The TEU's introduction of the subsidiarity principle as a general principle represented a reaction against the increased legislative activities entailed by the SEM programme, together with the extensions of EU competence agreed at Maastricht. Later, concerns as to the transparency of legislation and the legislative process, and anxieties as to the competitiveness of European business, also served to focus attention upon reform of EC legislation. But while the language(s) of subsidiarity, transparency and competitiveness have provided the reform rhetoric, no coherent reform initiative has emerged to match it.

A number of different reports have analysed EU regulatory policy from a number of different perspectives. As we note, the consequence has been not a single reform initiative, but a rather fragmented approach (consistent with the fragmented structure of EU governance). In some respects, these reports have cumulatively catalysed reform of regulatory policy. But in many ways, the appointment of committees and the reports produced by them are more to do with being *seen* to respond to political pressures rather than with the achievement of effective reform. In the following sections we explore:

- the Sutherland report on the internal market after 1992;
- the Strategic Programme for the SEM;
- the impact of subsidiarity in theory and practice;
- legislative consolidation/codification; and
- legislative simplification.

The Sutherland report   The appointment of former Commissioner Peter Sutherland to head a 'High Level Group' to consider the future development

Box 11.1: The Sutherland report

subsidiarity	five criteria to guide future action: – *need for EU action,* – *effectiveness of EU action,* – *proportionality,* – *consistency with existing rules,* – *communication of rules.*
transparency	– improved *consultation* and *communication* of initiatives, – *transparency* in rule-making, – *transparency* of internal market rules, – *consolidation and codification* of legislation.
access to justice	– improving the delivery of legal advice and redress.
administrative cooperation	– promotion of a partnership between national and EU administrators.

of the SEM represented a first attempt to set an agenda for the SEM post-1992. The report (High Level Group 1992), published just months before the 31 December 1992 deadline for completion of the SEM programme, was broad in scope and sought to establish markers for a more effective approach to rule-making, rule-implementation and rule-enforcement. It drew together a number of principles which have subsequently influenced the development of the SEM (represented in Box 11.1).

The Sutherland report attempted to keep the momentum of the SEM programme going at a time when the rule-making phase of the programme was coming to an end. Further, in its identification of future work (especially for the Commission), the report was suggestive of an ongoing relevance of EU institutions and activities. The report also paved the way for a more concrete attempt to develop a post-1992 strategy for the SEM in the form of the 1993 Commission Strategic Programme.

The Strategic Programme In 1993, the Commission produced its Strategic Programme, *Making the Most of the Internal Market* (CEC 1993d). The report was not an evaluation of the operation of the SEM but rather drew together a number of diverse threads of policy development covering the 'Completion of the Legal Framework'; the 'Management of the Single

Market'; the 'Development of the Single Market'; and a 'Dynamics and Open External Policy'. In this way, the report concretised some of the policy developments flagged by the Sutherland report (with areas such as administrative cooperation being targeted for more specific policy development, such as the Customs 2000 or KAROLUS programmes designed to improve cooperation and information flows between national administrations; see also CEC 1994d). Thus, the Strategic Programme is perhaps best viewed as an umbrella programme for more distinctive individual initiatives (e.g. on consolidation and codification of legislation: CEC 1993e) rather than as a broad, horizontal initiative.

Subsidiarity In a series of reports to the European Council (in particular following the 1992 Edinburgh and 1993 Brussels meetings) and in its annual report on the application of the subsidiarity principle, the Commission has set out the principles by which it applies the subsidiarity principle. The outcome of this Commission–European Council dialogue has been a process of legislative review (see Maher 1995) covering both past legislative action and future legislative proposals.

Legislation and future legislative proposals are reviewed in the light of three criteria drawn from Article 3b, EC (CEC 1993f):

• Does the EC possess legal competence to enact measures in the area?
• If the EC has competence, what is the need for action?
• If there is a need for action, is action proportionate to the demand for action?

EC competence has evolved and expanded with successive Treaty revisions, with the consequence that 'creative' uses of the principle of implied competence or the use of general or residual legal bases (like Articles 100 and 235, EC) are becoming increasingly unnecessary. We have already highlighted this in our discussion of the shipment of waste regulation (see Chapter 8). As that case study indicates, the issue has become less one of the *existence* of EC competence and more one of the *choice of legal basis*. While we are not suggesting that the issue of the existence of competence is unimportant (the EC does not have an inherent but only an attributed competence), we do suggest that a dispute over the choice of legal basis is a more likely topic for litigation than a challenge to the existence of EC competence. Support for this view can be found in the UK's unsuccessful legal challenge to the Working Time Directive. The UK's attempt to argue that the EC lacked competence to adopt the measure turned into an issue of whether Article 118a, EC was an *appropriate* legal basis for action.

If the subsidiarity principle is to have teeth it will be in the political arena with regard to the justification of the 'need for action'. In this respect, the subsidiarity principle merely poses the question rather than providing mechanisms for answering it. It is clear that the aim of the

Member States, post-SEM programme has been to require a higher level of justification from the Commission before it proposes legislation. The subsidiarity principle might have pointed the institutions in the direction of more widespread use of cost and risk assessment and determinations of the effectiveness of EU action. However, in order for such assessments to become routine, internal institutional reform would be required.

In 1993 the institutions concluded an Inter-Institutional Agreement on Procedures for Implementing the Principle of Subsidiarity. However, this simply re-stated the need for the institutions to justify their actions in the light of the subsidiarity principle rather than setting an agenda for institutional reform. Another potential source of institutional reform could come from the ECJ in that it could set down essential procedural requirements, conformity to which would be necessary to meet the subsidiarity standard. The unwillingness of the Court to do this is evidenced, once again, by the Working Time litigation. The UK had argued that the risks which the Directive sought to overcome were largely presupposed. In other words, the intensity of regulation was not to be a function of a case-by-case risk analysis, but was to be determined *a priori* by the Directive. Further, the relevant scientific Advisory Committee had not been consulted prior to the adoption of the Directive (this might have been appropriate in order to assess the level of risk to be regulated). But the Court found no problem with this lack of consultation or with the lack of more detailed risk assessment. Rather, because Article 118a permits the adoption of minimum *harmonised* measures, for the Court this necessarily presupposed the need for EC action. Once again we see that it will be up to the political institutions to reform themselves rather than reform being imposed by the Court.

The third aspect of subsidiarity follows logically from the second. Not only is an assessment of risks or needs required, but also an assessment of whether EU action would be proportionate to those risks or needs is necessary. 'Proportionality' can be read in a number of different senses:

- Does the risk or need require legislative action or will a lighter-touch solution suffice?
- If legislation is required, does it require the complete harmonisation of rules or will minimum standards be appropriate?
- Would legislative action, even if appropriate, none the less impose costs which are not justified because of the level of risk or need, or because of the difficulties in implementation and enforcement?

We would repeat that the subsidiarity principle begs these sorts of questions but does not of itself answer them, nor does it establish institutional mechanisms through which these sorts of questions can be answered. However, as a principle of EC law, it has always been possible to use the principle of proportionality to challenge measures. We are, perhaps, more accustomed to litigation using the proportionality principle to challenge national rules (e.g. in relation to the free movement of goods, workers and services). However, the principle can be also used to challenge EC measures.

Our analysis above has indicated the limited scope for the use of subsidiarity as a new legal norm by which to substantively review the adoption of Community rules. Rather we have suggested that where subsidiarity is, potentially, of more significance is within the political arena. But, as we have noted, some degree of institutional reform may be necessary in order for subsidiarity to change the regulatory culture of the institutions. As we indicate below, in the absence of institutional reform, the subsidiarity principle has been used as part of a more technocratic process of legislative review.

At the 1992 Edinburgh European Council, the Commission gave three undertakings as regards the implementation of the subsidiarity principle:

- legislative measures would be accompanied by *explanatory memoranda* justifying the need for the measure;
- there would be a withdrawal or revision of certain proposed measures; and
- there would be a review of existing legislation.

The Commission produced a list of twenty proposals which it considered could be withdrawn in the light of the subsidiarity principle. The EP was not impressed by this preemptive action and asked that most of the sacrificial lambs be saved from the altar. For their part, the Member States drew up their own lists of least-favoured measures. In June 1993 a joint Franco-British initiative suggested the withdrawal or revision of twenty-four measures covering both existing and proposed legislation. In November 1993, the German government produced a list of fifty-four items which it considered ought to be revised.

The Commission pointed out that many of the measures on both lists were already on the Commission's Edinburgh list and therefore these were not contentious. As regards the other measures on the Franco-British list, the Commission did agree to replace its proposed Directive on zoos with a 'soft law' alternative of a recommendation, while refusing to withdraw the other listed measures. Similarly, the Commission produced a response to the German list in June 1994 in which it resisted most of the demands for change. The Commission did, however, agree to withdraw its proposal on the liability of service providers and to re-examine proposed directives on tobacco advertising, speed limits for trucks and the maximum alcohol content for drivers.[14]

A more intriguing effect of the German list concerned those proposals which Germany did not wish to see withdrawn but in respect of which it felt some revision or simplification was required. In this sense, the German government sought to harness the subsidiarity dynamic to achieve leverage within the negotiation process. Three of the proposals listed were later modified and common positions (supported by Germany) agreed in the

Council. This provides evidence for Van Kersbergen and Verbeek's (1994) claim that the subsidiarity principle is less concerned with the general division of power between the EU and its Member States, and more a matter of the particular relationship between *individual* Member States and the EU on particular policy issues.

By 1994 eleven proposals had been withdrawn by the Commission. It is difficult to assess, quantitatively, the significance of this figure for two reasons. First, it is inappropriate to look at the number of measures withdrawn in a given year as a proportion of the measures proposed in that year, since some proposals may have been around longer than a year. Secondly, the number of Commission proposals has declined significantly as a consequence of the completion of the White Paper legislative exercise. Therefore, it is impossible to get a representative base-line year. Given that the impact of subsidiarity is felt most tangibly in the politics of particular proposals, the most one can offer is a qualitative analysis. The most significant proposal to be withdrawn concerned the liability of service providers. A Directive on product liability had already been adopted in respect of *goods*. The proposal would have established a parallel provision in respect of *services*. It is less clear, however, whether the withdrawal of this proposal had much to do with an application of the subsidiarity principle. Rather, its demise owed more to poor consultation, poor drafting and a lack of strong Commission support for the initial draft (see Shaw 1995b).

On the face of it, the subsidiarity principle does not appear *on its own* to have resulted in a radical reduction in legislative proposals, though it is possible that it has combined with other factors (e.g. low economic growth) so that there has been less wilingness to create new rules in certain areas (e.g. social policy).

If the Commission feared that the review of future proposals might compromise its right of initiative, its fear of the review of existing legislation was that all the past achievements would be undone. It would be ironic if the completion of the internal market led to a process by which the Community's *acquis communautaire* might be jeopardised. Thus, while agreeing – at the 1993 Brussels European Council – to a review of some 50,000 pages of legislation, the Commission noted that the review would not include legislation adopted in the preceding two years and nor should the *acquis* be called into question.

In its report to the Brussels Council (CEC 1993f), the Commission proposed a review of existing legislation under three headings:

- the *recasting* of rules and regulations: this involves the codification of rules and regulations in a given area (e.g. the 1992 Customs Code),
- the *simplification* of rules and regulations: the increased use of 'new approach' directives, European standards, mutual recognition and horizontal harmonisation measures.
- the *repeal* of rules and regulations.

As with the effect of subsidiarity on future proposals, the review of existing legislation has led not to a radical deregulation of EC legislation but more to a technical process of legislative consolidation, codification and simplification. The impact of subsidiarity has been subsumed, to a large extent, within the recommendations of the Sutherland report and the Commission's Strategic Programme and, in particular, in consolidation, codification and simplification initiatives. However, in respect of simplification, the dynamics engendered by the subsidiarity principle must also be viewed alongside the desire to reduce burdens on business in the light of competitiveness concerns. These initiatives are examined in the following sections.

Consolidation/codification We must, at the outset, clarify the terminology to be used. By 'consolidation' we refer to the process by which the Office for Official Publications produces a consolidated text of directives together with their amendments in all the official languages (the *Consleg* system). This does not require the adoption of new legislation. It is a form of informal codification designed to increase the transparency of legislation (especially in areas where the Community has adopted numerous technical amendments and cross-references to other directives). By 'codification' we mean the adoption of a single new legal instrument which codifies all the existing rules in a given area. This terminology differs from that which has been used by the Commission in the past. The Commission has referred to the process of compiling all the legal texts in one document (without legal change) as 'declaratory consolidation' (CEC 1993e), while referring to the process of codification which creates a new legal instrument as 'constitutive consolidation' (CEC 1993b). We think it preferable to refer to the former as *consolidation* and the latter as *codification*.

The process of consolidation is fairly non-contentious. It is a technical process to increase the transparency of legislation. Codification ought to be non-contentious as its function is to further increase transparency and ease of implementation by the production of a single binding legal text. However, as the Commission highlighted in 1993 in a follow-up to the Sutherland report, the results of the codification process have been 'mixed' (CEC 1993e). First, Member States have used the imminent codification of rules as a reason for not transposing unimplemented measures. This seems to have been the case in the area of public procurement (see Chapter 5). Secondly, Member States have also used the opportunity of legislative codification to re-open debates within the Council. It is this second point which exposes the Commission's fear that legislative review ought not to be used as an exercise by which to undermine the *acquis communautaire*.

In December 1994 the institutions concluded an inter-institutional agreement on an accelerated procedure for codification. A working party of representatives from the Community institutions has been established to scrutinise Commission proposals and to certify that proposals do not involve any changes of substance. There is an accelerated procedure for the approval of proposals by the Parliament and the Council. Thus, institutional reform has taken place to give effect to the re-casting of rules.

Simplification Legislative simplification has taken on a new meaning in the period which has followed legislative review under subsidiarity. The post-SEM, post-TEU period has been marked not simply by concerns of subsidiarity, but more significantly, with anxieties as to the competitiveness of European business (see CEC 1993c). Of importance to this competitiveness debate has been the effects of the regulatory climate (both national and EU) upon European businesses.

The language of 'de-regulation' has been prominent in the domestic politics of UK Conservative governments. Within Germany, the Free Democrat Economics Minister Günther Rexrodt also called for greater de-regulation of the regulatory environment, e.g. in urging Chancellor Kohl to embark on a more ambitious de-regulation of postal services than that which Kohl had envisaged. It is not surprising to find that the Anglo-German Deregulation Group should, therefore, be co-chaired by an ex-minister of the Thatcher government (Francis Maude) and by a former Parliamentary Secretary at the Economics Ministry (Norbert Lammert). In 1994, this Group called upon the EU institutions to (Anglo-German Deregulation Group 1994): 'institute a programme of deregulation at the Community level so that all citizens of Europe can benefit from improvements'. For the Commission, it is somewhat ironic that the EU is being blamed for its regulatory activities when, as the Commission argues (CEC 1995c), 'Community legislation completing the single market is by nature a deregulation exercise, since it is aimed at eliminating national measures which create barriers to trade.' Further, it has been the EU which has sought to liberalise markets in procurement, air transport, energy and telecommunications (often in the face of opposition of reluctance from the Member States).

But it is clear that the activities of the EU have come under renewed scrutiny in the light of competitiveness concerns. A number of different regulatory reform initiatives have been launched. In 1995, UNICE produced a report entitled *Releasing Europe's Potential Through Targeted Regulatory Reform* (UNICE 1995). In many ways the report is ambivalent. While aimed primarily at *EU* institutions, it none the less finds that the major source of regulation is *national*. The report is also supportive of the completion of the SEM as an important mechanism for the removal of national trade barriers. Where the report is most critical of EU action is in respect of social and environmental legislation. In both these areas the report calls for limitations on future EU action and for a review of existing legislation, e.g. on the transfer of undertakings and on waste regulation.

At the Madrid summit in 1995, the UK put forward its priorities for regulatory reform, calling for a change in the regulatory culture of the Commission. For its part, President Santer tabled the Commission's report on *Better Law Making* to the Madrid summit, in which the Commission repeated the initiatives it was already taking in the application of the subsidiarity and proportionality principles.

A potentially more significant development was the establishment in 1994 of a group of independent experts to assess the impact of both EC and national legislation on employment and competitiveness in Europe. The Molitor report (named after its chairman Bernhard Molitor) was produced in 1995 and has been greeted with general disappointment by all those involved. For the Commission, the report had the crucial failing of not considering the impact of *national* legislation and of concentrating instead on EC law (though its recommendations were considered to have national application). As regards the reform of EC legislation, the report did not move far beyond a repetition of the Commission's own legislative review initiatives. Member States like the UK sought support for their own initiatives from the Molitor report but could find little of substance in the report to back any specific claims. Indeed, the report's argument in favour of fundamental social rights was not exactly met with equanimity either by the UK government or by UNICE which has argued against the harmonisation of social rights.

What then do these reform initiatives add up to? In one sense, very little can be said to have come directly out of either the UNICE or Molitor reports. No great de-regulation dynamic has emerged. In this sense one can draw a parallel with the subsidiarity principle and suggest that contemporary concerns with competitiveness have not resulted in a radical de-regulation agenda at the EC level. Rather, if there has been an effect it is in catalysing the institutions to develop an increased awareness of the effect of EC rules on business. The language is not that of de-regulation, but of *legislative and administrative simplification*.

The idea of legislative and administrative simplification can be traced back to the mid-1980s and the establishment of the SME Task Force to monitor the effects of Community legislation on SMEs. The work of this Task Force was transferred to DG XXIII which is now responsible for the *fiche d'impact* assessment of the effect on business of Community proposals (identified in the annual legislative programme). However, DG XXIII is not in a position to force other DGs to consider the business impact of their proposals. Nor can vertical pressure come from the Secretary General's office (though General Guidelines for Legislative Policy have been circulated to DGs).

However, the language of legislative and administrative simplification has emerged in the mid-1990s as the EU's politically correct way of talking about regulatory reform without adopting the language of de-regulation.

In the context of the SEM, it has been taken up under the Commission's Simpler Legislation for the Internal Market (SLIM) initiative. Launched in 1996 (CEC 1996e), the SLIM initiative was a response to the failure of the Molitor report to say anything significant, and the willingness of the Internal Market ministers to want something significant to come out of simplification.[15] At an informal meeting in Florence under the Italian presidency, the Council asked the Commission to identify areas for pilot projects. DG XV produced four pilot areas and reported to the Council in December 1996. However, with the precedents of Molitor and UNICE in mind, the report suffers from the same problem as these other two reports in having been produced too quickly. Very little reform has emerged that was not, perhaps, already possible. The Commission has launched a second wave of SLIM projects and it remains to be seen whether the SLIM initiative will yet reap substantive reform.

Summary

A number of different policy streams can be identified which mirror attempts to reform EU regulatory policy. One stream is concerned with the Commission's own review of the future direction of the EU's governance structure post-SEM. Another reflects the anxieties of Member States about the transfers of rule-making competence to the EC associated with the TEU. A third underlines the economic environment in which EU governance operates and highlights competitiveness concerns. These pressures for reform have not, however, coalesced around a common theme or common movement. Rather, the languages of subsidiarity, transparency and competitiveness have been deployed to bring concerns to light, but without providing a conceptual core around which to build a consensus for reform.

Some institutional reform has been brought about to respond to these reform pressures but this has tended to be technical and modest. If there is a problem with the quality of Community legislation, the problem may lie with the fragmented decision-making structure of the Community itself. Policy coordination is difficult not only within aggregate structures like the Commission, but across the legislative institutions of the EU. This creates the paradox that if the policy at issue is regulatory reform, the institutional structure of the EU may be the biggest hurdle to such reform.

Conclusion

In the first half of this chapter we described and analysed potential systemic changes such as the TEU and the enlargement of the EU in the context of the evolution of the SEM. In the second half we focused more specifically upon initiatives which self-consciously reflected upon the evolving governance of the SEM.

The post-1992 dynamics have been shaped profoundly by the inter-institutional system of governance of the EU. The operationalisation of the subsidiarity principle, for example, cannot be understood as the naked input of Member States' political preferences through Treaty revision, but rather as a more iterative process of dialogue between the Commission and the European Council; between the Commission and the Member States; and between the Commission, the EP and Council. Attempts to reform EU regulatory policy are shackled by the very institutional structure which may be responsible for the problems they seek to solve.

Not only are policy inputs shaped through institutional structures, but the possible policy outcomes are also so shaped. It is striking the extent to which ideas of consolidation, codification, simplification, and indeed the idea of EU regulation as de-regulation have become the adaptable elements through which political pressures can be refracted and solutions suggested. Thus, anxieties as to the pressure of legislation on business can be translated into policy solutions which emphasise transparency (consolidation and codification) or harmonisation (EU re-regulation) rather than radical de-regulations of EC competence.

Our conclusion is that in seeking to find a direction for the EU in the wake of the completion of the SEM programme, the institutional (organisational, procedural and normative) structure of the EU has had an enormous impact upon the construction of policy problems and suggestions for their solution.

Notes

1 OJ C102 (4.4.96), 1.
2 OJ L254 (30.9.94), 64.
3 Case C-84/94, *United Kingdom* v. *Council of the EU (Working Time)* [1996] 3 CMLR 671.
4 A new Objective 6 status was developed for the distribution of Structural Funds in Scandinavia (Preston 1995: 453).
5 At one stage, the issue of approximating rules on takeovers and mergers was linked to the negotiation of the MCR (on which see Chapter 4).
6 The UK and Ireland remain outside the Schengen system which creates a common external border and removes controls internally between Schengen states.
7 Regulation 1683/95, OJ L164 (14.7.95), 1.
8 Regulation 2317/95, OJ L234 (3.10.95), 1.
9 See, e.g., Case C-91/92, *Paola Faccini Dori* [1994] ECR I-3325; Case C-192/94, *El Corte Ingles SA* v. *Cristina Blázquez Rivero* [1996] ECR I-1281.
10 Cases C-6, C-9/90, *Francovich and Bonifaci* v. *Italy* [1991] ECR I-5357.
11 Cases C-46, C-48/93, *Brasserie du Pêcheur* v. *Germany, R* v. *Secretary of State for Transport ex p. Factortame* [1996] ECR I-1029.

12 Case C-392/93, *R* v. *HM Treasury ex p. British Telecommunications plc* [1996] ECR I-1631.
13 Case C-5/94, *R* v. *MAFF ex p. Hedley Lomas* [1996] ECR I-2553.
14 Noted in *Agence Europe*, 13–14/6/94, 11.
15 See Council Resolution on legislative and administrative simplification in the field of the internal market, OJ C224 (1.8.96), 5.

12

Conclusion

Reviewing the policy agenda

In our Introduction we argued that the single market formed the centre-piece of economic and political integration from the mid-1980s. However, we also noted that the attention of policy-makers and students of integration has shifted to other topical concerns, notably EMU and the 1996/97 IGC. We raised the question of whether the SEM was froth rather than substance.

It should by now be clear that we believe the SEM to have been a key development in the history of integration. Politically, European integration was given major impulses by the SEM. In economic terms the SEM has led to a shift on the part of many economic actors from a national-market to a European-market focus. The Commission itself sees the SEM as 'the most ambitious and comprehensive supply-side programme ever launched' (CEC 1996f: 7). A fundamental reconstruction of European economic governance has been under way over the last decade or so as regulatory powers have been curtailed at the national level and reconstructed supranationally.

The narrower internal market programme, set out in the White Paper, *Completing the Internal Market* (CEC 1985a), was largely agreed by the end-1992 deadline: 260 of the 282 measures had been adopted by the Council by that date. As significantly, that narrower programme then dynamised other policy areas as political actors sought to demonstrate policy linkages, exploit new institutional powers, and construct new coalitions of Member State interests. The passing of the end-1992 deadline should not be regarded as the end-point for attention to the SEM. In terms of the measures contained in the White Paper, attention turned from 1993 onwards to the policy phase concerned with the transposition and implementation of the rules. If the preoccupation of policy-makers and analysts with issues such as EMU suggests that this implementation phase is of less interest politically, then that is to misjudge the essentially political nature of the regulatory arrangements that have been put in place. In particular, as was shown in the previous chapter, the terms of the SEM debate have themselves been adjusted over time. On a broader, systemic plane, the new concerns with subsidiarity and European competitiveness have introduced a changed normative context within which the SEM is considered. Further, at a sub-systemic level, the question of simplifying the regulatory burden of internal market legislation has led to subtle adjustments to strategies for the evolution of the rules. Thus the SEM remains an issue of continuing salience.

In any case, bearing in mind our wider understanding of the SEM, there remains a range of policy issues in earlier policy phases. This situation applies particularly to the liberalisation of several utilities sectors where the state has traditionally been the major provider. These sectors were scarcely mentioned in the Cockfield White Paper because more developed sectoral programmes were necessary. These utilities sectors are character-ised by the existence of a network-type infrastructure. Nicholas Argyris has argued that they characteristically have terminals, links and nodes and involve service-providers.[1] Emblematic of such utility sectors in this vol-ume is air transport. Thus, the airlines constitute the service-providers, airports are the 'nodes', airways (for which the state has traditionally provided air traffic control) form the 'links', and airports represent the 'terminals'. Air transport liberalisation has led the way in EU utilities liberalisation, with telecommunications following and the electricity mar-ket rather further behind. Railways and postal services have barely been addressed by the EU as yet but proposals are planned. Liberalisation of these sectors, it should be noted, is much more politically contested, not least because workforces in the sectors have perceived EU action as an assault on the notion of public service, and specifically upon their jobs. The industrial unrest occasioned amongst staff of Air France in October 1993 in response to the necessary job cuts to secure EU approval of state aid symbolised the greater politicisation of sectoral liberalisation. Liberal-isation of the utilities sectors is, therefore, at an earlier stage of the policy cycle, so there is still much distance to travel to complete the SEM.

If one interprets the SEM more widely still – including through reference to internal market flanking measures such as social and economic cohesion – then broader policy concerns fall under the spotlight, and there remains much policy activity in these domains.

How, then, can we summarise and explain what has happened since 1985?

Summarising the achievements of the SEM[2]

To summarise the story of the SEM, we need to cast our minds back to the state of the EC's common market in the early 1980s. The lamentable performance of the EC – as it then was – in achieving the goal of a common market was attributable to deficiencies in the policy-making arrangements

Box 12.1: The SEM: before and after

Before the SEM programme (mid-1980s)
- Goods were stopped and subject to frontier controls.
- There was no common market in goods, since most had to comply with different sets of national requirements, creating segmentation.
- The service sector was almost wholly excluded from competition or market integration.
- Controls over capital mobility were pervasive.
- There were major obstacles to labour mobility.
- Fiscal barriers were pervasive.

After the SEM programme (mid-1990s)
- Frontier controls on goods were abolished.
- There was increased harmonisation, increased use of European and international standards, and mutual recognition.
- Legislation was put in place to liberalise key service sectors.
- Capital controls have been abolished.
- Obstacles to labour mobility have been removed and there has been greater mobility of those not economically active (students and the retired).
- Some fiscal barriers remained.

---

and the lack of political will on the part of national governments. We give a summary of the situation before and 'after' the SEM programme in Box 12.1.

A first achievement of the SEM has already been reported on, namely the expansion of its scope beyond the White Paper to include pre-existing common market legislation, other closely related domains (notably the liberalisation of certain network-based service sectors), and flanking policy areas (competition policy, measures promoting regional cohesion and social policy). The SEM has thus taken on a much wider significance than the original *internal market* White Paper (see CEC 1996f: 35). The way in which the SEM's achievements are reported by the Commission in its 1996 report, *The Impact and Effectiveness of the Single Market*, also reveals the shifting self-construction of the policy area. Thus, one chapter of the report concentrates on the impact upon citizens (CEC 1996f: 11–14), with specific reference to:

- social policy (which the UK government did not see as integral to the internal market);
- consumer interests (for which the EC/EU was only given broad authority later, in the TEU); and

- environmental protection (which was almost entirely neglected at the time of the internal market White Paper, see Chapter 8; also Weale and Williams 1992).

This chapter of the Commission report reveals how important it is to make the connection between the evolution of a particular area and wider systemic developments in integration. The SEM had a galvanising effect on related policy areas but also had to reflect the evolving systemic context of integration.

In product markets the regulatory environment has been transformed over the decade from the SEM's launch. The abolition of border controls for goods has brought major benefits to cross-border trade, with the elimination of customs forms, including in trade with the EEA states (Iceland, Liechtenstein and Norway). The situation for fiscal formalities has been less impressive, owing to a failure to agree on a new VAT payments system. The regulatory environment for technical trade barriers has been changed dramatically. Harmonising legislation covers some 30 per cent of industrial output and new approach Directives a further 17 per cent. Eighty per cent of standardisation now takes place at European or international level, whereas it was 80 per cent at national level a decade ago. Un-harmonised national requirements affect only some 25 per cent of output but, even here, the principle of mutual recognition is at hand. Of course, the resultant situation does not provide a business-environmental paradise. There have been complaints about delays in the writing of European standards and about the arrangements for securing certification of products. Small and medium-sized firms are concerned about the regulatory burden they bear in complying with the SEM. The Commission's surveys indicate greater satisfaction with the SEM amongst manufacturers of goods rather than service-providers, and amongst the largest companies (more than 1,000 employees) rather than smaller ones (CEC 1996f: 15–16).

The service sector had largely been excluded from market integration prior to the White Paper. Here, too, the situation has been transformed, but developments are running behind those in the product markets. Most legislative measures have been coming into effect from 1993: scarcely surprising, since the legislative momentum in service sectors lagged behind that for manufactured goods. In the road haulage and air transport industries operators can utilise the new supranational regulatory frameworks freely to provide services across borders, with significant consequent change in industry behaviour. In telecommunications the legislation for liberalisation has developed apace, although it is not yet fully in effect and some national obstacles remain. Air transport and telecommunications have seen major re-structuring through international alliances as well as changes in domestic industry structure. In the financial services sector the introduction of a 'single banking licence' has reduced the costs of cross-border operations but more legislative action is deemed necessary. This situation is linked in part to the situation on capital controls. Although removed as a general principle, Member States' national fiscal laws have served to undermine the impact of this step for the financial services sector, constraining the pension funds sector in particular. Distortions in the fiscal treatment of investment income and other financial services products have also hampered a complete liberalisation of capital movements.

The Commission has undertaken extensive analysis as to the economic effects of the changes brought about by the SEM. Thirty-eight in-depth studies – some sectoral others horizontal – have been undertaken by independent experts.[3] This amounts to 'twice the amount of research that went into the famous Cecchini Report of 1988' (Monti 1996: 2). We cannot do justice here to the extensive findings so confine our comments to the broader macro-economic consequences. The calculations on these are problematic, for there is a recognition of two factors that hamper the attribution of economic changes to the SEM. First, it is difficult to isolate the SEM-effect from other significant changes in the European economy, notably the end of the Cold War and resultant economic reconstruction to the East; German unification; developments in the international economy; and the effects of other EU policies such as the structural funds. Secondly, much of the SEM legislation only came into force from 1994, while some will not take full effect till the next millennium. Hence, with the time lag associated with economic actors adapting to the changed regulatory context, the full effects will still not be felt for some time.

Bearing in mind these caveats, the Commission estimates the following effects:

- between 300,000 and 900,000 extra jobs than if the SEM had not been created;
- an extra increase in EU income of 1.1–1.5 per cent over the period 1987–93;
- a boost to investment of 1–3 per cent;
- inflation rates which are 1.0–1.5 per cent lower than they would have been in the SEM's absence;
- stimulated investment in the EU by an extra 2.7 per cent;
- increased economic convergence and cohesion between different EU regions;
- increased trade volumes between Member States of 20–30 per cent in manufacturing products;
- increased foreign direct investment into the EU: from 28 per cent of global foreign investment flows in the mid-1980s to 44 per cent in the early 1990s;
- continuing industrial reconstruction as revealed by increasing merger and acquisition activity (see *European Economy*, Supplement A, July 1996);

- increased cross-border public sector purchasing from 6 per cent to 10 per cent; and
- reduced costs for traders and hauliers by ECU 5 bn as a result of the ending of customs and fiscal checks at borders (CEC 1996f: 5; Monti 1996: 2–3).

Some of these benefits have been masked by developments in the business cycle, renewed concerns in the 1990s about the European economies' competitiveness, and the pain experienced by some economies in meeting the EMU convergence criteria.

Where has the SEM been less effective?

Some White Paper measures simply have not been adopted because of political deadlock. The areas affected are:

- company taxation;
- approximation of taxation treatment of investment income;
- an origin-based VAT system; and
- company law.

In procedural terms there are serious concerns about the 'holy trinity' of transposition, enforcement and redress. Although the Commission report states that the transposition rate for the White Paper measures was on average 90 per cent for the EU-15, it notes that 'fifty-six per cent . . . have been transposed in *every* Member State' (CEC 1996f: 23). That yields a rather different picture and one which is arguably more pertinent to those firms conducting business across the SEM. The comparability of enabling legislation also remains a concern. Enforcement is more complex still because the relevant agencies may be national, regional or local, thus making it extremely difficult to monitor the impact of the SEM 'on the ground' to ensure equivalence across the EU. The Commission's resources simply do not permit sufficient oversight of this dimension (see Chapter 11). Finally, the ability of private parties to secure redress through the courts is complex and variable because of differences in national legal systems.

A final issue worthy of mention here concerns over-zealous regulation: where national transposition introduces costs over and above those necessitated by the relevant EC Directive. This phenomenon, known in the UK as 'gold-plating', lies behind the recent emphasis in SEM policy on reducing the regulatory burden (see Chapter 11).

Despite the legislation to open up public procurement in the utilities (see Chapter 5) and more generally, the results in this area of activity have been much more limited. Although a major area of economic activity – 11.5 per cent of EU GDP in 1994 – the achievements have been limited, with only 10 per cent import penetration of import markets. A major explanation for this situation is 'the substantial delay in incorporating the 11 procurement Directives into national legislation and enforcing them effectively'

(CEC 1996f: 21). The 1996 Florence European Council underlined the importance of accelerating national transposition in this area. Finally, it is worth mentioning that the general impact of the single market upon small and medium-sized enterprises has been rather limited.

To summarise, the achievements of the SEM have been remarkable. The single market itself has become a rolling programme for the transformation of economic governance in the EU. As the Commission's report puts it, the 'single market remains politically centre-stage as a key instrument through which the priorities of the Union can be delivered' (Monti 1996: 144). This finding leads on to a further area of our conclusions. How did this story of economic transformation come about? How did the SEM/SEA package deal have such a galvanising effect on economic governance in the EC/EU?

Explaining the achievements

What lies at the heart of the achievements of the SEM is the transformation of the EC's governance capacity. This development occurred both at the systemic level, facilitated by the SEA, and at the level of the SEM policy 'sub-system' and the component policy issues. So how can we conceptualise what governance capacity is comprised of in the EC/EU context, so as to summarise and better understand the political and legal dynamics of the SEM?

Two well-established means of assessing governance capacity are in terms of democratic rule and policy outputs (see survey in Weaver and Rockman 1993b).[4] We initially concentrate on policy outputs but return to the question of democratic rule at the end of this section.

What determines governance capacity as measured by policy output? Three component parts can be identified: the constitutive goals of the system of governance; the institutional structure – formal and informal – for achieving those goals; and how these features interact with the wider policy community, principally socio-economic actors. We examine how each of these contributed to increased governance capacity.

Constitutive goals

Constitutive goals relate to the broad objectives of the EC: its functional scope, areal domain and membership (Young 1989: 29). How did these change with the SEM? It is worth making a differentiation between what happened politically, following what may be termed a 'political-decisional' dynamic of integration, and what happened in a more formalised manner following the 'judicial-normative' dynamics of integration.[5] It is critically important in European integration to have a grasp of both these dynamics if one is to be able to understand what is happening, and this, we hope, has been a characteristic of this study's new institutionalist approach.

The SEM comprised a subtle admixture of these two dynamics, but with both pointing in the direction of greater integration. The June 1985 Milan commitment to completion of the internal market fell into the political-decisional category by virtue of its non-binding, declaratory status, albeit building upon existing treaty commitments, but it included the important ingredients of a clear focus for EC policy and a deadline, the end of 1992. The SEA, by contrast, fell into the judicial-normative category because of its constitutional, treaty-reforming character. It may indeed be argued that this admixture of the two dynamics played some role in assuring the new dynamics of integration in the late 1980s. For example, it was certainly important in keeping the UK government engaged in the evolving integration process, given its persistent reservations about a purely constitutional-legal route to change, as displayed in its greater unease with the Maastricht and 1996/97 IGC episodes.

The internal market objective was not the sole basis for re-defining the constitutive goals of the EC. The notion that the internal market programme was a free-standing initiative was one confined to the British government, and Conservative ministers arguably fell victim to their own neo-liberal propaganda in advancing this line while neglecting the linked developments set in train with the SEA. In his account of getting agreement to the White Paper inside the Commission (i.e. *months before* the Milan European Council), Cockfield explains that he had to obtain support by means of promising other commissioners from the southern Member States to back their demands for a doubling of the structural funds (1994: 45). If this was necessary inside the Commission, where the deployment of naked national interests is barely compatible with commissioners' oaths of neutrality, then it is difficult to see how the contours of the overall political bargain could be in question amongst British participants in the European Council, where the defence of national interests is of paramount concern.

In terms of putting the internal market programme into operation we can identify a number of political-decisional factors, noted by Lord Cockfield himself (1994: 29–75). The first was the setting out of a clear programme for achieving the internal market. Cockfield argues that the use of a White Paper – something of a novelty within the EC at the time – was itself a device used to give the internal market initiative importance by including the 'philosophy or principles to be followed and the programme in detail' (Cockfield 1994: 34). The programme thus provided a fresh political strategy for achieving the existing goals of the EC. The second element was the 1992 deadline with its mobilising effect.[6] A third consideration was giving the programme some kind of 'philosophical framework', in part implicit in the Treaty, to capture the imagination of those affected. Implicitly this was neo-liberal but it was not expressed in such terms by the Commission, for that could have been counter-productive in some Member States with less normatively compatible traditions of economic management. Finally, the emphasis placed upon 'removing barriers' was regarded as getting to the root of the incomplete single market. This emphasis upon obstacles did not discriminate between the four freedoms, thus avoiding possible pressures to put, say, liberalising services as a lower priority than liberalising goods. The subsequent 'costs of non-Europe' study was a useful way of both providing valuable evidence for sustaining the programme's momentum and demonstrating its economic advantages to the wider business community, whose engagement was to be key. Each of these elements was political-decisional in character.

Not only did these factors represent practical steps for getting the internal market initiative off the ground but they also comprised a strong normative dimension. Thus, the Commission's 'mission' was re-stated and given greater purpose. And presidencies of the Council were concerned to post a good performance on the SEM 'scoreboard' during their six-month period.

In judicial-normative terms the EC's constitutive goals were broadened significantly by the SEA, extending beyond policy areas related to the SEM. Of particular relevance in the latter context were the Treaty changes relating to EC competences, especially on health and safety, the environment, and cohesion. These changes gave a firmer constitutional-legal basis for policy in these areas through flanking measures for the SEM. Later on the EEA and the 1995 enlargement of the EU formally enlarged the geographical scope of the SEM. The judicial process also contributed to the dynamism through its case law on free movement and its consequent impact on flanking policy areas.

Institutional structure
The institutional changes brought about by the SEA were central to putting the SEM into practice. The key decision was the introduction of QMV to core areas of the SEM, including legislative harmonisation, capital controls and the freedom to provide services, as well as to related policy areas, such as air transport liberalisation, health and safety and parts of regional policy and research and technology matters. Where QMV applies – and was further extended by the TEU – it is important to bear in mind that the *practice* of QMV does not necessarily follow. However, the new rules did lead to a change of behaviour on the part of national governments. It was no longer possible for one Member State to adopt dogged blocking tactics in the Council. That state would need to negotiate with a view to maximising its influence even if fundamentally opposed to the legislation concerned, cf. British tactics in negotiating the Maternity Directive (Chapter 9). If this case represented rule-driven behaviour, we should also recall the impact of norms on governments' 'rational' behaviour. Thus, the French government's decision on merger control to end its objection to the legislation – which was subject to unanimity – was sweetened by being able to

claim the credit for agreement being reached. The norms of conducting a good presidency do not coincide with those of defending the national interest!

To retain a balanced picture, it must be recalled that some of the most problematic areas of the SEM retain unanimous voting. Free movement of persons is the principal area of the SEM where progress has been obstructed by unanimity. Taxation matters are another case where unanimity has impeded progress, i.e. on the harmonisation of indirect taxes.

None the less, the institutional changes clearly enhanced the decision-making capacity of the EC/EU and particularly in respect of the White Paper programme. Data on the consequences of increased use of QMV have been provided in various forms. The Commission has published its scorecards on the internal market: something that was in part provided for in the SEA, in what became Article 7b, EC. This monitoring of implementation was also an important contributory factor to mobilising decision-making, not only at the rule-making stage but also in respect of transposition into national law of directives. The idea of 'league tables' on transposition helped to put pressure on those Member States neglecting their duties. Italy, for example, seemed more conscious of its record on implementation and pushed through 'omnibus' enabling legislation. The Commission has continued to make reports on single market rule-making and rule-implementation even after the passing of the end-1992 deadline. Analyses on the impact of QMV on decision-making have also been published, although studies of the overall situation – as opposed to a case-study approach such as our own – have been somewhat limited (see, for example Engel and Borrmann 1991).

The other principal constitutional change in the SEA was the introduction of new policy-making procedures engaging the EP. In the context of the SEM it was the new cooperation procedure which was the innovation. The cooperation procedure was not only introduced with regard to accelerating decision-making but also as a move towards enhancing governance capability according to the benchmark of democratic rule. However, contrary to initial fears that increased parliamentary involvement might result in legislative stalemates, there is little evidence of the EP's greater involvement hampering the decisional process. Indeed, engaging the EP in much of the SEM legislation may be judged as having harnessed additional resources in the EU's institutional system. In our case study on the Maternity Directive, the EP was shown to have had quite significant powers in both agenda-setting on equal opportunities and in brokering the final agreement in the trialogue with the Commission and the Council presidency.

Again, however, formal institutional changes do not amount to the whole story. The Commission's Directorate General for the internal market, along with the Council of Ministers were vested with new norms: in the former case, almost a new 'culture'. Self-congratulatory it may be but there is

Conclusion

surely some truth in Cockfield's noting that Fernand Braun (Cockfield's Director General for the internal market) considered that 'at long last and for the first time in many years ... [the staff] knew exactly what was expected of them' (Cockfield 1994: 42). Thus the normative change in the administrative culture of the Commission was also a contributory factor. Combined with dynamic leadership from key commissioners, especially Cockfield and Delors, together with their respective *cabinets*, the new normative context combined with new decisional rules in the Council and opportunities offered by ECJ rulings to dynamise individual policy issues (see also Pollack 1994). Commission President Delors utilised the changed political climate for pursuing a 'Russian dolls' strategy (Ross 1995: 39–50). Thus, inside the SEM/SEA were concealed successive Russian dolls: the Delors package of budgetary and economic cohesion reforms agreed in 1988; the re-launching of EMU in 1988; and the social dimension culminating in the 1989 Social Charter.

There were additional knock-on effects in respect of ideas on policy. The studies on the costs of non-Europe were largely based on mainstream neo-classical applied economics. This thinking began to assume some kind of ideational hegemony within the Commission and certainly in its Directorate General for the internal market. However, as Weale and Williams (1992) have pointed out, these ideas (and the costs of non-Europe studies) paid scant regard to environmental externalities. In consequence, the increased decisional capacity on internal market matters was not replicated immediately in the environmental policy domain. First, DG XI (Environment) had to set up a task force on environmental policy and the single market in order to seek to integrate the two policy areas to a greater degree (see Chapter 8). And that did not occur until 1989. Thus the SEM and SEA created a kind of dynamic instability to integration that mobilised related policy areas.

It has been noted that the Court has tended in the past to err on the side of the supranational institutions when making judgments about matters of competence (supranational versus national) (Weiler 1994). In the case of the SEM the Court handed down a number of legal judgments following agreement on the White Paper that helped speed up the policy process in the Council. This situation arose as greater awareness of the SEM led to an increase in resort to European law. To take the case of air transport liberalisation, the *Nouvelles Frontières* (1986) and *Ahmed Saeed* (1989) judgments declared the existing regulatory arrangements to be against the Treaties, thus expediting the passage of legislation to fill a regulatory void. Rulings such as these fed into a much more propitious institutional system. Thus, the Commission was able to build on such rulings in most of our case studies. Separately from such developments the *Francovich* ruling opened up new ways whereby private parties could seek enforcement of EC law where Member States had failed to transpose it at national level.

Interaction with wider policy community

Beyond these changes to the EC institutions two areas of developments are particularly interesting concerning, respectively, the response of member governments and that of interest groups.

For member governments there were two developments which supported an increase in the governance capacity of the EC. The first was that the single market's programmatic content and time-scale proved to form a convenient instrument in domestic politics. In France '1993' appeared to fulfil the need for 'le grand projet' in domestic industrial policy: a successor to the role played by economic plans in earlier times. In the UK the SEM objective was seen as an extension of the Conservative government's support for enterprise in the 'Europe – open for business' campaign. More characteristically for Germany, the approach was to hold a series of tripartite European conferences, aimed at building consensus between the social partners to address the challenges of the SEM. In addition, the need for member governments to ensure 'their' economy was well prepared for completion of the SEM reinforced the commitment to the goals and ensured the mobilisation of national institutional resources for their achievement.

Beyond government, business and its interest groups were also to the fore. We have already mentioned the growth in individual companies, transnational interest groups and freelance lobbyists based in Brussels. Taking a new institutionalist view of that development, we may regard it as one manifestation of the way in which non-governmental actors reacted to the change in the organisational configuration of the supranational state, resulting, for instance, in the emergence of new interest groups lobbying on equal opportunities policy.

Another manifestation, which is associated more with the growth of research and technology programmes at the supranational level, has been the way in which companies and research institutions have come to orientate themselves more towards the EC because of financial incentives. These developments are part of a pattern whereby the governance capacity of the EC/EU brings with it a constituency of supportive elites. The organisational configuration of the state was identified by Lindberg and Campbell (1991) as one of the impulses for lasting change in the governance of the American economy. Whether this proves to be repeated in the European case – as, indeed, was predicted by Lindberg (in different research) and by other neo-functionalists – remains to be seen. The European integration process is arguably too brittle to make such an assertion with complete confidence.

There were in fact two distinct developments under way in the relationship between institutions and the wider policy community. One was a response on the part of interest groups to the SEM/SEA. The other was a re-organisation of business activity in response to technological change and globalisation. Thus, the growth of M&A activity was not just a response to the SEM but was part of a global pattern. In that sense business strategies and the SEM were *both* responses to global developments. That they were in synchronisation with each other was helpful to promoting integration. This situation corresponds to William Wallace's notion of informal integration as 'intense patterns of interaction which develop without the impetus of formal political decisions, following the dynamics of markets, technology, communications networks, and social change' (W. Wallace 1990: 9). It therefore differs from formal integration, which is achieved politically: 'decision by decision, bargain by bargain and treaty by treaty'.[7]

The conclusion must be that the favourable conditions associated with the SEM/SEA bargain derived in part from the balance achieved between informal and formal paths to integration. The governance capacity of the EC/EU was enhanced by the strong, responsive participation of non-governmental actors, for that is essential for such a small agency as the Commission with its absence of field agencies in the Member States. Indeed, lobbying of the Commission became so extensive that efforts have been made to regulate access (McLaughlin and Greenwood 1995). However, the fact that corporate strategies were already being re-thought because of *global* developments made firms more willing to become associated with the SEM project. This situation is perhaps most clearly evident in the case of air transport where British Airways and KLM endorsed European liberalisation while simultaneously pursuing transatlantic alliances.

Policy outputs and democratic rule
The achievements associated with the SEM, we have argued, can be explained by the re-formulation of the EC's constitutive goals, the reform of its institutions and the informal integration surrounding these two developments. However, the changes in governance capacity have not been an unqualified success. One problem was that the SEM/SEA 'effect' reached its zenith in the late-1980s. This was important in order to get momentum with the legislative phase. However, the 'hype' rebounded on the SEM and the EU somewhat in the 1990s when integration entered a much more difficult phase characterised by the problems of securing popular support for the Maastricht Treaty. European integration became bogged down in controversies about the transparency of its decision-making process, the legitimacy of an elite-led process and intrusions upon national and sub-national governmental powers (the subsidiarity debate). The SEM was caught up in these problems, especially with a large part of technical harmonisation having been transferred to 'private interest government' in the form of standards-setting bodies, for which accountability mechanisms are opaque.

Helen Wallace summarised the situation of the early 1990s thus:

> technocracy and an elite-driven process seem no longer an adequate basis for
> EC governance. The gap between governed and governors within and between
> countries is serious and created havoc in the debate about Maastricht to which

technical and legalistic devices seem an inappropriate response ... Regulatory capture is endemic and stifles certain kinds of policy development. The privatization of public space and the dissensus about European public goods make it much harder for the EC to retain effective footholds. (H. Wallace 1994: 96)

The concentration in the SEM and SEA upon policy output rather than on democratic rule bears some responsibility for the 'turbulent times' of EU governance which she diagnosed. Moreover, this situation has not been seriously addressed thus far in the 1996/97 IGC, for which the prospects are scarcely helped by the absence of 'a big idea'. To the extent that difficulties persist concerning the quality of the EU's democracy, the SEM is at risk of being undermined.

The single market and theory

Our study has advanced a new institutionalist agenda for research on the EU. What conclusions can we make regarding the value of this approach?

First of all, *on the character of integration* we have demonstrated that an institutionalist focus enables inclusive analysis of European integration. Thus, it permits analysis of constitutive change. Predominantly such change occurs through developing new goals for the EC/EU system, such as in the SEM/SEA. It also takes place through the evolving jurisprudence of the Court. However, an institutionalist focus can shift down a level, to examine detailed regulatory policy-making. We argue that an ability to capture these features is important if the phenomenon of integration is to be dissected and re-connected adequately.

Secondly, we conclude on *integration theorising* that approaches which do not take account of the different levels and stages of integration offer incomplete accounts. Thus, theorising through reference only to grand bargains can scarcely capture all aspects of EU governance. To focus only on these decisions, where national governments are especially powerful, is an inadequate basis to argue that 'the state' retains control over the integration process (see Moravcsik 1993; 1994; Milward, 1992). Equally, individual case studies using 'micro-theoretical' approaches, such as the policy network literature, may illustrate specific circumstances but face serious challenges if they are to tell us much about the wider pattern of integration (Peterson 1995). A further issue concerns where theories seek to explain policy negotiation but then take no account of whether, and how, policy is put into practice. We have at least sought to base our interpretation in this study around a multi-level and multi-faceted analysis of the governance of the EU. Crucially, it is the analysis of the operationalisation of governance that is important.

Thirdly, we have demonstrated that an *institutional focus* can connect up the analysis of all levels of EU governance: from negotiating the SEA to the day-to-day regulation of mergers.

Fourthly, we have argued that *historical institutionalism* can offer a range of insights. It can provide an analytical underpinning to 'multi-level governance' and to the interaction between systemic and sub-systemic governance in the EU (see Chapter 3). Moreover, it can throw light on:

- the pattern of policy evolution;
- the interaction of the all-important political and legal dynamics of integration and policy;
- the ability of the supranational institutions to exploit institutional opportunity structures in order to set the policy agenda and influence policy;
- the important normative and cultural dimension of integration;
- the strategic and tactical responses of interests and national governments to the EU's institutional rules; and
- the differing patterns of governance across different policy areas arising from different institutional roles, rules and norms (governance regimes).

Fifthly, historical institutionalism has been shown to have some value in explaining seismic change as much as incremental development: the step-change of integration that occurred with the SEM/SEA bargain, and the resulting paradigm shift across a set of diverse policy issues. The key here is the way in which the European Council can act as a catalyst for change in European integration. Pairings of states or even the Commission can inject ideas that gather their own dynamic over a series of summit meetings. This catalysing effect is more than some kind of rational outcome of Member State preferences. Moreover, such change creates ripples throughout the whole EC/EU system, through both institutional reform and a normative shift.

Of course, we have not discovered the holy grail. Historical institutionalism cannot get to the very mainsprings of integration. It offers an explanation based on intermediating factors rather than going to the underlying sources of macro-social change. In more modestly doing this, however, we have argued that it offers a balanced and inclusive 'reading' of European integration.

Outlook

Like integration theorising, the SEM will be on the EU's agenda for some time yet. It remains to be completed. Indeed, the Commission has been consulting with interested parties in order to launch in June 1997 at the Amsterdam European Council a programme to complete and exploit the full potential of the SEM by 1 January 1999 (at the time of writing). The consequent interaction with EMU, the EU's next big project, scheduled for 1999, may bring additional economic benefits. Equally, there have been suggestions that potential non-EMU participants like the UK may find their access to the SEM hampered because that kind of an *à la carte* EU is not on offer. Into the next millennium, eastern enlargement raises key issues about the ability of future members to accept the SEM rules.

The empirical research agenda is likely to move towards much greater emphasis on 'regulating the SEM'. As this study has shown, there are quite diverse arrangements for regulating the SEM's operation. At one end of the spectrum is merger control, with almost wholly supranational arrangements: the Commission as regulator and the ECJ and the CFI as instances for appeal. At the other end are the arrangements relating to pregnant women at the workplace. Here national courts and industrial tribunals are responsible for overseeing implementation, with monitoring from national agencies such as the UK's EOC. The creation of a European Cartel Office in the competition domain would introduce further variation, and perhaps trigger pressure for similar agencies where the Commission has regulatory powers: an EU Aviation Authority perhaps?

One thing which historical institutionalism can predict is that institutions take on their own dynamics, norms and values. With such a diversity of regulatory arrangements for the SEM – executive and judicial, supranational and national – there is a very real danger that a highly fragmented and opaque set of arrangements is emerging for regulating economic governance in the EU. The 'logic' of global trade regulation by the WTO intrudes in this area, too. If one reflects on how the steering of the US economy was shifted to the federal level with the emergence of inter-state railroads, the result at least was a set of fairly similar regulatory institutions. In the EU the regulatory environment has become confused, more multi-faceted and potentially contradictory.

Given that historical institutionalism emphasises the iterative nature of policy-making, the story of the SEM is far from complete.

Notes

1 Nicholas Argyris, 'Regulatory reform in the EU utilities sectors, with particular reference to telecommunications', paper at UACES annual conference, 7 January 1997.

2 This section is based on the Commission's own extensive assessments of the impact and effectiveness of the SEM, as summarised in CEC (1996f). A 'glossier' version of the findings is to be found in Monti (1996); also see Ayral (1995).

3 For a listing of the surveys, see Monti (1996: 159–61).

4 Weaver and Rockman use the terms 'governmental capability' but these have been adapted here, not least because there is no 'government' at the supranational level.

5 The terms 'political-decisional' and 'judicial-normative' derive from Weiler (1982).

6 The 1992 deadline was introduced formally by the SEA in Article 8a (EEC) and is mentioned also in Article 100b. However, there is ambiguity because of the

SEA's 'Declaration on Article 8a of the EEC Treaty' which specifies that, 'setting the date of 31 December 1992 does not create an automatic legal effect'.
7 It should be pointed out that the distinctions made by William Wallace do not correspond to those of Joseph Weiler, outlined earlier. Weiler's distinctions are between different forms of what would most likely be classified by Wallace as formal integration.

References

Abbati, C. degli (1987), *Transport and European Integration*, Luxembourg, Office for Official Publications of the EC.

ACE (1991), *ACE News*, Sept.–Dec. issue, Brussels.

ACE (1992), Position of L'Association des Compagnies Aériennes de la Communauté Européenne (ACE) with Regard to the EC Commission's Phase Three Proposals, paper presented to the EP's Committee on Transport and Tourism public hearing, 21. 1. 92, Brussels.

AEA (1991), *Commission Proposals for the Third Phase – AEA Comments*, Brussels.

Allen, D. (1983), Managing the Common Market: The Community's Competition Policy, in Wallace *et al.* (1983), 209–36.

Allen, D. (1992), European Union, the Single European Act and the 1992 Programme, in D. Swann (ed.), *The Single European Market and Beyond*, London, Routledge, 26–50.

Alter, K. J. and Meunier-Aitsahalia, S. (1994), Judicial Politics in the European Community: European Integration and the Pathbreaking *Cassis de Dijon* Decision, *Comparative Political Studies*, 26:4, 535–61.

Anglo-German Deregulation Group (1994), *Deregulation Now*, London.

Argyris, N. (1989), The EEC Rules of Competition Policy and the Air Transport Sector, *Common Market Law Review*, 26:1, 5–32.

Armstrong, K. (1995), Regulating the Free Movement of Goods: Institutions and Institutional Change, in J. Shaw and G. More (eds), *New Legal Dynamics of European Union*, Oxford, Clarendon Press, 165–91.

Armstrong, K. (1996), Citizenship of the Union? Lessons from *Carvel* and *The Guardian*, *Modern Law Review*, 59:4, 582–8.

Armstrong, K. (forthcoming), New Institutionalism and EU Legal Studies, in C. Harlow and P. Craig (eds), *Law-Making in the European Union*, Dublin, Round Hall.

Armstrong, S. and Bulmer, S. (1996), United Kingdom, in D. Rometsch and W. Wessels (eds), *The European Union and Member States*, Manchester, MUP, 253–90.

Atkins, W. S. (1988), *The 'Cost of Non-Europe' in Public Sector Procurement*, Vol. 5, Luxembourg, Office for Official Publications of the EC.

Atkinson, M. and Coleman, W. (1989), Strong States and Weak States: Sectoral Policy Networks in Advanced Capitalist Economies, *British Journal of Political Science*, 19:1, 47–67.

Ayral, M. (1995), *Le marché intérieur de l'Union européenne*, Paris, La documentation française.

Balfour, J. (1994), Air Transport – A Community Success Story?, *Common Market Law Review*, 31:5, 1025–53.

Balfour, J. M. (1989), Freedom to Provide Air Transport Services in the EEC, *European Law Review*, 14:1, 30–46.

Barnard, C. (1995), A European Litigation Strategy: The Case of the Equal Opportunities Commission, in J. Shaw and G. More (eds), *New Legal Dynamics of European Union*, Oxford, Clarendon Press, 253–72.

Barrett, S. (1987), *Flying High: Airline Prices and European Regulation*, Aldershot, Avebury/Adam Smith Institute.

Bellamy, C. (1997), The European Judiciary: How it Works, European Union Policy Papers III, Manchester, EPRU.

Bright, C. (1992), Nestlé/Perrier: New Issues in EC Merger Control, *International Financial Law Review*, 11:9.

Brittan, Sir L. (1991), *Competition Policy and the Single European Market*, Cambridge, Grotius Publications.

Brown, L. N. and Kennedy, T. (1994), *The Court of Justice of the European Communities* (4th edn), London, Sweet & Maxwell.

Bulmer, S. (1992), Completing the European Community's Internal Market: The Regulatory Implications for the Federal Republic of Germany, in K. Dyson (ed.), *The Politics of Regulation in Germany*, Aldershot, Dartmouth Publishing, 53–77.

Bulmer, S. (1993), The Governance of the European Union: A New Institutionalist Approach, *Journal of Public Policy*, 13:4, 351–80.

Bulmer, S. (1994), Institutions and Policy Change in the European Communities: The Case of Merger Control, *Public Administration*, 72:3, 423–44.

Bulmer, S. (1996), The European Council and the Council of the European Union: Gatekeepers of a European Federal Order?, *Publius: The Journal of Federalism*, 26:4.

Bulmer, S. and Wessels, W. (1987), *The European Council: Decision-Making in European Politics*, London, Macmillan.

Burch, M. and Holliday, I. (1995), *The British Cabinet System*, Hemel Hempstead, Harvester-Wheatsheaf.

Burley, A.-M. and Mattli, W. (1993), European Before the Court: A Political Theory of Legal Integration, *International Organization*, 47:1, 41–76.

Burrows, N. (1990), Harmonization of Technical Standards: reculer pour mieux sauter?, *Modern Law Review*, 53:5, 597–603.

Button, K. and Swann, D. (1989), European Community Airlines – Deregulation and Its Problems, *Journal of Common Market Studies*, 27:4, 259–82.

Button, K. and Swann, D. (1992), Transatlantic Lessons in Aviation Deregulation: EEC and US Experiences, *The Antitrust Bulletin*, 37:1, 207–55.

Cameron, D. (1992), The 1992 Initiative: Causes and Consequences, in A. Sbragia (ed.) (1992), *Euro-politics: Institutions and Policymaking in the 'New' European Community*, Washington, D.C., The Brookings Institution, 23–74.

Cammack, P. (1989), Bringing the State Back In?, *British Journal of Political Science*, 19:2, 261–90.

Campbell, J. and Lindberg, L. (1991), The Evolution of Governance Regimes, in Campbell *et al.* (1991), 319–55.

Campbell, J., Hollingsworth J. R. and Lindberg L. (eds) (1991), *Governance of the American Economy*, Cambridge, CUP.

Caporaso, J. (1996), The European Union and Forms of State: Westphalian, Regulatory or Post-Modern?, *Journal of Common Market Studies*, 34:1, 29–52.

Caporaso, J. and Keeler, J. (1995), The European Union and Regional Integration Theory, in C. Rhodes and S. Mazey (eds), *The State of the European Union*, Harlow, Longman.

Carlsnaes, W. and Smith, S. (1994), *European Foreign Policy. The EC and Changing Perspectives in Europe*, London, Sage Publications.

CEC (1968), *General Programme for the Elimination of Technical Barriers to Intra-Community Trade Arising from Disparities among National Laws*, COM(68) 138 final, Brussels.

CEC (1979), *Memorandum on the Contribution of the European Communities to the Development of Air Transport Services*, COM(79) 311 final, Brussels. (Also published in *Bulletin of the EC*, Supplement no. 5/79.)

CEC (1980), *Commission Communication on the Removal of Technical Barriers to Trade*, COM(80) 30 final, Brussels.

CEC (1984), *Toward the Development of a Community Air Transport Policy*, COM(84) 72 final, Brussels.

CEC (1985a), *Completing the Internal Market*, COM(85) 310 final, Brussels.

CEC (1985b), *Technical Harmonization and Standards: A New Approach*, COM(85) 19 final, Brussels.

CEC (1986), *Public Procurement in the European Community*, COM(86) 375 final, Brussels.

CEC (1987a), *Towards a Dynamic European Economy: Green Paper on the Development of the Common Market for Telecommunications Services and Equipment*, COM(87) 290, Brussels.

CEC (1987b), *Fourth Environmental Action Programme*, Official Journal of the European Communities, OJ C328 (7.12.87).

CEC (1987c), *Communication on Its Programme Concerning Safety, Hygiene and Health at Work*, COM(87) 520 final, Brussels.

CEC (1988a), *Communication on a Community Regime for Procurement in the Excluded Sectors*, COM(88) 376 final, Brussels.

CEC (1988b), *Proposal for a Council Directive on the Procurement Procedures of Entities Providing Water, Energy and Transport Services*, COM(88) 377 final, Brussels.

CEC (1988c), *Seventeenth Report on Competition Policy*, Brussels, OOPEC.

CEC (1989a), *Global Approach to Certification and Testing*, COM(89) 209 final, Brussels.

CEC (1989b), *A Community Strategy for Waste Management*, SEC(89) 934 final, Brussels.

CEC (1989c), *Community Charter of Fundamental Social Rights*, COM(89) 248 final, Brussels.

CEC (1989d), *Communication from the Commission Concerning Its Action Programme Relating to the Implementation of the Community Charter of Basic Social Rights for Workers*, COM(89) 568 final, Brussels.

CEC (1989e), *Council Directive on the Introduction of Measures to Encourage Improvements in the Health and Safety of Workers* (89/391/EEC), 12 June, Brussels.

CEC (1990a), *Green Paper on the Development of Standardization: Action for Faster Technical Integration in Europe*, COM(90) 456 final, Brussels.

CEC (1990b), *Proposal for a Council Regulation on the Supervision and Control of Shipments of Waste Within, Into and Out of the European Community*, COM(90) 415 final, Brussels.

CEC (1991a), *Completion of the Civil Aviation Policy in the European Communities. Towards Single Market Conditions*, COM(91) 275 final, Brussels.

CEC (1991b), *Amendment to the Proposal for a Council Directive Concerning Measures to Encourage Improvements in the Safety and Health of Pregnant Workers, Women Workers Who Have Recently Given Birth and Women Who Are Breastfeeding*, COM(90) 692 final – SYN 303, Brussels.

CEC (1992a), *XXIst Report on Competition Policy*, SEC(92) 756 final, Brussels.

CEC (1992b), *Report by the Commission to the Council and the European Parliament on the Evaluation of Aid Schemes Established in Favour of Community Air Carriers*, SEC(92) 431, Brussels.

CEC (1992c), *Towards Sustainability, Fifth Environmental Action Programme*, COM(92) 23 final, Brussels.

CEC (1992d), *Re-examined Proposal for a Council Directive Concerning Measures to Encourage Improvements in the Safety and Health of Pregnant Workers, Women Workers Who Have Recently Given Birth and Those Who Are Breastfeeding*, COM(92) 259 final – SYN 303, Brussels.

CEC (1992e), *Council Directive 92/85/EEC on the Introduction of Measures to Encourage Improvements in the Safety and Health at Work of Pregnant Workers and Workers Who Have Recently Given Birth or Are Breastfeeding (Tenth Individual Directive Within the Meaning of Article 16(1) of Directive 89/391/EEC)*, 19 October.

CEC (1993a), *Community Merger Control: Report from the Commission to the Council on the Implementation of the Merger Regulation*, COM(93) 385 final, Brussels.

CEC (1993b), *XXIInd Report on Competition Policy*, COM(93) 162 final, Brussels.

CEC (1993c), *Growth, Competitiveness, Employment – The Challenges and Ways Forward into the 21st Century*, COM(93) 700 final, Brussels.

CEC (1993d), *Making the Most of the Internal Market: Strategic Programme*, COM(93) 632 final, Brussels.

CEC (1993e), *Follow-up to the Sutherland Report: Legislative Consolidation to Enhance the Transparency of Community Law in the Area of the Internal Market*, COM(93) 361 final, Brussels.

CEC (1993f), *Report to the European Council on the Adaptation of Community Legislation to the Subsidiarity Principle*, COM(93) 545 final, Brussels.

CEC (1994a) *Expanding Horizons*, a Report by the Comité des Sages for Air Transport to the European Commission, Brussels, DG VII.

CEC (1994b), *European Social Policy: A Way Forward for the Union*, COM(94) 333 final, Brussels.

CEC (1994c), *The Community Internal Market*, COM(94) 55 final, Brussels.

CEC (1994d), *Development of Administrative Co-operation in the Implementation and Enforcement of Community Legislation in the Internal Market*, COM(94) 29 final, Brussels.

CEC (1995a), *The Broader Use of Standardization in Community Policy*, COM(95) 412 final, Brussels.

CEC (1995b), *Medium Term Social Action Programme (1995–97)*, COM 95(134) final, Brussels.

CEC (1995c), *The Single Market in 1994*, COM 95(238) final, Brussels.

CEC (1995d), *White Paper: Preparation of the Associated Countries of Central and Eastern Europe for Integration into the Internal Market of the Union*, COM(95) 163 final, Brussels.

CEC (1996a), *Thirteenth Annual Report on Monitoring the Application of Community Law*, COM(96) 600 final, Brussels.

CEC (1996b), *Draft Proposal for a Council Regulation Amending Council Regulation 4064/89 on the Control of Concentrations Between Undertakings*, COM(96) 313 final, Brussels.

CEC (1996c), *Green Paper: Public Procurement in the European Union: Exploring the Way Forward*, Brussels.

CEC (1996d), *The Single Market in 1995*, COM 96(51) final, Brussels.

CEC (1996e), *Report of the Commission on the SLIM Pilot Project*, COM(96) 559 final, Brussels.

CEC (1996f), *The Impact and Effectiveness of the Single Market*, COM(96) 520 final, Brussels.

CEC (1996g), *Vertical Restrains in EU Competition Policy*, Green Paper, Brussels.

Cecchini, P., Catinat, M. and Jacquemin, A. (1988), *The European Challenge 1992. The Benefits of a Single Market*, Aldershot, Wildwood House.

Chalmers, D. (1996), *The Single Market: From Prima Donna to Journeyman*, in J. Shaw and G. More (eds), *New Legal Dynamics of European Union*, Oxford, Clarendon Press.

Charpentier, G. and Clark, R. (1975), *Les achats publics dans le marché commun*, Brussels.

Chayes, A. (1976), The Role of the Judge in Public Law Litigation, *Harvard Law Review*, 89:7, 1281–316.

Church, C. and Phinnemore, D. (1994), *European Union and European Community: A Handbook and Commentary on the Post-Maastricht Treaties*, Hemel Hempstead, Harvester-Wheatsheaf.

Closa, C. (1994), Citizenship of the Union and Nationality of Member States, in D. O'Keeffe and P. Twomey (eds), *Legal Issues of the Maastricht Treaty*, London, Wiley Chancery Law.

Cockfield, Lord A. (1994), *The European Union: Creating the Single Market*, Chichester, Chancery Law Publishing.

COFACE (1992) EC Directive on the Protection of Pregnant Women at Work, press release, Brussels.

COFACE (1993), Protection de la maternité, position paper, 17 March, Brussels.

Collie, L. (1993), Business Lobbying in the European Community: The Union of Industrial and Employers' Confederation of Europe, in S. Mazey and J. Richardson (eds), *Lobbying in the European Community*, Oxford, OUP.

Consumers' Association (1991), Developments in European Community Air Transport Policy: Memorandum by Consumers' Association, position paper to House of Commons Transport Committee, February, London, Consumers' Association.

Cook, J. and Kerse, C. (1991), *EEC Merger Control: Regulation 4064/89*, London, Sweet & Maxwell.

Corbett, R. (1987), The 1985 Intergovernmental Conference and the Single European Act, in R. Pryce (ed.), *The Dynamics of European Union*, London, Croom Helm, 238–72.

Corbett, R. (1992), The Intergovernmental Conference on Political Union, *Journal of Common Market Studies*, 30:3, 271–98.

Cowles, M. G. (1995), Setting the Agenda for a New Europe: The European Round Table and EC 1992, *Journal of Common Market Studies*, 33:4, 501–26.

Cox, A. (1993), *Public Procurement in the European Community: The Single Market and the Enforcement Regime After 1992*, Winteringham, Earlsgate Press.

Cox, A. (1994), Derogation, Subsidiarity and the Single Market, *Journal of Common Market Studies*, 32:2, 127–47.

Craig, P. and de Búrca, G. (1995), *EC Law: Text, Cases and Materials*, Oxford, OUP.

Cram, L. (1993), Calling the Tune Without Paying the Piper? Social Policy Regulation: The Role of the Commission in European Community Social Policy, *Policy and Politics*, 21:2, 135–46.

Dashwood, A. (1983), Hastening Slowly: The Community's Path Towards Harmonization, in Wallace *et al.* (1983).

de Búrca, G. (1996), The Quest for Legitimacy in the European Union, *Modern Law Review*, 59:3, 349–76.

Dehousse, R. and Weiler, J. (1990), The Legal Dimension, in W. Wallace (ed.), *The Dynamics of European Integration*, London, Pinter, 242–60.

Docksey, C. and Williams, K. (1994), The Commission and the Execution of Community Policy, in G. Edwards and D. Spence (eds), *The European Commission*, Harlow, Longman, 117–45.

Doganis, R. (1991), *Flying Off Course: The Economics of International Airlines* (2nd edn), London, Harper Collins Academic.

Earnshaw, D. and Judge, D. (forthcoming), The Life and Times of the European Union's Cooperation Procedure, *Journal of Common Market Studies*, 35:4.

Eberlie, R. (1990), The New Health and Safety Legislation of the European Community, *Industrial Law Journal*, 19:2, 81–97.

Economist, The (1989), Where Nationalism Dies Hard, 8 July, 18–19.

Egan, M. (1991), 'Associative Regulation' in the European Community: The Case of Technical Standards, paper presented to the European Community Studies Association biennial conference, 22–24 May.

Ehlermann, C.-D. (1995), Reflections on the European Cartel Office, *Common Market Law Review*, 32:2, 471–86.

Engel, C. and Borrmann, C. (1991), *Vom Konsens zur Mehrheitsentscheidungen: EG-Entscheidungsverfahren und nationale Interessenpolitik nach der Einheitlichen Europäischen Akte*, Bonn, Europa Union Verlag.

EOC (1993a), Formal Response of the Equal Opportunities Commission to the Trade Union Reform and Employment Rights Bill, Manchester.

EOC (1993b), Formal Response of the Equal Opportunities Commission to the Department of Social Security Consultative Document Changes in Maternity Pay: Proposals for Implementing the Pregnant Workers Directive, Manchester.

Esser, J. (1995), Germany: Challenges to the Old Policy Style, in J. Hayward (ed.), *Industrial Enterprise and European Integration*, Oxford, OUP, 48–75.

EP (1992), Recommendation of the Committee on Women's Rights on the Common Position Established by the Council with a View to the Adoption of a Directive on the Introduction of Measures to Encourage Improvements in the Safety and Health at Work of Pregnant Workers and Workers Who Have Recently Given Birth, PE 156.167/fin., 24 April, Luxembourg.

Evans, P. Rueschemeyer, D. and Skocpol, T. (eds) (1985), *Bringing the State Back In*, Cambridge, CUP.

EWL (1992), Work Programme for Year 1992–1993, Brussels.

Farquhar, B. (1995), Consumer Representation in Standardisation, *Consumer Law Journal*, 3:2, 56–68.

Farr, S. (1992), *Harmonisation of Technical Standards in the EC*, London, Chancery.

FATUREC (1991), submission to the President of the Council of Ministers, 21 October, London.

Featherstone, K. (1994), Jean Monnet and the 'Democratic Deficit' in the European Union, *Journal of Common Market Studies*, 32:2, 149–70.

Fine, F. (1987), The Philip Morris Judgment: Does Article 85 Now Extend to Mergers?, *European Competition Law Review*, 8:4, 333–43.

Finnemore, M. (1993), International Organizations as Teachers of Norms: The United Nations Educational, Scientific and Cultural Organization and Science Policy, *International Organization*, 47:4, 565–97.

Forsyth, M. (1981), *Union of States: The Theory and Practice of Confederation*, Leicester, LUP.

Freeman, G. (1985), National Styles and Policy Sectors: Explaining Structured Variation, *Journal of Public Policy*, 5:4, 467–96.

Garrett, G. (1992), International Co-operation and Institutional Choice: The European Community's Internal Market, *International Organization*, 46:2, 533–60.

Garrett, G. (1995), The Politics of Legal Integration in the European Union, *International Organization*, 49:1, 171–81.

Garrett, G. and Weingast, B. (1993), Ideas, Interests and Institutions: Constructing the European Community's Internal Market, in J. Goldstein and R. Keohane (eds), *Ideas and Foreign Policy: Beliefs, Institutions and Political Change*, Ithaca, N.Y., Cornell University Press, 173–206.

Göhler, G. (1987), Politische Institutionen und Politikwissenschaft, in Göhler (ed.), *Grundfragen der Theorie Politischer Institutionen: Forschungsstand – Probleme – Perspektiven*, Opladen, Westdeutscher Verlag, 15–47.

Gormley, L. (1989), Actually or Potentially, Directly or Indirectly? Obstacles to the Free Movement of Goods, *Yearbook of European Law*, 9, 197–208.

Granell, F. (1995), The European Union's Enlargement Negotiations with Austria, Finland, Norway and Sweden, *Journal of Common Market Studies*, 33:1, 117–41.

Green, N., Hartley, T. and Usher, J. (1991), *The Legal Foundations of the Single European Market*, Oxford, OUP.

Haas, E. (1957), *The Uniting of Europe*, Stanford, Stanford University Press.

Hall, P. (1992), The Movement from Keynesianism to Monetarism: Institutional Analysis and British Economic Policy in the 1970s, in S. Steinmo, K. Thelen and F. Longstreth (eds), *Structuring Politics: Historical Institutionalism in Comparative Analysis*, Cambridge, CUP, 90–113.

Hall, P. and Taylor, R. (1996), Political Science and the Three New Institutionalisms, *Political Studies*, 44:5, 936–57.

Harlow, C. (1996), Francovich and the Problem of the Disobedient State, *European Law Journal*, 2:3, 199–225.

Hawkes, L. (1992), The EC Merger Control Regulation: Not an Industrial Policy Instrument: The De Havilland Decision, *European Competition Law Review*, 13:1, 34–8.

Hayes-Renshaw, F. and Wallace, H. (1996), *The Council of Ministers*, Basingstoke, Macmillan.

High Level Group (1992), The Internal Market After 1992: Meeting the Challenge, Brussels.

Hildebrand, P. M. (1993), The European Community's Environmental Policy 1957 to '1992': From Incidental Measures to International Regime?, in D. Judge (ed.), *A Green Dimension for the European Community: Political Issues and Processes*, London, Frank Cass & Co.

Hix, S. (1994), The Study of the European Community: The Challenge to Comparative Politics, *West European Politics*, 17:1, 1–30.

Hix, S. (1995), Parties at the European Level and the Legitimacy of EU Socio-Economic Policy, *Journal of Common Market Studies*, 33:4, 527–54.

HM Government (1984), Europe – The Future, *Journal of Common Market Studies*, 23:1, 74–81.

Hoffman, Lord, L. (1997), A Sense of Proportion, John Maurice Kelly Memorial Lecture, Faculty of Law, University College Dublin.

Hoffmann, S. (1966), Obstinate or Obsolete: The Fate of the Nation State and the Case of Western Europe, *Daedalus*, 95, 862–915.

Hoffmann, S. (1982), Reflections on the Nation-State in Western Europe Today, *Journal of Common Market Studies*, 21:1/2, 21–37.

Holloway, J. (1981), *Social Policy Harmonisation in the European Community*, Farnborough, Gower.

Hosli, M. (1996), Coalitions and Power: Effects of Qualified Majority Voting on the Council of the European Union, *Journal of Common Market Studies*, 34:2, 255–73.

House of Lords Select Committee on the European Communities (1985), *Parental Leave and Leave for Family Reasons*, Session 1984–85, Third Report, HL 84, London, HMSO.

House of Lords Select Committee on the European Communities (1991), *Protection at Work of Pregnant Women and Women Who Have Recently Given Birth, and Child Care*, Session 1991–92, Second Report, HL Paper 11, 26 November, London, HMSO.

Huntoon, B. D. (1989), Emerging Controls on Transfers of Hazardous Waste to Developing Countries, *Law and Policy in International Business*, 21, 247–71.

Hurrell, A. and Menon, A. (1996), Politics Like Any Other? Comparative Politics, International Relations and the Study of the European Union, *West European Politics*, 19:2, 386–402.

IOCU (1991), *EC Commission's Proposals for a 3rd Package of Liberalisation Measures Leading to a Single Internal Market: Market Entry, the Preservation of Multi Airline Competition*, 11 September, The Hague.

Jachtenfuchs, M. (1995), Theoretical Perspectives on European Governance, *European Law Journal*, 1:2, 115–33.

Jacobs, F., Corbett, R. and Shackleton, M. (1992), *The European Parliament* (2nd edn), Harlow, Longman.

Jacqué, J. P., and Weiler, J. H. H. (1990), On the Road to European Union – A New Judicial Architecture: An Agenda for the Intergovernmental Conference, *Common Market Law Review*, 27, 185–207.

James, P. (1993), The European Community. A Positive Force for Health and Safety?, in D. Mayes (ed.), *Aspects of European Integration. Environment, Regulation, Competition and the Social Dimension*, London, NIESR, 30–5.

Jeffery, C. (1994), The Länder Strike Back: Structures and Procedures of European Policy-Making in the German Federal System, Discussion Papers in Federal Studies No. FS 94/4, Leicester, Centre for Federal Studies.

Joerges, C. (1988), The New Approach to Technical Harmonization and the Interests of Consumers: Reflections on the Requirements and Difficulties of the Europeanization of Product Safety Policy, in R. Bieber, R. Dehousse, J. Pinder and J. Weiler (eds), *1992: One European Market*, Baden-Baden, Nomos Verlagsgesellschaft.

Judge, D. and Earnshaw, D. (1994), Weak European Parliament Influence?, *Government and Opposition*, 29:2, 262–76.

Judge, D., Earnshaw, D. and Cowan, N. (1994), Ripples or Waves: The European Parliament in the European Community Policy Process, *Journal of European Public Policy*, 1:1, 27–52.

Kassim, H. (1995), Air Transport Champions: Still Carrying the Flag, in J. Hayward (ed.), *Industrial Enterprise and European Integration: from National to International Champions in Western Europe*, Oxford, Clarendon Press, 188–214.

Katzenstein, P. (ed.) (1978), *Between Power and Plenty: Foreign Economic Policies of Advanced Industrial States*, Madison, Wis., University of Wisconsin Press.

Keatinge, P. and Murphy, A. (1987), The European Council's Ad Hoc Committee on Institutional Affairs (1984–85), in R. Pryce (ed.), *The Dynamics of European Union*, London, Croom Helm, 217–37.

Kendall, V. (1991), Standardization and its Problems, *Economist Intelligence Unit, European Trends*, 3, 70–4.

Keohane, R. (1989), Neoliberal Institutionalism: A Perspective on World Politics, in R. Keohane, *International Institutions and State Power*, Boulder, Colo., Westview Press, 1–20.

Keohane, R. and Hoffmann, S. (1991), Institutional Change in Europe in the 1980s, in Keohane and Hoffmann (eds), *The New European Community: Decision-making and Institutional Change*, Boulder, Colo., Westview Press, 1–39.

Kerremans, B. (1996), Do Institutions Make a Difference? Non-Institutionalism, Neo-Institutionalism, and the Logic of Common Decision-Making in the European Union, *Governance*, 9:2, 217–40.

Kirchner, E. J. (1992), *Decision-making in the European Community. The Council Presidency and European Integration*, Manchester, MUP.

Kloss, D. (1992a), Health and Safety at Work in S. Bulmer, S. George and A. Scott (eds), *The United Kingdom and EC Membership Evaluated*, London, Pinter Publishers, 203–4.

Kloss, D. (1992b), Equal Treatment of Men and Women, in S. Bulmer, S. George and A. Scott (eds), *The United Kingdom and EC Membership Evaluated*, London, Pinter Publishers, 205–11.

Kohler-Koch, B. (1996), Catching Up With Change: The Transformation of Governance in the European Union, *Journal of European Public Policy*, 3:3, 359–80.

Krämer, L. (1992), *Focus on European Environmental Law*, London, Sweet & Maxwell.

Krasner, S. (1983), Structural Causes and Regime Consequences: Regimes as Intervening Variables, in S. Krasner (ed.), *International Regimes*, Ithaca N.Y., Cornell University Press, 1–21.

Kratochwil, F. (1989), *Rules, Norms and Decisions. On the Conditions of Practical and Legal Reasoning in International Relations and Domestic Affairs*, Cambridge, CUP.

Kummer, K. (1992), The International Regulation of Transboundary Traffic in Hazardous Wastes: The 1989 Basel Convention, *International and Comparative Law Quarterly*, 43:3, 530–62.

Leibfried, S. and Pierson, P. (eds) (1995), *European Social Policy: Between Fragmentation and Integration*, Washington, D.C., The Brookings Institution.

Leibfried, S. and Pierson, P. (1996), Social Policy, in Wallace and Wallace (1996), 185–207.

Lindberg, L. (1963), *The Political Dynamics of European Economic Integration*, Stanford, Stanford University Press.

Lindberg, L. (1994), Comment on Moravcsik, in S. Bulmer and A. Scott (eds), *Economic and Political Integration in Europe: Internal Dynamics and Global Context*, Oxford, Blackwell Publishers, 81–5.

Lindberg, L. and Campbell, J. (1991), The State and Economic Governance, in Campbell *et al.* (1991), 356–95.

Lindberg, L. and Scheingold, S. (1970), *Europe's Would-Be Polity*, Englewood Cliffs, NJ: Prentice-Hall.

Lowi, T. (1964), American Business, Public Policy, Case Studies and Political Theory, *World Politics*, 16, 677–715.

Lowi, T. (1972), Four Systems of Policy, Politics and Choice, *Public Administration Review*, 32:4, 298–310.

Lowndes, V. (1996), Varieties of New Institutionalism: A Critical Appraisal, *Public Administration*, 74:2, 181–97.

Ludlow, P. (1991), The European Commission, in Keohane and Hoffmann (1991), 85–132.

McGee, A. and Weatherill, S. (1990), The Evolution of the Single Market – Harmonisation or Liberalisation, *Modern Law Review*, 53:5, 578–96.

McGowan, F. and Seabright, P. (1989), Deregulating European Airlines, *Economic Policy*, 9, 283–344.

McLaughlin, A. and Greenwood, J. (1995), The Management of Interest Representation in the European Union, *Journal of Common Market Studies*, 33:1, 143–56.

McMillan, J. (1985), Qu'est-ce que c'est la normalisation?, *Revue du marché commun*, 284, 93–8.

Maher, I. (1994), National Courts as European Community Courts, *Legal Studies*, 14:2, 226–43.

Maher, I. (1995), Legislative Review by the EC Commission: Revision without Zeal, in J. Shaw and G. More (eds), *New Legal Dynamics of European Union*, Oxford, Clarendon Press.

Majone, G. (1989), *Evidence, Argument and Persuasion in the Policy Process*, New Haven and London, Yale University Press.

Majone, G. (1991), Cross-National Sources of Regulatory Policymaking in European and the United States, *Journal of Public Policy*, 11:1, 79–106.

Majone, G. (1992), Regulatory Federalism in the European Community, *Environment and Planning C: Government and Policy*, 10, 299–316.

Majone, G. (1993), The European Community Between Social Policy and Social Regulation, *Journal of Common Market Studies*, 31:2, 153–70.

Majone, G. (1994), The Rise of the Regulatory State in Europe, *West European Politics*, 17:3, 77–101.

Majone, G. (1996), *Regulating Europe*, London, Routledge.

March, J. and Olsen, J. (1984), The New Institutionalism: Organizational Factors in Political Life, *American Political Science Review*, 78, 734–49.

March, J. and Olsen, J. (1989), *Rediscovering Institutions: The Organizational Basis of Politics*, New York, The Free Press.

March, J. and Olsen, J. (1996), Institutional Perspectives on Political Institutions, *Governance*, 9:3, 247–64.

Margue, T.-L. (1991), L'ouverture des marchés publics dans la Communauté, *Revue du Marché Unique Européen*, 4, 111–221.

Marks, G., Hooghe, L. and Blank, K. (1996), European Integration from the 1980s: State-Centric *v.* Multi-Level Governance, *Journal of Common Market Studies*, 34:3, 341–78.

Marks, G., Nielsen, F., Ray, L. and Salk, J. (1996), Competencies, Cracks and Conflicts: Regional Mobilization in the European Union, in G. Marks, F. Scharpf, P. Schmitter and W. Streeck (eds), *Governance in the European Union*, London, Sage, 40–63.

Mattli, W. and Slaughter, A.-M. (1995), Law and Politics in the European Union: A Reply to Garrett, *International Organization*, 49:1, 183–90.

Mazey, S. (1988), European Community Action on Behalf of Women: The Limits of Legislation, *Journal of Common Market Studies*, 27:1, 63–84.

Mazey, S. and Richardson, J. (1993), Introduction: Transference of Power, Decision Rules, and Rules of the Game, in S. Mazey and J. Richardson (eds), *Lobbying in the European Community*, Oxford, OUP, 3–26.

Mazey, S. and Richardson, J. (1994), The Commission and the Lobby, in G. Edwards and D. Spence (eds), *The European Commission*, Harlow, Longman, 169–201.

Meehan, E. (1993), *Citizenship and the European Community*, London, Sage Publications.

Micklitz, H. (1986), Perspectives on a European Directive on the Safety of Technical Consumer Goods, *Common Market Law Review*, 23, 617–40.

Milward, A. (1992), *The European Rescue of the Nation-State*, London, Routledge.

Milward, A., Lynch, F., Romero, F., Ranieri, R. and Sørensen, V. (1993), *The Frontier of National Sovereignty: History and Theory 1945–1992*, London, Routledge.

Monnet, J. (1978), *Memoirs*, London, Collins.

Monti, M. (1996), *The Single Market and Tomorrow's Europe. A Progress Report from the European Commission*, London, Kogan Page.

Moravcsik, A. (1991), Negotiating the Single European Act, in R. Keohane and S. Hoffmann (1991) (eds), *The New European Community: Decisionmaking and Institutional Change*, Boulder, Colo., Westview Press, 41–84.

Moravcsik, A. (1993), Preferences and Power in the European Community, *Journal of Common Market Studies*, 31:4, 473–524.

Moravcsik, A. (1994), Why European Integration Strengthens the Nation-State, paper presented at Conference of Europeanists, Chicago.

Moravcsik, A. (1995), Liberal Intergovernmentalism and Integration: A Rejoinder, *Journal of Common Market Studies*, 33:4, 611–28.

Naveau, J. (1992), *Droit Aérien Européen: les nouvelles règles du jeu*, Paris, Institut du Transport Aérien.

Neven, D., Nuttall, R. and Seabright, P. (1993), *Merger in Daylight: The Economics and Politics of European Merger Control*, London, CEPR.

Ninni, A. (1990), Recent Changes in the Power Equipment Industry and the Opening Up of Public Procurement Markets in the EEC, *Energy Policy*, May, 320–30.

Norton, P. (ed.) (1996), *National Parliaments and the European Union*, London, Frank Cass.

Nugent, N. (1994), *The Government and Politics of the European Union* (3rd edn), Basingstoke, Macmillan.

OECD (1988), *Deregulation and Airline Competition*, Paris.

O'Keeffe, D. (1994), Union Citizenship, in D. O'Keeffe and P. Twomey (eds), *Legal Issues of the Maastricht Treaty*, London, Wiley Chancery Law.

Pearce, J. and Sutton, J. (1986), *Protection and Industrial Policy in Europe*, London, Routledge and Kegan Paul/RIIA.

Pelkmans, J. (1987), The New Approach to Technical Harmonization and Standardization, *Journal of Common Market Studies*, 25:3, 249–69.

Pelkmans, J. (1991), The Internal EC Market for Air Transport: Issues After 1992, in D. Banister and K. Button (eds), *Transport in a Free Market Economy*, Basingstoke, Macmillan, 195–215.

Pelkmans, J. (1994), The Significance of EC-1992, *The Annals of the American Academy of Political and Social Science*, 531, 94–111.

Pelkmans, J. and Vollebergh, A. (1986), The Traditional Approach to Technical Harmonization: Accomplishments and Deficiencies, in J. Pelkmans and M. Vanheukelen (eds), *Coming to Grips with the Internal Market*, Maastricht, EIPA.

Pescatore, P. (1987), Some Critical Remarks on the 'Single European Act', *Common Market Law Review*, 24:1, 9–18.

Peters, B. G. (1992), Bureaucratic Politics and the Institutions of the European Community, in A. Sbragia (ed.), *Euro-politics: Institutions and Policymaking in the 'New' European Community*, Washington, D.C., The Brookings Institution, 75–122.

Peters, B. G. (1994), Agenda-Setting in the European Community, *Journal of European Public Policy*, 1:1, 9–26.

Peterson, J. (1995), Decision-Making in the European Union: Towards a Framework for Analysis, *Journal of European Public Policy*, 2:1, 69–93.

Pierson, P. (1996), The Path to European Integration: A Historical Institutionalist Analysis, *Comparative Political Studies*, 29:2, 123–63.

Pollack, M. (1994), Creeping Competence: The Expanding Agenda of the European Community, *Journal of Public Policy*, 14:2, 95–145.

Preston, C. (1995), Obstacles to EU Enlargement: The Classic Community Method and the Prospects for a Wider Europe, *Journal of Common Market Studies*, 33:3, 451–63.

Rehbinder, E. and Stewart, R. (1985), *Environmental Protection Policy*, Berlin, Walter de Gruyter.

Reif, K.-H. (1993), Cultural Convergence and Cultural Diversity as Factors in European Identity, in S. Garcia (ed.), *European Identity and the Search for Legitimacy*, London, Pinter, 131–53.

Rhodes, M. (1991), The Social Dimension of the Single European Market: National Versus Transnational Regulation, *European Journal of Political Research*, 19, 245–80.

Rhodes, M. (ed.) (1995), *The Regions and the New Europe*, Manchester, MUP.

Rhodes, R. A. W. (1996), The New Governance: Governing without Government, *Political Studies*, 44:5, 652–67.

Richardson, J. (ed.) (1982), *Policy Styles in Western Europe*, London, Allen & Unwin.

Rieger, E. (1996), The Common Agricultural Policy: External and Internal Dimensions, in Wallace and Wallace (1996), 97–129.

Risse-Kappen, T. (1996), Exploring the Nature of the Beast: International Relations Theory and Comparative Policy Analysis Meet the European Union, *Journal of Common Market Studies*, 34:1, 53–80.

Rose, R. (1993), *Lesson-Drawing in Public Policy?*, Chatham, N.J., Chatham House.

Rosenau, J. N. (1992), Governance, Order and Change in World Politics, in J. Rosenau and E-O. Czempiel (eds), *Governance Without Government: Order and Change in World Politics*, Cambridge, CUP.

Ross, G. (1995), *Jacques Delors and European Integration*, Oxford, Polity Press.

Rubery, J. (1992), Pay, Gender and the Social Dimension to Europe, *British Journal of Industrial Relations*, 30:4, 606–21.

Ruggie, J. G. (1993a), Territoriality and Beyond: Problematizing Modernity in International Relations, *International Organization*, 47:1, 139–74.

Ruggie, J. G. (1993b), Multilateralism: The Anatomy of an Institution, in Ruggie (ed.), *Multilateralism Matters: The Theory and Praxis of an Institution*, New York, Columbia University Press, 3–47.

Sabatier, P. (1988), An Advocacy Coalition Framework of Policy Change and the Role of Policy-Oriented Learning Therein, *Policy Sciences*, 21:2/3, 129–68.

Sandholtz, W. (1992), ESPRIT and the Politics of International Collective Action, *Journal of Common Market Studies*, 30:1, 1–21.

Sandholtz, W. and Zysman, J. (1989), 1992: Recasting the European Bargain, *World Politics*, 42:1, 95–128.

Sbragia, A. (1993), The European Community: A Balancing Act, *Publius: The Journal of Federalism*, 23, 23–38.

Scharpf, F. (1988), The Joint-Decision Trap: Lessons from German Federalism and European Integration, *Public Administration*, 66:3, 239–78.

Schattschneider, E. E. (1960), *The Semisovereign People: A Realist's View of Democracy in America*, New York, Holt, Rinehart & Winston.

Schmidt, A. (1992), Transboundary Movements of Waste under EC Law: The Emerging Regulatory Framework, *Journal of Environmental Law*, 4:1, 57–80.

Schmidt, V. (1996), Loosening the Ties that Bind: The Impact of European Integration on French Government and its Relationship to Business, *Journal of Common Market Studies*, 34:2, 223–54.

Schneider, V. (1992), Organized Interests in the European Telecommunications Sector, in J. R. Grote and K. Ronit (eds), *Organized Interests and the European Community*, London, Sage Publications.

Schnöring, T. (1991), National Differences in Telecommunications R & D in Europe, *Intereconomics*, May/June, 128–38.

Schreiber, K. (1991), The New Approach to Technical Harmonization and Standards, in L. Hurwitz and C. Lequesne (eds), *The State of the European Community*, Harlow: Longman.

Scott, J. (1995), GATT and Community Law: Rethinking the 'Regulatory Gap', in J. Shaw and G. More (eds), *New Legal Dynamics of European Union*, Oxford, Clarendon Press.

Sedelmeier, U. and Wallace, H. (1996), Policies Towards Central and Eastern Europe, in Wallace and Wallace (1996).

Shackleton, M. (1991), The European Community Between Three Ways of Life: A Cultural Analysis, *Journal of Common Market Studies*, 29:6, 575–601.

Shaw, J. (1991), Pregnancy Discrimination in Sex Discrimination, *European Law Review*, 16:3, 313–20.

Shaw, J. (1993), *European Community Law*, Basingstoke, Macmillan.

Shaw, J. (1994), Twin Track Social Europe – The Inside Track, in D. O'Keeffe and P. Twomey (eds), *Legal Issues of the Maastricht Treaty*, London, Wiley Chancery Law, 295–311.

Shaw, J. (1995a), Decentralization and Law Enforcement in EC Competition Law, *Legal Studies*, 15:1, 128–63.

Shaw, J. (1995b), The Birth, Life and Death of a Proposal: The Ill-fated Services Draft, paper presented to the European Community Studies Association conference, Charleston, S. Carolina, 11–14 May.

Shaw, J. (1996a), European Citizenship: The IGC and Beyond, paper presented to the Irish Centre for European Law conference, *Political Union and the Agenda of the IGC*, Trinity College Dublin, 30 November.

Shaw, J. (1996b), *Law of the European Union* (2nd edn), London, Macmillan.

Skowronek, S. (1982), *Building a New American State. The Expansion of National Administrative Capacities*, Cambridge, CUP.

Sloot, T. and Verschuren, P. (1990), Decision-Making Speed in the European Community, *Journal of Common Market Studies*, 29:1, 75–85.

Smith, M. (1994), Beyond the Stable State? Foreign Policy Challenges and Opportunities in the New Europe, in Carlsnaes and Smith (1994), 21–44.

Snyder, F. (1993), The Effectiveness of Community Law: Institutions, Processes, Tools and Techniques, *Modern Law Review*, 56:1, 19–54.

Sohrab, J. A. (1990), The Single European Market and Public Procurement, *Oxford Journal of Legal Studies*, 10, 522–38.

Springer, B. (1992), *The Social Dimension of 1992: Europe Faces a New EC*, New York, Praeger Publishers.

Stein, E. (1981), Lawyers, Judges and the Making of a Transnational Constitution, *American Journal of International Law*, 75:1.

Steiner, J. (1990), *Textbook on EEC Law* (2nd edn), London, Blackstone Press.

Stevens, H. (1997), Liberalisation of Air Transport in Europe, 1983–1993: A Case Study in European Integration, working paper, LSE, European Institute.

Sun, J.-M. and Pelkmans, J. (1995), Regulatory Competition in the Single Market, *Journal of Common Market Studies*, 33:1, 67–89.

Sunstein, C. (1990), Paradoxes of the Regulatory State, *University of Chicago Law Review*, 57:2, 407–41.

Szysczak, E. (1994), Social Policy: A Happy Ending or a Reworking of the Fairy Tale?, in D. O'Keeffe and P. Twomey (eds), *Legal Issues of the Maastricht Treaty*, London, Wiley Chancery Law, 313–27.

Task Force EC (1990), '1992' – *The Environmental Dimension: Task Force Report on the Environment and the Internal Market*, Bonn, Economica Verlag GmbH.

Teague, P. (1989), *The European Community: The Social Dimension. Labour Market Policies for 1992*, London, Kogan Page.

Teasdale, A. (1993), The Life and Death of the Luxembourg Compromise, *Journal of Common Market Studies*, 31:4, 567–79.

Temple Lang, J. (1997), The Duties of National Courts under Community Constitutional Law, *European Law Review*, 22:1, 3–18.

Tesauro, G. (1995), The Community's Internal Market in the Light of the Recent Case-law of the Court of Justice, *Yearbook of European Law*, 15, 1–16.

Thelen, K. and Steinmo, S. (1992), Historical Institutionalism in Comparative Politics, in S. Steinmo, K. Thelen and F. Longstreth (eds), *Structuring Politics: Historical Institutionalism in Comparative Analysis*, Cambridge, CUP, 1–32.

Tilly, C. (ed.) (1975), *The Formation of Nation States in Western Europe*, Princeton, Princeton University Press.

Trepte, P.-A. (1993), *Public Procurement in the EC*, Bicester, CCH Editions.

UNICE (1987), Merger Control at Community Level, UNICE declaration of 10 November 1987, Brussels.

UNICE (1989a), Draft Regulation Regarding the Control of Concentrations, UNICE note of 17 November 1989, Brussels.

UNICE (1989b), Draft Regulation on Concentration Control, UNICE position paper of 14 December, Brussels.

UNICE (1990), UNICE Comments on the Proposal for a Directive Concerning the Protection at Work of Pregnant Women or Women Who Have Recently Given Birth (COM(90)406-Syn303), 12 November, Brussels.

UNICE (1995), *Releasing Europe's Potential Through Targeted Regulatory Reform*, Brussels.

Vallance, E. and Davies, E. (1986), *Women of Europe: Women MEPs and Equality Policy*, Cambridge, CUP.

Van de Voorde, E. (1992), European Air Transport after 1992: Deregulation or Re-regulation?, *The Antitrust Bulletin*, 37:2, 507–28.

Van Kersbergen, K. and Verbeek, B. (1994), The Politics of Subsidiarity in the European Union, *Journal of Common Market Studies*, 32:2, 215–36.

Von Wilmowsky, P. (1993), Waste Disposal in the Internal Market: The State of Play after the ECJ's Ruling on the Walloon Import Ban, *Common Market Law Review*, 30:3, 541–70.

Waelbrock, M. (1982), The Emergent Doctrine of Community Pre-emption – Consent and Re-delegation, in T. Sandalow and E. Stein (eds), *Courts and Free Markets: Perspectives from the United States and Europe*, Oxford: Clarendon Press.

Wallace, H. (1994), European Governance in Turbulent Times, in S. Bulmer and A. Scott (eds), *Economic and Political Integration in Europe: Internal Dynamics and Global Context*, Oxford, Blackwell Publishers, 87–96.

Wallace, H. (1996a), The Institutions of the EU: Experience and Experiments, in Wallace and Wallace (1996), 37–68.

Wallace, H. (1996b), Politics and Policy in the EU: The Challenge of Governance, in Wallace and Wallace (1996), 3–36.

Wallace, H. and Young, A. (1996), The Single Market: A New Approach to Policy, in Wallace and Wallace (1996), 125–55.

Wallace, H. and Wallace, W. (eds) (1996), *Policy-making in the European Union*, Oxford, OUP.

Wallace, H., Wallace, W. and Webb C. (eds) (1983), *Policy-Making in the European Community* (2nd edn), Chichester, John Wiley.

Wallace, W. (1990), Introduction: the Dynamics of European Integration, in W. Wallace (ed.), *The Dynamics of European Integration*, London, Pinter/RIIA, 1–24.

Warner, H. (1984), EC Social Policy in Practice: Community Action on Behalf of Women and its Impact in the Member States, *Journal of Common Market Studies*, 23:3, 141–67.

Weale, A. and Williams, A. (1992), Between Economy and Ecology? The Single Market and the Integration of Environmental Policy, *Environmental Politics*, 1:4, 45–64.

Weale, A. and Williams, A. (1993), Between Economy and Ecology? The Single Market and the Integration of Environmental Policy, in D. Judge (ed.), *A Green Dimension for the European Community: Political Issues and Processes*, London, Frank Cass & Co.

Weatherill, S. (1994), Beyond Preemption? Shared Competence and Constitutional Change in the European Community, in D. O'Keeffe and P. Twomey (eds), *Legal Issues of the Maastricht Treaty*, London, Wiley Chancery Law.

Weatherill, S. (1996), After *Keck*: Some Thoughts on How to Clarify the Clarification, *Common Market Law Review*, 33:5, 885–906.

Weatherill, S. and Beaumont, P. (1995), *European Community Law* (2nd edn), Harmondsworth, Penguin.

Weaver, R. Kent and Rockman, Bert A. (1993a), Assessing the Effects of Institutions, in Weaver *et al.* (1993b), 1–41.

Weaver, R. Kent and Rockman, Bert A. (eds) (1993b), *Do Institutions Matter? Government Capabilities in the United States and Abroad*, Washington, D.C., The Brookings Institution.

Webb, C. (1983) Theoretical Perspectives and Problems, in Wallace *et al.* (1983), 1–41.

Weiler, J. H. H. (1982), Community, Member States and European Integration: Is the Law Relevant?, *Journal of Common Market Studies*, 21:1/2, 39–56.

Weiler, J. H. H. (1991), The Transformation of Europe, *The Yale Law Journal*, 100:8, 2405–83.

Weiler, J. H. H. (1994), Journey to an Unknown Destination: A Retrospective and Prospective of the European Court of Justice in the Arena of Political Integration, in S. Bulmer and A. Scott (eds), *Economic and Political Integration in Europe: Internal Dynamics and Global Context*, Oxford, Blackwell Publishers, 131–60.

Weiler, J. H. H. (1997), The Reformation of European Constitutionalism, *Journal of Common Market Studies*, 35:1, 97–131.

Wellens, K. and Borchardt, G. (1980), Soft Law in European Community Law, *European Law Review*, 14:5, 267–321.

Werts, J. (1992), *The European Council*, Amsterdam, North-Holland.

Wessels, W. (1992), Staat und (westeuropäische) Integration: die Fusionsthese, *Politische Vierteljahresschrift*, Sonderheft 23 (Die Integration Europas, ed. M. Kreile), 36–61.

Wessels, W. (1997), An Ever Closer Fusion? A Dynamic Macropolitical View on Integration Processes, *Journal of Common Market Studies*, 35:1, 267–99.

Westlake, M. (1995), *The Council of the European Union*, London, Cartermill Publishing.

Wheatcroft, S. and Lipman, G. (1986), *Air Transport in a Competitive European Market*, Travel and Tourism Report No. 3, London, Economist Intelligence Unit.

White, E. (1989), In Search of the Limits to Article 30 of the EEC Treaty, *Common Market Law Review*, 26:2, 235–80.

Wilks, S. (1996), Regulatory Compliance and Capitalist Diversity in Europe, *Journal of European Public Policy*, 3:4, 536–59.

Wilks, S. and McGowan, L. (1994), Discretion in European Merger Control: The German Regime in Context, *Journal of European Public Policy*, 2:1, 41–67.

Wilks, S. and McGowan, L. (1995), Disarming the Commission: The Debate over a European Cartel Office, *Journal of Common Market Studies*, 33:2, 259–73.

Wilks, S. and Wright, M. (1987) (eds), *Comparative Government-Industry Relations: Western Europe, the United States and Japan*, Oxford, Clarendon Press.

Wils, W. (1993), The Search for the Rule in Article 30: Much Ado About Nothing, *European Law Review*, 18, 475–92.

Wincott, D. (1995), The Role of the Law or the Rule of the Court of Justice? An 'Institutional' Account of Judicial Politics in the European Community, *Journal of European Public Policy*, 2:4, 583–602.

Winter, J. A. (1991), Public Procurement in the EEC, *Common Market Law Review*, 28, 741–82.

Woolcock, S. (1989), European Mergers: National or Community Controls?, RIIA Discussion Paper No. 15, London, RIIA.

Woolcock, S. (1994), The European *acquis* and Multilateral Trade Rules: Are they Compatible?, in S. Bulmer and A. Scott (eds), *Economic and Political Integration in Europe: Internal Dynamics and Global Context*, Oxford, Blackwell Publishers, 199–218.

Woolcock, S. and Hodges, M. (1996), EU Policy in the Uruguay Round, in Wallace and Wallace (1996), 301–24.

Woolcock, S., Hodges, M. and Schreiber, K. (1991), *Britain, Germany and 1992: The Limits of Deregulation*, London: Pinter/RIIA.

Wright, M. (1988), Policy Community, Policy Network and Comparative Industrial Policies, *Political Studies*, 36:4, 593–612.

Wurzel, R. (1993), Environmental Policy, in J. Lodge (ed.), *The European Community and the Challenge of the Future* (2nd edn), London, Pinter.

Young, D. and Metcalfe, S. (1994), Competition Policy, in M. Artis and N. Lee (eds), *The Economics of the European Union: Policy and Analysis*, Oxford, OUP, 119–38.

Young, O. (1989), *International Cooperation: Building Regimes for Natural Resources and the Environment*, Ithaca, N.Y., Cornell University Press.

Index